Drive Around

917.11

Thomas
Cook

Vancouver
& British Columbia

The best of Vancouver's big-city
attractions plus Victoria's heritage
buildings and the magnificent scenery
of British Columbia's mountains,
forests and rivers

Maxine Cass and Fred Gebhart

Thomas Cook
Publishing

www.thomascookpublishing.com

Written by Maxine Cass and Fred Gebhart, updated by Maxine Cass

Published by Thomas Cook Publishing
A division of Thomas Cook Tour Operations Limited.
Company registration no. 1450464 England
The Thomas Cook Business Park, Unit 9, Coningsby Road,
Peterborough PE3 8SB, United Kingdom
Email: books@thomascook.com, Tel: + 44 (0) 1733 416477
www.thomascookpublishing.com

Produced by Cambridge Publishing Management Limited
Burr Elm Court, Main Street, Caldecote CB23 7NU

ISBN: 978-1-84848-064-3

© 2005, 2007 Thomas Cook Publishing
This third edition © 2009
Text © Thomas Cook Publishing
Road maps supplied and designed by Lovell Johns Ltd, OX8 8LH
Road map data © MapQuest.com Inc., Mountville PA 17554
City maps prepared by RJS Associates, © 2007 Thomas Cook Publishing

Maps prepared by Polly Senior cartography

Series Editor: Adam Royal
Production/DTP: Steven Collins

Printed and bound in India by Replika Press Pvt Ltd

Cover photography: Front: © John Arnold Images Ltd/Alamy. Back: Thomas Cook

About the authors

Maxine Cass studied Medieval European History at the University of California, Santa Barbara, has lived in Greece and Senegal, and has become a widely published photojournalist and writer. Maxine is the author of the *AAA Photo Journey to San Francisco* and *Time for Food: San Francisco*, and contributes to publications in Europe, the US, Canada and Asia, as well as collaborating with other authors on the *Drive Around Guides*, *On the Road Around* and *Discover Guides* series. Maxine and her husband and co-author, Fred Gebhart, live in San Francisco.

Fred Gebhart has travelled BC as a teenager as well as an adult. A freelance photojournalist for two decades, Fred covers the western side of North America for publications in Asia and Europe, and Australasia for North American readers.

Acknowledgements

The authors and publishers would like to thank the following people and organisations for their assistance:

Emily Armstrong; Banff Lake Louise Tourism; Chelsea Barr; John Bateman; BC Ferries; Cindy Burr; Stacey Butterfield; Catherine Callery; Monica Campbell-Hoppé; Canadian Tourism Commission; Michelle Comeau; Sarah Cotton; Brooke Darling; Teresa Davis, Tourism Campbell River & Region; Anthony Everett; Fairmont Hotels & Resorts; Catherine Frechette; Gabriola Island Chamber of Commerce; Lou Gebhart; Kristine George; Jennifer Gerstenberger; Steve Giordano; Lori Grant; Janice Greenwood-Fraser; Dick Griffith & Miranda Richter, Air Canada; Michael & Manon Hobbs and the Duen; Jasper Tourism & Commerce; Helen Kelleher-Empey; Lana Kingston, Tourism Vancouver Island; Kootenay Rockies; Annik LaRoche; Laurel Point Inn, Victoria; Holly Lenk; Kate Colley Lo; Louise MacDougall; Paul & Virginia McCarthy; Heather McGillivray; Shelley Malo; Mendo; Geoff Moore and Kim Pratt, Cariboo Chicotin Coast Tourism Association; Shannon Neidig; Pan Pacific Hotel, Vancouver; Panther; Penticton & Wine Country Tourism; Prince George Development Corp.; Mary Ellen Quesada; Francis Ratcliffe; Cathy Ray, Tourism Victoria; Kelly Reid; Jennifer Rhyne; The Rocky Mountaineer; Krista Rodger; Judy Love Rondeau; Mika Ryan; John Samms, Tourism Canmore; Laura Serena; Diana Sorace; Kerry Stansfield; Liz Steele; Lisa Strachan; Thompson Okanagan Tourism; Tourism Alberta; Tourism British Columbia; Tourism Kamloops; Tourism Kelowna; Tourism Prince Rupert; Tourism Vancouver; Tourism Victoria; Tourism Whistler; Doug Treleaven; Linda Trudeau; Vancouver, Coast & Mountains Tourism Region; Anda Verge; VIA Rail; Nora Weber; Heidi Wesling; Bruce Wishart; and Laura Woodbridge.

Contents

About Drive Around Guides

Thomas Cook's Drive Around Guides are designed to provide you with a comprehensive but flexible reference source to guide you as you tour a country or region by car. This guide divides Vancouver and British Columbia into touring areas – one per chapter. Major cultural centres or cities form chapters in their own right. Each chapter contains enough attractions to provide at least a day's worth of activities – often more.

Ratings

To make it easier for you to plan your time and decide what to see, every area is rated according to its attractions in categories such as Architecture, Entertainment and Children.

Chapter contents

Every chapter has an introduction summing up the main attractions of the area, and a ratings box, which will highlight the area's strengths and weaknesses – some areas may be more attractive to families travelling with children, others to wine-lovers visiting vineyards, and others to people interested in finding churches, nature reserves or good beaches.

Each chapter is then divided into an alphabetical gazetteer, and a suggested tour. You can select whether you just want to visit a particular sight or attraction, choosing from those described in the gazetteer, or whether you want to tour the area comprehensively. If the latter, you can construct your own itinerary, or follow the authors' suggested tour, which comes at the end of every area chapter.

The gazetteer

The gazetteer section describes all the major attractions in the area – the villages, towns, historic sites, nature reserves, parks or museums that you are most likely to want to see. Maps of the area highlight all the places mentioned in the text. Using this comprehensive overview of the area, you may choose just to visit one or two sights.

One way to use the guide is simply to find individual sights that interest you, using the index or overview map, and read what our authors have to say about them. This will help you decide whether to visit the sight. If you do, you will find plenty of practical information, such as the street address, the telephone number for enquiries and opening times.

Alternatively, you can choose a hotel, perhaps with the help of the accommodation recommendations contained in this guide. You can

Symbol Key

- ℹ️ Tourist Information Centre
- 🔄 Advice on arriving or departing
- 🅿️ Parking locations
- 🔄 Advice on getting around
- ➡️ Directions
- 🔟 Sights and attractions
- 🅒 Accommodation
- 🍴 Eating
- ⬤ Shopping
- 🏅 Sport
- 🔺 Entertainment

Practical information

The practical information in the page margins, or sidebars, will help you locate the services you need as an independent traveller – including the tourist information centre, car parks and public transport facilities. You will also find the opening times of sights, museums, churches and other attractions, as well as useful tips on shopping, market days, cultural events, entertainment, festivals and sports facilities.

then turn to the overall map on pages 10–11 to help you work out which chapters in the book describe those cities and regions that lie closest to your chosen touring base.

Driving tours

The suggested tour is just that – a suggestion, with plenty of optional detours and one or two ideas for making your own discoveries, under the heading *Also worth exploring*. The routes are designed to link the attractions described in the gazetteer section, and to cover outstandingly scenic coastal, mountain and rural landscapes. The total distance is given for each tour, as is the time it will take you to drive the complete route, but bear in mind that this indication is just for the driving time: you will need to add on extra time for visiting attractions along the way.

Many of the routes are circular, so that you can join them at any point. Where the nature of the terrain dictates that the route has to be linear, the route can either be followed out and back, or you can use it as a link route, to get from one area in the book to another.

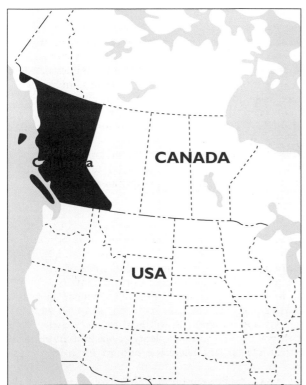

As you follow the route descriptions, you will find names picked out in bold capital letters – this means that the place is described fully in the gazetteer. Other names picked out in bold indicate additional villages or attractions worth a brief stop along the route.

Accommodation and food

In every chapter you will find lodging and eating recommendations for individual towns, or for the area as a whole. These are designed to cover a range of price brackets and concentrate on more characterful small or individualistic hotels and restaurants. In addition, you will find information in the *Travel facts* chapter on chain hotels, with an address to which you can write for a guide, map or directory. The price indications used in the guide have the following meanings:

$	budget level
$$	typical/average prices
$$$	de luxe.

Introduction

Above
Fraser River

Even if you've been to British Columbia before, you may have missed the best the province has to offer. If this is your first visit, chances are that you'll still miss some of the most amazing country to be found in North America. BC is simply too big, too grand and too empty to take in at one visit. It's not that the province doesn't try. The provincial tourist authority calls itself Super, Natural British Columbia, trying to convey the immense variety bursting from within its boundaries. But the grand sense of space and discovery that comes from so few people scattered across such an immense territory is also BC's biggest stumbling block. Beyond Vancouver, BC's economic heartland, Victoria, its political capital, and a handful of smaller population centres, the province is almost empty.

British Columbians are justifiably proud of the rolling grasslands of the Chilcotin Plateau stretching westward from Williams Lake, but few have actually *seen* the vast prairies and the occasional rough-hewn fence snaking along the only road for 200km in any direction. The magnificently decaying totem poles that still dot the Queen Charlotte Islands a century after smallpox decimated the population are famous around the globe. But more Americans, Britons, Germans, Italians and Japanese actually visit Gwaii Haanas National Park each year than Canadians.

That's not to deny BC's obvious urban allure. Vancouver is one of the cleanest, most scenic and most walkable big cities in North America, a combination of late 19th-century urban planning and 21st-century affluence, surrounded by snowcapped mountains and sparkling ocean inlets. Victoria is a classic capital that has adapted to the modern era without sacrificing its grand façades, open views or British style.

BC is schizophrenic. Greenpeace was born of ecological angst in Vancouver, yet both city and province remain heavily dependent on the continuing exploitation of forest, fish and mineral resources that are rapidly disappearing. The sea otters and fur seals that first lured outsiders to the BC coast have been hunted to extinction. Coastal and interior rainforests that once stretched for days in any direction are being systematically reduced to scattered holdings in isolated parklands.

Seemingly endless shoals of silvery salmon that gave coastal and interior First Nation groups the wealth and leisure to produce some of the finest art the world has seen have been reduced to annual trickles by overfishing at sea and clear-cutting (the practice of cutting down every tree, leaving the landscape barren) on land. Toxic runoff from mining operations in the Kootenays and other regions that have been closed for three generations continues to poison the land.

The unrelenting and very public battle between preservation and continued exploitation gives BC a sense of tension and endless struggle. Look carefully from viewpoints such as Meadows in the Sky, vast wildflower fields at the top of Mount Revelstoke, and it's easy to believe that nature reigns supreme and serene. Turn your gaze beyond park boundaries, and entire mountainsides have been shorn of trees and riven with erosion scars.

It seems a miracle that any sense whatsoever of the natural grandeur of forest, lake and mountains, the isolation and unabashed awe recorded by travellers less than 150 years ago, can still be found. It's more a testament to commercial and political avarice than to any far-sighted policy of preservation.

Early businessmen and politicians contrived to turn immense tracts of crown lands into semi-private playgrounds along railways and roadways and called them National Parks. Banff, Glacier, Jasper and Yoho may have been created for the enjoyment of the rich and the enrichment of the Canadian Pacific Railway, but all have become spiritual and physical refuges for the public.

It's not the first time that private enrichment schemes have backfired. BC's original First Nation inhabitants were systematically deprived of land, liberty and tradition by government policies designed to open the land to White settlers, loggers and miners. But the traditions and peoples that generations of government agents worked so hard to suppress have re-emerged as potent political, economic and cultural forces – fuelled in large part by modern angst over those not-so-long-ago transgressions.

Change has become a permanent part of the BC landscape. The First Nations were overtaken by fur traders and explorers in the 18th century, who were themselves displaced by lumbermen followed by farmers in the 19th century, only to be overtaken by First Nations claims in the 20th century.

Nature continues a tug-of-war, with points won and lost on all sides. The once-mighty Columbia River has long-since been banished into a chain of placid lakes behind a series of dams extending south into the United States. At Rogers Pass, railway builders abandoned the surface to unrelenting snowfall and endless avalanches and drove tunnels nearly 400m beneath the inhospitable pass. Faced with similar problems in the Cascades, the Kettle Valley Railway simply gave up and closed.

Whether resource industries simply give up or find new routes in the 21st century remains to be seen. The battle between exhausting natural resources or preserving them for future uses is already straining BC's social and economic fabric. Either way, the outcome will mean the passing of traditional ways of life that someone holds dear. If BC finally breaks with tradition to favour conservation, the awe-inspiring scenery that has been creating legends for the last 100 centuries will still be around for another visit.

Travel facts

Above
Cycle trails are ubiquitous

Accommodation

Chain hotels and motels provide the most reliable accommodation, while bed and breakfast may be good value outside major cities. Expect to pay $100–250 per night in major cities, $60–125 in smaller towns, single or double occupancy.

Whether you're considering a hotel, motel, bed & breakfast, houseboat, dude ranch (equipped for horse riding), guest ranch or fishing camp, to book accommodation, contact **Super, Natural British Columbia**, *tel: (800) 435-5622; www.hellobc.com* and **Travel Alberta**, *tel: (800) 252-3782 or (780) 427-4321; www1.travelalberta.com*. Both provinces have lodging information and can make bookings. Local tourist offices also have lists of area accommodations.

Prices vary as much as 50 per cent from value season to high season (about mid-May to early September, and winter at ski resorts), when cities and tourism areas are booked out months in advance.

Airports

Most international visitors arrive at Vancouver International Airport (YVR) *www.yvr.ca*. Calgary International Airport (YYC) *www.calgary.com* provides access to the Rocky Mountain National Parks from Alberta. For flight information and bookings, contact individual airlines, not the airport. Luggage trolleys are free for international arrivals; expect to pay $1–2 at local airports. Major airports have foreign exchange and banking services as well as car hire/rental facilities. An Airport Improvement fee is levied unless passengers have same-day flight connections.

Children

Most attractions offer reduced prices for children (or students). Major hotels and motels can arrange for babysitters, a pricey service. Children stay free in their parents' room with many motel chains.

Picnics offer mealtime flexibility, so does a small cooler filled with cold drinks and snacks. Most towns have roadside restaurants with long hours, cheap children's menus and familiar names.

Climate

Western Canadians are proud of the damp coastal weather that nurtures lush forests and the dramatic climate that transforms the interior with a snowy winter blanket or sizzling summer temperatures. Weather and temperature can vary widely along the coast, fog one hour, drizzle the next, crisp blue sky followed by scudding clouds. Prepare for rain and snow from October to April, and plunging temperatures and heavy snow any month in the Canadian Rockies. Coastal BC climate is moderated by the Pacific Ocean. Victoria and the Gulf Islands are famed as Canadian sun spots, sheltered by Vancouver Island's mountains and Washington's Olympic Mountains.

Currency

Canadian dollars come in denominations of $1 and $2 coins, and $5, $10, $20, $50 and $100 notes (bills). Bills vary in colour, but are the same size. There are 100 cents to the dollar. Coins are: 1 cent (penny), 5 cents (nickel), 10 cents (dime), 25 cents (quarter), 1 dollar (loonie) and 2 dollars (toonie or twonie).

The safest forms of money are traveller's cheques and credit or debit cards. Carry at least one, preferably two, major credit cards, such as **American Express**, **MasterCard** or **VISA**. Car hire companies, hotels and motels require a credit card or a substantial cash deposit, even if the bill has been prepaid or will be settled in cash. Some shops, motels, restaurants and petrol (gas) stations will accept only cash.

Thomas Cook Bureaux provide full foreign exchange facilities and will change currency and traveller's cheques.

Banks can exchange foreign currency or traveller's cheques, but expect delays at small town branches. Traveller's cheques from well-known issuers are acceptable everywhere.

Customs allowances

Visitors to Canada of legal age (19) may bring 1.5 litres of wine or 1.14 litres of spirits or a combination of wine and spirits, or 8.5 litres of beer and ale. Tobacco allowances are 200 cigarettes, 50 cigars, 200g of loose tobacco, and 200 tobacco sticks. Rules may change so check before travelling: *www.cbsa.gc.ca/publications/pub/rc4161-eng.html*. Check with customs officials at home for returning duty-free allowances. Because of taxes, alcohol is cheaper at duty-free shops. Tobacco and perfume are cheaper at supermarkets and department stores than at airport and duty-free shops.

Drinking laws

The minimum drinking age is 19 in British Columbia and 18 in Alberta and it is strictly enforced. Beer, wine and spirits can be purchased in BC-owned Liquor Stores; beer and wine are also available

Electricity

Canada uses 110V, 60 Hz current with two- or three-prong plugs. Power and plug converters are seldom available.

Beware of buying electrical equipment – it probably won't operate on the 220V 50 Hz power the rest of the world uses. Exceptions are battery-operated items such as radios, cameras and portable computers.

Be equally wary of regionally-coded DVDs, which will in most instances only play on players manufactured in the same region. Canada is in region 2: the U.S., U.S. territories and Canada. The region code is usually specified on the back of individual DVD packages.

in privately owned beer and wine stores. Look for beer, wine and spirits in provincially licensed private Liquor Stores in Alberta. Licensed establishments, bars, lounges, saloons, taverns or pubs may open between 0800 and varying times after midnight.

Laws against drinking and driving are severe and strictly enforced (see Drinking and driving laws, pages 25 and 26).

Eating out

Canadians enjoy eating out as an occasion, a chance for social mixing and to see how the rest of the world lives. Even in casual spots, smart-casual clothing and footwear are required.

Salmon and berry dishes have been part of the Western Canadian diet for generations, and are dependable. Sustainable, often organic, and above all locally produced fruits, vegetables, fish, meat and poultry are a matter of pride; though foodstuffs may be local, prices may be expensive. Imported foodstuffs or exotic game such as caribou will reflect availability and transport costs. Portions are hearty, in keeping with pioneer traditions of serving without stint.

Breakfast often includes rashers of Canadian bacon or sausages with hash browns (shredded fried potatoes), eggs, pancakes and toast. Bagels, fruit or bran muffins, scones or English muffins (crumpets), porridge or cereal are other possibilities. A 'Continental breakfast' is juice, coffee or tea and bread or pastry.

Lunch and dinner menus feature appetisers (starters), salads, soups, pastas, entrées (main courses) and desserts. Salads come at the beginning of the meal. Sunday brunch (usually 1100–1400), self-service buffets piled high with hot and cold dishes, can be good value for hearty eaters. Many fast-food outlets have drive-up windows. Look for A&W, Burger King, KFC (Kentucky Fried Chicken), Little Caesar's, McDonald's, Pizza Hut and Taco Bell.

Coffee and tea are widely available and, except when served at coffee shops or coffee houses in major cities, often weaker than that served in Europe. Iced tea may be sweet; ask if you prefer it plain, without sugar and unflavoured. Plain water is served free of charge upon request.

Entry formalities

A passport is now required for US citizens arriving by air, land or sea. Non-Canadian visitors need a passport and may be required to obtain a visa before arrival. Check with the Canadian Embassy or Consulate (and www.goingtocanada.gc.ca/requirements/index.aspx) for passport, visa and proof of return travel requirements before departing for Canada.

Canada prohibits revolvers, pistols, fully automatic firearms and other weapons and self-defence sprays such as mace and pepper spray. Firearms such as hunting rifles and shotguns must be declared at

Festivals

Western Canada's events are the mirror of the community, from wine festivals (Okanagan Spring (Apr–May) and Fall (Sep–Oct) Wine Festivals) and fruit (Peach Festival, Penticton – Aug), to boating events (Victoria Classic Boat Festival®, Victoria Inner Harbour – Sep), rodeos (Cloverdale Rodeo – May) and First Nations powwows (Squilax Pow Wow, Squilax, North Shuswap – Jul; Kamloopa Pow Wow, Kamloops – Aug) and sophisticated music, film and theatre festivals in Vancouver (TD Canada Trust Vancouver International Jazz Festival – late Jun–early Jul; Vancouver Folk Music Festival – mid-Jul; HSBC PowerSmart Celebration of Light (fireworks) – late Jul–early Aug; Vancouver International Film Festival – late Sep–early Oct) and Victoria (Shakespeare in the Summer – mid-Jul–mid-Aug; Victoria Fringe Theatre Festival – Aug–early Sep, Vancouver Island Blues Bash – early Sep).

entry. Narcotics and certain pharmaceutical products may not be imported. Carry documentation such as a doctor's prescription to prove that medications are legitimate.

Food

Rich, delicate salmon is king on any Western Canadian menu, from raw to grilled (broiled), poached, creamed, sauced or doused with Eastern Canada's contribution, maple syrup. Fish is delicious whether farmed or wild. Alberta contributes lean beef and buffalo for meat-eaters; autumn brings caribou, venison and elk (wapiti) to the menu.

The Okanagan Valley's fruitbasket grows peaches, pears, apples, cherries, plums, nectarines, grapes and vegetables, while the Lower Fraser Valley produces berries – blueberries, raspberries, blackberries, gooseberries and huckleberries.

Health

In the event of a life-threatening emergency, telephone 911 (free) for an ambulance. If a life is at stake, treatment will be swift and professional, as government-run health programmes cover everyone. Non-Canadians pay for treatment, and non-emergency care cost is reasonable, though emergency care can be exorbitant. Most travel agents selling international travel offer travel insurance policies covering Canadian medical costs.

Bring prescription medication for the entire trip, plus a few extra days. Carry a copy of the prescription showing the generic (chemical) name and formulation, not just a brand name.

Canada is basically a healthy place. No inoculations are required and common sense is enough to avoid most health problems. Eat sensibly and don't drink water that hasn't come from the tap or a

Information

Super, Natural British Columbia (Tourism British Columbia) *Walk-in visitor information centre: Plaza Level, 200 Burrard St, Vancouver, BC V6C 3L6; tel: (800) 435-5622 or (604) 583-2000; www.hellobc.com.* In UK *http://uk. britishcolumbia.travel/en-ca* or via **Canadian Tourism Commission,** *www.canada. travel/splash.en-gb.html*

Travel Alberta *Walk-in visitor information centre: 999 8th St SW, Suite 760, Calgary, AB T2R 1J5; tel: (800) 252-3782 or outside North America (780) 427-4321; www1.travelalberta.com*

Parks Canada *Tel: (888) 773-8888; www.pc.gc.ca, (Provincial)* **BC Parks** *all information through www.env.gov.bc.ca/bcparks*

Insurance

Travel insurance should cover you, your belongings and your holiday. Buy cover for delayed or cancelled flights, as well as weather problems and medical evacuation.

Language

Canada is officially bi-lingual in English and French; all public signage and documents will be in both languages (*see also* page 282).

bottle. Most ground water is contaminated with *Giardia lamblia*, which results in a severe bacterial infection of the gut.

Sunglasses, broad-brimmed hats and sunscreen help prevent sunburn, sunstroke and heat prostration. Drink plenty of non-alcoholic liquids, especially in warm weather.

Maps

The **Canadian Automobile Association** (CAA) prints useful road maps in conjunction with the **American Automobile Association** (AAA), free to members at CAA offices. The RAC and other automobile clubs have reciprocal agreements with the CAA. **MapArt** *70 Bloor St E, Oshawa, ON L1H 3M2; tel: (905) 436-2525 or (877) 231-6277; www.mapart.com,* produce easy-to-use regional and city maps. Detailed, 3-dimensional maps of Rocky Mountain National Parks are designed by **Gem Trek Publishing** *#301, 2614 Bridge St, Victoria, BC V82 459; tel: (250) 380-0100; www.gemtrek.com*

Museums

Most museums charge an entry fee, and are closed one day a week. Rural museums sometimes open only on weekends or in summer.

National and Provincial Parks

National Parks and Historic Heritage Sites charge daily entry fees per person. Camping fees are extra. Save money and purchase the personal **National Parks Pass** ($67.70), **National Historic Sites** ($53.00), or both passes in the **Discovery Package** ($84.40), for entry to 27 parks and 78 historic sites. Fees are less for seniors over 64 years, children 6 to 16, and family groups. **BC Provincial Parks** fees vary, and differ seasonally.

Opening times

Standard office and business hours are 0830/0900–1630/1700 Monday–Friday. Most banks are open Monday–Friday 1000–1600, and Saturday mornings. ATMs are open 24 hours. Shops are open Monday–Wednesday and Saturday 0900/1000–1800, and Thursday and Friday until 2100. Sunday hours are 1100/1200–1700.

Tourist offices outside Vancouver and Victoria have limited hours or may be closed from mid-September–mid-May. Petrol (gas) stations are open long hours, but may close between 2200 and 0630. Pub, saloon and restaurant hours vary greatly between areas, but are likely to close earlier in winter. Call churches, synagogues, temples or mosques in advance for services and opening hours.

Public holidays

The following public holidays are observed in British Columbia and Alberta:

New Year's Day (1 Jan);
Alberta Family Day (third
Mon in Feb);
Good Friday (Mar/Apr);
Easter Monday (Mar/Apr);
Victoria Day (Mon on
or prior to 24 May);
Canada Day (1 Jul);
BC Day and Alberta
Heritage Day (first Mon
in Aug);
Labour Day
(first Mon in Sep);
Thanksgiving Day
(second Mon in Oct);
Remembrance Day
(11 Nov);
Christmas Day (25 Dec);
Boxing Day (26 Dec).

Post offices and government offices close on public holidays.

Packing

Outside a handful of restaurants in the major cities and resorts that require business attire, dress is casual and practical. Take rainwear and at least one change of warm clothing (sweater/pullover and jacket) and sturdy shoes, or consider buying them at one of Canada's fine-quality outdoor outfitters.

Dress in layers as temperatures can change dramatically during the day, especially in the mountains and near the ocean. A backpack can be pre-packed or stocked upon arrival with a hat, sunscreen, insect repellent, sunglasses, prescription medicine, contraceptives, an umbrella, raincoat, electricity adaptor, alarm clock and a camera.

Postal services

Every town has at least one **Canada Post/Postes Canada** office, listed in the phone directory blue pages and on *www.canadapost.ca*. Most are open at least Mon–Fri 0900–1700. Hotel concierges, drug stores and tourist shops often sell stamps.

Letters or parcels sent abroad (even to the USA) should go airmail to avoid delays. Domestic letters generally arrive in three to seven days.

Public transport

• **BC Transit** have extensive bus and related systems throughout the province, including Vancouver, *tel: (604) 953-3333; www.translink.bc.ca*, and for Victoria and beyond, *tel: (250) 385-2551; www.transitbc.com*
• **BC Ferries**, *tel: (250) 386-3431* or *(888) 223-3779; www.bcferries.com*, serve Victoria, Vancouver Island, the Gulf Islands and Queen Charlotte Islands, Prince Rupert and Bella Coola, with stops along Inside Passage, and other BC coastal areas.

Reading

• *Best Weekend Getaways from Vancouver*, by Jack Christie, 2008, Douglas & McIntyre, Vancouver.
• *British Columbia: An Illustrated History*, by Geoffrey Molyneux, 2003, Raincoast Books, Vancouver.
• *British Columbia Wine Country*, by John Schreiner and Kevin Miller, Revised Edition 2007, Whitecap Books, Vancouver.
• *Haida Gwaii: Journeys Through the Queen Charlotte Islands,* by Ian Gill, 2004, Raincoast Books, Vancouver.
• *Handbook of the Canadian Rockies*, by Ben Gadd, 1999, Corax Press, Jasper.
• *Lilies & Fireweed: Frontier Women of British Columbia*, by Stephen Hume, 2004, Harbour Publishing, Madeira Park, BC.

- *Looking at Indian Art of the Northwest Coast*, by Hilary Stewart, 2004, Douglas & McIntyre, Vancouver.
- *More English than the English: A Social History of Victoria*, by Terry Reksten, 1986, Orca Book Publishers, Victoria.
- *Native Peoples and Cultures of Canada,* by Alan D McMillan, 1995, Douglas & McIntyre, Vancouver.
- *Native Sites in Western Canada,* by Pat Kramer, 2002, Altitude Publishing Canada Ltd, Canmore, Alberta.
- *Notes from The Century Before: A Journal from British Columbia,* by Edward Hoagland et al, 2002, The Modern Library, New York.
- *Official Guide to Pacific Rim National Park Reserve,* by JM MacFarlane et al, 1996, Blackbird Naturegraphics, Inc, Calgary.
- *Raven Steals the Light,* by Bill Reid and Robert Bringhurst, 1996, Douglas & McIntyre, Vancouver.
- *Totem Poles*, by Pat Kramer, 2004, Altitude Publishing Canada Ltd, Canmore, Alberta.
- *A Traveller's Guide to Historic British Columbia,* by Rosemary Neering, 2002, Whitecap Books, Vancouver.
- *The West Beyond the West: A History of British Columbia*, by Jean Barman, Revised Edition 2007, University of Toronto Press, Toronto.

Safety and security

- Dial 911 on any telephone for free emergency assistance from police, fire and medical authorities.
- Never discuss travel plans or valuables in public. Walk with assurance in well-lit places and give the impression that you are not worth robbing (eg don't wear expensive jewellery). A wallet in a back pocket or an open handbag is an invitation to theft. Report incidents to local police immediately, and get a report for your insurance company.
- Unwatched luggage can vanish in an instant and is subject to confiscation by authorities. Hotel bell staff may keep guest luggage for a few days, but always get receipts.
- If your car breaks down, turn on the flashing emergency lights, raise the bonnet and wait inside the vehicle. Have your keys out to unlock car doors before entering a car park on foot, and check around and inside the vehicle before entering. Don't pick up hitchhikers and never leave the car with the engine running.
- Lock room doors, windows and sliding glass doors from the inside. Ground-floor rooms are convenient but easier to break into. When leaving the room at night, leave a light on. When someone knocks at

Limerick
County Library

Smoking

As of 2007 smoking is banned in all public places – including outdoor areas of restaurants and bars – in British Columbia.

Stores

Major department store chains include The Bay. Among discount chains are Zellers and Wal-Mart.

the door, use the peephole to see who it is. If someone claims to be on the hotel staff, check with the front desk. Money, cheques, credit cards, passports and keys should be with you or in the hotel safe deposit box. Photocopy the important pages of your passport and visas. Carry the copies and extra passport photos separately from the documents themselves.

Shopping

Food souvenirs include smoked or tinned salmon; local Okanagan Valley wines; dried cherries, berries and apples; berry conserves and syrups.

Canadian-made clothing and footwear are well made, attractive and practical. Outdoor outfitters and discount stores carry a wide range of goods, many sport-specific. Mountie (RCMP) souvenirs come in wood, on tea towels or as stuffed bears or beavers.

First Nations artwork is usually pricey; ask for the artist's certificate of authentication when you purchase an artefact. Aboriginal peoples produce masks; baskets; stone, wooden and soapstone carvings; jewellery; paintings; and hand-made grey or white Cowichan sweaters.

Sport

Vancouver offers several professional sports: NLL Vancouver Ravens lacrosse; NHL Vancouver Canucks hockey and WHL Vancouver Giants hockey; CFL BC Lions football; USL Vancouver Whitecaps men's soccer and NWL Vancouver Canadians baseball. Playing fields abound throughout British Columbia. Golf, marathons, bicycling, fishing, alpine and Nordic skiing, sailing, windsurfing and the very Canadian sport of curling are popular for individual recreation. Vancouver, Whistler and Victoria are the principal venues for the 2010 Olympic and Paralympic Winter Games, *www.vancouver2010.com* (*see page 23*), and visitors will see signs of construction and refurbishment in the southwestern region of the province until then.

Right
Whistler Mountain Bike Park's 250km of trails offer something for every level of rider

Time

Most of British Columbia is on Pacific Standard Time (PST), GMT −8. Alberta and roughly the Rocky Mountain section of BC are on Mountain Standard Time (MST), GMT −7. Both provinces jump ahead to Daylight Time (PDT) GMT −7/(MDT) GMT −6, from the second Sunday in March until the first Sunday in November.

Tipping

Tipping is standard except in the very rare restaurant where a service charge is added. Servers expect 15–20 per cent of the food and drink charge; bartenders at least $1 per drink.

Hotel porters get $1–$2 per bag and the bellperson who shows you your room several dollars more. Expect to pay $1–5 for valet parking each time your car is delivered. Don't tip ushers in cinemas, theatres and similar establishments, but do tip tour guides, taxi drivers, and for any other services.

Toilets

Canadians know them as washrooms. Restrooms, bathrooms and toilet are terms imported from the USA. Men and Women are also common designations. Ultra-trendy bars, parks and recreational areas may have unisex washrooms.

Snow sports

For up-to-date reviews of snow-sports resorts, check *www.skisnowboard. com/resorts.html*

Taxes

British Columbia's provincial sales tax is 7 per cent; Alberta has none. Most services are subject to a Canadian Goods and Services Tax (GST), of 5 per cent. Both provinces charge a room tax.

Telephones

Public telephones (pay phones) are marked by a white telephone on a blue background. Dialling instructions are posted on the telephone or in the telephone directory white pages. Local calls cost 50¢; toll-free (800, 866, 877 and 888 area codes) and 911 (emergency) calls are free. To talk to an operator, dial 0. To locate local numbers, dial 411. For long-distance information, dial 1 + area code + 555-1212. There is a charge for all information calls.

Many hotels and motels add steep surcharges to phone calls, even when calling toll-free numbers from rooms; use a pay phone in the lobby. Prepaid phonecards are widely available, and may be a bargain.

For international enquiries or assistance, dial 00. For international calls, dial 011 (access code) + country code + city code (omit the first zero if there is one) + local number.

Internet access varies, as does wireless (wifi) coverage. Many hotels charge for an internet connection; a concierge may know of a local internet café.

Travellers with disabilities

While Federal and provincial laws require that public business and services be readily accessible by people with a disability, not all are. For specific information, contact **SATH** (Society for Accessible Travel & Hospitality), *347 5th Ave, Suite 605, New York, NY 10016; tel: (212) 447-7284; www.sath.org* or **RADAR**, *12 City Forum, 250 City Rd, London EC1V 8AF; tel: (020) 7250-3222; www.radar.org.uk*

Wheelchair accessibility information is free from the **Canadian Paraplegic Association/British Columbia Paraplegic Association** *780 SW Marine Dr, Vancouver, BC V6P 5Y7; tel: (604) 324-3611 or (877) 324-3611;* **CPA Alberta** *#305, 11010–101 St, Edmonton, AB T5H 4B9; tel: (780) 424-6312 or (888) 654-5444; www.canparaplegic.org.* **SPARC** *201-221 E. 10th Ave, Vancouver BC, V5T 4V3; tel: (604) 718-7744; www.sparc.bc.ca/application_forms* provide disabled parking permits on a province-wide basis.

2010 Olympic and Paralympic Winter Games
www.vancouver2010.com/en

Olympic Winter Games:
12–28 Feb 2010

Paralympic Winter Games:
12–21 Mar 2010

2010 Vancouver Olympic and Paralympic Winter Games

British Columbia will host 6,800 or so of the world's best athletes and support officials in 2010 for the Olympic and Paralympic Winter Games. Competition venues offer sea-level staging in Vancouver and close by in Richmond, with mountain events in West Vancouver and Whistler. The Vancouver and Whistler hubs are linked on land by the Sea-to-Sky Highway, which will be widened and modernised during 2009.

Seventeen sports fill the competition schedule: alpine skiing, biathlon, bobsleigh, cross-country skiing, curling (one of Canada's sports obsessions!), figure skating, freestyle skating, ice hockey, ice sledge hockey, luge, Nordic combined, short track speed skating, skeleton, ski jumping, snowboarding, speed skating and wheelchair curling.

Whistler's three venues host half the sports. Alpine skiing is slotted for Whistler Creekside in Whistler. Bobsleigh, luge and skeleton teams will be at the Whistler Sliding Centre at Blackcomb Mountain. Three stadiums in the Callaghan Valley 15km from Whistler are preparing for biathletes, cross-country skiers, ski jumpers and Nordic combination competitors.

The Richmond Oval, bank side on the Fraser River, will be the venue for speed skaters. Fans and supporters of freestyle skiing and snowboarding will head to Cypress Mountain in West Vancouver. Vancouver's four in-city venues host the other sports, including ice hockey at Canada Hockey Place in downtown Vancouver; figure skating and short track speed skating at the Pacific Coliseum in Hastings Park; ice hockey and ice sledge hockey at the UBC Thunderbird Arena; and curling and wheelchair curling at the Vancouver Olympic Centre/Vancouver Paralympic Centre near Queen Elizabeth Park, easily reached by the new Canada Line light rail that by late 2009 should connect Vancouver International Airport with downtown Vancouver.

Downtown Vancouver's BC Place Stadium, with North America's largest air-supported stadium roof, hosts the Olympic Winter Games opening and closing ceremonies and the Paralympic Winter Games opening ceremony. Fifty-five thousand spectators will watch multimedia ceremonies and medal award presentations there. An outdoor Whistler Celebration Plaza hosts Whistler venue award ceremonies and the Paralympic Winter Games Closing Ceremony.

The 2010 Vancouver games have three mascots: Sumi, a mountain animal guardian spirit with an orca whale hat, thunderbird wings and black bear legs; the sea bear Miga that combines orca whale, bear and Kermode (Spirit Bear) and hails from near Tofino (Vancouver Island); and Quatchi, a forest-dwelling hockey-loving sasquatch, or Bigfoot.

Tickets went on sale in October 2008. The www.vancouver2010.com website details ticketing procedures for Canadians and advises others on how to obtain tickets. The best advice is to pinpoint your favourite event(s), find the date and venue on the schedule and plan and book your 2010 Olympic or Paralympic holiday early, then travel to see what awaits elsewhere in BC.

Driver's guide

Automobile Clubs

There are no reciprocal agreements between the AA and RAC, and the equivalent CAA in Canada. You should ensure that you purchase sufficient insurance when you hire a car.

Autoroutes

The Coquihalla Highway between Hope and Kamloops is BC's only toll road, with a standard $10 toll for a car or RV. The tollbooth accepts some credit cards and debit cards as well as cash.

Accidents

Legally, you must STOP if involved in a collision or accident and call the local police or Royal Canadian Mounted Police (RCMP). For most areas in BC, the emergency number is 911 to alert the police or emergency medical services. You can also dial 0 to be directed to the authorities. Emergency service numbers are listed inside the phone directory front cover. Call your own insurance company and, if in a hired car, your car-hire company. Collisions in BC resulting in death, injury or property damage apparently exceeding $1,000 are the responsibility of the driver, who is personally responsible for alerting police within 24–48 hours (depending on the jurisdiction) and the Insurance Corporation of British Columbia (ICBC): *tel: (800) 910-4222* or *(604) 520-8222; www.icbc.com*. ICBC, whose offices are listed in the telephone directory and on the ICBC website, is the province's issuer of driving licences as well as the provider of accident insurance. If you are involved in an accident, British Columbia and Alberta require you to produce your driving licence, vehicle licence number, vehicle registration number, insurance carrier and cover policy number along with your contact information to police and other parties to the incident. Exchange your information with the other driver(s) and get the names and contact information of any witnesses. Note as many details as you can, such as the time, location and weather. Photographs can be helpful later. You should remain at the accident site until police arrive and the law requires you to render all reasonable assistance. Pull over to the side of the roadway if possible and set out emergency triangles to warn other drivers.

Right
Kabuki Kabs, Victoria

Documents

Your home-country driving licence is valid in British Columbia and Alberta. You should always carry it while driving and have your picture identification with you at all times.

The vehicle registration, proof of liability and collision insurance coverage, with any hire car contract, must be in the car and accessible at all times.

Provisional licences are not valid. Car hire companies require that all drivers be at least age 25.

Drinking and Driving

Driving while impaired (DWI), often called DUI (driving under the influence of alcohol or drugs) is illegal. The criminal blood alcohol limit is .08mg. Strict enforcement permits a breath sample to be taken by a police officer; a blood sample may be required later. Police and the RCMP establish random checkpoints and may be particularly attentive near winery tasting rooms and entertainment venues. Penalties include fines and imprisonment.

If your vehicle collides with a parked vehicle, leave a note with your name, address, licence plate number and insurance information securely affixed to the other vehicle. For a collision with an animal – 10 per cent of all BC accidents are with animals – do not try to move it but call the nearest humane society or authorities.

Breakdowns

If you have a breakdown, stop your vehicle on the hard shoulder, getting it as far to the right as possible. On ordinary roads, consider using the verge but beware of roadside ditches. Turn hazard lights on and raise the bonnet. If it's dark or visibility is limited, place flares and reflective warning triangles where they can be seen by other drivers. (Remember, it can be very dangerous to walk on the hard shoulder of any freeway or highway.) Place an SOS note on the windscreen. You and your passengers may be safer out of the vehicle and well up the verge away from the traffic, but for security, stay in the locked car if you are in an isolated area, it is night-time, or it is hard to see for any reason.

You may call for a breakdown lorry, called a tow truck, usually dispatched from a local petrol (gas) station. Breakdown insurance is strongly recommended and one phone call is all it takes to hand the whole problem over to an operator who is expert in sorting things out. Your insurance company may call a towing service it has under contract for emergency roadside assistance repairs or towing to a repair garage. You are responsible for payment or for signing the form that affirms to your insurance company that you have had the service. Most car-hire companies either pay for repairs directly or reimburse the cost shown on repair receipts. If a hire car is going to be out of service for more than a few hours, ask the hire company for a replacement vehicle.

Caravans and camper vans (Trailers and RVs)

Recreational vehicles or RVs, often called motorhomes, are a popular way to travel in Western Canada, though hire companies restrict access to some highways and may limit cross-border travel to the USA. Hire options include a choice of daily kilometre limits and seasons; high season is July–August.

The higher cost of hiring and operating an RV is offset by savings on accommodation and meals, and the convenience of not packing and unpacking at each stop.

Maintenance takes time and attention away from touring. Check the vehicle inside and out for its condition. Get operating manuals and a full demonstration for all systems before leaving with a hired RV. Buy a pair of sturdy rubber gloves to handle emptying the waste-holding tanks and wear old clothes for the task. For sanitary and

Essentials

You should travel with three red, reflective warning triangles, road flares, a torch, a first aid kit and a jack for tyre repair. If the vehicle has a spare tyre, make sure that it is properly inflated. Have chains for snow season travel.

Fines

Drivers can be fined for moving violations like speeding, illegal turns or other infractions, for parking violations, and for DWI, driving while impaired under the influence of alcohol or illegal drugs. Police authorities will issue a citation, often called a ticket, on the spot. The citation specifies the police authority, jurisdiction (city, town), legal code reference number, a short description of the violation, the vehicle reference, the police officer's identification, your information if it is a moving violation, and where and how the ticket can be paid or challenged.

On-the-spot fine payments are *never* made, and anyone offering to pay a fine when cited may be assumed to be offering a bribe to a police officer, an extremely serious offence.

Citations are registered in a computer database by car licence that is linked to the vehicle identification number. The car or RV hire company will be notified of any citations issued to its vehicles.

environmental reasons, sewage system disposal must be done at authorised dump stations.

The size of an RV or trailer cannot exceed 12.5m in length. These vehicles drive more like lorries than cars and are generally treated as lorries by traffic laws. They are blown about more by the wind than cars and are more subject to rollover and drift. Taller and wider dimensions can create hazards at gas stations, tollbooths, parkades and with low-hanging trees and signs. On BC Ferries, the cost of passage for RVs is based on vehicle length.

Woodall's (*www.woodalls.com*) is a fine reference for 15,000 camping spots in North America; the Canada listings are also in *Woodall's Canada Campground Guide*. There are private RV parks and camping in some National Parks and BC (provincial) Parks during the summer, generally April to September. To book a BC Parks camping pitch, *tel: (800) 689-9025; www.discovercamping.ca*. Travel Alberta handles camping information requests; *www1.travelalberta.com* or check *www.cd.gov.ab.ca/enjoying_alberta/parks/planning/gateway/camping.aspx* (Alberta Provincial Parks).

Wherever you park along the side of a road or on city streets, the vehicle must always be pulled off the roadway and should only be parked in a safe, well-lit place in view of passers-by. Always lock the vehicle. Canada's wonderful outdoors presents the challenge of bears searching for easy food supplies. Observe all provincial and park recommendations for storing and carrying food to avoid temptation for the bear and an unpleasant confrontation.

Driving in British Columbia and Alberta

Major roads across Canada are superbly maintained and most signs are in both English and French, with distances in kilometres. The greatest challenge, other than winter driving, is that pedestrians always have the right of way at zebra crossings (crosswalks) and intersections.

Away from the coast in winter, blowing snow can reduce visibility to zero, and snow, ice and wet roadways slow or halt traffic for hours. BC highways require mandatory use of chains (traction devices) when a posted highway sign states: *Winter Tires or Chains Are Required Beyond This Point*. Alberta requires chains or snow tyres 'when conditions warrant', but all mountain national parks require chains or tyres. It's wise to keep the petrol (gas) tank at least half full at all times. Carry extra water, food, warm clothing and a torch if driving in winter or marginal weather conditions outside of urban areas. Useful snow country equipment includes an ice scraper and small shovel. Parked cars should be equipped with a front engine compartment plug, plugged into an electrical source and the engine block heater turned on when temperatures fall to –10°C.

The green sign with a white maple leaf marks the Trans-Canada Highway (Highway 1) that runs 7,821km from Victoria on Vancouver

Lights

Headlights must be on at all times. Driving only with parking lights is illegal.

Mobile phones

Mobile or cell(ular) phone use while driving is not illegal, but a hands-free device is recommended over one that requires dialling and distracts attention from the road. A cell phone can be useful to call 911 in an emergency or for breakdown assistance.

Road information

British Columbia Ministry of Transportation; *tel: (800) 550-4997; www.drivebc.ca*, and in Alberta, the Alberta Motor Association (AMA); *tel: (877) 262-4997; www.ama.ab.ca/road-report/highways.htm*, has road condition information. Local radio stations also broadcast weather and driving information. In urban areas, most stations have regular traffic reports during morning and evening rush hours.

Government of Canada Weather Information numbers are in the telephone directory blue pages. Check weather online for British Columbia at *www.weatheroffice.gc.ca/forecast/canada/index_e.html?id=BC*

Island to Kamloops, Golden, Banff National Park, Calgary, and on to St John's, Newfoundland in the east. The Yellowhead Highway, with its road sign of a silhouette of the Iroquois fur trapper, Tête Jaune (Yellow Head), is a northern alternative to some of the Trans-Canada Highway. The Yellowhead (Highway 16) leaves Highway 1 west of Winnipeg, and is the main route through Edmonton, Jasper, Prince George and ends at Prince Rupert. Highway 3, the Crowsnest Highway, is marked with a black crow on a white signpost and crosses the BC–Alberta boundary in the south. The Icefields Parkway, with hanging and walk-on glaciers, alpine lakes, waterfalls and river vistas between Lake Louise and Jasper, is one of Canada's most scenic drives. Vancouver, Whistler and Victoria are the principal venues for the 2010 Olympic and Paralympic Winter Games.

Driving rules

Traffic drives on the right in Canada. Car headlights must be on at all times while driving, even in daylight. Horns are seldom used.

When cars arrive at an intersection at nearly the same moment, the vehicle to the right proceeds first. Unless otherwise posted, a vehicle can turn right from the right-hand lane after a full stop. Before turning, drivers should, but don't always, signal the direction of the intended turn. Buses stopping at the right side of the road and pulling out into traffic proceed first, and bicycles, like pedestrians, should generally be yielded the right of way. Roadways are marked with a solid white line for 'do not pass', and with a broken line on the side where vehicles may pass. In mountainous areas, curves are not infrequent, dictating slower speeds and no passing. Oncoming traffic on narrow roads is required to let the uphill driver proceed. If stuck in mud or snow, gently rock the vehicle by changing from forward to reverse gears. Beware of agricultural vehicles moving more slowly than regular traffic, which will be marked with a reflector, but may scatter hay or splash snow or slush across the windscreen. Stop when a school bus lowers its red and white STOP sign or flashes its lights – and do not pass.

Fuel

Petrol (gas, gasoline) and diesel are sold at gas stations in litres. For drivers from the USA, who are used to gas sold in US gallons (3.78 litres), pump prices may be bewildering. There are several major gas companies, but prices vary only minimally, and can be higher outside of cities and major towns. Most vehicles take unleaded petrol that comes in regular, premium and super grades. Buy regular unless the car-hire company or vehicle operations manual specifies otherwise. Most stations are self-service although some offer a high-priced, full-service alternative. Pump prices include all taxes. Cash and credit cards are accepted, though for safety, most stations will not accept

Seat belts

The driver and all passengers must wear seat belts or a child safety restraint that meets Canadian Motor Vehicle Safety Standards. Check *www.icbc.com/road_safety/ carseat_kindof.asp; tel: (877) 247-2551*, for up-to-date information on child seat requirements. Safety seats can be hired with the car or purchased for under $100 at a discount store. In an RV, passengers riding behind the driver's seat need not wear belts, but should be safely seated when the vehicle is in motion.

bills over $20. Try to keep the tank at least half full at all times and fill up in the daytime when you can be sure stations are open.

Information

Both Tourism British Columbia and Travel Alberta and their Visitor InfoCentres provide fine free provincial maps. The six Canadian Rockies National Parks have maps and visitor information in *The Mountain Guide*, a free brochure that is available at the parks or online at *www.pc.gc.ca/docs/v-g/pm-mp/guidem-mguide/index_e.asp*. Auto club maps are useful for specific areas and many area or district chambers of commerce have local maps.

Parking

Parking garages, parking lots and parkades (car parks) are indicated by a white P on a blue background. Prices are posted at the entrance and some urban parkades accept credit cards. Kerbside parking is usually limited, either by posted signs or by coin-operated parking meters, where the per-hour rate may be higher than in lots and parkades.

Kerbs may be colour-coded: red is no stopping or parking at any time; white is for passenger loading/unloading only; green is limited time parking (usually 10 minutes); yellow is a commercial loading zone; blue is special permit handicapped parking. Parking is not permitted within 5m of a fire hydrant; near a disabled kerb ramp; at bus stops, intersections or zebra crossings (crosswalks); blocking a driveway; on pavements (sidewalks), or on highways.

Security

Lock the vehicle when you're inside as well as when you leave it. Always park in well-lit areas at night, in the open and within view of passers-by. Check for intruders before getting in your vehicle at night – and an RV anytime. Never leave the engine running when the driver is not behind the wheel. The RCMP can always render assistance. Should you have the misfortune to become a victim of crime, your insurers will require you to report the circumstances to the police and obtain a police report that you have done so.

Speed limits

The highway speed limit is 80–100kph for cars, posted less for trucks and RVs. Slow down in towns and cities, where the speed limit is 50kph or lower. If driving conditions are poor, drivers are required to keep to a safe speed, no matter how slow. Police use radar and aircraft to track, stop and ticket (cite) speeders, but be alert – you could be stopped – even when traffic normally flows at least 10kph above the posted limit.

CANADIAN ROAD SIGNS

Yield (Give Way)

No Entry

Curve (bend)

No Left Turn

No U-turn

Divided highway
(dual carriageway)

Stop sign ahead

Signs unique to the British Columbia area

Logging trucks use
or cross the road

Deer or elk cross
the road

Moose cross
the road

This sign denotes a
severe road condition such
as a turn which requires
drivers to slow down

Freeway sign showing
distance to exit

Rural road destinations
are shown with finger
boards

B.C. Provincial

Trans-Canada
(Highway 1 and
Highway 16)

Thanks to the following website for its kind permission to reproduce the B.C. signs:
www.bchwys.ca

Getting to Vancouver and British Columbia

Unless you already live within driving distance of British Columbia, flying is the most practical way to get there, with rail a close second. **VIA Rail** operates a popular transcontinental railway service to Vancouver and Prince Rupert. Summer schedules are timed for daylight transit through the Rocky Mountains and through the Skeena River Valley to Prince Rupert.

There is also a ferry service from Seattle and other cities in Washington State to Vancouver and Victoria, as well as a rail service from the US via **AMTRAK**.

Motor coach travel is possible, though slow and cramped. Air travel is even more cramped, but travel time is counted in hours rather than days.

If your primary interest is the Rocky Mountains, consider flying into Calgary, Alberta, rather than Vancouver. Banff is two hours by car from Calgary compared to 12 to 14 hours of driving from Vancouver via Hwy 1, the TransCanada Highway. If you *are* driving from Vancouver, consider overnighting in Revelstoke, about halfway to Banff National Park.

No matter where you're flying into, don't let airline flight schedules mislead you into a full first day of touring. Vancouver may be only 10–12 air hours from much of Europe or Asia, but jet lag intensifies the effects of long-distance air travel. Expect to arrive fatigued, disoriented, short-tempered and otherwise *not* ready to drive.

Night-time flights are attractive because they seem to offer an extra day of sightseeing upon arrival. Resist the temptation. Most travellers do better by timing their flights to arrive in the late afternoon or early evening, then getting a good night's sleep before tackling the sights. Since many airport-area hotels and motels offer a free shuttle service to and from the airport, you can take a shuttle to the hotel, sleep off the flight, shuttle back to the airport the next morning and pick up the hire car at no additional cost.

One of the best 'cures' for jet lag is simply spending lots of time in the outdoors and letting the sun help you

Below
Floatplane

adjust to the new time zone. Drinking lots of water during the flight and going easy on the alcohol also help.

Many fly-drive programmes offer what looks like an easy first-day drive, ie Vancouver International Airport to Whistler, north of Vancouver. It's a two-hour jaunt that can stretch to half a day in weekend or holiday traffic. Better to spend the first night in an airport-area hotel and hit the road refreshed in the morning – especially if you're not accustomed to urban traffic or driving on the right side of the road.

The reverse is equally true. Don't plan a tight schedule that gets you into Vancouver or Calgary and on to the airport the requisite two or more hours before an international departure. Unexpected traffic can leave you stranded on a freeway as your plane takes off overhead. Allow a safety margin by spending your last night in Canada near the departure airport, or at least in the same city, and plan extra time to clear airport security.

Try to arrive with a few dollars in Canadian currency and coins. Luggage trolleys are free in the international arrivals area but must be paid for in some domestic airports. Some trolley stands accept credit cards, usually VISA or MasterCard, but other stands require cash – and currency exchange facilities are located outside the arrivals area.

ATMs, automated teller machines, offer the best currency exchange rates and never close. Star and Cirrus are the most common international ATM networks, but check with your card issuer before leaving home to ensure that you have the proper four-digit PIN (personal identification number) for Canadian outlets. International airports have currency exchange facilities in the international terminal that are open long hours. Domestic terminals and smaller airports generally have no exchange facilities. US dollar and pound sterling traveller's cheques from Thomas Cook and other major issuers are accepted almost everywhere, but traveller's cheques in other currencies must generally be cashed at a bank. Personal cheques drawn on banks outside Canada are generally not accepted.

Canadian airports don't have duty-free shopping for incoming travellers, but it's no great loss. Prices for alcohol and other duty-free items are almost always lower in Liquor Stores, supermarkets and discount stores than in duty-free shops.

Some car-hire companies have cars at Vancouver International Airport itself (in a car park just outside International Arrivals), others require that you take a coach to an off-airport facility to pick up your hire car – be sure to ask when making your car reservation.

If hiring an RV, ask the hire company about airport pick-up and drop-off when making your booking. Most hire companies provide free transport to and from their offices, which are usually located some distance from the airport.

Above
Whistler Mountain

Setting the scene

The land

British Columbia. It was named in the 19th century after a river, the Columbia, itself named after an 18th-century American ship that took its name from a 15th-century Italian, Christopher Columbus, who never came anywhere near his 21st-century namesake.

Like its name, BC is a hodge-podge of geography: massive glaciers and bone-dry deserts; rich alluvial plains and sheer granite canyons. Home to one of the greatest cities in North America, BC also lays claim to some of the least developed and least populated land on the continent. It's also a latecomer to the travel scene.

Early explorers

A Chinese manuscript tells of a storm-whipped voyage eastward to a land of enormous trees and red-skinned people around 220 BC, but landfall could have been among the towering redwood forests of Northern California and Oregon as easily as the red cedar and Sitka spruce stands of British Columbia. Chinese and Japanese shipwrecks along the North American coast have been dated as early as the 5th century AD, matching Asian ceramics found up and down the length of the Columbia River. Sir Francis Drake *may* have visited Vancouver Island in 1579 on his voyage to plunder Spanish possessions around the world, but any sure evidence was lost when Drake's logbook burned in an Admiralty fire.

That leaves Juan de Fuca, a Greek sailing for Spain in 1592, as the first outsider to visit BC officially. De Fuca gave his name to the strait between Vancouver Island and Washington State, due south, but neither the First Nations who lived there nor the Europeans who read of them much noticed or cared – possibly because stormy weather prevented de Fuca from landing and seeing BC first hand. It wasn't until Danish captain Vitus Bering sailed east from Russia in the early 1700s that Europe began to pay serious attention to the northwest edge of North America.

What Bering found were enormous populations of sea otters, much prized by merchants in China for their rich, silky fur. Russian hunters and merchants flocked to Alaska to trade with local Native groups for otter pelts. This sparked a race for commerce that brought Spanish, English and American traders to the coast.

Spain got there first. Juan Perez arrived from Mexico in 1774, claiming the Queen Charlotte Islands and Nootka Sound, on the western coast of Vancouver Island. Bruno de Heceta and Juan

Francisco de la Bodega y Quadra sailed north in 1775, a trip most notable for what didn't happen. Heceta noted, but didn't bother to explore, 'the mouth of some great river'. It was the Columbia, the easiest way to reach the interior of British Columbia until the transcontinental railway arrived a century later.

Search for the Northwest Passage

The British had their own commercial and strategic agenda. The Admiralty as well as commercial explorers had been searching for a direct route westward across the Atlantic to Asia for nearly two centuries. Parliament had a standing offer of £20,000 to the person who discovered a northern sea route to China and Asian lands south. Innumerable navigators had failed to find the Northwest Passage from the Atlantic side, so Captain James Cook went looking for the Pacific Ocean end of the fabled passage.

The fur trade

Cook never found the passage east, but he did find safe anchorage at Nootka Sound, then controlled by Spain. His officers and men traded with the Mowachat First Nation to obtain sea otter pelts for clothing and bedding against the coming winter.

Cook eventually sailed south for Hawaii, where he was killed in 1779. Charles Clark, the expedition's second-in-command, headed for home by way of Macao. When Macanese merchants discovered the well-worn otter skins, they paid such astronomical prices that the crew threatened to mutiny if they didn't return to Nootka Sound. Clark put down the rebellion and sailed for home, where news of the voyage set off a fur rush. Ships from Boston and New York joined the fray once America's war for independence from Britain ended in 1783. The crush of traders nearly led to war between Britain and Spain, but cooler, more commercial minds prevailed. Both countries mounted expeditions to map the Northwest coast in preparation for diplomatic talks.

Spain sent Bodega y Quadra; Britain sent George Vancouver, who had sailed to Vancouver Island as midshipman under Cook. America wasn't part of the talks, but legal technicalities weren't enough to keep trader Robert Gray away. It was Gray who found and charted the mouth of the Columbia River in 1792, establishing US claims to the region. Later the same year, British and Spanish authorities signed the Nootka Accord, agreeing that the Northwest Coast should be open to traders of all nations.

The Nootka Accord was the high point of European exploration of BC by sea as war engulfed Europe and over-hunting destroyed the otter trade. Spain eventually traded its claims to the Pacific Northwest to America in return for Washington's recognition of Spanish title to California.

As far as Britain was concerned, all the important activity in Western Canada took place on land. British traders had been trading for furs across Eastern Canada for 200 years. In 1670, the Hudson's Bay Company (HBC) had wrangled rights to everything west from Hudson Bay, a vast, unknown territory called Rupert's Land. Anthony Henday paddled up the North Saskatchewan River from Hudson Bay in 1754 and became the first known White to glimpse Canada's Rocky Mountains. He returned the next spring, canoes nearly swamped under the weight of furs, and set off an overland rush. Competitors followed, including a French-Canadian consortium, the North West Company (NWC) and numerous American companies. The race to find a way through BC to the Pacific Ocean was on.

North West Company partners Alexander Mackenzie, Simon Fraser and David Thompson grabbed an early lead. Mackenzie made his way west to the mouth of the Bella Coola River in 1793, the first White to cross the continent north of Mexico. He returned with tales of a land so filled with wild animals that it looked like a 'stall-yard'.

Americans Meriwether Lewis and William Clark explored west from American territory, reaching the mouth of the Columbia River before returning home in 1806. Fraser battled through treacherous rapids along the Fraser River to the Pacific in 1808. Thompson paddled the entire length of the Columbia in 1811, but reached the Pacific Ocean four months late. He arrived to find American traders who had sailed around Cape Horn building a fort at modern day Astoria.

American presence

That initial American presence seemed of no great import. The NWC peacefully took over Astoria when war broke out between the US and Britain in 1812. When the war ended, the 49th Parallel divided the United States and British America east of the Rockies, and the two countries jointly occupied the unmapped West. When the HBC took control of the NWC in 1821, Britain emerged triumphant with the only economic force that spanned the continent. But British power existed only on paper. On the ground, the West was beyond control.

The Americans, however, were getting restless. In 1825, Britain and the US both recognised Russian authority south to 54°40', the current boundary between Southern Alaska and Northern BC. Americans began talking of 'Manifest Destiny', the idea that they were empowered by divine right to occupy the continent from ocean to ocean. Missionaries who were moving westward to 'civilise the savages' began sending back enticing reports of rich farmland beyond the Rocky Mountains.

The HBC was just as busy, building and strengthening forts at Spokane, Okanagan, Nisqually, Langley and elsewhere to block American expansion. Company farms along the Columbia River and Puget Sound in what is now Oregon and Washington fed both inland

Opposite
Totem pole, Stanley Park, Vancouver

Above
Fort Steele Heritage Town

forts and a growing export trade to Alaska, Hawaii and Asia. HBC's chief factor, Dr John McLoughlin, systematically directed American immigrants south into present-day Oregon, hoping to retain the Columbia River, the only practical route into British Columbia, the company's most profitable territory. But the HBC also hedged their position. In 1841, company governor George Simpson and head trader James Douglass moved to Fort Victoria, on the southern tip of Vancouver Island. It was a foresightful move.

US Army surveyors were already mapping a wagon route westward over the Rocky Mountains by way of passes far lower and easier than any in British America. The US Navy paid a 'goodwill' visit to the Pacific Northwest, updating its charts from the Columbia River region north to Vancouver Island and noting the HBC's lack of coastal defences. In 1843, America moved.

The US Senate officially declared Oregon Territory, an enormous tract west of the Rockies, north of California and south of Alaska, to be American. Americans were told it was their patriotic duty and God-given destiny to move west. More importantly, they were given an irresistible lure: 260 hectares for every White US male and 130 hectares for his wife, free for the taking.

Fortunately for Britain, the initial settlers headed south into the Willamette River Valley, south of the Columbia River. But US–British tensions heightened in 1844 when James Polk won the presidential election on the slogan of '54°40' or Fight!', challenging Britain for control north in the West. Since neither country was anxious for a third war, diplomats simply extended the existing boundary, the 49th Parallel, to the Pacific Ocean, then west down the middle of the Strait of Juan de Fuca between Vancouver Island and Washington State.

The HBC lost the Columbia River, the only viable route from interior BC to the coast. Furs from the interior began moving eastward over the Yellowhead Pass, through the Northern Rockies and downriver through Alberta. In coastal areas, the company turned to commerce and farming.

Britain leased all of Vancouver Island to the HBC in 1849 in order to create a colony. Just months later, the Gold Rush in California sent demand for grain, timber, coal and every sort of manufactured product through the roof. Successive gold strikes in Oregon and Washington kept farming and lumbering busy even as a new Royal Navy station at Esquimalt, next to Victoria, boosted coal mining at Nanaimo. Demand for salmon kept salteries, and later canneries, busy.

Settlers, however, were in short supply. Would-be immigrants headed for Oregon and Washington in the western US, where land was less expensive and easier to get to. Until the Canadian Pacific Railway arrived in 1886, the only practicable route to BC was a brutal five-month voyage around the tip of South America. Victoria remained a prosperous but tiny town surrounded by vast forests. Gold changed history, just as it had done in California, Oregon and Washington.

The Gold Rush

HBC traders had been accepting occasional amounts of the precious metal from their First Nation trading partners for years, but the company had never revealed its discoveries, fearing further encroachment by American interests. Faced with growing piles of the stuff in Victoria vaults and rumours of gold finds on the Fraser River starting to circulate, the HBC decided to act. After enacting strict mining licence laws and laying in supplies, the company sent 20kg of raw gold to the nearest mint, San Francisco, early in 1858. The next summer, more than 30,000 miners flooded north from America.

HBC made a fortune supplying the Gold Rush. The company was also terrified that America would take control as easily as it had seized California from Mexico in 1846. Although British on the map, both Vancouver Island and New Caledonia, as the mainland was called, were effectively outside all political control.

The fears were warranted. American miners demanded immediate changes to mining regulations and government practices. A special US Commissioner sent to the Fraser River gold fields to look after American interests reported that it was only a matter of time until both Vancouver Island and the mainland became American by force of population alone. Unless, of course, Washington wanted to act sooner.

While the Americans debated, the British acted. In June 1858, the House of Commons declared the mainland a Crown Colony. Queen Victoria chose the name British Columbia and assigned key officials. A provisional government was declared at Fort Langley in November, then moved to New Westminster (now part of Greater Vancouver), a

Aboriginal Tourism Association of British Columbia (ATBC)
#704 100 Park Royal S, West Vancouver, BC V7T 1A2; tel: (877) 266-2822 or (604) 921-1070; www.aboriginalbc.com, promotes British Columbia First Nations cultures, museums, and tours offered by members and acts as an information resource.

site Royal Engineers judged more defensible against an expected American invasion. Gold Commissioners and magistrates imposed strict order in the mining camps, a startling contrast to the lawlessness and self-rule that predominated in US mining communities of the time.

The new provincial government also adapted a US-style land distribution system, allowing White settlers to buy up to 65 hectares at bargain rates – the entire Lower Fraser River Valley was settled, cleared and planted within nine years. Cattle ranches sprang up across the province as drovers brought herds north from Washington and discovered fine meadows ready for the taking.

Merchants prospered, but every economic downturn prompted new calls for union with America, the land most BC residents had so recently left. Talk of a State of British Columbia increased when America purchased Alaska from Russia in 1867, bolstered by half-hearted attempts by Washington to claim BC as compensation for British support of the (defeated) Confederacy during the US Civil War.

It was an uneasy time, even as continuing gold discoveries opened the Cariboo, the Kootenays and almost every corner in between. BC's political leaders were firmly British, but business lived or died by commercial decisions made in San Francisco, not London markets. Ordinary citizens were either recent American immigrants or Canadian-born with little loyalty to any government beyond the strictly local. Talk of union with America faded after BC voted to join the new Dominion of Canada in 1870, a vote bought by promises of an all-Canadian transcontinental railway and strengthened economic ties east across the Rockies. When the rails finally arrived in 1886, an obscure lumber town called Vancouver was suddenly catapulted to fame and fortune as Western Canada's richest, most successful and most cosmopolitan city.

First Nations

The biggest losers were BC's original First Nations inhabitants. Smallpox and other European disease brought to Mexico by Spanish explorers and conquerors had been steadily moving north and west following long-established trade routes. Epidemics had begun to sweep through mainland tribes about the time Spanish and English traders first appeared off Vancouver Island and entire villages were wiped out. Survivors had little chance against government policies and agents intent on clearing land for White settlement. HBC agents commonly purchased tribal lands, but prices were pitiful and promises to protect traditional hunting and fishing areas were routinely violated.

Colonial and Dominion officials treated tribes as well as individuals as incompetent imbeciles by policy, regularly confiscating land and resources 'for their own good'. In 1874, a BC/Canadian Indian Reserve Commission began setting aside lands for First Nations groups. The region's original inhabitants ended up with 0.34 per cent of the

2010 Olympic and Paralympic Winter Games
www.vancouver2010.com/en.
In 2010, Vancouver, Whistler and other British Columbia venues will host the Olympic Games (*12–28 Feb*) and Paralympic Winter Games (*12–21 Mar*). To attend events and travel in British Columbia in February or March 2010, book early (*see p23*).

Above
Thunderbird Totem

province. The railways alone were given 8 per cent of BC's most commercially profitable and agriculturally useful land.

Along the coast, First Nations' traditional practices were outlawed in an effort to destroy indigenous culture and increase dependence upon the government. Generations of children were forcibly removed from their families to be raised in church- and government-run residential schools, where the use of Native languages was strictly forbidden. Claims for monetary compensation, return of traditional lands and enforcement of long-ignored treaty terms are meeting with a fair degree of success in modern courts.

The railway and the 20th century

The development boom came to an abrupt end with the Panic of 1893. Stock market failures around the world were echoed in bank and railway failures, which brought down businesses and farms dependent upon capital and transportation – which included most of BC. Recovery had to wait for the Yukon Gold Rush of 1898. World War I put a damper on growth, but the economy boomed again into the 1920s, as irrigation spread into the Okanagan and other areas thought too dry for successful agriculture. World War II saw the development of the chain saw and other mechanised equipment that allowed the timber industry to leap into a post-war housing boom.

The last patch of virgin forest near Victoria was reduced to a wasteland in the 1970s, sparking furious protests. Plans to expand logging in the Queen Charlotte Islands led to the most massive campaign of civil disobedience in Canadian history – and to the formation of a new national park, Gwaii Haanas, in 1987. Similar efforts in the 1990s to log virgin forests in Clayquot Sound, off the west coast of Vancouver Island, sparked more protests.

Salmon runs, once the mainstay of BC life, have all but disappeared. Overfishing by fleets from the United States, Canada and other Pacific nations is partly to blame, but the despoliation of spawning beds by logging and other human activity is even more destructive.

The decline of resource industries is producing a new economic ethic. Although couched in references to Mother Earth and First Nations beliefs, the new model is based on harsh economic choices: resources can be used up, as the sea otter trade, the fur trade, fisheries, mining and a growing number of timber companies have shown. Or the resources can be preserved for some less intensive but longer-term use. Sport fishing, for example, boosts the local economy more than commercial fishing. Recreational use of forests is more profitable in the long run than clearcutting. Mountain climbers, skiers and sightseers spend more money to enjoy an undamaged mountain than mining companies pay to turn it into ore and toxic waste. The outcome of this ongoing battle is shaping the face and the psyche of BC in the 21st century.

Highlights and touring itineraries

Top ten sights

Not the top ten places visitors to BC actually *go* to, but the top ten that we recommend not to miss.

• **Barkerville Historic Town** (*page 186*)
The *real* Cariboo Gold Rush that refused to die.

• **Fort Steele Heritage Town** (*page 253*)
A frontier town that has brought the 1890s vividly back to life.

• **Fraser River Canyon & Hell's Gate** (*pages 190–1 and 193*)
The toughest terrain you're ever likely to drive.

• **Gwaii Haanas National Park Reserve, Queen Charlotte Islands** (*pages 117–18*)
Leave the car behind to see nature on the edge.

• **The Hazeltons – (Old) Hazelton, 'Ksan and Kispiox** (*pages 216–17*)
Where the heart of the First Nations beats most powerfully.

• **The Paint Pots, Kootenay National Park** (*page 261*)
The colours and the setting are magical.

• **Nelson** (*pages 246–7*)
It looks as good in person as it did on the silver screen.

• **Meadows in the Sky, Mount Revelstoke National Park** (*page 235*)
Wildflower carpets that disappear into empty summer skies.

• **Inner Harbour & Thunderbird Park, Victoria** (*pages 69–70*)
Everyone's vision of what BC *should* look like.

• **Takakkaw Falls, Yoho National Park** (*pages 265–6*)
First Nations visitors were as awe-struck as modern travellers.

The best of BC

These three circular tours start and end in Vancouver, but there's no reason not to pick up either of the last two routes from Calgary. Suggested overnight stops are shown in **bold**.

Two weeks

The Great Western BC Marathon. You'll need time at home to recover from this holiday.

Day 1 Arrive in **Vancouver** (*see page 42*).
Day 2 **Vancouver**.
Day 3 BC Ferries to **Victoria** (*see page 62*).
Day 4 The Island Highway to **Campbell River** (*see page 98*).
Day 5 The Island Highway to **Port Hardy** (*see page 101*).
Day 6 BC Ferries' **Discovery Coast** (*see page 106*) route to Bella Coola.
Day 7 Bella Coola over The Hill to **Anahim Lake/Nimpo Lake** (*see pages 198–201*).
Day 8 Hwy 20 to **Riske Creek** (*see page 202*).
Day 9 Hwy 97 to Barkerville, overnight in **Wells** or **Quesnel** (*see page 192*).
Day 10 Hwy 97 to **100 Mile House** (*see page 191*).
Day 11 Hwy 97 to **Cache Creek** (*see page 187*).
Day 12 Hwy 1 through the Fraser River Canyon to Hells Gate and **Hope** (*see page 127*).
Day 13 Hwy 1 to **Vancouver**.
Day 14 Home.

The Great Interior BC Marathon. You'll need a few days to rest up from this one, too.

Day 1 Arrive in **Vancouver** (*see page 42*).
Day 2 Hwy 1 to **Hope** (*see page 127*).
Day 3 Hwy 1 through the Fraser River Canyon and Hells Gate to **Kamloops** (*see page 138*).
Day 4 Hwy 1 through the Shuswap Lakes to **Revelstoke** (*see page 236*).
Day 5 Hwy 1 over Rodgers Pass and Glacier National Park to **Golden** (*see page 233*).
Day 6 Hwy 1 through Yoho National Park to **Lake Louise/Banff/Canmore** (*see pages 271 and 273*).

Day 7 Hwy 93 through Kootenay National Park to **Radium Hot Springs** (*see page 261*).

Day 8 Hwy 95 to Fort Steele Heritage Town and **Cranbrook** (*see page 250*).

Day 9 Hwy 3/3A to Creston, the Kootenay Lake Ferry and **Nelson** (*see page 246*).

Day 10 Hwy 3A/3 to Castlegar and **Grand Forks** (*see page 243*).

Day 11 Hwy 3/97 to **Penticton** (*see page 153*).

Day 12 Hwy 97/3A/3 to Keremeos, Princeton and **Manning Provincial Park** (*see page 132*).

Day 13 Hwy 3 to Hope and **Vancouver**.

Day 14 Home.

Four weeks

See most of BC in a busy month.

Day 1 Arrive in **Vancouver** (*see page 42*).

Day 2 **Vancouver**.

Day 3 BC Ferries to **Victoria** (*see page 62*).

Day 4 Island Highway to Nanaimo and **Campbell River** (*see page 98*).

Day 5 Island Highway to **Port Hardy** (*see page 101*).

Day 6 BC Ferries to **Prince Rupert** (*see page 206*).

Day 7 BC Ferries/fly to **Skidegate**, Queen Charlotte Islands (*see page 120*).

Days 8 & 9 **Gwaii Haanas National Park Reserve** (*see page 117*).

Day 10 BC Ferries/fly to **Prince Rupert** (*see page 206*).

Day 11 Yellowhead Highway (Hwy 16) to the Hazeltons and **Smithers** (*see page 218*).

Day 12 Yellowhead Highway (Hwy 16) to Fort St James and **Prince George** (*see page 222*).

Day 13 Hwy 97 to Barkerville and **Wells/Quesnel** (*see page 192*).

Day 14 Hwy 97/1 to **Kamloops** (*see page 138*).

Day 15 Hwy 1 through the Shuswap Lakes to **Revelstoke** (*see page 236*).

Day 16 Hwy 1 over Rodgers Pass and Glacier National Park to **Golden** (*see page 233*).

Day 17 Hwy 1 through Yoho National Park to **Lake Louise/Banff/Canmore** (*see pages 271 and 273*).

Day 18 Hwy 93 through Kootenay National Park to **Radium Hot Springs** (*see page 261*).

Day 19 Hwy 95 to Fort Steele and **Cranbrook** (*see page 250*).

Day 20 Hwy 3 to **Creston** (*see page 243*).

Day 21 Hwy 3A to the Kootenay Lake Ferry and **Nelson** (*see page 246*).

Day 22 Hwy 3A/3 to Castlegar and **Grand Forks** (*see page 243*).

Day 23 Hwy 3/97 to **Penticton** (*see page 153*).

Day 24 Hwy 97/97C to Kelowna, Meritt, Kamloops and **Cache Creek** (*see page 187*).

Day 25 Hwy 1/99 to Hat Creek and **Lillooet** (*see page 191*).

Day 26 Hwy 12/1 to Lytton, down the Fraser River Canyon to **Hope** (*see page 127*).

Day 27 Hwy 1 to **Vancouver**.

Day 28 Home.

Ratings

Beaches	●●●●●
Food	●●●●●
Outdoor activities	●●●●●
Scenery	●●●●●
Children	●●●●○
History	●●●●○
Museums	●●●●○
First Nations	●●●○○

Vancouver

Canada's third-largest city is a small town at heart. Decades of immigration have given Vancouver more foreign-born citizens than any other North American city, yet it remains an essentially Canadian place. Yes, black is the uniform of the day, and hard-eyed attitude the public posture *du jour*, but Vancouver remains a polite, tidy town where everyone seems to know everyone else and quite prefers it that way. Harbour vistas vie with Sydney, Hong Kong and San Francisco for the world's best, while urban views stand in for big-city streetscapes from Los Angeles to London, Moscow and Shanghai. Cosmopolitan Vancouver works hard to remain an overgrown village on the edge of a vast rainforest. Serious mountains rise within sight of City Hall, while *laissez-faire* beaches are just a quick bus ride away and a young, bustling population is ready to enjoy both at the slightest excuse, along with some of North America's best dining. Vancouver is also renowned as a gay-lesbian friendly place and annually processes one million passengers from around the world who are en route to Alaska through the Canada Place and Ballantyne Cruise Ship Terminals.

Arriving and departing

ⓘ Tourism Vancouver/ Vancouver Touristinfo Centre *Plaza Level, 200 Burrard St, Vancouver, BC V6C 3L6; tel: (604) 683-2000; www.tourismvancouver.com. Open daily 0830–1800, with tourist information, bookings for accommodation and sightseeing tours, a partner travel agency for air and cruise ship reservations, and the Tickets Tonight half-price ticket service.*

Visitor Information Centre *Vancouver International Airport international and domestic arrivals level. Open daily.*

Most air services use Vancouver International Airport (YVR) (*www.yvr.ca*). Vancouver's rapid transit Skytrain adds the Canada Line (*www.canadaline.ca*) in late 2009 for 25-minute transit from YVR to Vancouver's Waterfront Station. Regional carriers offer a seaplane service from the harbour.
• **VIA Rail** *Pacific Central Station, 1150 Station St; tel: (888) 842-7245; www.viarail.ca*, provides national rail service.
• **Rocky Mountaineer Vacations** *1755 Cottrell St at Terminal Ave; tel: (604) 606-7245 or (877) 460-3200 (00 800-0606-7372 from the UK); http://rockymountaineer.com*, offer rail tours to Whistler on the *Whistler Mountaineer* and the Rocky Mountains.

Lions Gate Bridge

Grouse Mountain

Capilano Suspension Bridge

First Narrows

Stanley Park Drive

99

1A

Stanley Park

Beaver Lake

Lions Gate Bridge Road

Burrard Inlet

N

Aquarium

Stanley Park Drive

Lost Lagoon

SeaBus

West End

Lagoon Drive

Gilford Street

Coal Harbour

Georgia Street

Pender Street

Canada Place

Waterfront Station

English Bay

Beach Avenue

Denman Street

Barclay Street

Robson Street

Nelson Street

Broughton Street

Comox Street

Pendrell Street

Barclay Heritage Square

Jervis Street

Bute Street

Vancouver Art Gallery

Lookout Tower

Water Street

Gastown

Davie Street

Hastings Street

Chinatown

Burnaby Street

Thurlow Street

Cambie St.

Pender Street

Carrall St.

English Bay

Harwood Street

Bute Street

Burrard Street

Hornby Street

Granville Street Mall

Robson Street

Dunsmuir Street

Howe Street

Nelson Street

Smithe Street

Georgia Street

Vancouver Maritime Museum

Vancouver Museum

Vanier Park

Beach Avenue

Pacific Street

Granville Street

Seymour Street

BC Place Stadium

Museum of Anthropology

Burrard Street Bridge

Yaletown

Science World

4th Ave

Granville Street Bridge

Granville Island

Steveston

False Creek

VanDusen Botanical Garden

Cambie Street Bridge

Main Street

Nitobe Memorial Garden

University of British Columbia Botanical Garden

Bloedel Floral Conservatory

Vancouver International Airport

0		500m
0		500 yards

ⓘ The Georgia Straight *1701 W Broadway; tel: (604) 730-7000; www.straight.com,* a free weekly newspaper, has the best listing of local events, cultural attractions, performances, cinemas and other happenings.

Tickets Tonight *Tourism Vancouver Touristinfo Centre, Plaza Level, 200 Burrard St; tel: (604) 684-2787; http:// ticketstonight.ca/ticketstonight; open daily 1000–1800,* sells half-price tickets to performing arts, cultural events and sports throughout Greater Vancouver on the day of the event. You can also buy full-price tickets in advance.

Below
Vancouver cityscape

• **Highway access** is Hwy 1 (the TransCanada Hwy) from the east and Hwy 99 from the south and north.
• **BC Ferries** *tel: (250) 386-3431* or *(888) 223-3779; www.bcferries.com,* provide a ferry service from Tsawwassen (south of the city) to Victoria and Horseshoe Bay (northwest of the city) to Nanaimo, both on Vancouver Island.

Getting around

Public transport
TransLink *tel: (604) 953-3333; www.translink.bc.ca,* is Canada's largest public transport system, a combination of bus, light rail (SkyTrain) and ferry (SeaBus). All major tourist sites in the lower Mainland area are accessible by public transit, though schedules may not be convenient.
Aquabus Ferries *tel: (604) 689-5858; www.theaquabus.com,* and **False Creek Ferries** *tel: (604) 684-7781; http://granvilleislandferries.bc.ca,* provide a ferry service around False Creek from Science World west to the Maritime Museum.

Driving is practical throughout Vancouver, although traffic slows during rush hours *(0730–0930 and 1600–1800).* Left-turn lanes are rare and roadways can be narrow, especially in residential areas with kerbside parking. Metered parking is generally available; most car parks accept either coins or credit cards. Watch for cyclists.

Sights

🅱 **Barclay Heritage Square** *Barclay, Nicola, Haro and Broughton Sts. Open daily.*

Roedde House Museum *$ 1415 Barclay St; tel: (604) 684-7040; http:// roeddehouse.org. Open Tue–Fri, Sun 1400–1600 for guided tours.*

Bloedel Floral Conservatory & Queen Elizabeth Park $ *W. 33rd Ave and Cambie St; tel: (604) 257-8584; www. city.vancouver.bc.ca/parks/ parks/bloedel/index.htm. Conservatory open daily 1000–1700.*

Canada Place *Harbourside at the foot of Howe St; www.canadaplace.ca. Open daily.*

Capilano Suspension Bridge $$ *3735 Capilano Rd, North Vancouver; tel: (604) 985-7474; www. capilanosuspensionbridge. com. Open 0830–dusk in summer, 0900–1700 in winter. Call for exact hours.*

Chinatown *Gore, Keefer, Carrall and E Hastings Sts.*

Dr Sun Yat-Sen Classical Chinese Garden $$ *578 Carrall St; tel: (604) 662-3207; www. vancouverchinesegarden.com. Open Tue–Sun.*

Barclay Heritage Square

Vancouver's most elegant heritage area preserves nine of the city's few remaining Victorian-era (1890–1908) homes. Most are closed to the public, but the **Roedde House**, built in 1893, has become a period museum. All nine homes are surrounded by spectacular period gardens.

Bloedel Floral Conservatory

Perched atop Vancouver's highest hill in **Queen Elizabeth Park**, the silvery tridetic dome of Bloedel houses the city's largest tropical plant collection and 100 species of free-flying birds. A courtyard behind Bloedel is popular for *tai chi* and similar exercise activities morning and evening. Walking trails offer broad vistas of Vancouver, the harbour and the mountains beyond.

Canada Place

The sail-like, white roofline of Canada Place marks Vancouver's main cruise ship terminal, convention centre hotel and CN IMAX cinema. Look for cruise ships at dock during the May–September Alaska cruise season, and vast vistas across Burrard Inlet all year.

Capilano Suspension Bridge

This 137m footbridge sways 70m above the Capilano River canyon to a shady forest park on the far side. The original bridge opened in 1889, creating the first tourist attraction on what was then the deserted North Shore of Burrard Inlet. Today's bridge is laced with steel cables that can carry the weight of several fully loaded Boeing 747 passenger planes and did support a fallen 40-tonne Douglas fir in 2006, but the swaying, bouncing span feels more like a thrill ride when the spring melt turns the river below into a thundering torrent. **Treetops Adventure** is an hour's walk at the rainforest mid-storey along 250m of seven cable suspension bridges, suspended between eight Douglas fir trees. Free guided eco-tours add another dimension to the bridge crossing. The world's largest private display of totem poles can be seen at Kia'palano, the First Nations Cultural Centre, along with daily demonstrations of weaving, beadwork and cedar carving.

Chinatown

Vancouver's Chinatown is the third-largest Chinese community in North America after San Francisco and New York. What began as a refuge against periodic persecution has become a wealthy community infused by massive immigration from across Asia. Vegetables, fruits, fish and other goods spill from shops on to pavements that are jammed with shoppers all day, the most interesting and safest time to visit. **Dr Sun Yat-Sen Classical Chinese Garden**, the first classical Chinese garden built outside China, is an island of tranquillity.

English Bay West of
False Creek, between
Stanley Park and Point Grey.

False Creek East beneath
the Burrard Bridge, past
Granville Island to Science
World.

Gastown Water St, between
Columbia and E Cordova Sts;
http://gastown.org

Granville Island South
side of False Creek, beneath
the Granville Bridge;
tel: (604) 666-5784;
www.granvilleisland.com.
Open daily.

Grouse Mountain $$$
6400 Nancy Greene Way,
North Vancouver; tel: (604)
984-0661 or (604) 980-
9311;
http://grousemountain.com.
Skyride trams depart every
15 minutes, 0900–2200.

**Lookout Tower at
Harbour Centre** $$
555 W. Hastings St;
tel: (604) 689-0421;
http://vancouverlookout.com.
Open summer 0830–2230,
winter 0900–2100.

English Bay

The protected waters of English Bay, Captain James Vancouver's anchorage in 1792, are popular for kayaking and sailing. The shoreline, especially **Vanier**, **Hadden** and **Kitsilano Beach Parks** on the south and the **Seawall Promenade** into **Stanley Park** on the east, is popular for walking, cycling and rollerblading.

False Creek

This shallow inlet stretching east from English Bay along the south side of the inner city has become one of Vancouver's premier recreation areas. The one-time industrial slum has been reborn as a series of marinas, parks and low-rise housing developments with stunning water views, all linked by a walking and cycling trail stretching from Kitsilano Beach to Vanier Park, around False Creek to the Seawall Promenade and circling Stanley Park.

Gastown

Once Vancouver's red-light district, Gastown has become a less risqué, but no-less-popular, entertainment district where it's best to be cautious, especially at night. Many of Gastown's original brick buildings have been renovated as bars, restaurants and offices. Don't miss the **steam clock** at the corner of Water and Cambie streets, signalling the quarter hour with steam-powered chimes.

Granville Island

One million cubic metres of mud dredged from False Creek nearly a century ago created a metal-bashing haven called Industrial Island. Island factories produced decades-worth of rivets, chain, nails, cement and industrial pollutants. Industry was eased out in the 1960s, the site cleaned up and renamed. As Granville Island, it has become a popular refuge for boaters, artists, shoppers and entertainers. The **Public Market** (open daily 0900–1900) is Vancouver's best.

Grouse Mountain

Skim the slopes of 1,242m Grouse Mountain by the Skyride aerial tramway, or hike the Grouse Grind, a rugged walk that gains 850m in 2.9km. Either way, clear-weather views offer the best panorama of Vancouver ground-side of a helicopter. Peak facilities include restaurants, a cinematic exploration of lower BC from the air, in The Theatre In The Sky, a free-flight 'Birds in Motion' demonstration by an eagle, hawk, owl and peregrine falcon (May–Sep), a lumberjack skills demonstration (May–mid-Oct), kilometres of walking paths, helicopter rides, tandem paragliding, downhill mountain biking and the **Refuge for Endangered Wildlife** for orphaned grizzly bears and grey wolves. Grouse is open for winter skiing (snow line tel: (604) 986-6262), snowboarding, ice skating and sleigh rides.

🏛 Museum of Anthropology $$
6393 Northwest Marine Dr (University of British Columbia); tel: (604) 822-5087; www.moa.ubc.ca. Mid-May–early Oct open daily 1000–1700, Tue until 2100; early Oct–late May open Wed–Sun 1100–1700, Tue until 2100.

Nitobe Memorial Garden & UBC Botanical Garden $
6804 Southwest Marine Dr; tel: (604) 822-9666; www.nitobe.org or www.ubcbotanicalgarden.org. Open daily.

Below
Granville Street Bridge

Lookout Tower at Harbour Centre
Want to get your bearings? This tower 50 seconds' ride above a downtown mall has a 360-degree view of Vancouver, its waterways and mountains. Snacks and coffee are served, and a wireless internet connection provides contact with the world from on high.

Museum of Anthropology (MOA)
Canada's top anthropology museum has one of the world's finest collections of First Nations artefacts and art, with modern and antique totems, feast dishes and carvings in wood, stone, gold and other media. Don't miss the outdoor totem poles, directly behind the museum. MOA intends to double its space by 2009, with additional gallery space, room for travelling exhibits, and an enlarged museum shop with more superb Northwest art. Renovation will continue through 2010.

Nitobe Memorial Garden and University of British Columbia Botanical Garden
Nitobe is a calm Japanese tea and stroll garden 200m from MOA. The Botanical Garden has more than 400 species of rhododendrons, a 16th-century Physick Garden and thousands of other plants from around the world.

① Science World at TELUS World of Science $$ *1455 Quebec St; tel: (604) 443-7443; www.scienceworld.bc.ca. Open Mon–Fri 1000–1700, Sat–Sun 1000–1800.*

Stanley Park *West end of Georgia St; tel: (604) 257-8400; http://vancouver.ca/parks/parks/stanley. Open daily.*

Vancouver Aquarium Marine Science Centre $$$ *Tel: (604) 659-3474; www.vanaqua.org. Open late Jun–early Sep 0930–1900, early Sep–late Jun 0930–1700. Call for exact hours.*

Steveston $ *West end of Steveston Hwy, Richmond.*

Gulf of Georgia Cannery National Historic Site $ *12138 4th Ave, Richmond; tel: (604) 664-9009; www.pc.gc.ca/lhn-nhs/bc/georgia/index_e.asp. Open early May–early Oct. Call for hours.*

Vancouver Art Gallery $$ *750 Hornby St; tel: (604) 662-4719; www.vanartgallery.bc.ca. Open daily 1000–1730, Tue–Thu to 2100.*

Vancouver International Airport art *First Nations artwork is scattered throughout the international and domestic terminals; tel: (604) 207-7077; www.yvr.ca/guide/todo/art/index.asp*

Science World at TELUS World of Science
BC's largest science museum uses hands-on displays to explain the natural world for kids, who usually have to push their way through crowds of fascinated adults to reach the exhibits. There's an OMNIMAX® domed theatre and Centre Stage live shows that demonstrate natural forces and concepts – usually with audience participation.

Stanley Park
Vancouver has one of the world's finest urban parks, 400 hectares of forest laced with 80km of walking and cycling paths. The most popular path is a 10km shoreline loop. Highlights include totem poles, sweeping vistas across Vancouver and the North Shore, restaurants, picnic grounds, a rose garden, beaches and horse-drawn carriage tours. Major restoration and tree planting has been done since a major windstorm in 2006. **Vancouver Aquarium**, one of the best aquaria in the region, specialises in the Pacific Northwest, with a special area for beluga whales.

Steveston
This former salmon cannery town at the mouth of the Fraser River is still Canada's largest commercial fishing port and a popular local getaway. The **Gulf of Georgia Cannery National Historic Site** is a restored fish-processing plant, all that remains of what was once the world's largest concentration of salmon canneries.

Vancouver Art Gallery
This one-time courthouse showcases West Coast artists, as well as travelling exhibitions. The neoclassical exterior is often a shooting location for television and cinema productions.

Vancouver International Airport art
Vancouver Airport (YVR) has BC's best free collection of First Nations art. Most of the monumental eye-catchers are in the International

Above
Science World

Vancouver Maritime Museum
$$ 1905 Ogden Ave; Vanier Park; tel: (604) 257-8300; www.vancouvermaritimemuseum.com. Open daily Victoria Day–Labour Day 1000–1700; rest of year, Tue–Sat 1000–1700, Sun 1200–1700.

Vancouver Museum $$ Vanier Park, 1100 Chestnut St; tel: (604) 736-4431; www.vanmuseum.bc.ca. Open Tue–Sun (Mon in summer) 1000–1700, Thu to 2100.

VanDusen Botanical Garden $$ 5251 Oak St at 37th Ave; tel: (604) 878-9274; www.vandusengarden.org. Open 1000 daily.

Vanier Park Chestnut St, at English Bay; tel: (604) 257-8400. Open daily.

West End Between Burrard St and Stanley Park.

Terminal, including a trio of totems between the terminal and the car park, and *The Spirit of Haida Gwaii, The Jade Canoe*, a 6m bronze by Bill Reid, with traditional Haida themes on the departure level.

Vancouver Maritime Museum

Canada's finest Pacific museum is filled with uniforms and memorabilia, including Captain George Vancouver's navigational instruments and Captain Cook's 1779 charts-in-progress when he was killed in Hawaii. One highlight is the **St Roch National Historic Site**, a 1928 ship built for arctic patrol, docked inside the museum. Among other achievements, the *St Roch* was the first vessel to circumnavigate North America.

Vancouver Museum

Canada's largest civic museum includes vast collections of local artefacts as well as First Nations and Pacific Rim art collections.

VanDusen Botanical Garden

One of Canada's most comprehensive collections of ornamental plants. Plantings are rotated to provide maximum colour in all seasons. The gardens and facilities are being refurbished; a pathway lined with spraying water will lead into the partially hidden garden site.

Vanier Park

Vanier occupies much of the headland on the west side of False Creek inlet. Lawns, marinas, a walking and cycling path and broad views across English Bay make it a popular city escape all year round. The Vancouver Maritime Museum and the Vancouver Museum are both located in the park.

West End

Elegant homes belie the second most densely populated area in North America (after New York City). This neighbourhood is west of the downtown business high-rises. Youngish residents enjoy their proximity to Stanley Park's running areas, biking and recreation.

First Nations art

After decades of suppression by Christian missionaries and government policy, BC's Aboriginal arts, crafts and cultures have returned to the mainstream. Academic interest at the University of British Columbia and Victoria's Royal BC Museum sparked a revival of totem-pole carving in the 1940s and 1950s. The new totems helped fuel a renaissance of cultural and artistic forms that had all but disappeared outside museum collections. Fifty years later, modern interpretations of traditionally bold, stylised First Nations motifs are everywhere.

Vancouver International Airport has a fine collection of modern First Nations art and several retail shops sell hand-made artefacts; UBC's Museum of Anthropology (MOA) has an even larger collection. MOA's gift shop is filled with affordable reproductions of display pieces. The Bill Reid Gallery of Northwest Coast Art (639 Hornby St; tel: (604) 682-3455; http://billreidgallery.ca) displays Reid's own work and that of other aboriginal artists. Commercial gallery prices are higher.

Accommodation and food

Hotel space can be tight and expensive in summer but prices drop once the cruise ships head south in September and October. Tourism Vancouver offer a booking service.

The Fairmont Hotel Vancouver $$$ *900 W Georgia St; tel: (604) 684-3131 or (800) 257-7544; www.fairmont.com/hotelvancouver*, is the *grande dame* of Vancouver hotels, worth every penny.

The Listel Hotel $$$ *1300 Robson St; tel: (604) 684-8461 or (800) 663-5491; www.thelistelhotel.com*, is a delightful hotel with art gallery décor.

Opus Hotel $$$ *322 Davie St; tel: (604) 642-6787 or (866) 642-6787; http://opushotel.com*, in the trendy Yaletown District, is ultra posh with an online Lifestyle Concierge™ service that recommends dining and clubs, arts and culture venues, and sightseeing.

Pacific Palisades Hotel $$$ *1277 Robson St; tel: (604) 688-0461 or (800) 663-1815; www.pacificpalisadeshotel.com*, combines a trendy location with Miami South Beach colours, a film production suite, and a variety of packages for families to ecotravellers.

Pan Pacific Vancouver $$$ *999 Canada Place; tel: (604) 662-8111 or (877) 324-4856; www.panpacific.com*, rises above Canada Place with the best harbour views in town.

Sutton Place $$$ *845 Burrard St; tel: (604) 682-5511 or (866) 378-8866; www.vancouver.suttonplace.com*, is a highly successful version of traditional luxury.

Below
Al fresco dining is popular in Vancouver

Vancouverites eat out more often and drink more wine than any other city in North America. The city's young, well-travelled population, vibrant immigrant communities, fresh seafood and healthy economy have transformed food from fuel to celebration. West Coast or Northwest Cuisine is the code for fresh local ingredients (most often seafood) with a light touch on the sauces.

Alibi Room $$ *157 Alexander St, Gastown; tel: (604) 623-3383; www.alibi.ca*, styles its menu on English bistro, and dining on the patio or upstairs overlooking Vancouver's origins is a plus.

Del-Hi Darbar Restaurant $$ *2120 Main St (near 5th); tel: (604) 877-7733*, has wonderful *dhosas* and enormous portions of South Indian delights.

Greens and Gourmet $$ *2582 W Broadway; tel: (604) 737-7373*, is vegetarian with a wide variety of hot dishes and freshly squeezed juices.

Kalamata Greek Taverna $$ *388 W Broadway; tel: (604) 872-7050,* has the sparkle, bustle and sunny flavours of Greece.

Kamei Royale Japanese Restaurant $$ *1030 W Georgia St; tel: (604) 687-8588,* has cosy booths, supreme service and marvellous sushi.

Salmon House $$ *2229 Folkestone Way; tel: (604) 926-3212; www.salmonhouse.com,* on a West Vancouver hillside has a three-course *prix fixe* menu with ingredients sourced only from the province.

Bridges Restaurant $$–$$$ *Granville Island; tel: (604) 687-4400; www.bridgesrestaurant.com,* has reliable seafood and the city's most popular patio.

CinCin $$$ *1154 Robson St (near Bute); tel: (604) 688-7338; www.cincin.net,* is an award-winning Italian restaurant.

Dundarave Fish Market $$$ *2423 Marine Dr; tel: (604) 922-1155; www.dundaravefishmarket.com,* offers patrons the chance to select fresh fish from the counter, which are then prepared to order.

Raincity Grill $$$ *1193 Denman St (at Morton); tel: (604) 685-7337; www.raincitygrill.com,* pushes the edge with locally sourced West Coast dishes and a great selection of BC wines by the glass.

Star Anise $$$ *1485 W 12th Ave (near Granville); tel: (604) 737-1485; www.staranise.ca,* serves the city's most successful fusion of Asian and West Coast flavours.

Top of Vancouver Revolving Restaurant $$$ *555 W Hastings St; (604) 669-2220; www.topofvancouver.com,* at 167m above street level offers above-it-all views over a 60-minute revolution.

Shopping

Vancouver has a reputation for good shopping. **Robson Street** is Canada's answer to Beverly Hills, with blocks of brand name and trendy shops from Burrard to Cardero Streets. **Chinatown** has bargains on Asian imports. **A&B Sound** *556 Seymour St; tel: (604) 687-5837; www.absound.ca* and **HMV** *788 Burrard St; tel: (604) 669-2289; www.hmv.ca/hmvcaweb/en_CA/home.do,* are locked in perpetual competition over music DVDs. **Duthie Books** *2239 W 4th Ave; tel: (604) 732-5344; http://duthiebooks.com,* has the city's best selection of Canadiana and travel books. **Mountain Equipment Co-op** *130 W Broadway; tel: (604) 872-7858; www.mec.ca,* is a good stop for outdoor gear. **Lululemon** *2113 W 4th St; tel: (604) 732-6111; www.lululemon. com/vancouver/kitsilano,* began its now-worldwide yoga clothing production at this store; ask for recommended local fitness, Pilates or yoga studios. First Nations art and artefacts shops sell museum quality. Amongst the best is **Hill's Native Art** *165 Water St, Gastown; tel: (604) 685-4249 or (866) 685-5422; www.hillsnativeart.com*

On the water

The best way to see Vancouver is from the water. **Vancouver Harbour Cruises** $ *tel: (604) 688-7246* or *(800) 663-1500; www.boatcruises.com*, offer daily one-hour harbour cruises aboard the city's only authentic paddlewheeler mid-April–early October.

Suggested tour

Total distance: 80km.

Time: Allow a half-day for driving and 2 days to see the sights. Pick up the circular tour anywhere, but try to avoid commuter traffic (*0730–0930 and 1600–1800*).

Links: The city tour links with ferry routes to Vancouver Island from **Horseshoe Bay** and the lower Fraser River valley on Hwy 1 eastbound toward **Harrison Hot Springs**, **Hope** and the **Okanagan Valley**.

Route: Start at **Fourth Ave**, on the western edge of Vancouver. This trendy shopping district stretches from Burrard St to Balsam St, where it becomes a residential area headed west towards **Jericho Beach Park**. Watch for cyclists as the road veers to the right and becomes NW Marine Drive towards **Locarno Park**, **Locarno Beach** and **Spanish Banks Beach**, all looking onto English Bay. The parks offer expansive vistas to North Vancouver and east to the inner city and Stanley Park. There is ample parking, particularly near Locarno Park, as well as picnic and recreational facilities.

Pacific Spirit Regional Park begins just west of Spanish Banks. The 770-hectare park surrounds the **University of British Columbia** campus on **Point Grey**. At the first stop sign, turn right on to Chancellor Dr and the car park for the **MUSEUM OF ANTHROPOLOGY (MOA)** ❶, on the right. The outdoor totem exhibition area is over a small rise behind the car park and behind the museum building. Walk the 200m west along Marine Dr to **NITOBE MEMORIAL GARDEN**, on the left.

Marine Dr curves south around Point Grey. Just past the **UBC Botanical Garden**, 2km beyond MOA, move into the left lane. At the first traffic signal, turn left on to 16th Ave. Follow 16th Ave east back into Vancouver and the pleasant, tree-shaded residential neighbourhoods of **Shaughnessy Heights**. The road is a broad parkway, but residential parking frequently blocks the kerb lane.

Follow 16th Ave to Arbutus St and turn north (left). Several blocks north of W 4th Ave are still paved with brick, which becomes slippery in rain. Continue downhill towards **Kitsilano Pool**, Hutton Park and Vanier Park, with English Bay behind.

Follow signs for the **VANCOUVER MARITIME MUSEUM** ❷ and **VANCOUVER MUSEUM**, skirting the edge of **VANIER PARK**. Parking is extremely limited; try the Maritime Museum and the Vancouver Museum.

From the Vancouver Museum, turn south (left) on to Chestnut for one block, then go west (right) on Greer Ave, following signs for the bicycle route on to the **Burrard Bridge**.

After crossing the bridge, continue straight on Burrard St for 10 blocks to Georgia St. Turn east (right) for one block to Hornby St and turn south (right). **The VANCOUVER ART GALLERY** ❸ is on the right. To the right is the **BC Provincial Courts** building, with an urban park and waterfalls rising above street level. Turn south (right) on to Howe St and west (right) on to Smithe St. Follow Smithe across Burrard to Thurlow and turn south (left) for two blocks to Nelson St. Turn west (right) on to Nelson for four blocks to Nicola St, then go north (right) one block to Barclay. Turn east (right) on Barclay to **BARCLAY HERITAGE SQUARE** ❹ and the **Roedde House Museum**.

Take the first left turn after the museum. Continue north to Robson St and turn west (left) to Denman St. Turn north (right) on Denman, following signs for ferries to **Nanaimo** and the **Sunshine Coast**. At Georgia St, turn north (left) towards **Stanley Park**. Stay in the right-hand lane and veer right into the park.

Parking regulations are enforced all year; buy parking coupons at the yellow dispensers. The first car park on the left is convenient for visits to the **VANCOUVER AQUARIUM** ❺ and **horse-drawn tours** of the park. One kilometre beyond is the main parking area and **Totem Pole Display** ❻. Just ahead and on the right are broad views back to the sail-like roofline of **CANADA PLACE**. Expect to see cruise ships docked at Canada Place from May to October. Ships returning from Alaska dock around 0800 and depart 1600–1800 the same day. The **Nine O'clock Gun**, on the waterfront just past a bronze statue of a runner, is fired at 2100 each evening. The cannon originally signalled the close of commercial fishing each day.

Turn right onto Stanley Park Drive up to **Brockton Point**. Just beyond **Brockton Point** is Vancouver's answer to Copenhagen's *Little Mermaid*, **Girl in a Wetsuit**, a bronze statue of a woman diver in a wetsuit. Follow Stanley Park Drive north until you reach Lions Gate Bridge Road (Highway 1A). Follow the road up to the suspension bridge, **Lions Gate Bridge** ❼, which leads to North Shore. The entrance to **Lions Gate Bridge**, from within Stanley Park, is closed 1530–1830 to minimise park traffic.

Cross the bridge and turn east (right) on to Marine Dr, following signs for **North Vancouver**, **Capilano Canyon** and Grouse Mountain. Turn north (left) at the first traffic signal, Capilano Road. CAPILANO SUSPENSION BRIDGE is 3km uphill, on the left. The swaying pedestrian bridge, built a century ago for fishing and logging access, was Vancouver's first tourist attraction. Continue 4km north on Capilano Rd, which becomes Nancy Greene Way, to GROUSE MOUNTAIN and the Skyride tram.

Return downhill to Hwy 1. Take the highway eastbound to the **Second Narrows Bridge** and cross **Burrard Inlet**. Take the first exit, following signs for the bicycle route on to McGill St. Follow McGill past **Exposition Park** and along the waterfront for 3km. Turn north (right) on to Wall St and continue through residential areas above the docks for another 2km, then go north (right) on to Dundas St to Heatley Avenue.

Turn south (left) on to Heatley Avenue to E Pender St. Turn west (right) through the heart of CHINATOWN ❽, past the Chinese Cultural Centre behind the large gate on the south (left) side of the street with the Dr Sun Yat-Sen Classical Chinese Garden behind.

Turn north (right) on to Abbott St to E Cordova St and turn east (right) along the edge of GASTOWN ❾ for two blocks to Columbia St. Go two blocks north (left) on Columbia and turn west (left) on to Alexander St. At the first stop sign, where the brick pavement begins, turn north (right) on to Water St. A flamboyant statue of **Gassy Jack** who built the first bar in Gastown is on the left. Approach the Steam Clock on the north (right) at Cambie St.

At the end of Water St, turn south (left) into Richards St, immediately west (right) on to W Hastings St, then south (left) on to Howe St. The **Four Seasons Hotel** is on the east (left) at Georgia St. Cross Georgia. West (right) is the Vancouver Art Gallery. Continue south on Howe St and cross the **Granville Street Bridge**.

Stay in the right-hand lane and follow signs for 4th Ave W, turning on to Pine St, then north (right) following signs for GRANVILLE ISLAND ❿. When leaving Granville Island, follow signs for 4th Ave W. Follow 4th Ave one block back to Burrard St.

Lions Gate Bridge

Grouse Mountain

⑦

Capilano Suspension Bridge

First Narrows

ley Park Drive

Stanley Park

99
1A

Lions Gate Bridge Road

Beaver Lake

Stanley Park Drive

Burrard Inlet

N

Brockton Point

Aquarium ⑤

⑥

Lost Lagoon

West End

Lagoon Drive

Coal Harbour

SeaBus

Gilford Street

Denman Street

Georgia Street

Pender Street

Canada Place

Waterfront Station

English Bay

Beach Avenue

Barclay Street

Robson Street

Nelson Street

Comox Street

Pendrell Street

Broughton Street

Jervis Street

Bute Street

④ Barclay Heritage Square

Vancouver Art Gallery

Lookout Tower

Water Street

⑨ Gastown

English Bay

Davie Street

Burnaby Street

③

i

Cambie St

Hastings Street

⑧

Pender Street

Chinatown

Harwood Street

Bute Street

Thurlow Street

Burrard Street

Hornby Street

Howe Street

Granville Street Mall

Robson Street

Georgia Street

Dunsmuir Street

Carrall St

Vancouver Maritime Museum

②

①

Beach Avenue

Pacific Street

Granville Street

Seymour Street

Nelson Street

Smithe Street

BC Place Stadium

Vancouver Museum

Museum of Anthropology

Vanier Park

Burrard Street Bridge

Yaletown

Science World

4th Ave

Nitobe Memorial Garden

University of British Columbia Botanical Garden

Granville Street Bridge

⑩ Granville Island

Steveston

False Creek

Bloedel Floral Conservatory

VanDusen Botanical Garden

Cambie Street Bridge

Main Street

0   500m
0   500 yards

The Gulf Islands

Ratings

Art and craft	●●●●●
Nature	●●●●●
Outdoor activities	●●●●●
Parks	●●●●●
Scenery	●●●●●
Wildlife	●●●●●
Coastal villages	●●●●○
Beaches	●●●○○

An island archipelago spans the Strait of Georgia, misnamed the Gulf of Georgia by Captain George Vancouver in 1792. Of the 200 or so Gulf Islands (the San Juans are the same group on the US side of the boundary), five of the major Gulf Islands house 12,000 permanent residents. Within a few hours' reach of Victoria or Vancouver by BC ferry, float plane or water taxi, the dry, sunny climate, small retiree and day commuter population, scenery, outdoor activities and arts communities lure visitors to posh inns and bed and breakfasts. Nostalgic vestiges of alternative lifestyles that thrived in relative island isolation in the 1960s can still be found along the rustic side routes and in crafts markets.

Rugged cliffs and smooth beaches lure sailors, kayakers and canoeists on to the water to view pods of orcas and dolphins. Panoramic views from mountaintops entice hikers and cyclists to explore island roads.

Gulf Islands National Park Reserve of Canada, *2220 Harbour Rd, Sidney, BC V8L 2P6; tel: (250) 654-4000; www.pc.gc.ca/pn-np/bc/gulf*, designated Canada's 40th national park in 2003, protects parts of 15 southern Gulf Islands, including Mayne, North and South Pender and Saturna, along with many islets in the Strait of Georgia Lowlands area.

GALIANO ISLAND

ⓘ Galiano Island Chamber of Commerce
Tel: (250) 539-2233; www.galianoisland.com

Ⓣ Taxi Galiano $
Tel: (250) 539-0202; www.taxigaliano.com, provides island-wide taxi, shuttle and tour guiding services.

How did an island, inhabited for centuries by Coast Salish peoples, get a Spanish name? Answer: Spaniard Dionisio Alcala Galiano sailed a survey ship to the island in 1792.

Spreading 27km long over a narrow, hilly, 57sq km land area, the second-largest and northernmost main Gulf Island concentrates its thousand or so inhabitants in several population centres. Ferries call at **Sturdies Bay**. The one main route, Montague Road, goes to Montague Harbour, the other main activity centre, then becomes Porlier Pass Road, stopping short of the island's northern tip.

Many visitors choose to bring or hire bikes, take the **Go Galiano Island Shuttle**, walk, or kayak/canoe between places. Most of Galiano's parks provide views of the Strait of Georgia and vistas across to other tiny isles such as the Ballingall Islets, which shelter harbour seals and provide sanctuary for birds.

Dionisio Point Provincial Park
Water access to island's northern tip; tel: (250) 539-2115; www.env.gov.bc.ca/bcparks/explore/parkpgs/dionisio.html

Montague Harbour Marine Provincial Park
10km northwest of Sturdies Bay at Montague Harbour; tel: (250) 539-2115; www.env.gov.bc.ca/bcparks/explore/parkpgs/montague.html

Galiano Bluffs Park
Bluff Rd.

Bodega Ridge *From Cook Rd on northwest of island; tel: (250) 539-2115; www.env.gov.bc.ca/bcparks/explore/parkpgs/bodega.html*

Water-access-only **Dionisio Point Provincial Park**, backed by forest, has rocky headlands looking out to Porlier Pass. **Montague Harbour Marine Provincial Park** offers a range of activities – walking white-shell beaches or Gray's Peninsula salt-water marsh; scuba-diving; spotting shellfish and sea stars at low tide; hiking 180m through a fir, western red cedar and arbutus forest; First Nations middens; or taking in vistas from a rocky precipice. **Galiano Bluffs Park** has fine views to Victoria and the San Juan Islands; for another awesome vista, hike up **Bodega Ridge**.

MAYNE ISLAND

Mayne Island Community Chamber of Commerce
www.mayneislandchamber.ca. In summer, get a map-brochure at the Village Bay ferry dock.

Miners Bay Gaol (Mayne Island Museum) *$ C4, Miners Bay.*

Ferries land at **Village Bay**, a transit depot for the commercial centre at **Miners Bay**, named after prospectors on their way to the Fraser and Cariboo gold rushes between 1858 and the 1860s. Look for fine late-Victorian-era houses. Since then, the 21sq km island has fostered apple and tomato farming and remains an island getaway for Vancouverites.

Right
Bedwell Harbour

Active Pass Lighthouse *Georgina Point. Hours vary.*

Mount Parke Regional Park *Off Montrose Rd, via Fernhill Rd; www.crd.bc.ca/parks/mount_parke.htm. Open daily.*

Miners Bay Gaol (Mayne Island Museum) belies its history as the 1896 Plumper Pass lockup (gaol), exhibiting wreck artefacts. **Georgina Point Heritage Park** is a good picnicking and birdwatching spot, with **Active Pass Lighthouse**, operational since 1885. Cycle Mayne's hills, hike 270m up **Mount Parke** for a view east to Vancouver and west to Vancouver Island, or stroll the **Japanese Gardens** at **Dinner Bay Park**.

PENDER ISLANDS

Pender Island Chamber of Commerce *Pender Island; tel: (250) 629-3988 or (866) 468-7924; www.penderislandchamber.com*

Mount Norman Regional Park *South Pender Island, south of the causeway; www.crd.bc.ca/parks/documents/mount_norman_brochur.pdf. Open daily.*

Driftwood Center *Bedwell Harbour Rd at Razor Point Rd* has provisions and along with the Community Hall *(tel: (250) 629-3669; www.penderislands.org)* hosts the Apr–Oct Saturday **Farmers Market**.

A narrow causeway joins the 24sq km of Pender's North and South Islands. Ferries put in at **Otter Bay**, North Pender; almost all of the 2,000 residents live further south near **Magic Lake**. While all the Gulf Islands have beaches, the Penders' sheltered coves are numerous and easily accessible. Try another panoramic Gulf Island hike up 217-m **Mount Norman**.

For a break from kayaking, horse riding, swimming and hiking from May to October, visit the (North) Island service area, **Driftwood Center**, for a Saturday **Farmers Market**.

SALT SPRING ISLAND

Salt Spring Island Chamber of Commerce *121 Lower Ganges Rd, Ganges; tel: (250) 537-5252, (250) 537-4223 or (866) 216-2936; www.saltspringtoday.com. Open daily.*

Gulf Islands' Spinning Mill $ *351A Rainbow Rd, Ganges; tel: (250) 537-4342; www.gulfislandsspinningmill.com. Tours by appointment.*

Salt Spring is a 180sq km island getaway with many of the arts and amenities of a thriving metropolis without the urban angst. Sheep are reared for meat and wool, providing work for some of Salt Spring's 10,000 residents. **Gulf Islands' Spinning Mill** offers tours of its wool, mohair, llama and alpaca production.

The town of **Ganges** is the bustling hub of this island. Local farmers rub elbows with potters and musicians at the **Salt Spring Island Saturday Market** (*http://saltspringmarket.com*) in Centennial Park each Saturday from late March–October. In summer, **ArtCraft** pulls together 200-plus island artisans' work for unique souvenir shopping from mid-May–mid-September, or visit Salt Spring's 40 or more art galleries.

Ferries call at **Long Harbour**, **Vesuvius Bay** and **Fulford Harbour**.

Wineries joined the attractions, with the first island-grown releases in 2003: **Salt Spring Vineyards** *151 Lee Rd at 1700 block Fulford-Ganges*

ArtCraft *Mahon Hall, 114 Rainbow Rd, Ganges; tel: (250) 537-0899; www.gulfislandsartscouncil.com. Open daily mid-May–mid-Sep.*

Ruckle Provincial Park *Via Beaver Point Rd; tel: (250) 539-2115; www.eng.gov.bc.ca/bcparks/ explore/parkpgs/ruckle.html. Open daily.*

Mount Maxwell Provincial Park *Southwest of Ganges, Cranberry Rd to Maxwell Rd; tel: (250) 539-2115; www.env.gov.bc.ca/bcparks/ explore/parkpgs/mt_max. html. Open daily.*

Mill Farm Regional Park Reserve *Southwest island section via rough Musgrave Rd; www.crd.bc.ca/parks/reserves/ millfarm.htm. Open daily.*

Right
Salt Spring Island

Opposite
Otter Bay

Rd; tel: (250) 653-9463; www.saltspringvineyards.com and **Garry Oaks Winery** *1880 Fulford-Ganges Rd; tel: (250) 653-4687; http://garryoakswine.com*

The parks introduce what nature offers in the Gulf Islands. The shore **Ruckle Provincial Park** is rocky, its 486 hectares encompassing a sheep farm, several settler homes, fields and forest walks. Hikers enjoy views towards Vancouver Island from **Mount Maxwell Provincial Park.** Rough roads access the hang-glider heaven atop 698m **Mount Bruce** in **Mill Farm Regional Park Reserve.**

SATURNA ISLAND

Saturna Island *www. saturnatourism.com*

East Point Regional Park *East Point Rd. Open daily.*

Mount Warburton Pike *via Staples Rd, west section of the island. Open daily.*

Saturna Island Family Estate Winery *8 Quarry Rd; tel: (250) 539-5139 or (877) 918-3388; www.saturnavineyards.com. Open May–Oct or by appointment.*

Astronomy aside, the island's 350 residents proudly claim East Point's sandstone formations as the 1791 discovery site of the island by the Spanish schooner *Santa Saturnina*. Saturna's few inhabitants are spread over 96sq km, leaving most businesses close to the **Lyall Harbour** dock, where ferries connect to other Gulf Islands.

Orca-spotting is phenomenal in summer from **East Point Regional Park**, near an 1889 lighthouse. Salmon and raptors, including peregrine falcons, hawks, osprey and eagles, engage in preying upon the small, but numerous, offshore fish. Look for deer and racoons amid forests of fir, spruce and alder, half-hidden in ferny undergrowth.

For vista spotters, 490m **Mount Warburton Pike** can be climbed or reached via a dirt road, and island arts and crafts run the gamut from tarot readings to goldsmithing, woodworking and *raku* (lead-glazed, Japanese-style pottery), even winemaking at **Saturna Island Family Estate Winery.**

Above
Canoeing in the Gulf Islands

Accommodation and food in the Gulf Islands

There is no shortage of bed and breakfasts, inns, lodges and country manors to select from, but prices can be high. Advance bookings are essential in summer and at holiday periods. Check with InfoCentres and Provincial Parks for camping; Saturna Island has no public camp pitches. Every ferry landing has a store for provisioning and most have at least one restaurant/pub nearby. Fine dining is often part of a B&B stay.

Gulf Islands Brewery $ *www.gulfislandsbrewery.com*, on Salt Spring Island produces a number of beers for local restaurant and pub consumption, including Salt Spring label Pale Ale, Golden Ale and Porter. Heatherdale, resembling Scottish-style fraoch ale, brews with plants from the Butchart Gardens in Victoria in place of hops, with brews served only at the gardens.

Hummingbird Pub $$ *47 Sturdies Bay Rd, Galiano Island; tel: (250) 539-5472*, is a good spot to meet local people, with live entertainment in summer. Take the pub's summertime-only red and white shuttle from Montague Bay.

Hastings House Country House Hotel $$$ *160 Upper Ganges Road, Salt Spring Island; tel: (250) 537-2362 or (800) 661-9255; www.hastingshouse.com*, may be the poshest collection of lodging buildings in Western Canada, including the original HBC post and a local artists' sculpture garden, secluded on 9 hectares. *Open mid-Mar–mid-Nov.*

Gulf Islands Online
www.gulfislands.net

BC Ferries 1112 Fort St,
Victoria, BC V8V 4V2;
tel: (250) 386-3431 or
(888) 223-3779;
www.bcferries.com

BC Provincial Parks
www.env.gov.bc.ca/bcparks

Gulf Islands Water Taxi $ Tel: (250) 537-2510; www.saltspring.com/watertaxi. Summer season connections between Salt Spring and Galiano or Mayne.

Oceanwood Country Inn $$$ *630 Dinner Bay Rd, Mayne Island; tel: (250) 539-5074; www.oceanwood.com,* is a 12-room, Tudor-style waterfront inn with a solarium and fine dining room, complemented by fresh garden ingredients and one of the best wine cellars in Western Canada.

Poets Cove Resort & Spa $$$ *9801 Spaulding Rd, South Pender Island; tel: (888) 512-7638* or *(250) 629-2100; http://poetscove.com,* is elegant with a marina, spa, canoeing, kayaking, diving and eco-tours.

Suggested tour

Time: Via BC Ferries, distance depends on route, season and number of islands visited. In summer, June–Labour Day, from Tsawwassen, off BC Hwy 99, 45 minutes south of Vancouver, the run around four islands – but not Saturna Island – could take 5 hours; 6 hours on the direct Tsawwassen–Swartz Bay (Vancouver Island) run, with a return to one of the islands; or as little as 4 hours. Check with BC Ferries before planning a route and verify routing again on the day of travel for exact schedules.

Links: Vancouver (Tsawwassen – *see page 44*) is the mainland BC link to the Gulf Islands. From Salt Spring Island to Vancouver Island, sail from Vesuvius Bay to Crofton or from Fulford Harbour to **Swartz Bay** (*see page 80*).

Route: Ferry schedules will shape a tour, especially outside the mid-May–September busy season. The best strategy is to start big and work towards wilderness, ie begin with **SALT SPRING ISLAND** ❶, exploring Ganges' art and ambience, hike the trails for **Mount Maxwell Provincial Park** vistas, and work through the other islands as time and routes permit, to **GALIANO's** ❷ kayak-loving shoreline and **SATURNA ISLAND's** ❸ relative isolation.

Victoria

Ratings

Architecture	●●●●●
Food and drink	●●●●●
Gardens	●●●●●
Children	●●●●○
Historical sights	●●●●○
Outdoor activities	●●●●○
Scenery	●●●●○
Shopping	●●●○○

Victoria doesn't *look* like Western Canada's oldest industrial city. British Columbia's capital has swapped the noise and the grit of old-fashioned metal bashing for cleaner, more modern technologies without sacrificing one of Canada's greatest concentration of heritage buildings. Older neighbourhoods are filled with lovingly restored storefronts, rambling mansions and social welfare programmes that city founders couldn't have imagined in their worst nightmares.

Victoria wallows in its reputation for espousing the ludicrous and the off-beat. City dwellers from Vancouver to Halifax dismiss Victorians as refugees from the *real* Canada, but these self-satisfied refugees have never forgotten the winters they left behind. Canada's mildest climate, quick access to the out-of-doors and neighbourhoods like LoJo (shopping) and the Design District have attracted a youthful mixture of urban escapees, artists, ardent environmentalists and would-be entrepreneurs willing to meet established politicians and entrenched industrialists in a social ferment that aims to change the political and economic future.

Arriving and departing

ⓘ Tourism Victoria Visitor Centre *812 Wharf St, Victoria, BC V8W 1T3; tel: (250) 953-2033; www.tourismvictoria.com. Open daily 0900–1700, longer in summer. Reservations, tel: (800) 663-3883.*

Downtown Victoria Ambassadors, in green and white shirts, provide free maps and information, *tel: (250) 414-6972; www.tourismvictoria.com/ ambassadors. Open Jun–Sep.*

Victoria International Airport (YYJ) *tel: (250) 953-7500; www. victoriaairport.com* is 20km and 30 minutes north of downtown Victoria, near Sidney. Taxi **$$$** to downtown. **AKAL Airport Shuttle Bus $$** *tel: (250) 386-2525; www.victoriaairportshuttle.com.* Coach service every 30 minutes or **BC Transit $** *tel: (250) 385-2551; http://bctransit.com*

The **Inner Harbour** has seaplane and helicopter services to Vancouver, Seattle, the San Juan Islands, the Gulf Islands and other destinations.

By sea

Three million people visit Victoria each year, most of them by water. Advance booking is required on most routes.

• **BC Ferries** *1112 Fort St; tel: (250) 381-1401 or (888) 223-3779; www.bcferries.com,* serve Swartz Bay and neighbourhoods like LoJo

Johnson Street Bridge

Butchart Gardens

Craigflower Manor and Schoolhouse

Bastion Square

Pandora Street

Johnson Street

Victoria Harbour

Market Square

Inner Harbour

Yates Street

View Street

Fort Street

Wharf Street

Government Street

Douglas Street

Blanshard Street

Quadra Street

Vancouver Street

Chinatown

Victoria Bug Zoo

Inner Harbour

The Fairmont Empress

Broughton Street

Courtney Street

Belleville Street

Fairfield Road

Rockland Avenue

Art Gallery of Greater Victoria

Craigdarroch Castle

Cook Street

Parliament Buildings

Royal British Columbia Museum

Thunderbird Park

Richardson Street

Government House Gardens

Superior Street

Michigan Street

Superior Street

Fairfield Road

Fairfield Road

Oswego Street

Simcoe Street

Michigan Street

Menzies Street

Niagara Street

Toronto Street

Douglas Street

Heywood Avenue

Linden Avenue

Moss Street

Carr House

Fort Rodd Hill and Fisgard Lighthouse National Historic Sites

Beacon Hill Park

Cook Street

Dallas Road

0   500m
0   500 yards

Juan de Fuca Strait

Scenic Marine Drive ■

Monday Magazine
818 Broughton St;
tel: (250) 382-6188;
www.mondaymag.com, free
each Friday in shops and
newspaper boxes, has
Victoria's best listing of
current events and reviews.

**Washington State
Ferries**
www.wsdot.wa.gov/ferries.
For recorded information
or to book vehicle transit
between Anacortes–
Sidney, tel: (888) 808-7977
or in Washington State,
(206) 464-6400, or online.

(Lower Johnson Street, shopping) and the Design District, at the north end of the Saanich Peninsula; 30 minutes by car from downtown, with vehicle and passenger service from Vancouver and the Gulf Islands. Ferry services connect with **BC Transit** in both Victoria and Vancouver.

• **Black Ball Transport** (*MV Coho*) *430 Belleville St; tel: (250) 386-2202; http://cohoferry.com*, has a car and passenger service between Victoria's Inner Harbour and Port Angeles, Washington.

• **Victoria–San Juan Cruises** *tel: (800) 443-4552 or (360) 738-8099; www.whales.com*, has passenger service between Bellingham, Washington and Victoria via Roche Harbor (San Juan Island, Washington) mid-May–Sep.

• **Victoria Clipper** *254 Belleville St, Victoria; tel: (250) 448-5000 or (800) 888-2535; www.clippervacations.com/ferry*, has a daily passenger ferry service to Seattle with the fastest ships on the route.

• **Washington State Ferries** *2499 Ocean Ave, Sidney; tel: (250) 656-1831; www.wsdot.wa.gov/ferries*, has a vehicle and passenger service to Anacortes, Washington. Fares may be paid in either US or Canadian currency.

By land
• All road transport between Victoria and the mainland requires a ferry connection. **Pacific Coach Lines** *700 Douglas St; tel: (250) 385-4411 or (800) 661-1725; www.pacificcoach.com*, operate between central Victoria and central Vancouver.
• The *Malahat 450 Pandora Ave; tel: (888) 842-7245; www.viarail.ca*, has a daily return rail service between Victoria and Courtenay via Nanaimo (*see p168*).

Getting around

Walking is the best way to explore touristic Victoria, a compact area around the Inner Harbour. It's also practicable to explore all but the most distant parts of the city by public transport. **BC Transit** *tel: (250) 385-2551; www.bctransit.com*, **Victoria Tourist Information (BusLine)** *tel: (250) 382-6161; www.busonline.ca*, has a dense network of bus routes throughout Greater Victoria with several discount ticket and pass schemes available at the Tourism Victoria Visitor Centre.

Driving
Narrow streets, busy traffic and limited street parking make it difficult to explore downtown by car. The best bet is to park and explore on foot, then drive to more distant attractions. There is ample parking off the west side of Wharf Street along the Inner Harbour, as well as parking garages east of Government Street. Parking meter time limits are strictly enforced, especially downtown.

Below
Victoria's Inner Harbour

Afternoon tea

Every hotel, restaurant and café offers its own version of afternoon tea. **Blethering Place Tea Room and Restaurant $$** *2250 Oak Bay Ave (Oak Bay); tel: (250) 598-1413; www.blethering.com*, is favoured by the 'Tweed Curtain' set (the older population). **The Fairmont Empress (Hotel) $$$** *721 Government St; tel: (250) 389-2727; www.fairmont.com/empress/ GuestServices/Restaurants/AfternoonTea.htm*, is overpriced and overtouristed, but it's hard to beat the city's most sumptuous setting. **James Bay Tea Room and Restaurant $$** *332 Menzies St (behind Parliament Buildings); tel: (250) 382-8282; http://jamesbaytearoomandrestaurant.com*, attracts nearby residents, as well as government and legislative workers. **The White Heather Tea Room $$** *1885 Oak Bay Ave; tel: (250) 595-8020, open Tue–Sat*, a local favourite, serves tea, Not So Wee Tea, and the Big Muckle Giant Tea for Two.

Downtown traffic is usually heavy, but flows smoothly in other areas. Major arteries, particularly Hwy 17 and Hwy 1A, are jammed during rush hours, 0730–0900 and 1600–1800 Monday–Friday. Left turns are extremely difficult anywhere downtown, while scenic country roads on the Saanich Peninsula can be narrow, winding and slow.

Sights

Afternoon Tea
A Victoria tradition, The Fairmont Empress (Hotel) serves more than 100,000 of these light meals yearly. Cups of strong tea wash down finger sandwiches, crumpets and scones arrayed on multi-tiered trays amid pots of whipped cream and conserves. An early 19th-century Duchess of Bedford gets credit for afternoon tea. Desperate to counteract 'that sinking feeling around 5pm', she tried snacking on small sandwiches and tea. The custom caught on, evolving into today's afternoon tea and the more formal version known as 'high tea'.

Art Gallery of Greater Victoria $$
1040 Moss St; tel: (250) 384-4101; http://aggv.bc.ca. Open daily 1000–1700, Thu 1000–2100.

Art Gallery of Greater Victoria
Victoria's city art museum concentrates on contemporary Canadian artists, as well as North American and European historical artists and notable Asian artists. The gallery shop is particularly well stocked with affordable reproductions.

Bastion Square *Wharf St between Yates and Fort Sts. Open daily.*

Maritime Museum of British Columbia $$
28 Bastion Sq; tel: (250) 385-4222; http://mmbc.bc.ca. Open daily 0930–1630, to 1700 mid-Jun–mid-Sep.

Bastion Square
The Square (actually a long rectangle) is the site of Victoria's first gaol, as well as the original Provincial Court House, used between 1889 and 1962. The Victoria Law Courts Building now houses the **Maritime Museum of British Columbia**, filled with ship models, figureheads, tools, naval uniforms and the 1860 *Tilikum*, an 11m dugout canoe converted to a schooner that sailed from Victoria to England and back between 1901 and 1904.

🅑 **Beacon Hill Park**
*Juan de Fuca Strait
between Douglas and Cook
Sts; tel: (250) 361-0628; www.
victoria.ca/visitors/leisure_
parksbcn.shtml and www.
beaconhillpark.ca. Open daily.*

Butchart Gardens $$$
*800 Benvenuto Ave,
Brentwood Bay; tel: (250)
652-5256 or (866) 652-
4422; www.butchartgardens.
com. Open daily 0900;
closing varies with the
season. Reduced prices in
winter.*

Carr House $
*207 Government St;
tel: (250) 383-5843;
www.emilycarr.com. Open
daily Jun–Aug 1100–1600;
same hours Tue–Sat rest of
year.*

Chinatown *Between
Herald, Government,
Pandora and Store streets.*

Fan Tan Alley *Chinatown,
between Fisgard St and
Pandora Ave. Open daily.*

Craigdarroch Castle $$
*1050 Joan Cres; tel: (250)
592-5323;
http://craigdarrochcastle.com.
Open mid-Jun–Labour Day,
0900–1900; rest of year,
1000–1630.*

Coloured bricks set into the pavement along View Street west to Bastion Square and south along Government Street to Fort Street then west towards the harbour mark the original stockade where Victoria began.

Beacon Hill Park

This 25-hectare park is named after Beacon Hill, the highest seaside point in Victoria, where signal fires once burned to warn sailors off reefs guarding the harbour entrance. The park is a collection of formal gardens, a farm animal petting area, small lakes and playing fields sloping down to cliffs overlooking the Strait of Juan de Fuca. Runners, dog walkers and sightseers flock to the seaside walkway with its wide vistas across the Strait to the Olympic Mountains in Washington. The Trans Canada Highway 'Mile 0' mile marker is a popular photo spot.

Butchart Gardens

Originally a limestone quarry, since 1904 Butchart, a national historic site, has become one of the most popular gardens in Canada. Its 22 manicured hectares are divided into Italian, Japanese, rose and sunken gardens, plus other landscape creations. The gardens are colourful all year and spectacular in summer – as are the crowds. There is less of a crush before 1100 and after 1500.

Carr House

The cream-coloured Victorian building is the birthplace of Emily Carr, one of Canada's most famed artists and authors. She took the country by storm in the 1930s with wild, haunting images of forests and totem poles before turning to books that re-created late 19th-century Victoria. A description of Carr's father, 'more English than the English', became an unofficial goal for three generations of Victorians. The house is open for tours.

Chinatown

The oldest Chinese community in Canada began in 1858 when Victoria was BC's only serious settlement. Don't miss **Fan Tan Alley**, the width of an adult armspan in places. Small shops set into the walls sell everything from haircuts and antique jewellery to New Age crystals and incense in what were once brothels, opium dens and gambling parlours.

Craigdarroch Castle

The castle was the grandest home atop the grandest hill in Victoria, a 39-room rough stone castle built by Nanaimo coal baron Robert Dunsmuir. The house was completed in 1890, months after Dunsmuir's death, but his family lived there until 1909. The intricately ornamented mansion is resplendent in carved wood, polished marble and fine paintings, elegantly restored after decades' service as a hospital, music academy, offices and decaying derelict.

Opposite
Bastion Square's Law Courts
Building now houses the
Maritime Museum

Craigflower Manor and Schoolhouse $
110 Island Hwy (Hwy 1A and Admiral Rd); tel: (250) 386-1606; www. conservancy.bc.ca/content. asp?sectionack=craigflower. Open daily May–Sep 1100–1700.

The Fairmont Empress (Hotel) $ *721 Government St; tel: (250) 384-8111 or (800) 257-7544; www.fairmont.com/empress*

Above
The Fairmont Empress (Hotel)

Craigflower Manor and Schoolhouse

This 1856 farmhouse, a national historic site, was the command centre for one of the Hudson's Bay Company's most successful farms. Most of the furnishings came to BC with Scottish families brought by the HBC to colonise the area. Guides in period costume conduct tours of the interior as well as heritage gardens, orchards, oatfields and the Kosapsom (First Nation) village site.

The Fairmont Empress (Hotel)

Opened in 1908 by the same architect who built Parliament House, the ivy-covered Empress sits surrounded by gardens on what was once a rubbish-filled tidal flat. The posh Edwardian décor in The Fairmont Empress's original lobby (south end of the building) is worth visiting, if only for a drink, but beware of Tea Time in summer, when the hotel is swamped with tourists. Corridors in The Fairmont Empress's first underground level are lined with photographs showing the world's upper crust at play around Victoria during the first half of the 20th century.

Fort Rodd Hill and Fisgard Lighthouse National Historic Sites
$ 603 Fort Rodd Hill Rd, west of Esquimalt off Hwy 1A; tel: (250) 478-5849; www.pc.gc.ca/lhn-nhs/bc/fortroddhill/index_e.asp; www.pc.gc.ca/lhn-nhs/bc/fisgard/index_e.asp. Open daily mid-Feb–Oct, 1000–1730; Nov–mid-Feb 0900–1630.

Government House Gardens 1401 Rockland Ave; tel: (250) 387-2080; http://ltgov.bc.ca/gardens. Open daily dawn–dusk. Free (donations welcome).

Inner Harbour Between Parliament Buildings, The Fairmont Empress (Hotel), Johnson Street Bridge and West Victoria.

Market Square 560 Johnson St; tel: (250) 386-2441; www.marketsquare.ca. Open daily.

Parliament Buildings South end of Inner Harbour; www.leg.bc.ca/info/2-2.htm. Open during business hours.

Fort Rodd Hill and Fisgard Lighthouse National Historic Sites

The massive seaside fortress protected the naval base and coaling station at Esquimalt, just west of Victoria, between 1878 and 1956, when missiles replaced coastal defence guns. Fisgard Lighthouse National Historic Site, white atop a rocky islet connected to the mainland by modern walkway, is the oldest lighthouse on the west coast of Canada. The lightkeeper's house has become an excellent lighthouse and **shipping museum** with broad ocean views.

Government House Gardens

You can't tour the official residence of BC's Lieutenant Governor, but the 14 hectares of azaleas, blossoming shrubs, formal flowerbeds, heather, ivy, lawns and rhododendrons are open to the public – unless the British royal family happens to be in residence.

Inner Harbour

Nearly all of touristic Victoria is packed into a ten-block area along the south and east sides of the Inner Harbour, where the city began about 160 years ago. Ferries from the US dock inside the harbour, as do seaplanes from Vancouver and the rest of Vancouver Island, whale-watching boats, sea kayakers and dozens of pleasure boaters, while tiny ferries dart from shore to shore like water bugs. The best views are from the harbour side of Government Street, across from The Fairmont Empress (Hotel), and from the waterside pedestrian promenade.

Market Square

The collection of nine red-brick heritage buildings, now an open shopping arcade, was originally shops and storehouses for the docks and industrial areas built to supply successive waves of gold miners, fishing fleets, seal hunters, coal ships and general cargo vessels that sailed into Victoria.

Parliament Buildings

The imposing buildings at the south end of the Inner Harbour were built by British architect Francis Mawson Rattenbury. Ratz, as he preferred to be called, arrived in Victoria in 1892 and promptly won an Empire-wide competition to build the province's new Parliament House at the age of 25.

He also built the opulent Edwardian Empress Hotel, Crystal Garden and other ornate edifices in Victoria, before a lurid divorce and lusty remarriage to a woman 30 years younger. Stuffy Victoria ostracised both the avant-garde wife, who dared to smoke cigarettes in public, and her new husband. Ratz was murdered by his wife's young lover in 1935, after fleeing to England to escape Victoria's withering disdain.

**Royal British
Columbia Museum**
$$ 675 Belleville St; tel: (250)
356-7226 or (888) 447-
7977;
http://royalbcmuseum.bc.ca.
Open daily 0900–1700.

Thunderbird Park
Belleville and Douglas Sts;
tel: (250) 356-7226. Open
daily.

Victoria Bug Zoo $$
631 Courtney St;
tel: (250) 384-2847;
http://bugzoo.bc.ca.
Open daily with longer hours
in summer.

Royal British Columbia Museum

Centrepiece of this sprawling museum is a First Nations collection. Enter through the full-sized Kwakiutl chief's house with displays of totems, carvings and chiefly regalia. Even more striking are artefacts, including story-telling masks, from the apex of First Nations arts and handicrafts in the lucrative decades after first contact with White fur traders and merchants. Many tribes disappeared as smallpox and other diseases decimated BC's Native population between 1843 and 1885. One outbreak of smallpox alone that spread from Victoria in 1862 killed 20,000, a third of the Province's non-White population.

Thunderbird Park

Next to the museum is Thunderbird Park, created to display totem poles in 1941. As the outdoor poles began to crumble from the effects of weather and time, museum curators sought out carvers to create replacements. Mungo Martin, Chief of the Kwakwaka'waku (Kwakiutl) band near Fort Rupert, organised a carving group in the 1950s that successfully re-created what had already become a lost art. Many of the poles towering above the park are replicas of Martin's original creations, while the originals stand protected inside the museum.

Victoria Bug Zoo

The City of Victoria hangs 1,500 flower baskets from downtown lampposts from June to September in an ever-so-civilised bow to summer, colour, and a city symbol. For a feel of the wilder side, this bug zone is home to an astounding variety of insects and spiders. Bug guides help with holding a tickling 400-leg millipede. The bug haven is Canada's largest ant farm and the spot to see leaf-cutter ants in action if a jungle is not on your itinerary. Check the white-eyed assassin bugs, giant stag and giant rhinoceros beetles, walking sticks, or glow-in-the-dark scorpions. For the brave who can make a home for one, the Bug Zoo has an Arthropod Sales division, offering, if available, Mexican red-legged or Indian ornamental tarantulas, giant whip scorpions, or Oriental praying mantis. The gift shop is wacky, including cricket-infused lollipops. When sated with the natural world's oddities, The Fairmont Empress Tea is only a block away.

Right
Thunderbird Park

Accommodation and food

Hotel space is tight in summer. Budget–moderate motels line Hwy 1/1A (Douglas Street) north of downtown. Most rooms can be booked through **Tourism Victoria** *tel: (800) 663-3883; www.tourismvictoria.com*

Days Inn on the Harbour $$ *427 Belleville St; tel: (250) 386-3451 or (800) 665-3024; www.daysinnvictoria.com*, is across the street from the Inner Harbour ferry docks, a 10-minute walk from The Fairmont Empress.

Executive House Hotel $$ *777 Douglas St; tel: (250) 388-5111 or (800) 663-7001; www.executivehouse.com*, rises directly behind The Fairmont Empress with sweeping harbour views from the upper floors.

The Fairmont Empress (Hotel) $$$ *721 Government St; tel: (250) 384-8111 or (800) 257-7544; www.fairmont.com/empress*, is the most prestigious and most central address in town.

Laurel Point Inn $$$ *680 Montreal St; tel: (250) 386-8721 or (800) 663-7667; www.laurelpoint.com*, overlooks the Inner Harbour entrance with modern luxury.

The Victoria population demands and gets the kind of variety, quality and value you'll find in Vancouver. Booking is essential in summer.

The Bay Centre $ *Government St, Fort–View Sts; tel: (250) 952-5690; www.thebaycentre.ca*. Food Court has quick lunch or dinner.

Sticky Wicket Pub $ *Strathcona Hotel, 919 Douglas St; tel: (250) 383-7137 or (800) 663-7476; www.strathconahotel.com*, is a sports bar for families, complete with a pair of rooftop volleyball courts.

Rebar Modern Food $$ *50 Bastion Square; tel: (250) 361-9223; http://rebarmodernfood.com*, dishes up vegetarian with seasonal menus within chartreuse walls embellished with Chinese lanterns.

Spinnakers Gastro Brewpub and Restaurant $$ *308 Catherine St; tel: (250) 386-2739 or (877) 838-2739; http://spinnakers.com*, is Canada's first brewpub. It has harbour views and serves its own malt vinegar and local products.

Swans Suite Hotel $$ *506 Pandora Ave; tel: (250) 361-3310 or (800) 668-7926; www.swanshotel.com*, has Swan's Brewpub and one of BC's best breweries, **Buckerfields Brewery**, on the premises.

Wharfside Eatery $$ *1208 Wharf St; tel: (250) 360-1808; www.wharfsideeatery.com*, offers great harbour views with tasty fish and pizza.

Deep Cove Chalet $$$ *11190 Chalet Rd, Sidney, along Saanich Inlet; tel: (250) 656-3541; http://deepcovechalet.com*, is the best French restaurant on Vancouver Island with one of the largest wine cellars in the province.

ⓘ The City of Victoria has four *Secrets of the City* self-guided Heritage Walk brochures with maps and descriptions that may be downloaded from its website (*www.victoria.ca/ visitors/wlkngt.shtml*): *Fools Rush In* (Gold Rush era); *Forbidden City* (Chinatown); *Happy Hauntings*; *Law and Disorder*.

Suggested tour

Total distance: 60km, or 110km with all detours.

Time: Allow a half-day for driving and 2 days to see all the sights, starting from the southwest corner of Beacon Hill Park, Douglas Street and Dallas Road. Pick up the circular tour anywhere, but avoid rush hours (*0730–0900 and 1600–1800*), especially downtown.

Links: Victoria connects with the **Gulf Islands** (*see page 56*) and with routes to **South Vancouver Island** (*see page 76*) or **Central Vancouver Island** (*see page 86*).

Route: Follow Dallas Road east through BEACON HILL PARK ⓘ along the **Juan de Fuca Strait** separating the US and Canada. The wooden sign marking Mile 0 of the TransCanada Highway is scenic, but the highway now extends west to **Tofino**.

A shoreline walking and cycling path is as popular with runners as it is with photographers entranced by the **Olympic Mountains** across the strait.

Detour 1: Dallas Road continues past **Ross Bay Cemetery**, where most early Victoria citizens can be found. Dallas Road changes names to Hollywood Crescent just beyond the cemetery, then becomes Crescent Road as it curves around **Gonzales Bay**, usually called **Foul Bay** for the leavings of its sea birds.

Take King George Terrace to the right, following green Scenic Drive signs. The **King George Lookout**, part of **Trafalgar Park**, has Victoria's best sea-level view across the Strait to **Port Angeles**, Washington, 37km due south.

King George Terrace ends at Beach Drive. Go right (east) on Beach Drive along the shores of **McNeil Bay** to the **Municipality of Oak Bay**. Tudor motifs are so popular that the municipal limit is half seriously called the 'Tweed Curtain'. Beach Drive swings north through the **Victoria Golf Club**, favoured by strollers. Visitors occasionally meet Doris Gravlin, the resident ghost, usually wearing a long white dress. Gravlin's body was found in a sand trap in the 1930s. Her husband was suspected of murder, but he drowned before the investigation was completed.

Just north are **Haynes Park** and the **Oak Bay Marina**. The **Oak Bay Rose Garden** and more than 500 plants from the private estate that once occupied the area fill the southeast corner of **Windsor Park**, west on Currie Road opposite the breakwater.

Continue north past **Willows Park** and through the massive stone gates of **Uplands**. The posh 1912 housing estate was designed by the Olmsted brothers, who designed New York's Central Park. The

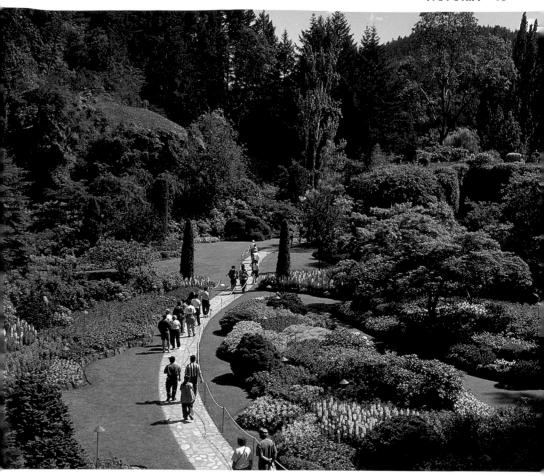

Above
Butchart Gardens

30-hectare **Uplands Park**, part of the original estate plan, is the largest tract of undeveloped Garry oak habitat in Victoria. Known as Oregon white oak in the US and British Columbia's only native oak, immense groves of Garry oaks once flourished in the drier meadows of Victoria. Many of the graceful trees became furniture or house beams. Most of the park is undeveloped. Continue 5km north to **Loon Bay**, the **Royal Victoria Yacht Club** and another massive stone gate marking the northern boundary of Uplands. Beach Drive becomes Cadboro Bay Road at Sinclair Road (*end of detour*).

Detour 2: Follow Cadboro Bay Road to Arbutus Road. Turn left (north) on to Arbutus and keep to the main roads headed north and west through **Mount Douglas Park** to Royal Oak Drive. Take Royal Oak Drive to Hwy 17 northbound. Go left (west) at Keating Cross Road, following signs to **Butchart Gardens**. Return to Victoria via Hwy 17A, passing east of NRC-Centre of the Universe, the Dominion Astrophysical Observatory interpretive centre, on the way to Hwy 17.

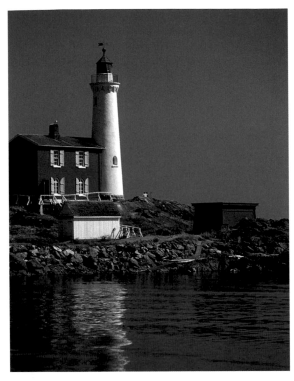

Above
Fisgard Lighthouse, Fort Rodd Hill

Continue south on Hwy 17 towards Victoria. Shortly after the dual carriageway ends, turn right on to Cloverdale Road, following signs and lane markings for 'Victoria by way of Douglas St'. At the second traffic signal, turn left on to Douglas to pass **Mayfair Shopping Centre**, one of the largest shopping malls on Vancouver Island, and a strip of motels.

The bright pink and grey brick **Victoria City Hall** is on the west side of Douglas at Pandora Street.

Continue five blocks to Broughton Street and turn right (west) at the red-brick **St Peter's Presbyterian Church**, right again at Broad Street and again on to Fort Street, one-way eastbound. Follow Fort Street 2km past **Antique Row** to Moss Street. Turn right (south), following green signs for the Art Gallery of Greater Vancouver (*end of detour*).

Head east to skirt Beacon Hill Park, then north up Cook Street, right in Richardson Street and left in Moss Street to reach the **ART GALLERY OF GREATER VICTORIA ❷**. From the Gallery, turn right on to Will Spencer Place, left on to Moss and right on to Fort Street. Turn right into Joan Crescent to **CRAIGDARROCH CASTLE ❸**.

Exit right into Joan Crescent. Continue to Rockland Avenue, turn right and then immediately left into **GOVERNMENT HOUSE GARDENS ❹**. Leave Government House to the left (west) on Rockland. Continue across Moss Street, Cook and Vancouver Streets, where Rockland becomes Courtney Street, to Quadra Street and **Christ Church Anglican Cathedral**, built in 13th-century Gothic style. Turn left (south) on to Quadra, which becomes Arbutus Way in **BEACON HILL PARK**. Continue on to Circular Drive, or follow Park Way to the top of Beacon Hill for views across Victoria and Juan de Fuca Strait and return to Circular Drive. Follow the circle left to Douglas Street and go left. Go right (west) on to Niagara Street two blocks to Government Street and turn right (north). **CARR HOUSE ❺** is ahead on the right (east).

Continue north past the **James Bay Inn** towards Belleville Street, with the **PARLIAMENT BUILDINGS ❻** on the left and the **ROYAL BRITISH COLUMBIA MUSEUM ❼** on the right. Across Belleville, the **INNER**

HARBOUR ❽ is on the left and **THE FAIRMONT EMPRESS HOTEL** ❾ on the right. Move to the right lane following Government Street north, passing the **Tourism Victoria Visitor Info Centre** on the left.

Continue past Fort Street with **The Bay Centre** on the right and **Munro's Books** on the left. At View Street, **BASTION SQUARE** ❿ and the **Maritime Museum** are to the left.

Detour: Turn left (west) on to Yates Street, then right (north) on to Wharf Street one block later, and move into the left or middle lane. Turn left (west) and cross the sky-blue **Johnson St Bridge** over **Victoria Harbour** to Esquimalt. Follow Esquimalt Road west to Admirals Road and turn right (north) to Hwy 1A at **CRAIGFLOWER MANOR AND SCHOOLHOUSE**. Turn left (west) on to Hwy 1A. Go straight to Ocean Boulevard, the first traffic signal beyond the **Juan de Fuca Recreation Centre** (on the south side), following signs for **FORT RODD HILL** and **FISGARD LIGHTHOUSE**. Return via Hwy 1A, which becomes Douglas Street.

South Vancouver Island

Ratings

Beaches	●●●●
Nature	●●●●
Parks	●●●●
Scenery	●●●●
Walking	●●●●
Children	●●●
Food	●●●
History	●●●

Don't expect to visit Victoria without exploring South Vancouver Island. Routes from Victoria's airport and major ferry terminals include a scenic drive through peaceful farming country north of the city. To the west lie increasingly wild stretches of forest and storm-wracked beach as the Strait of Juan de Fuca opens into the Pacific Ocean. Much of the oceanfront is protected in a series of parks linked by a rugged walking trail.

Inland forests have long since been logged, regrown and logged again in a seemingly endless cycle that despoils land and streams. It isn't until Port Renfrew and the roadless areas north that timber companies relinquish their hold. The variety of outdoor leisure activities, from boating and birding to strolling the lush glades of Butchart Gardens, mountain biking former railway lines and wilderness hiking, have made South Vancouver Island a playground for Victorians of all persuasions.

BOTANICAL BEACH

Botanical Beach, Juan de Fuca Provincial Park *3.5km south from Port Renfrew on gravel road; tel: (250) 474-1336; www.env.gov.bc.ca/bcparks/explore/parkpgs/juanfuca.html. Open daily.*

Botanical Beach, at the mouth of the Strait of Juan de Fuca, is one of BC's best known, if seldom seen, beaches. Sandstone cliffs drop to a cobble beach and rich tide pools that have been studied by generations of marine biologists from around the globe. At low tide, the pools are filled with green sea urchins, purple sea stars, scuttling red crabs, the waving green tentacles of anemones and swarms of silvery fish. The best and safest time to visit is near the end of a falling tide (use tide tables for Tofino) just before slack water. Rising tides sweep in rapidly, with massive rogue waves scouring what had been dry land an eyeblink earlier.

Rough tides and massive winter storms have eroded cliffs and headlands into swirling stone sculptures topped with Sitka spruce and shore pine. Several easy trails, including Mill Bay, Botany Bay and Shoreline, offer fine views even at high tide. All three trails converge on the Juan de Fuca Marine Trail, which leads 47km to China Beach.

DEVONIAN REGIONAL PARK

Devonian Regional Park *William Head Road, 1km west of My-Chosen Café; tel: (250) 478-3344; www.crd.bc.ca/parks/devonian/index.htm. Open daily dawn–dusk.*

My-Chosen Café $$ *4492 Happy Valley Road; tel: (250) 474-2333, is a local favourite, especially at weekends.*

An easy 1km nature trail on this former farm leads from the car park past **Sherwood Pond** (once used to water cattle) to the beach at **Perry Bay**, a favourite spot to watch for seals, sea lions and whales. A 5km trail leads east to **Witty's Lagoon**, but the trail is walkable only at low tide.

Right
Devonian Regional Park

DOMINION ASTROPHYSICAL OBSERVATORY
CENTRE OF THE UNIVERSE

Dominion Astrophysical Observatory NRC Centre of the Universe *Observatory Hill, 5071 W Saanich Rd; tel: (250) 363-8262; www.hia-iha/nrc-cnrc.gc. ca/cu/main_e.html. Open daily, call for hours and programmes.*

The 1.82m reflecting telescope inside the white dome atop **Observatory Hill** was the world's largest when it opened in 1918 and is still in active use. A scenic access road spirals around the hill to a car park just outside the observatory dome. The observatory interpretive centre calls itself 'The Centre of the Universe'. A planetarium and multimedia shows like *Falling Asteroid Blues* further engage visitors.

EAST SOOKE REGIONAL PARK

East Sooke Regional Park *Off Rocky Point Rd; tel: (250) 478-3344; www. crd.bc.ca/parks/eastsooke/ index.htm. Open daily 0800–sunset.*

South Vancouver Island's prime park has 1,435 hectares of semi-wild shore and forest laced with walking trails. The foreshore is framed by twisted arbutus and stunted pines, backed by Sitka spruce, red cedar, hemlock and Douglas fir. Look for bald eagles perched at the edge of the forest, river otters and mink scurrying through piles of tangled driftwood and cormorants diving offshore. Sea lions are common from September to May. Walking routes range from pre-picnic walks to an all-day, 10km trek along the park shoreline. Tiny spits and offshore islands protect dozens of pocket-sized beaches and picnic spots.

GALLOPING GOOSE REGIONAL TRAIL

Galloping Goose Regional Trail $ *Multiple entry points between Victoria and Leechtown; tel: (250) 478-3344; www. crd.bc.ca/parks/galloping-goose/index.htm. Open daily dawn–dusk.*

This linear park (55km long by 10m wide) follows the railbed of the *Galloping Goose*, a 1920s passenger railway that once ran from Victoria to Leechtown, an abandoned mining camp north of Sooke. The trail meanders through a variety of landscapes from urban streets to dense forest. Popular stretches are Roche Cove Regional Park (off Gillespie Road in Metchosin) to Matheson Lake Regional Park, about 4km, and through Sooke Potholes Provincial Park (*see page 82*).

JUAN DE FUCA MARINE TRAIL

Juan de Fuca Marine Trail *Between China Beach, west of Jordan River, in Juan de Fuca Provincial Park (near Port Renfrew), BC Parks; tel: (250) 474-1336; www.env.gov.bc.ca/bcparks/ explore/parkpgs/juanfuca.html*

Park and trail cover 47km of spectacular beaches, dazzling marine views, lush coastal forest and rich wildlife habitat. Experienced hikers should allow four days to walk the entire trail, but shorter sections make easy day hikes. **China Beach**, just west of Jordan River, has crashing surf 20 minutes from the trail head. **Botanical Beach** (*see page 76*), the west end of the trail, is famed for its tide pools and easy walks along the **Mill Bay**, **Botany Bay** and **Shoreline** trails. Other trail access points include **Sombrio Beach** and **Parkinson Beach**.

LOCHSIDE REGIONAL TRAIL

Lochside Regional Trail *Lochside Dr and Beacon Ave to Quadra St in Victoria; tel: (250) 476-3344; www.crd.bc.ca/parks/lochside/index.htm*

Scrap the railway but keep the right of way. That's the idea behind the 29km **Lochside Regional Trail**, named after its starting point. By either name, the walking and cycling trail connects with the Galloping Goose Trail at Quadra Street near Greenridge Circle in Victoria. Much of the trail is gravel, passing through forest, fields, hobby farms with pig and turkey pens, open-air museums, and even a field for flying model aeroplanes. Allow three hours one way to cycle to or from Victoria.

POINT NO POINT

Point No Point Resort $$ *10829 West Coast Rd (21km west of Sooke); tel: (250) 646-2020; www.pointnopoint.com*

The point of Point No Point (named by early chartmakers who either saw or didn't see the point, depending on their position) is a 400m rock pile pounded by ferocious waves. The inn of the same name is a traditional stopping point for modern Victorians on the way to or from Port Renfrew.

PORT RENFREW

Port Renfrew Chamber of Commerce *1 Parkinson Rd, Port Renfrew; www.portrenfrew.com or www.portrenfrewcommunity.com*

This tiny village at the mouth of the San Juan River is the end of the road on South Vancouver Island. It's also the terminus (or the beginning) of the Juan de Fuca Marine Trail south and east to China Beach, the West Coast Trail north to Bamfield and a maze of logging roads that converge on Cowichan Bay and Duncan (*see pages 87–9*). Expect at least a smattering of hikers, paddlers, beachcombers, fishers and hunters all year, though traffic is heaviest from June to mid-September when hundreds of West Coast Trail walkers pour through town.

Right
Port Renfrew's Botanical Beach

Food in Port Renfrew

Don't expect big-city cuisine in this frontier town that caters to outdoor recreationists.

Lighthouse Pub $$ *Parkinson Rd; tel: (250) 647-5505; www.portrenfrew.com/lighthouse,* is a good alternative restaurant.

Port Renfrew Hotel & Pub $$$ *17310 Parkinson Rd; tel: (250) 647-5541; www.portrenfrewhotel.ca,* has waterfront cabins looking out on the Strait of Juan de Fuca entrance.

RED CREEK FIR

ⓘ **Red Creek Fir** *12km from Port Renfrew; www.portrenfrew.com/redfir. htm.* Ask for directions and (especially) road conditions; accessible only by 4-wheel drive.

Thought to be the largest standing Douglas fir in Canada, this 74m-high tree was probably closer to 90m tall before the top blew off in a windstorm sometime in the past 900 or so years. Its 349sq-m of wood were left when loggers clearcut the area in 1987. Another record holder is a Douglas fir in the upper Coquitlam watershed that was measured at 94m tall in 1996.

SAANICH PENINSULA

ⓘ **Saanich Peninsula Chamber of Commerce** *West side Hwy 17, halfway between Swartz Bay Ferry Terminal and Sidney; #203, 2453 Beacon Ave, Sidney; tel: (250) 656-3616; www.spcoc.org.* Open daily.

ⓘ **BC Aviation Museum $** *1910 Norseman Rd (at Victoria International Airport), Sidney; tel: (250) 655-3300; www.bcam.net.* Open May–Sep daily 1000–1600, Oct–Apr daily 1100–1500.

Pointing north from Victoria like a thumb, the Saanich Peninsula is largely open, rolling country. Much of the peninsula is protected from future development within regional parks or agricultural preserves, but Victoria's expanding population has led to traffic congestion and pollution problems. Hwy 17, which leads from the BC Ferries landing at Swartz Bay to central Victoria, is the main traffic artery. Hwy 17A, W Saanich Road, is a more scenic alternative, but considerably slower.

At the tip of the peninsula and Hwy 17 are **Swartz Bay** and the **BC Ferries terminal**. Just south is **Victoria International Airport** and the **BC Aviation Museum**, which showcases the history of flight in Canada. The emotional highlight is a replica of the Gibson Twin built by Victorian William Gibson in 1910 – the craft flew 60m before crashing into a Garry oak tree, beating the American Wright brothers' 1903 flight record of 36m.

Right
Vintage seaplane

SAANICH HISTORICAL ARTIFACTS SOCIETY

Saanich Historical Artifacts Society $
7321 Lochside Dr, Saanichton; tel: (250) 652-5522; www.horizon.bc.ca/~shas. Open mid-Jun–mid-Sep daily 0930–1600, Oct–May daily 0930–1200.

The 12-hectare site looks like a junk yard from the highway, but the antique farming equipment, model railway, sawmill and almost everything else are maintained in perfect working order. Facilities include a small lake, forest hiking trails, a nature pond and picnic facilities.

Accommodation on the Saanich Peninsula

Brentwood Bay Lodge & Spa $$$ 849 Verdier Ave, Brentwood Bay; tel: (250) 544-2079 or (888) 544-2079; www.brentwoodbaylodge.com, has luxury ocean-view suites with outside balconies and fireplaces, a wood-fire grill restaurant, art gallery, 65-slip marina and a scuba-diving centre.

SIDNEY

The Marine Ecology Centre Port Sidney Marina, 9835 Seaport Place; tel: (250) 655-1555; www.mareco.org/home/default.asp. Open daily 1200–1700.

Sidney Spit Marine Park Sidney Island, 3km from Sidney.

Princess Margaret Marine Park Portland Island, 8km from Sidney. Both former provincial marine parks are in **Gulf Islands National Park Reserve**, 2220 Harbour Rd, Sidney, BC, V8L 2P6; tel: (250) 654-4000; www.pc.gc.ca/pn-np/bc/gulf/index_e.asp

The town was built in the 1890s at the terminus of the Victoria and Sidney Railway. The railway is long gone, but the high street, Beacon Avenue, is a pleasant place to wander. Look for bookshops along Beacon Avenue and Third Street, as well as a variety of speciality shops. The waterfront includes several restaurants with pleasant outdoor decks, pubs, parks, a marina and a popular fish market.

The Marine Ecology Centre is a combination aquarium and marine research station dedicated to local marine life. Volunteers are usually on hand to explain exhibits in the touch tanks and aquaria as well as beneath a battery of microscopes. Exhibits are designed for children, but there are details and information enough to keep professional researchers entranced.

Just offshore are the former **Sidney Spit Marine Park** and **Princess Margaret Marine Park**, now included in **Gulf Islands National Park Reserve**. Both are accessible by private boat or by ferry from the marina at the end of Beacon Avenue. The parks offer calm, sandy beaches, open lagoons, meadows and forests teeming with birds, deer and other wildlife, and camping.

SOOKE

Sooke Region Visitor Centre
Sooke Region Museum, see overleaf.

Sooke is the southernmost harbour in Western Canada, a bustling fishing, logging and tourist town. The harbour is protected by **Whiffen Spit**, a narrow strip of sand, gravel and driftwood nearly 5km long. Both Sooke Harbour and Sooke Basin, a large sheltered backwater, are popular with kayakers.

Sooke Region Museum $
2070 Phillips Rd, Sooke; tel: (250) 642-6351 or (866) 888-4748; http://sookeregionmuseum.com. Open daily 0900–1700.

Moss Cottage $
2070 Phillips Rd, Sooke; tel: (250) 642-6351. Moss Cottage is part of Sooke Region Museum (see above).

Adrena Line Zipline Adventure Tours $$
Beneath the 17 Mile Pub Liquor Store, 5128C Sooke Rd; tel: (250) 642-1933 or (866) 947-9145. Operates Apr–Oct, call for hours.

Sooke was the site of Vancouver Island's first successful steam-powered sawmill and one of BC's last commercial fish traps. **Sooke Region Museum** tells both stories in lavish detail, as well as recounting a short-lived gold rush at Leechtown and the large First Nations villages that once dominated the area. **Moss Cottage** is the oldest structure in Sooke, built in 1870 with lumber from the original Muir Mill, itself built around a boiler salvaged from a shipwreck in 1849. The cottage, furnished as a working-class home from 1902, is open all year. Guides explain the displays in summer. **Adrena Line Zipline Adventure Tours** nearby in the Sooke Mountains offer two-hour guided tours along eight zip lines 20–30m above the ground.

Accommodation and food in Sooke

Mom's Café $$ *2036 Shields Rd; tel: (250) 642-3314*, is a busy local eatery, known for beer batter halibut.

Sooke Harbour House $$$ *1528 Whiffen Spit Rd; tel: (250) 642-3421 or (800) 889-9688; www.sookeharbourhouse.com*, is one of the most acclaimed restaurant-hotels in Western Canada, specialising in all-local products including two dozen types of crab and vegetables from the kitchen garden.

SOOKE POTHOLES PROVINCIAL PARK

Sooke Potholes Provincial Park
Sooke River Rd, 5km north of Sooke; tel: (250) 474-1336; www.env.gov.bc.ca/bcparks/explore/parkspgs/sooke.html. Open daily.

The potholes, natural glacier-formed holes in the sandstone bedrock of the Sooke River filled with cool, clear water, have been a popular summer swimming destination since the 1860s. It is also a place where people come to ride bikes and watch spawning coho and chinook salmon. Expect crowds on hot summer days, but winter visitors are rare.

WEST COAST TRAIL

West Coast Trail
Pacific Rim National Park Reserve, Ucluelet or Parks Canada West Coast Trail InfoCentres at Pachena Bay/Gordon River; tel: (250) 726-7721; www.pc.gc.ca

West Coast Trail Express $ Tel: (250) 477-8700 or (888) 999-2288; www.trailbus.com, has shuttle transportation to the West Coast and Juan de Fuca Trails, May–Sep.

Port Renfrew is the end or the beginning of the rugged 6-day, 75km trek through bogs, beaches, forests, rivers, rain and sun along the western edge of Vancouver Island. Created as a life-saving route for sailors shipwrecked on the treacherous coast in the 19th century, the Trail has become one of the most popular hikes in Canada. From June through September a limited number of hikers are allowed to start each day, with groups leaving from Port Renfrew or Pachena Bay (3km from Bamfield) and Nitinat, the midway point. Most permits are booked up months in advance, but a handful are available, especially in shoulder seasons, on a first-come, first-served basis each day at 1300. The trail is part of the Pacific Rim National Park Reserve.

Witty's Lagoon Regional Park

Witty's Lagoon Regional Park
Metchosin Rd; tel: (250) 478-3344; www.crd.bc.ca/parks/wittys/index.htm. Open 0800–sunset.

Witty's perfectly encapsulates the West Coast with luxuriant forests, clear creeks, a waterfall, long sandy beaches backed by wracks of driftwood, bald eagles, blue herons, 158 other bird species, seals and passing whales. A 5km trail leads to the **Devonian Regional Park** (*see page 77*) at low tide.

Suggested tour

Total distance: 260km.

Time: Allow a half-day to drive east from Victoria and a full day to drive west, or 2–4 days to explore.

Links: Combine the south end of Vancouver Island with a visit to Victoria or island routes north.

Route: The south island tour has two sections, east up the Saanich Peninsula (70km return) and west to Port Renfrew (190km return). Drive each section as a day trip from Victoria, or allow at least one overnight in Sooke or Port Renfrew.

Below
Dusk on Vancouver Island

From downtown Victoria, follow Hwy 17 north along the Saanich Peninsula towards the **Victoria International Airport** and the BC Ferries landing at **Swartz Bay**. The rolling countryside becomes

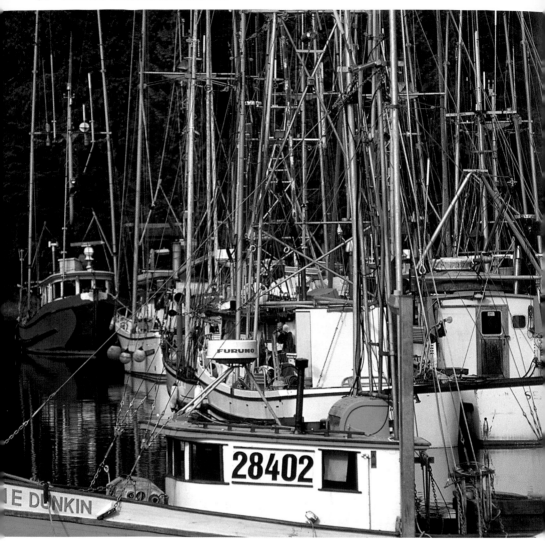

Above
A popular pastime on
Vancouver Island

increasingly agricultural beyond Victoria. Follow exit signs to **SIDNEY** ❶, a lively seaside town and terminus for Washington State Ferries from the US. Return southbound on Hwy 17 to Keating Cross Road and turn right (west) to **Butchart Gardens** (*see page 66*).

From Butchart Gardens, return southbound to W Saanich Road and turn right (south). The country road winds through 6km of scenic hills, farms and townships to **Observatory Hill** and the **DOMINION ASTROPHYSICAL OBSERVATORY** ❷. Continue on W Saanich Road and follow signs for Hwy 17. Take Hwy 17 into central Victoria or follow Hwy 1A (Gorge Road) westbound (right) to avoid the central city and continue the south island tour.

For the western tour, continue along Hwy 1A or the Victoria City Tour Detour to Fort Rodd Hill and Fisgard Lighthouse (*see page 69*) to **Craigflower Manor and Schoolhouse** (*see page 68*) and **Fort Rodd Hill/Fisgard Lighthouse**. From the Fort Rodd Hill car park, continue straight for 2km to Esquimalt Lagoon. Just offshore is **Royal Roads**, a protected anchorage first charted by Spanish sailors in 1790. At the west end of the lagoon, turn right on to Lagoon Road. At the top of the hill, turn left on to Metchosin Road. Pass Albert Head Lagoon Park and **WITTY'S LAGOON REGIONAL PARK ❸**, 3km to **My-Chosen Café** and veer right on to William Head Road. Turn right up the narrow avenue of **Lombard Poplars** just past **DEVONIAN REGIONAL PARK ❹**. Turn left on to Rocky Point Rd and right 3km later on to Matheson Lake Park Road. Pass East Sooke Regional Park to Gillespie Road. Turn right (north) on to Hwy 14 and turn west (left).

Pass Sooke River Road and the **SOOKE POTHOLES ❺**, the **Sooke River Hotel**, the Sooke Region Museum and continue into Sooke, a small fishing and resort town. Hwy 14 continues west into increasingly mountainous country past the **Shearingham Light** and **Shirley**, **POINT NO POINT ❻**, the lumber town of **Jordan**, and into **PORT RENFREW ❼**.

Take Hwy 14 back to **Victoria**.

Detour: In good weather, you can follow unpaved logging roads from Port Renfrew to **Lake Cowichan** and **Douglas**, then south along the Island Highway to **Victoria**. Allow half a day for the return trip. Ask about logging road closures and driving conditions in Port Renfrew before setting out.

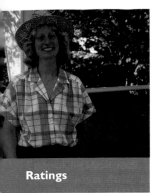

Ratings

First Nations art	●●●●●
Historical sights	●●●●●
History	●●●●●
National parks	●●●●●
Nature	●●●●●
Beaches	●●●●○
Children	●●●●○
Outdoor activities	●●●●○

Central Vancouver Island

Rolling hills, lush valleys, mossy forests, protected harbours, tranquil lakes, art from several First Nations bands and trackless beaches define the central section of Vancouver Island. So do clearcuts, tree plantations, slag heaps and abandoned mining towns. The coal mines that once made Nanaimo one of the richest cities in Canada are long closed, the grimy, sooty waterfronts transformed into sparkling marinas and busy bayside walking paths. Chemainus, Duncan and similar towns once dependent on forest industries have been reborn as tourist centres with museums, murals, totem poles and other artistic productions. Across Vancouver Island, great swathes of beach, island and forest have been preserved within the Pacific Rim National Park Reserve, much of it unreachable except by foot or by boat. In between lies an irregular chequerboard of natural forest, farmed forest, burgeoning dormitory communities and quiet villages. The area is becoming BC's second wine region, with wineries, cider makers and mead brewers on Vancouver Island and some of the Gulf Islands (*www.wineislands.ca*).

CHEMAINUS

ⓘ Chemainus Chamber of Commerce *Visitor Information Centre, 9796 Willow St (across from Waterwheel Park); tel: (250) 246-3944; www.chemainus.bc.ca. Open mid-May–early Oct daily 0900–1700, early Oct–mid-May Mon–Fri 0900–1700, Sat 1000–1600.*

Chemainus calls itself 'The Little Town that Did!' in memory of its successful transition from timber to tourism. When its mainstay mill closed in the early 1980s, the city paid local artists to paint **murals** on the buildings to lure coach tours. The ploy worked, sparking a business boom and 39 murals.

Centre of the boom is **Waterwheel Park** and the **Chemainus Valley Museum**, with local artefacts from the past century. Pick up a Mural Map at the Visitor Information Centre. The 39 paintings depict local history from the original First Nations inhabitants of the area to the arrival of Europeans and the development of local timber and agricultural industries. A new sawmill has reopened, but lumber plays second fiddle to a growing arts community, with galleries and performing arts theatre.

Accommodation and food in Chemainus

Waterwheel Park
Willow St. Open daily.

**Chemainus Valley
Museum $** *Waterwheel
Park; tel: (250) 246-2445.
Open daily mid-Feb–mid-Dec
1000–1600.*

Dancing Bean Coffee Company $ *9752 Willow St; tel: (250) 246-5050;
www.dancingbean.ca,* has live music ($), local art or photographic
exhibitions, coffee, tea, wine, and salads and sandwiches to accompany
homemade soup.

Chemainus Festival Inn $$ *9573 Chemainus Rd; tel: (877) 246-4181* or
(250) 246-4181; http://festivalinn.ca, is across the road from an 18-hole
golf course.

Fuller Lake Motel $$ *9300 Smiley Rd, Canada Hwy; tel: (250) 246-3282*
or *(888) 246-3255; www.chemainus-fullerlakemotel.com,* is the largest
motel in the area, and is non-smoking.

COWICHAN BAY & DUNCAN

Tourism Cowichan
*175 Ingram St, Duncan,
BC, V9L 1N8; tel: (250) 746-
1099 or (888) 303-3337;
http://visit.cowichan.net*

This tiny bayside town was once the heart of the entire Cowichan
region, stretching from the Malahat Hills north nearly to Nanaimo and
west to the Pacific Ocean. Meaning 'warm land' in the Cowichan First

True Grain Bread $ 1725 Cowichan Bay Rd; tel: (250) 746-7664; www.truegrain.ca, stone-grinds its grains and touts Old World-style loaves.

Bluenose 11 $$ North end of the village; 1765 Cowichan Bay Rd; tel: (250) 748-2841, with a deck with a bay view.

Rock Cod Café $$ 1759 Cowichan Bay Rd; tel: (250) 746-1550; www.rockcodcafe.com, is the local favourite for fresh seafood.

Cowichan Bay Maritime Centre $ 1761 Cowichan Bay Rd; tel: (250) 746-4955; www.classicboats.org. Open daily 0900–dusk.

Duncan-Cowichan Chamber of Commerce/Visitor Information Centre 381A TransCanada Hwy; tel: (250) 746-4636 or (888) 303-3337; http://duncancc.bc.ca. Open daily Jul–Aug 0900–1800, Apr–Jun Mon–Sat 0900–1700, Sep–Apr Tue–Sat 0900–1600.

Quw'utsun' Cultural & Conference Centre 200 Cowichan Way; tel: (250) 746-8119 or (877) 746-8119; www.quwutsun.ca. Open daily mid-Apr–Sep 0900–1600, Oct–Apr call for hours.

BC Forest Discovery Centre 2892 Drinkwater Rd, Hwy 1, just north of Duncan; tel: (250) 715-1113 or (866) 715-1113; www.bcforestmuseum.com. Open 1000–1700 daily Jun–Sep, Mar–May Thur–Mon, Oct Sat–Sun. Train rides $.

Nations language, Cowichan Bay was a major timber and farm port until railway builders opened a station in Duncan in the late 19th century.

Most buildings in this one-road town have their front doors on Cowichan Bay Road and their back doors on Cowichan Bay. The **Cowichan Bay Maritime Centre** is a combination museum and wooden-boat-building centre. Best views of the town are from the Centre's 100m pier. Pavilions along the pier display historic photographs and boat-related memorabilia.

Duncan became the Cowichan's main town when the railway arrived in the 1880s. A busy commercial and agricultural centre, it is best known for the 40 or so totem poles scattered around town and the **Quw'utsun' Cultural and Conference Centre**. Don't miss the multimedia programmes and exhibits on local Cowichan tribal history. In summer, a daily **Salmon BBQ** includes dances and story-telling with an excellent meal.

BC Forest Discovery Centre is the forest industry's own vision of BC history. Exhibits include a working lumber mill and steam train, as well as forest machinery and easy-to-understand displays of how trees are cut, sorted and processed. Rail buffs can ride steam and other trains.

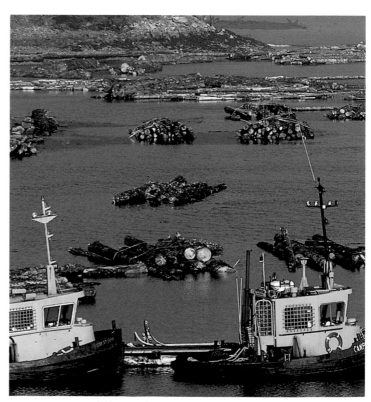

ⓘ Cowichan Valley Museum $ *130 Canada Ave; tel: (250) 746-6612; www. cowichanvalleymuseum.bc.ca. Open Jun–Sep Mon–Sat 1000–1600; Oct–May Wed–Fri 1100–1600, Sat 1300–1600.*

Somenos Marsh Conservation Area *East side of Hwy 1, north of Duncan; www.somenosmarsh.com*

Opposite
Logging boats

Cowichan Valley Museum offers domestic and industrial artefacts in period settings in a 1912 railway station. The photographic collection is one of BC's best local archives. Park at the museum and follow the yellow footsteps around town to see the entire totem collection.

Somenos Marsh Conservation Area is good for summer and winter birdwatching.

Food in Duncan

Bistro One Sixty One $$ *161 Kenneth St; tel: (250) 746-6466,* uses local ingredients in a romantic atmosphere.

Just Jakes $$ *45 Craig St; tel: (250) 746-5622; www.justjakes.ca,* strives to be down to earth with a local flavour, including the owner's own curry sauce for grilled prawns.

Vigneti Zanatta Winery & Vinoteca Restaurant $$ *5039 Marshall Rd; tel: (250) 748-2338; www.zanatta.ca,* focuses on local food and wines, most grown on the property. Call for restaurant hours.

GABRIOLA ISLAND

ⓘ Gabriola Island Chamber of Commerce and Visitor InfoCentre *#3–575 North Rd, Gabriola, BC V0R 1X0; tel: (250) 247-9332 or (888) 284-9332; www.gabriolaisland.org*

Gabriola Island, reached by ferry from Nanaimo, is the northernmost Gulf Island, with 4,500 permanent residents, an artists' colony, tide pools, beaches, petroglyphs and the **Malaspina Galleries**, cavernous sandstone formations on the northwest side. Activities include fishing, diving in clear cold waters, kayaking, beachcombing, hiking, biking, or golf. There is no public transport; visitors bring a car or bicycle.

MACMILLAN PROVINCIAL PARK

ⓘ MacMillan Provincial Park *Cameron Lake; tel: (250) 474-1336; www.env.gov.bc.ca/bcparks/explore/parkpgs/macmillan.html. Open daily.*

This roadside park includes **Cathedral Grove**, one of BC's only surviving stands of virgin forest accessible by highway. The park is named after Harvey MacMillan, BC's first Chief Forester and later head of what is now MacMillan Bloedel, one of BC's largest timber companies. The virgin grove stands in stark contrast to MacMillan Bloedel clearcuts and plantation projects nearby.

MALAHAT DRIVE ON ISLAND HIGHWAY

Malahat Drive winds through the Malahat Hills separating the Saanich Peninsula from the Cowichan region. Views eastward to the mainland are stunning in clear weather.

NANAIMO

ⓘ Tourism Nanaimo
*2290 Bowen Rd;
tel: (800) 663-7337 or
(250) 756-0106; www.
tourismnanaimo.com. Open
daily May–Aug 0900–1700,
Mon–Fri rest of the year.*

⇄ Nanaimo has three **BC
Ferries terminals,**
*tel: (888) 223-3779 or (250)
753-9344.*

Nanaimo Harbour Ferry
$ *Tel: (877) 297-8526;
www.nanaimoharbourferry.
com,* takes visitors to
Newcastle Island.

ⓑ The Bastion
*http://nanaimomuseum.
com/bastionpage.htm*

New Nanaimo Museum $
*100 Museum Way; tel: (250)
753-1821;
http://nanaimomuseum.com.
Call for opening hours.*

Petroglyph Provincial Park
*Hwy 1 pullout; tel: (250) 474-
1336; www.env.gov.bc.ca/bcparks/
explore/parkpgs/petrogly.html*

The town developed as a coal centre and remains Vancouver Island's
major export centre. The coal docks, foundries and other industries that
once lined the harbour have been replaced by marinas, parks and the
5km **Harbourfront Walkway**. Ask for self-guiding walking maps of
historic areas and buildings at the Tourist InfoCentre. **The Bastion** is the
sole surviving Hudson's Bay Company bastion, or fortress, in BC. The
white wooden redoubt houses a small museum. Guardsmen in 1850s
naval uniforms parade and fire a cannon at noon each day in summer.
New Nanaimo Museum uses local artefacts to reproduce a coal mine
and First Nations history. **Petroglyph Provincial Park**, *on Hwy 1* just
south of Nanaimo, has thousand-year-old petroglyphs and is a chance for
petroglyph rubbing as a souvenir.

Accommodation and food in Nanaimo

Dinghy Dock Pub & Family Restaurant $ *8 Pirate's Lane; (pub) tel: (250)
753-2373; (ferry to pub) tel: (250) 753-8244; www.dinghydockpub.com,*
offers an informal dining experience either while at anchor or on the
rising or falling tide.

Painted Turtle Guesthouse $ *121 Bastion St; tel: (866) 309-4432 or (250)
753-4432; www.paintedturtle.ca,* is a hostel hotel in the centre of town.

Coast Bastion Inn $$ *11 Bastion St; tel: (250) 753-6601 or (800) 716-
6199; www.coasthotels.com,* is just up the street from The Bastion.

Right
Nanaimo

NEWCASTLE ISLAND PROVINCIAL MARINE PARK

**ⓑ Newcastle Island
Provincial Marine
Park** *Just off Nanaimo; tel:
(250) 754-7893;
http://newcastleisland.ca*

This 306-hectare island sheltering Nanaimo Harbour has been home
to Snuneymuxw First Nation villages, coal mines, fish processing
plants and a resort. Accessible by ferry from Nanaimo, it has become a
favourite getaway for picnicking, walking, swimming and camping.

PACIFIC RIM NATIONAL PARK RESERVE

Park Visitor Information Centre *Hwy 4, at Ucluelet–Tofino junction.*

Pacific Rim National Park Reserve *West coast of Vancouver Island; tel: (250) 726-7721; www.pc.gc.ca/pn-np/bc/ pacificrim/index_E.asp*

This is three parks in one – the **West Coast Trail** (*see page 82*), stretching north from Port Renfrew, the **Broken Group Islands**, more than 100 islands in Barkley Sound, and **Long Beach**, between Ucluelet and Tofino – the only section accessible by road. The 30km of sandy beaches, rocky headlands, forests and bogs are busy in summer and deserted from November to April, except for seagulls, sea lions and crabs hiding in the tangled driftwood.

Wickaninnish Centre (*end of Wilk Rd, 3.5km from Hwy 4, refurbished by late 2009*) is the main interpretive centre, with a museum, restaurant and elevated walkways with expansive views. The surf-swept sand of Long Beach stretches 10km north.

PORT ALBERNI

Alberni Valley Chamber of Commerce *2533 Port Alberni Hwy; tel: (250) 724-6535; www.avcoc.com. Open daily.*

Alberni Pacific Railway $$ *3100 Kingsway Ave at Argyle St near Harbour Quay; tel: (250) 723-1376; www. alberniheritage.com/railway. Operates Thu–Mon late Jun–early Sep; occasional trips in other seasons.*

Alberni Valley Museum $ *Echo Centre, 4255 Wallace St; tel: (250) 723-2121; www. alberniheritage.com/museum.. Open Tue–Sat 1000–1700, Thu to 2000.*

Maritime Discovery Centre $ *2750 Harbour Rd; tel: (250) 723-6164; www. alberniheritage.com/maritime. Open daily third week of Jun–Labour Day 1000–1700.*

Lady Rose and Frances Barkley $$ *5425 Argyle St, Alberni Harbour Quay; tel: (250) 723-8313 or (800) 663-7192; www. ladyrosemarine.com*

Forty kilometres from the Pacific Ocean at the head of a fjord-like inlet, Port Alberni is shifting from mining and timber to tourism, although logging tours remain popular attractions.

Alberni Pacific Railway provides steam train service to the McLean Mill National Historic Site in summer. The restored 1929 2-8-2 Baldwin Locomotive No 7 spent its working life in island logging. Summer tours stop at **Chase & Warren Estate Winery** (*www.chaseandwarren.ca*); some trips feature the Beaufort Gang Train Robbery.

Alberni Valley Museum has a major collection of local Nuu Chah Nulth First Nations artefacts, as well as an operating steam engine, water wheel and similar practical items.

The **Maritime Discovery Centre** in a coastal lighthouse on the waterfront shows off Vancouver Island's wilder west coast history.

The ships **MV *Lady Rose*** and **MV *Frances Barkley*** provide freight, passenger and sightseeing services to Ucluelet via Bamfield and the Broken Group. Expect to see marine life all year and hikers, kayakers and boaters coming and going to one of BC's most popular marine parks in summer.

McLean Mill National Historic Site (*www.alberniheritage.com/mill*) is the only remaining steam-powered mill in British Columbia. The mill has been restored to its operating condition in 1965 when it was typical of the remote lumber camps and sawmills that dotted Vancouver Island. There is a stage show to introduce the mill to visitors who are treated like workers arriving at the mill for the day's labours.

Accommodation and food in Port Alberni

Dolce Vita Bar & Grill $$ *4505 Gertrude St; tel: (250) 724-5050,* specialises in seafood, Greek and Italian dishes.

McLean Mill National Historic Site *5633 Smith Road; tel: (250) 723-1376; www.alberniheritage.com/mill. Open daily late Jun–early Sep.*

Little Bavaria $$ *3035 4th Ave; tel: (250) 724-4242 or (800) 704-2744; http://littlebavariarestaurant.com*, is the only German restaurant in town.

Swale Rock Café $$ *5328 Argyle St; tel: (250) 723-0777*, serves seafood to a largely local crowd. Try the fried bread and blackberry preserves.

Best Western Barclay $$$ *4277 Stamp Ave; tel: (250) 724-7171 or (800) 563-6590; http://bestwesternbarclay.com*, is the largest hotel in town.

The Hospitality Inn $$$ *3835 Redford St; tel: (250) 723-8111 or (877) 723-8111; www.hospitalityinnportalberni.com*, has big-city facilities.

TOFINO

Tofino-Long Beach Chamber of Commerce/Tofino Visitor Information Centre *1426 Pacific Rim Hwy; tel: (250) 725-3414; www.tourismtofino.com. Call in advance.*

Eagle Aerie Gallery *350 Campbell St; tel: (250) 725-3235; www.royhenryvickers.com. Open daily.*

House of Himwitsa *$–$$ 300 Main St; tel: (250) 725-2017 or (800) 899-1947; www.himwitsa.com. Open daily.*

Whale Centre & Maritime Museum $$ *411 Campbell St; tel: (250) 725-2132 or (888) 474-2288; www.tofinowhalecentre.com. Whale watching daily Mar–mid-Oct.*

This one-time timber town has become a busy tourist centre for Pacific Rim National Park Reserve and **Clayoquot Sound**, a UNESCO Biosphere Reserve. Tofino has also become a centre for First Nations artists and galleries. **Eagle Aerie Gallery** exhibits works by Roy Vickers, one of Canada's most commercially successful First Nations artists.

House of Himwitsa is a combination First Nations gallery, restaurant and motel.

The **Whale Centre & Maritime Museum** sponsors whale-watching excursions to supplement displayed artefacts from local shipwrecks and First Nations history. Storm watchers fill hotels in winter.

Accommodation and food in Tofino

Common Loaf Bake Shop $ *180 First St; tel: (250) 725-3915*, is the town's best bakery and café.

Best Western Tin Wis Resort Lodge $$ *1119 Pacific Rim Hwy; tel: (250) 725-4445 or (800) 661-9995; www.tinwis.com*, overlooks a calm cove that was a traditional launching point for First Nations whalers.

Pacific Sands Beach Resort $$$ *Cox Bay; tel: (250) 725-3322 or (800) 565-2322; www.pacificsands.com*, has beachfront villas just north of Pacific Rim National Park.

Weigh West Marine Resort $$$ *634 Campbell St; tel: (250) 725-3277 or (800) 665-8922; www.weighwest.com*, is a waterfront hotel and restaurant popular with visiting fishermen.

Wickaninnish Inn $$$ *Chesterman Beach; tel: (250) 725-3100 or (800) 333-4604; http://wickinn.com*, gets international attention as one of BC's finest restaurants and most luxurious inns.

UCLUELET

ⓘ Ucluelet Chamber of Commerce/ Downtown Visitor Centre *Unit 3, 1645 Cedar Rd; tel: (250) 726-4641; http://uclueletinfo.com. Open daily in summer. Call in advance.*

ⓑ Amphitrite Point Lighthouse *South of downtown. Open daily.*

He-Tin-Kis Park
1km south of downtown. Open daily.

Government Wharf
Foot of Main St.

The logging and fishing village of Ucluelet is trying to switch to tourism, but Tofino gets most of the traffic. Ucluelet is smaller, quieter and more focused on outdoor activities such as kayaking, fishing, whale-watching and boating. **Amphitrite Point Lighthouse** has stunning views of Barkley Sound. Look for migrating grey whales between March and April, raging storms in winter and spectacular sunsets all year.

He-Tin-Kis Park boardwalk trails wander through old-growth cedar and spruce forests to open shoreline vistas, while **Government Wharf** is a convenient spot to watch bald eagles, seals and sea lions.

Accommodation and food in Ucluelet

Canadian Princess Resort $$$ *Harbourfront; tel: (250) 598-3366* or *(800) 663-7090; www.canadianprincess.com*, is a historic steamship turned resort, restaurant and mothership for salmon and halibut fishing and nature trips into Barkley Sound.

Snug Harbour Inn $$$ *460 Marine Dr; tel: (250) 726-2686* or *(888) 936-5222; www.awesomeview.com*, offers plush cliffside suites overlooking a private beach.

Suggested tour

Total distance: 320km.

Time: Allow a full day to drive from Victoria to Tofino; up to a week for sightseeing.

Links: Continue north to **Port Hardy** and **ferry routes** to the mainland (*see page 106*), take the ferry from **Nanaimo** back to **Vancouver** (*see page 42*), or return to Victoria.

Right
Chemainus mural

Rainforest archipelago

Clayoquot Sound, a UNESCO Biosphere Reserve, is the largest surviving temperate rainforest in North America, thanks to Canada's largest-ever civil protest. A provincial decision to allow logging in 1993 sparked hundreds of arrests, road blockades and world-wide boycotts of BC products before most logging permits were rescinded. The 65km-long sound includes 3,000sq km of islands, rivers and forests accessible only by air or boat. **Meares, Vargas** and **Flores** are the largest and most popular islands. **Hot Springs Cove**, the only natural hot springs on Vancouver Island, is another popular destination. Sea and air operators in Tofino and Ucluelet offer daily trips, weather permitting.

Route: Follow signs for Hwy 1 north from Victoria past **Portage Inlet** and **Thetis Lake Park**. The road swings north through **Goldstream Provincial Park** before it climbs up the Island Highway on a section known as the **MALAHAT DRIVE ❶**. Broad vistas across the **Saanich Peninsula** to the mainland and the **Cascade Range** are stunning in clear weather, but lay-bys at the 352m summit are accessible only from the northbound lanes. Continue on Highway 1 as it runs north through the rolling agricultural lands from Duncan to Nanaimo.

Detour: The scenic route follows the direct route 50km north to Cowichan Bay Road and a rest area 18km north of the **Malahat Summit**. Turn west (left) through 6km of rolling farmland and forests dotted with tiny lakes to **COWICHAN BAY ❷** and continue north. The road becomes Tzouhalem Road at a T-junction just north of the roadside historical marker lauding the landing of the first shipload of English settlers in 1862. A second marker is dedicated to poet Robert W Service, who worked and wrote locally in the early 1900s.

Continue north, then west, to **Maple Bay**. Take Maple Bay Road northeast (right) through 6km of exclusive housing estates to Genoa Bay Road and turn right (east). The narrow road climbs through a range of granite hills to emerge at tiny **Genoa Bay**.

Return to Maple Bay, with **Salt Spring Island** (*see pages 58–9*) just offshore. Take Herd Road north and west to Osborne Bay Road and turn north (right) to Champlain Street. Go east (right) into **Crofton**. Go back up Champlain Street to Crofton Road and turn north (right) to Chemainus Road, 2km beyond the Fletcher Challenge pulp and paper mill. Continue north to **CHEMAINUS ❸**.

Chemainus Road runs 10km to the Island Hwy. Turn right (north) towards Nanaimo. At Cedar Point Road, turn right (east) through pastoral farmland to Yellowpoint Road and go east (right). Continue past **Roberts Memorial Provincial Park**, a popular summer swimming spot, and back on to Cedar Point Road. At MacMillan Road, turn right to visit the **Harmac Pulp Mill** or continue on to the Island Hwy and NANAIMO ❹.

Hwy 1 becomes Hwy 19 at Nanaimo, but keeps the Island Hwy name. Continue north along a narrowing strip of flat land along the coast. Just before **Parksville**, take Hwy 4 west towards Port Alberni. The settlement just south of the highway with goats grazing on the roof is **Coombs**, a convenient rest and ice cream stop. The highway climbs past MACMILLAN PROVINCIAL PARK ❺, one of the rare bits of virgin forest left along any highway in BC, then drops down to **PORT ALBERNI** ❻, the island's most interior Pacific port.

The road continues past **Sproat Lake**, home to the world's largest water bombers (used to fight forest fires), and twists through the increasingly rugged **MacKenzie Range** and **Hydro Hill**, an 18 per cent grade. At the T-junction, go left to UCLUELET ❼ or right to **PACIFIC RIM NATIONAL PARK** and the end of the road at TOFINO ❽.

North Vancouver Island

Ratings

Beaches	●●●●●
Children	●●●●●
First Nations art	●●●●●
Mountains	●●●●●
Nature	●●●●●
Outdoor activities	●●●●●
Scenery	●●●●●
Wildlife	●●●●●

The northern portion of Vancouver Island stretches from warm, gentle beaches hundreds of metres wide and kilometres long to treacherous cliffs rising sheer from the turbulent ocean. Logging trucks and heavy equipment share the few northern roads and infrequent hamlets with hunters, fishers, RVs and long-distance cyclists, all of them outnumbered by bear, deer and bald eagles.

Just offshore, the Inside Passage between Vancouver Island and the mainland narrows from a broad marine highway at Parksville to a narrow, twisting channel dotted with jagged rocks and turbulent eddies from Campbell River northward.

Pods of orcas patrol the cold, fish-rich waters, dodging fleets of cruise ships, humpback whales and sea kayakers. On shore, look for the ornate, richly coloured totem poles created by the First Nations bands which have emerged from generations of repression and cultural twilight to become a major social and economic force once again.

ALERT BAY

ℹ **Village of Alert Bay Visitor Centre** 116 Fir St; tel: (250) 974-5024; www.alertbay.ca. Open daily Jul–Aug; Sep–Jun Mon–Fri.

⇄ **BC Ferry** Tel: (888) 223-3779 or (250) 386-3431; www.bcferries.com, from Port McNeill.

🏛 **'Namgis Burial Ground** Fir St, south of the ferry landing; roadside viewing.

Alert Bay was a hotbed of First Nations resistance to discriminatory laws in the 19th and early 20th centuries. The fishing and tourist community on Cormorant Island is an ethnic mix today, but the look and feel are solidly Kwakwaka'wakw, the name of the kwak'wala-speaking people of Vancouver Island and the adjacent mainland inlets. Don't miss the '**Namgis Burial Ground** with its stunning totem poles (the cemetery is closed to the public, but clearly visible from the street), and the **U'mista Cultural Centre**, a model Big House built to display half of a potlatch (*see box, page 101*) collection that was confiscated by government agents in 1922 and returned in 1978 after decades of wrangling. The rest of the collection is in the **Nuyumbalees Cultural Centre** (*Quathiashi Cove; tel: 250 285-3733; www.nuyumbalees.com. Open daily May–Sep; Oct–Apr Wed–Sat*) on Quadra Island (across from Campbell River). U'mista also has an excellent selection of First Nations artists, many shown online.

Accommodation and food in Alert Bay

Nimpkish Hotel $$ *318 Fir St; tel: (888) 646-7547* or *(250) 974-2324; http://nimpkishhotel.com,* has a deck for easy whale watching.

Tsa-Kwa-Luten Lodge $$ *#1 Lighthouse Rd, Quathiaski Cove, Quadra Island; tel: (250) 285-2042* or *(800) 665-7745; http://capemudgeresort.bc.ca,* is known for its restaurant with a view.

BEAVER COVE

Beaver Cove $
12km off Hwy 19.

Beaver Cove handles 1.4 million cubic metres of logs annually, Canada's largest dryland sort where logs are separated by species, grade and intended use. The sorted logs are dumped in huge ponds or 'booming grounds' in the cove to be chained together, or 'stowed up' into rafts 21m wide by 121m long. The rafts are then towed to pulp and lumber mills for processing. Watch from a lay-by at the top of the hill.

CAMPBELL RIVER

Campbell River Visitor Information Centre *1235 Shoppers Row, Tyee Plaza; tel: (250) 830-0411 or (877) 286-5705; www.visitorinfo. incampbellriver.com. Tourism Campbell River and Region, 900 Alder St; tel: (250) 830-1115; www.campbellriver. travel. Open all year.*

Campbell River & District Public Art Gallery *1235 Shoppers Row; tel: (250) 287-2261; www.crartgallery.ca. Open Sep–May Tue–Sat 1200–1700; Jun–Aug Mon–Sat 1000–1700.*

The Museum at Campbell River $ *470 Island Hwy at 5th Ave; tel: (250) 287-3103; www.crmuseum.ca. Open daily mid-May–Sep; Oct–mid-May Tue–Sun.*

Timber is the main industry, but Campbell River is better known for fishing and outdoor adventure. The town has become the hub for North Island hiking and trekking, fishing charters, dive trips, canoeing, kayaking, whale watching and other outdoor activities and the First Nations themed **Wei Wai Kum Cruise Ship Terminal**.

Campbell River & District Public Art Gallery features local artists and representations of the local area by outside artists. **The Museum at Campbell River** looks across Discovery Passage to Cape Mudge on Quadra Island. Exhibits cover local First Nations history, European exploration and exploitation, and local natural history. Museum field trips to historic sites are popular so book ahead

Scuba diving is stunning all year, with protected waters for beginners, racing tidal currents for thrill seekers and some of North America's richest marine environments. Several ships have been scuttled nearby to serve as artificial reefs and scuba dive destinations. During the spring–autumn salmon runs, look for snorkelling trips that put even non-divers face-to-face with salmon migrating upstream to spawn. Don't even dream about scuba diving the tricky and cold tidal waters without a local guide.

Accommodation and food in Campbell River

Seafood is always a good choice in a town that has fancied itself the Salmon Capital of BC for most of the past century.

Town Centre Inn $ *1500 Dogwood St; tel: (250) 287-8866 or (800) 287-7107; www.towncentreinn.com*, offers good value with full breakfast.

Heron's Landing Hotel $$ *492 S Island Hwy; tel: (250) 923-2848 or (888) 923-2849; www.heronslandinghotel.com*, is a boutique hotel with ocean views.

Lookout Seafood Bar & Grill $$ *921 Island Hwy; tel: (250) 286-6812; www.lookoutseafoodgrill.ca*, has had views of Discovery Passage since the 1920s.

Royal Coachman Inn $$ *84 Dogwood St; tel: (250) 286-0231; www.royalcoachmaninn.ca*, is a Tudor-style pub with a full menu, an off-track wagering lounge and the slogan 'haggard and thin they staggered in, fat and stout they waddled out'.

Anchor Inn & Suites $$$ *261 Island Hwy; tel: (250) 286-1131 or (800) 663-7227; http://anchorinn.ca*, offers ocean views and themed suites including African Safari, Arabian, English, Western and Arctic.

Harbour Grill $$$ *#112 1334 Island Hwy; tel: (250) 287-4143; www.harbourgrill.com*, overlooks Discovery Harbour and the restaurant website links to the summertime Alaska cruise ship schedule, to better time dining to cruiser viewing.

CAPE SCOTT PROVINCIAL PARK

ℹ️ **Northern Vancouver Island Trails Society** *www. northernvancouverislandtrails society.com*

🏞️ **Cape Scott Provincial Park** *64km from Port Hardy by public and logging roads; www.env.gov.bc.ca/bcparks/ explore/parkpgs/cape.html*

Cape Scott, the northernmost tip of Vancouver Island, is a tough two-day 27km return trek from the trailhead. An easy 45-minute trail leads to the sandy shores of San Josef Bay. The 46km North Coast Trail goes from Nissen Bight to Shushartie Bay. Watch for bears, cougars, Roosevelt elk, and for river otters and mink near San Josef Bay. Be prepared for dramatic weather changes such as severe storms that can damage and close trails. Check the website for up-to-date hiking information.

COURTENAY AND THE COMOX VALLEY

ℹ️ **Tourism Comox Valley** *2040 Cliffe Ave, Courtenay, BC, V9N 2L3; tel: (250) 334-3234 or (888) 357-4471; http://discovercomoxvalley.com. Open daily.*

🏛️ **Courtenay and District Museum & Palaeontology Centre $** *207 Fourth St; tel: (250) 334-0686; www.courtenaymuseum.ca. Call for days and hours.*

⛷️ **Mt Washington Alpine Resort $$** *1 Strathcona Parkway; tel: (250) 338-1386 or (888) 231-1499; www.mountwashington.ca. Open year-round.*

Courtenay and the Comox Valley are amongst the sunniest parts of Vancouver Island, sheltered behind the highest peaks on the island.

Courtenay and District Museum is across the street from the Native Sons Hall, Canada's largest free-span log structure. Highlight is a 14m, 80-million-year-old elasmosaur fossil, the largest marine dinosaur ever found in Canada west of the Rockies.

Mt Washington Alpine Resort has the highest vertical ski drop on the island. Views of the surrounding mountains are breathtaking in any season. Resort facilities and chairlift are open all summer, and alpine hiking and mountain biking are good ways to experience the landscape.

Right
Twilight over North Vancouver Island

CUMBERLAND

🛈 **Chamber of Commerce** *2680 Dunsmuir Ave; tel: (250) 336-8313; www.cumberlandbc.org. Open Jul–Aug daily 0900–1600; Sep–Jun Mon–Fri 0900–1600.*

🏛 **Museum & Archives** $ *2680 Dunsmuir Ave; tel: (250) 336-2445; www. cumberlandmuseum.ca. Open Mon–Sat 0900–1600.*

Cumberland was the heart of a massive coal field opened by Nanaimo coal baron Robert Dunsmuir, who built Craigdarroch Castle in Victoria (*see page 66*). Dunsmuir encouraged ethnic strife amongst British, Chinese, Italian, Japanese, Mexican and other workers to minimise union activities. The last mines closed in the 1960s, but slag heaps, derelict buildings, abandoned mine sites and a downtown mural showing a once-active Chinese community remain. **Cumberland Museum and Archives** explores the dramatic history of the region, including fatal mine accidents, bitter strikes, martial law and an awe-inspiring collection of period photographs.

PARKSVILLE AND QUALICUM BEACH

🛈 **Parksville and District Chamber of Commerce** *Hwy 19; tel: (250) 248-3613; http:// chamber.parksville.bc.ca*

Oceanside Tourism Association *Tel: (250) 248-6300; www. visitparksvillequalicumbeach. com*

Qualicum Beach Chamber of Commerce Visitor Centre *2711 W Island Hwy; tel: (250) 752-9532; www.qualicum.bc.ca. Open daily.*

🏛 **Craig Heritage Park Museum** $ *Parksville; tel: (250) 248-6966; www.parksvillemuseum. ca. Open May–Sep daily late.*

Qualicum Beach Historical & Museum Society $ *587 Beach Rd; tel: (250) 752-5533; www.qualicumbeach.com. Open mid-May–mid-Sep, Tue–Sat 1100–1600.*

Englishman River Falls Provincial Park *Errington Rd; tel: (250) 474-1336; www.env.gov.bc.ca*

Parksville and Qualicum Beach are a burgeoning holiday destination backed by kilometres of broad, sandy beach. Each receding tide leaves hundreds of shallow pools that warm to tropical temperatures in the summer sun. Anonymous strip malls line much of Hwy 19A, but the twinned towns are worth a visit.

Craig Heritage Park Museum offers local history and artefacts in heritage buildings moved to the site.

Qualicum Beach adjoins Parksville but has more open beachfront. **Qualicum Beach Historical & Museum Society** explores local history and the history of electrical power in BC in the town's original brick powerhouse.

Englishman River Falls Provincial Park has scenic waterfalls as well as easy forest walks, picnicking and swimming.

Potlatch

The potlatch ceremony, for naming of children, memorialising the dead, transferring rights and privileges, marriages, or the raising of memorial totem poles, was a central feature of First Nations life among coastal bands. Usually held in the quiet winter months, potlatch reinforced traditional chiefly authority through performances of sacred rituals and cemented political power by redistributing prodigious quantities of food, trade goods, clothing and household items in front of witnesses. The more wealth a leader could give away, the greater his power and influence.

The practice was banned in 1884 as sinful, wasteful and supportive of what Christian missionaries termed a 'decrepit' culture. A few First Nations communities complied, others continued to hold potlatches in secret. In more remote areas, the ban was simply ignored. In 1918, a government agent complained that 'During these gatherings, they lose months of time, waste their substance, contract all kinds of diseases and generally unfit themselves for being British subjects in the proper sense of the word'.

In 1922, federal officials raided potlatch ceremonies and confiscated an enormous collection of ceremonial and sacred objects. The potlatch ban was quietly dropped in the 1950s, along with prohibitions against other traditional First Nations practices, but the 1922 hoard of masks, headdresses, blankets, baskets, boxes and other regalia wasn't returned until the 1970s. The collection was divided between the U'mista Cultural Centre at Alert Bay and the **Nuyumbalees Cultural Centre** Museum at Cape Mudge, Quadra Island. Potlatch ceremonies are again being held publicly, especially in the Queen Charlotte Islands (see page 116), and Alert Bay (see page 96).

PORT HARDY

Port Hardy & District Chamber of Commerce 7250 Market St; tel: (250) 949-7622; www.ph-chamber. bc.ca. Open Jun–Sep Mon–Fri 0830–1800, Sat–Sun 0900–1700; Oct–May Mon–Fri 0900–1700.

Tourism Port Hardy www.porthardy.travel

Port Hardy Museum and Archives $ 7110 Market St; tel: (250) 949-8143. Call for hours.

Port Hardy is the end of the road on North Vancouver Island and a centre for North Island outdoor adventures. The walkway along **Hardy Bay** is a favourite gathering spot for bald eagles and other birds. BC Ferries' terminal is just south at **Bear Cove**.

Port Hardy Museum and Archives concentrates on local Kwakwaka'wakw First Nations history and later White arrivals.

Accommodation and food in Port Hardy

Ferry traffic is extremely heavy in summer. Book accommodation well in advance or expect to sleep in the back seat.

Glen Lyon Inn & Suites $$ 6435 Hardy Bay Rd; tel: (250) 949-7115 or (877) 949-7115; www.glenlyoninn.com, has rooms and suites facing Hardy Bay.

Pioneer Inn $$ 8405 Byng Rd; tel: (250) 949-7271 or (800) 663-8744; www.vancouverisland.com/pioneerinn, is a quiet choice outside of town.

Sporty Bar & Grill $$ 7800 Market St; tel: (250) 949-7811; http://thesporty.com, has starters to burgers, pizza and seafood specialities.

Left
Port Hardy thunderbird

STRATHCONA PROVINCIAL PARK

Strathcona Provincial Park
Tel: (250) 474-1336;
www.env.gov.bc.ca/bcparks/
explore/parkpgs/strathco.
html

Strathcona Park Lodge $ Adjacent to Strathcona Provincial Park;
tel: (250) 286-3122;
www.strathcona.bc.ca

Strathcona Provincial Park stretches nearly across Vancouver Island to include the tallest mountain on the island (Mt Golden Hinde, 2,200m) and the tallest waterfall in Canada (Della Falls, 440m). The **Strathcona Park Lodge** is the best-developed accommodation and activity centre in the largely wilderness park. Visiting in winter? Cross-country skiing and snowshoeing are popular in Paradise Meadows, and Mount Washington Alpine Resort (*see page 99*), adjacent to **Strathcona Provincial Park**, is known for downhill skiing, and maintains groomed cross-country trails ($) within the park.

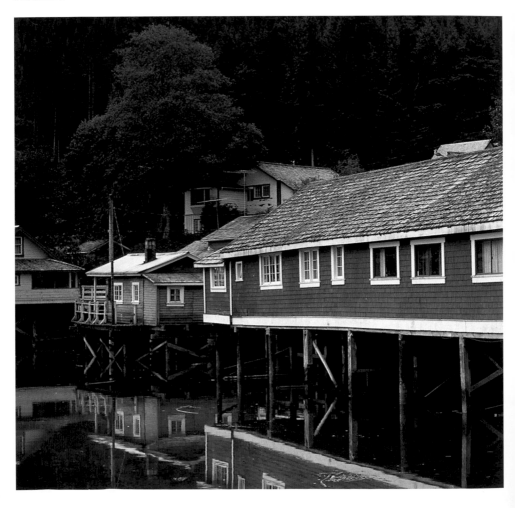

TELEGRAPH COVE

Telegraph Cove Resort $$$
*Telegraph Cove;
tel: (800) 200-4665; http://
telegraphcoveresort.com*

Telegraph Cove was named after a telegraph line at the turn of the 20th century. Surviving buildings, most on stilts above the water, are either museum pieces or part of a busy resort and ecotravel centre with whale-watching trips by boat or kayak, and excursions to see grizzly and black bears.

Suggested tour

Total distance: 360km.

Time: Allow 6 hours to drive from Parksville to Port Hardy; 2–3 days to enjoy the sights. In a hurry to get north? Take the 4-lane Inland Highway Route, Hwy 19, from Nanaimo to Campbell River and continue north to Port Hardy. The scenic Seashore Route along the Strait of Georgia, now Hwy 19A, will take longer, but will visit every interesting hamlet along the water.

Links: From Port Hardy, ferry routes lead north to Bella Coola and Prince Rupert (*see page 206*) or retrace Vancouver Island routes south.

Route: Follow Hwy 19 or 19A from Nanaimo to the adjoining beach towns of **PARKSVILLE ❶** and **QUALICUM BEACH ❷**. Hwy 19 continues inland, bypassing the beach and cutting at least an hour off the drive to Campbell River, but Hwy 19A along the **Strait of Georgia** is far more interesting.

Detour: From Hwy 19 in **COURTENAY ❸**, go east (right) on to 17th Ave towards **COMOX ❹**, and right again on Comox Road, passing a wildlife viewing area on the Comox River. To visit **Comox Spit** and for expansive good-weather views back along the coast, turn right into Balmoral Avenue and right again on to Croteau Road.

Return to Comox Road and turn right on to Lazo Road to **Lazo**, following the blue and white 'scenic drive' signs – watch out for deer grazing along the verges. The road curves around the Canadian Forces Base Comox, with a golf course (open to the public) and the Comox Valley Regional Air Terminal. Ryan Road leads directly back to Hwy 19, or follow back roads to **Little River** and BC Ferries routes to the mainland at **Powell River**, then back to Hwy 19 by way of the **Seal Bay Nature Park**.

Take Hwy 19a north from Courtenay to **CAMPBELL RIVER ❺** past the turn for **STRATHCONA PROVINCIAL PARK ❻** along a 10km paved sea walk through Campbell River, with angling at the Campbell River Fishing Pier. Continue north 7km to **Seymour Narrows**, one of the most perilous passages between Vancouver and Prince Rupert. Swift currents churn the Narrows into a boiling mass of white water at flood tide.

Left
Telegraph Cove

Above
Port Hardy totem pole

🛈 **Schoen Lake
Provincial Park**
www.env.gov.bc.ca/bcparks/
explore/parkpgs/schoen.html

There's a convenient overlook on the north side of Hwy 19.

With strong coastal currents such as those in Johnstone Strait, and much of Vancouver Island and mainland BC's coast accessible only by water, booking an adventure tour is usually the only way to see nature at close range. In addition to whale-watching boat tours from major towns, guided kayaking with established operators like **Northern Lights Expeditions** *tel: (800) 754-7402; www.seakayaking.com* and **Sea Kayak Adventures** *tel: (800) 616-1943; http://seakayakadventures. com*, ensures safety and naturalist and cultural interpretation.

Detour: Turn north (right) 29km north of **McNair Lake**, following signs for **Sayward**, one of the few remaining company-owned towns in BC. The road passes clearcuts, tree farms and isolated towns on the way to Sayward, then continues to **Kelsey Bay**. The bay, protected by the rusting hulks of sunken barges, was once the terminus for the BC Ferries route to Prince Rupert that now departs from Port Hardy. Return to Hwy 19 and turn north (right).

Hwy 19 continues north past **Schoen Lake Provincial Park**, a wilderness park best visited by high-clearance vehicles. **Hoomac Lake**, 4km north, is a more convenient rest break. A few hectares of old-growth forest have been left around the lake shore as habitat for elk and other animals that don't take well to tree farms. One of the few gas stations and restaurants between Campbell River and Port McNeill is in the town of **Woss**, 7km north of the lake and 2km west. The highway skirts **Nimpkish Lake** for 20-plus km beyond the Woss turn-off.

Detour: Turn south (right) off Hwy 19 at the **North Island Discovery Centre**; *tel: (250) 956-3844; www.island.net/~nifctour*. Book summer forest and mill tours by phone in advance. Continue past the centre to a T-junction at the end of the paved road. Turn left, following signs for the Telegraph Cove Resort. Just beyond is **BEAVER COVE** ❼ and a massive dryland sort. Watch the action from a lay-by near the top of the hill just beyond the dryland sort entrance.

Continue another kilometre to a second T-junction. Turn left for **TELEGRAPH COVE ❽**. Return to Hwy 19 and turn north (right).

The highway passes the **Nimpkish Fish Hatchery,** *tel: (250) 956-4712,* with excellent explanations of how poor logging practices and overfishing have blighted salmon runs in recent decades.

An imposing totem pole just across the Nimpkish River was carved in 1966 to commemorate the 1866 political union of Vancouver Island and mainland BC. Six kilometres north is the turn for **Port McNeill** and the ferry to **ALERT BAY ❾**. Continue north past the turn-off for **Bear Cove** and the BC Ferries terminal, and into **PORT HARDY ❿**.

Ferry voyages

Ratings

Children	●●●●●
History	●●●●●
Mountains	●●●●●
Nature	●●●●●
Scenery	●●●●●
Villages	●●●●●
Wildlife	●●●●●
Food and drink	●●●○○

BC Ferries are the most popular cruise company in Canada. Strictly speaking, the privately owned ferries are simply transportation for vehicles and foot passengers, but even the most prosaic ferry run from Vancouver to Vancouver Island can take on the air of a cruise when the summer sun shines bright and temperatures climb.

On the north coast, a ferry trip is more adventure than transportation. Plying the waters of the Inside Passage between Port Hardy and Bella Coola or Port Hardy and Prince Rupert, a ferry voyage is the best way, and most often the only way, to enjoy some of North America's most dramatic coastal vistas in a region where roads are all but unknown. Expect to see snow-capped peaks dropping steeply into icy blue fjords lined with dark green forests – and don't be surprised to see nothing at all if a storm blows through.

DISCOVERY COAST PASSAGE: PORT HARDY TO BELLA COOLA

Below
Bella Coola harbour

Unlike most BC Ferries runs that cater to commuters, commercial traffic and local residents, the Discovery Coast Passage route was created for tourists. This summer-only service aboard the *Queen of Chilliwack* was named 'Discovery' after Alexander Mackenzie, who, in 1793, was the first European to cross North America north of Mexico. Mackenzie emerged from the mountains at Bella Coola to discover that he had finally found the Pacific Ocean.

There are more ghost towns – reminders of the days when timber and fishing ruled the BC Coast – than modern settlements along the route, but the often-narrow, always-scenic channels are seldom empty. Cruise ships and fishing boats make regular runs between Alaska, to the north, and Canadian ports to the south. Pleasure craft throng the protected inlets and passages of the **Hakai Luxvbalis Conservancy**, one of the more popular areas in BC for sea kayaking.

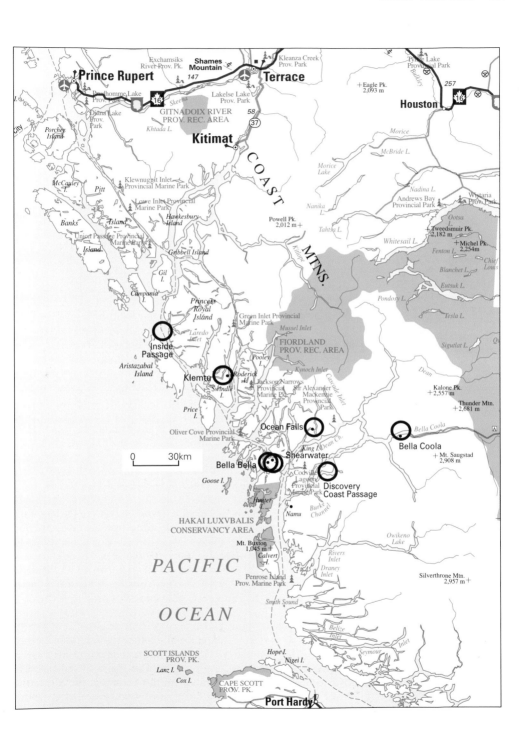

Hakai Luxvbalis Conservancy Area

The Heiltsuk First Nation has inhabited the coast and islands of what is now known as the Hakai Recreation Area for 10,000 years, believed to be the oldest continuously inhabited area of Western North America's coastline. In 2003, the Heiltsuk and the BC provincial government settled differences and agreed to co-manage the 122,998 hectares of environmentally precious land and marine areas, technically, the Hakai Luxvbalis Conservancy Area. Hakai ('wide passage') is BC's largest marine park.

Wolves and deer swim between islands and one hundred bird species fish the waters. Premier human activities are fishing for salmon, halibut and rockfish, and scuba diving.

Discovery Coast Passage, Port Hardy–Bella Coola $$$
www.bcferries.com/schedules/ discovery. This summer-only route operates early Jun–early Sep.

BC Ferries *Tel: (888) 223-3779 or (outside North America) (250) 386-3431; www.bcferries.com*

Hakai Luxvbalis Conservancy Area
www.env.gov.bc.ca/bcparks/ explore/parkpgs/hakai_luxv. html

The entire voyage takes between 15 and 33 hours, depending on how many of four potential port calls the *Queen* makes. Allow about 50 hours for a return voyage from either Port Hardy or Bella Coola. The ship stays reasonably close to schedule, but don't expect slavish devotion to the timetable. The 114m car ferry also carries kayaks and other small craft that can be dropped off and picked up at irregular stops along the trip. There may be detours when the captain spots a pod of orcas or a humpback whale nearby.

For the best sightseeing, sail the Discovery Coast Passage southbound, Bella Coola–Port Hardy, to enjoy the panorama of mountains surrounding North Bentinck Arm (near Bella Coola) in daylight. For easier driving, take a northbound sailing, Port Hardy–Bella Coola. The trip *up* The Hill, a steep gravel section of Hwy 20 just east of Bella Coola, is considerably less thrilling than twisting down the unpaved hairpin curves.

In Port Hardy (*see page 101*), passengers and vehicles board at the Bear Cove ferry dock. In Bella Coola, foot passengers board at the ferry dock, but vehicles must check in at the Co-op Parking lot or Tweedsmuir Travel, not at the ferry terminal, to pick up a boarding pass before driving to the dock. Check current procedures with BC Ferries when making your booking.

Boarding starts 90–120 minutes before sailing at both ports, but it's better to board early than late – early arrivals get the coveted seats next to the *Queen's* oversized view windows. Seating is first-come, first-served, so passengers in the know race aboard to drop a jacket or a backpack on their preferred window seat, usually in the forward lounge. Hotels, motels and bed and breakfasts at either end of the route can arrange transport to and from the dock for foot passengers.

Reservations are required for vehicles and for foot passengers – space is limited and the season short. There may be space on the first few and last few sailings at the last moment, but book four to six months in advance. Reservations can be changed (if space is available on the new date), but each change costs $30 per segment. You can check availability, make reservations and buy tickets by credit card online or by telephone.

Summer weather is usually good, but the coastal climate is fickle. Rain, fog and wind are at least as common as sunshine, which comes and goes almost without warning. Stick to comfortable, layered clothing and flat shoes for walking about on deck, up and down outside stairways and on shore. Long trousers, long sleeves, closed shoes and a warm jacket with a hood are likely to be as useful as sunglasses and sun block, even if the weather forecast predicts nothing but sunshine.

Seas will likely be calm no matter what the weather. Except for a short stretch of open water in the Queen Charlotte Sound just north of Port Hardy, a maze of islands protects the entire route from ocean swells and large wind waves.

The Discovery Coast Passage is a tourist cruise, but the *Queen* is no cruise ship: no disco, no casino, no swimming pool, no sauna, no beauty parlour, no dressy dinners. There is a gym, a couple of stationary bicycles on the solarium deck, as well as a full-service cafeteria, bar, lounge, laundry, showers, video arcade and gift shop. There is also plenty of outside deck space to enjoy the passing scenery while looking for orcas, humpback whales, eagles, seals, dolphins and passing vessels of all sizes. Binoculars and telephoto camera lenses are a must.

The *Queen* has no passenger cabins, but the reclining seats are extremely comfortable for night-long napping. Blankets, sheets and pillows can be hired on board, or bring your own. You can also pitch your own tent on the outer decks (or perhaps indoors, depending on the weather). A popular option is to overnight in Klemtu, Ocean Falls or Shearwater and pick up the ship on a later sailing, but rooms on shore are extremely limited. Book shoreside accommodation first (and explain that you're arriving aboard the *Queen*), then book passage to match your dates ashore.

BC Ferries has a same-day Port Hardy to Bella Coola service on Thursday, with the opposite route on Monday. The Tuesday departure lies over at McLoughlin Bay and Shearwater and returns on Wednesday, with stops at Klemtu, McLoughlin Bay, Shearwater and Ocean Falls on Saturday; tourists returning on Friday skip Klemtu.

Port calls stretch from 30 minutes to half a day, depending on the port and day of the week. Arrival and departure times are posted near the Purser's Office, forward of the cafeteria. There are shore excursions in most ports, usually walking tours, traditional dancing, salmon feasts or paddle trips. Buy shore tours as soon as possible after boarding. The better the weather, the earlier excursions sell out.

You can also explore ashore on your own, but watch the time. The *Queen* doesn't wait for late returners. The only departure warning is a long whistle blast 15 minutes before pulling away from the dock.

Bella Bella/McLoughlin Bay

**Bella Bella/
McLoughlin Bay**
*Heiltsuk Band;
www.bellabella.net*

Koeye Lodge $$$
*Tel: (250) 957-2567;
www.koeyelodge.com*

The Heiltsuk Band, based at Bella Bella, is opening the door to tourism slowly and cautiously. For now, tourists are generally restricted to McLoughlin Bay, 3km south of the village. The Purser may say that Bella Bella is too far to walk during the short port call, but it's not too far for several local artists to set up shop at the dock when the *Queen* calls, including famed silversmith Peter Gladstone. McLoughlin Bay is also a popular stop for kayakers setting off for or returning from camping trips through the Hakai Luxvbalis Conservancy Area (*see page 108*).

If the weather is reasonable, that is, blowing anything less than a full gale, walk a few hundred metres down the crushed shell beach to the traditional-style longhouse. Built by Heiltsuk carvers Frank and Kathy Brown, the longhouse is a combination local history museum, First Nations art gallery and simple restaurant specialising in salmon roasted on cedar planks over an open fire.

The area has old totem poles, deserted fish canneries, ravens, eagles, orcas, herons, dolphins and often bear and deer. A 1.5-hour speedboat trip arrives at **Koeye Lodge** south of Bella Bella where visitors settle in for a day or several in a lodge or rustic cabins to sea kayak, take a boat tour, see Heiltsuk pictographs, tour now abandoned Namu Village formerly occupied for 10,000 years, and to walk through old-growth rainforest. The Heiltsuk call the grizzly bear Qaikas Nan, that can be spotted fishing for spawning salmon in August–September while floating by boat or kayak down the Koeye River estuary. Eco-tours support Heiltsuk programmes that teach traditions and species conservation to younger band members.

Klemtu

Klemtu *Kitasoo
Xaixais Band Council;
Tel: (250) 839-1255;
www.kitasoo.org*

**Spirit Bear
Adventures $$$**
*Tel: (877) 644-2346 or
(250) 839-2346;
www.klemtutourism.com.
Weekly 4- (Fri, Mon) and
7-day (Fri) tours Aug–mid-
Oct.*

This is one of the most popular overnight stops on the Discovery Coast Passage.

Most of Klemtu's 300 or so residents turn out to welcome the *Queen*. Main Street is among the longest boardwalks in Canada, skirting two sides of a bay that is alive with bald eagles, dolphins and orcas on the hunt for salmon and other fish. A three-hour walking tour of town stops at a busy carving shed and a traditional First Nations feast (no alcohol permitted) guaranteed to finish before the ship sails. Bring your own kayak, rent one, or charter boats from band operators for fishing, sightseeing, hiking and camping on nearby islands.

The **Great Bear Rainforest** protects 400km of BC coastline, primarily to preserve the lives and habitat of the white Kermode bear that aboriginal peoples revere as the Spirit Bear. These black bears with black noses and eyes and a rare genetic trait that makes the fur white, are most numerous on Princess Royal Island (where Klemtu is at the south tip) in the Kitasoo Spirit Bear Conservancy rainforest lands.

Klemtu is a base for authorised First Nations eco-tours, **Spirit Bear Adventures**, into Kermode bear territory.

OCEAN FALLS

Ocean Falls
www.britishcolumbia.
com/regions/towns/?townID=
3570

Named after Link Falls, a waterfall that thunders directly into the sea, Ocean Falls was once a thriving pulp mill town at the head of Cousins Inlet. Three thousand people lived here in the mid-20th century, enough to fill a hospital, high school, hotel and Olympic-sized swimming pool. When the mill closed in 1980 and jobs evaporated, so did most of the people. A few families remain at the original town site, which spreads uphill from the ferry dock, a few more in nearby Martin Valley, but the population more than doubles when *Queen* passengers hit the streets on walking tours. Fishing and sightseeing boat charters are also available, as are a few bed-and-breakfast rooms – book onshore accommodation first, then matching sailing dates.

There's home-made soup, ice cream and espresso at the one café in town, a fire hall, a modern school and the mouldering remains of a long-closed hotel, but most of Ocean Falls is vanishing beneath a creeping carpet of blackberry bushes, alders and seedling pines. It's hard to miss the occasional splash of colour, usually a bright blue hydrangea in what was once a carefully tended front garden.

Today's residents wouldn't change much about their town. A hydroelectric dam built for the mill still churns out power, but with no logging and no toxic pulp waste pouring into the ocean, salmon, halibut, eagles, dolphins and other wildlife have returned.

SHEARWATER/DENNY ISLAND

Shearwater/Denny Island *Shearwater Resort & Marina;* tel: (800) 663-2370; www.shearwater.ca

Flying boats based at Denny Island, opposite Bella Bella, once patrolled the Queen Charlotte Channel for World War II submarine invaders. The base is long gone (so is an early 20th-century fish-packing plant), but with the newer name of Shearwater, the sheltered bay has become a base for tourism, sport fishing and maritime traffic. The Shearwater Resort includes a small hotel, fishing charters, eco-tourism centred on whale and dolphin spotting, birdwatching, and viewing black, grizzly and Kermode (spirit) bears, restaurant, pub, marina and bed-and-breakfast accommodation.

Look for commercial fishing boats, sailing boats and luxury motor yachts tied up to the dock. Crew and passengers are most likely tied up to the bar inside, the only full-service stop between Port Hardy and Bella Coola. The *Queen* ties up long enough for a meal or a drink at the resort. The alternative is to spend several days cycling and hiking the island, boating nearby waters, or booking an eco-adventure.

INSIDE PASSAGE: PORT HARDY TO PRINCE RUPERT

**ℹ Inside Passage,
Port Hardy–Prince
Rupert** $$$ *Tel: (888)
223-3779 or (outside North
America) (250) 386-3431;
www.bcferries.com/schedules/
inside*

Eagles, whales and mouth-dropping scenery on all sides make this all-year car-ferry route the most popular 15-hour cruise in Canada. Look for sheer mountains cloaked with red cedar and Sitka spruce rising from glacier-carved channels, low islands swept clean by winter storms and lighthouses marking channels less than 250m wide.

The entire trip takes place during daylight hours from mid-May to the end of September, when most sailings leave at 0730 and arrive at 2230 the same day. Check with BC Ferries for off-season schedules.

Vehicle spaces *must* be reserved in advance. Foot passengers must also book space, especially June to August when tour groups flock to north-coast ferry trips. A reserved seating lounge guarantees a seat for the voyage. Last-minute vehicle space *may* be available mid-September to mid-May, but make reservations four to six months in advance for summer travel.

In Port Hardy, board at Bear Cove, just south of town. In Prince Rupert, follow Second Avenue (Hwy 16) to the ferry dock. Boarding starts 90–120 minutes before sailing. There's no rush to be first on board in winter, when there are few passengers. In summer, be prepared to scramble for window seats in the forward cabins with the best views or opt for an outdoor seat.

Weather is usually warm and clear (but not always sunny) in summer, while storms are common in winter. The Inside Passage route is calm and well protected by dozens of islands off the BC coast, but rain, wind, fog and snow blast down from the Arctic in winter.

In any season, most passengers opt to spend the trip in comfortable reclining chairs or in the many lounge areas set with tables and chairs. Private cabins are available at an additional charge. There's also a dining room, complete with white linen tablecloths. Most passengers go for the less expensive cafeteria that serves everything from snacks to full meals. Ferries also have a licensed lounge, video arcade, games, free videos in public rooms and a well-stocked gift shop.

Suggested tours

Time: Allow up to 33 hours to travel the **Discovery Coast** between **Port Hardy ❶** and **Bella Coola ❷** or 15 hours along the **Inside Passage** between **Port Hardy** and **Prince Rupert ❸**.

Links: Both ferry routes meet at **Port Hardy** (*see page 101*), at the north end of Vancouver Island, for the drive south toward **Victoria** (*see page 62*). From **Bella Coola** (*see page 200*), it's possible to drive the **Cariboo-Chilcotin** to **Williams Lake** (*see page 202*) and either north to **Prince Rupert** (*see page 206*) or south towards **Vancouver** (*see page 42*). **Prince Rupert** is the mainland terminus of the **Yellowhead**

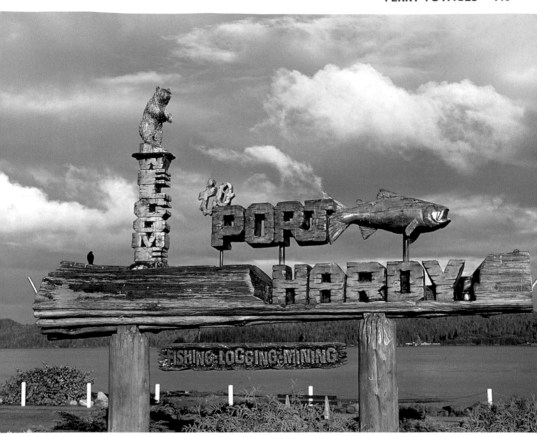

Above
Port Hardy welcome sign

Highway (*see page 214*), which continues westwards in the **Queen Charlotte Islands** (*see page 116*) or eastwards to the **Rocky Mountains** and **Jasper National Park** (*see page 275*).

The Inside Passage

Fewer than 5,000 people live on BC's central and northern coast, half of them in Bella Coola (*see page 200*) and another quarter in Queen Charlotte City, in the Queen Charlotte Islands (*see page 116*). Two hundred years ago, the waters and islands between Port Hardy and Prince Rupert were the realm of First Nations bands who lived well from the bounty of temperate coastal forests and the rich sea. A century ago, the same waters teemed with floating logging camps, pulp mills and fish canneries. Changing economic conditions closed most of those outside industries, leaving the Inside Passage once again a largely First Nations area where humans are vastly outnumbered by the wildlife and the scenery draws visitors from around the globe.

Route: Both ferry trips fit into a circular driving tour from **Vancouver** to **Victoria** by ferry, up **Vancouver Island** to **Port Hardy** by highway, ferry to the mainland at **Bella Coola** or **Prince Rupert**, then south by road to **Vancouver**. Allow 7–10 days for the entire route. It's also possible to combine both ferry voyages by driving to either Port Hardy or Bella Coola, taking one ferry route into **Port Hardy** and then taking the second route back to the mainland. Allow 10–14 days for the two ferry trips, plus long-distance driving on the mainland and any excursions on Vancouver Island.

Both routes are served by car ferries, but don't take *car* too literally. If it's street-legal in BC, BC Ferries will carry it: cars, vans, RVs, motor coaches, motorcycles, bicycles, trucks and foot passengers. Both tours can be taken in either direction and both can be made with a combination of train, coach and air connections to avoid driving altogether.

Below
McLoughlin Bay (Bella Bella)

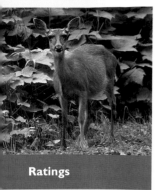

Ratings

First Nations	●●●●●
History	●●●●●
Nature	●●●●●
Outdoor activities	●●●●●
Parks	●●●●●
Beaches	●●●●○
Children	●●●●○
Walking	●●●●○

Queen Charlotte Islands

Also known as *Haida Gwaii*, Home of the People, the Queen Charlottes are BC's most remote islands. By any name, this isolated, storm-swept, rainforested archipelago 100km west of Prince Rupert is the best-known corner of Canada that almost nobody has ever seen. There are fewer than 150km of paved roads, more black bears and eagles than humans and barely enough vehicles to fill a small car park in downtown Vancouver.

Home to the Haida, proud, artistic warriors who once ruled the Pacific Northwest coast from cedar canoes, the Charlottes are an ecological wonder snatched from the jaws of timber cutters. Nearly overwhelmed by epidemics, discrimination and logging, the Haida rebounded as a vibrant traditional culture and artistic tradition. Gwaii Haanas National Park preserves links to 10,000 years of Haida history in a wilderness of moss-covered forests and village sites dotted with totem poles slowly crumbling back to earth.

Getting there

ⓘ Queen Charlotte Visitor Centre
3220 Wharf St; tel: (250) 559-8316; www.qcinfo.ca. Open Mon–Tue, Thu–Sat 0930–1630, with a booking service.

Ⓩ Sandspit Airport (YZP) *Tel: (250) 637-5313.*

Principal access is by air from Vancouver to Sandspit or to Masset or with **BC Ferries**, *tel: (888) 223-3779; www.bcferries.com,* 6 hours from Prince Rupert to Skidegate Landing.

Getting around

There is no public transport. Hire a car from the Sandspit Airport or Queen Charlotte City, or bring your own vehicle by ferry. Weather is highly variable – rain, fog and sun alternating with blustery winds and dead calm, even in summer.

Right
Kayaking in Gwaii Haanas National Park

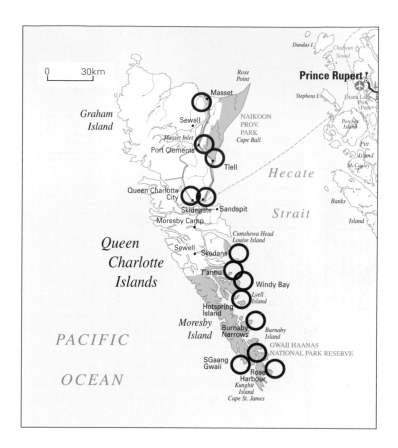

GWAII HAANAS NATIONAL PARK RESERVE/HAIDA HERITAGE SITE

One of North America's most spectacular natural areas became a park in 1987 following a stand-off between the Haida and logging companies on Lyell Island. The 1,500-sq km park protects rich marine environments, as well as trackless areas of old-growth cedar and spruce forest carpeted with moss and orchids, deep fjords, sandy scimitars of beach, enormous colonies of puffins and sea lions, some of the world's largest nesting populations of falcons and bald eagles, and over 500 Haida sites.

Credit isolation for the park's splendour. The only access is by water or air, and only when weather, currents and 7m tides allow. Parks Canada approves operators for day-trips as well as multi-day boat trips and guided or self-guided kayak trips.

On the water, expect to see orcas, humpbacks and other whales, dolphins, porpoises and clouds of seabirds. Black bears roam the intertidal areas, black-tailed deer the meadows and open forests. Bald eagles are common.

Ⓗ Gwaii Haanas National Park Preserve/Haida Heritage Site $$

Haida Heritage Centre, 60 Second Beach Rd, Skidegate; tel: (250) 559-8818; www.pc.gc.ca/pn-np/bc/ gwaiihaanas/index_e.asp. Open Mon–Fri 0800–1200, 1300–1630. Entry by commercial tour or individual permit. For permit reservations tel: (250) 387-1642 or (800) 435-5622. All visitors must attend a park and Haida Gwaii heritage orientation session before entering the park.

Ⓖ Rose Harbour Guest House $$

Rose Harbour, Gwaii Haanas National Park; tel: (250) 559-2326; www.roseharbour.com, has bed-and-breakfast accommodation with hot water.

Most Haida village sites have been reclaimed by the forest, but a few remain visible. All were once marked by forests of totem poles, most removed to museums as smallpox and other epidemics swept Haida Gwaii in the 19th century and villages were abandoned. A few poles remain, decaying, weather-beaten and returning to the earth in keeping with Haida tradition. Haida Gwaii watchmen (guardians) live at major village sites to discourage vandals and over-eager collectors.

Burnaby Narrows This twisting passage is navigable by small boats at high tide and dry at low tide. Walking is banned to protect the profusion of sea stars, urchins, mussels and other species.

Hotspring Island The only natural hot spring in the Charlottes was a traditional Haida healing place. Several soaking pools overlook the waters of Ramsay Passage.

Rose Harbour The tiny community of Rose Harbour is a convenient stop-over for quick trips: fly in from Queen Charlotte City, visit SGaang Gwaii by speedboat and fly out. Rose is also a convenient base for kayak trips.

SGaang Gwaii (Ninstints, Anthony Island) This abandoned village at the south end of Haida Gwaii was named a UNESCO World Heritage Site in 1981. The world's largest collection of totem poles in their original location still stands along the beach.

Skedans Skedans is the most accessible village site for day-trips.

T'annu There are no standing totem poles, but many visible house sites draped with moss. The ashes of famed Haida artist Bill Reid are buried in his ancestral village.

Windy Bay A modern longhouse here was the focus of Haida battles with logging companies in the 1980s.

Gwaii Haanas on the water

Expert kayakers rate Gwaii Haanas National Park amongst the best water on earth – as famous for swirling currents, racing tides and blasting storms as for protected shores, stunning scenery and rich wildlife. An on-the-water experience confirms why a proposed 5,000km Gwaii Haanas National Marine Conservation Area Reserve that would extend 10km from the shoreline is in the works. Kelp and creatures and formations of a rich, temperate climate intertidal area would be preserved.

Bluewater Adventures (tel: (604) 980-3800 or (888) 877-1770; http://bluewateradventures.ca) sails a 21m ketch around the islands. **Duen Sailing Adventures** (tel: (250) 652-8227 or (888) 922-8822; www.thenaturalcoast.com) has sailed the waters for more than a decade, with onshore excursions for forest hikes and kayaks for the water. **Butterfly Tours** (tel: (604) 740-7018 or (866) 568-3770; www.butterflytours.bc.ca) is all about single-person kayaking.

MASSET

Village of Masset
*400m from the
'Welcome to Masset' sign,
east side of Hwy 16;
tel: (250) 626-3982;
http://massetbc.com. Open
Mon–Fri 0900–1600.*

**Old Masset Village
Council** *348 Eagle Rd;
tel: (250) 626-3337.*

**Naikoon Provincial
Park** *Tel: (250) 626-
5115, (250) 626-3337 or
(250) 557-4390;
www.env.gov.bc.ca/bcparks/
explore/parkpgs/naikoon.html*

**Delkatla Wildlife
Sanctuary** *East of Masset;
www.massetbc.com/html/
delkatla_sanctuary.html*

Villager Cafe $$
*Orr St; tel: (250) 626-
3694, has Chinese dishes.*

**Copper Beech
House $$**
*1590 Delkatla; tel: (250)
626-5441; www.
copperbeechhouse.com, is
Masset's most comfortable
bed and breakfast.*

Masset is a fishing and tourist town at the north end of Graham Island. **Old Masset**, 2km west, is Canada's largest Haida community with modern totem poles, artist workshops and galleries. To the east is **Naikoon Provincial Park**, stretching to **Rose Spit**, where Haida legend says humans appeared, and south to Tlell. Don't miss **Tow Hill**, a 100m outcrop of basalt columns with active tidal blowholes at the base. Sandy beaches backed by mossy forest and bog stretch nearly 100km from Tow Hill to Rose Spit and south. **Delkatla Wildlife Sanctuary** east of Masset is a premier spot for viewing trumpeter swans, sandhill cranes, great blue herons, and many other species pausing on the Pacific Flyway.

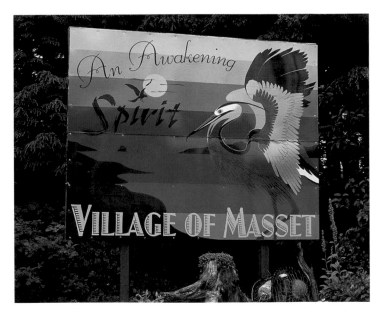

Right
Masset welcome sign

PORT CLEMENTS

**Village of Port
Clements**
*Tel: (250) 557-4295;
http://portclements.com*

**Port Clements
Museum $**
*45 Bayview Dr; tel: (250)
557-4576;
www.portclementsmuseum.org.
Call for hours.*

Port Clements is a tiny logging supply centre. The top attraction is the **Port Clements Museum**, an eclectic collection of early logging paraphernalia and household items.

The pleasant **Golden Spruce Trail**, 5km south on the gravel logging road, leads in 10 minutes to the site of a unique golden spruce tree destroyed by a vandal in 1997. Eight kilometres south is the **Haida Canoe**, a partially carved wooden canoe abandoned in the forest over a century ago.

QUEEN CHARLOTTE CITY

ⓘ **Queen Charlotte Visitor Centre** 3220 Wharf St; tel: (250) 559-8316; www.qcinfo.ca. Open Mon–Tue, Thu–Sat 0930–1630, with a booking service.

The administrative centre for the Charlottes is also the archipelago's largest town. Serious people live here, trying to pursue the area's traditional fishing and lumbering, while Haida arts and crafts are for sale in local galleries.

Accommodation and food in Queen Charlotte

Premier Creek Lodging $–$$ *3101 3rd Ave; tel: (250) 559-8415 or (888) 322-3388*, is a 1910 heritage building with a garden that overlooks the ocean.

Hecate Inn $$ *321 3rd Ave; tel: (250) 559-4543 or (800) 665-3350; www.qcislands.net/hecateinn*, is a family-owned motel in the islands.

Howler's Pub & Bistro $$ *2600 3rd Ave; tel: (250) 559-8600*, has Charlotte's best beer selection and restaurant views.

Sea Raven Restaurant $$ *3301 Oceanview Dr; Sea Raven Motel; tel: (250) 559-8503*, has the town's best seafood selection.

SKIDEGATE

🏛 **Haida Heritage Centre at K̲aay Llnagaay $$** 60 Second Beach Rd; tel: (250) 559-7885; www.haidaheritagecentre.com. Open daily mid-Jun–mid-Sep 1000–1800, mid-Sep–Apr Tue–Sat 1000–1700, May–mid-Jun Mon–Sat 1000–1800. Summer guided tours $. **Haida Gwaii Museum** tel: (250) 559-4643, is part of the Centre.

Pronounced 'skid-e-git', this one-time mission settlement is a Haida village. A modern five-longhouse cedar complex with six traditional totem poles in front, the **Haida Heritage Centre at K̲aay Llnagaay** provides an introduction to intensely rich Haida culture and artistic traditions. The **Haida Gwaii Museum** is known for its totem pole collection and art by modern artisans like Bill Reid, historic photographs, and Queen Charlotte Islands natural history displays. One longhouse named after Bill Reid and his famous *War Canoe* is a Haida artist education centre; in the open-sided Carving Shed, carvers craft cedar totem poles. An Eating House café serves Haida food and more standard fare. For more cultural immersion in summer, guides provide tours inside and outside the centre. Just off Hwy 16 is the **Spirit Lake Trail**, a moderate 3km, 90-minute hike through second-growth and old-growth forest around two small lakes.

TLELL

🏛 **Naikoon Provincial Park $** Tel: (250) 626-5115 or (250) 626-3337; www.env.gov.bc.ca/bcparks/explore/parkpgs/naikoon.html

This one-time ranching town has become an artistic centre, where roadside signs announce galleries. Tlell is also the southern entry for **Naikoon Provincial Park** with camping, hiking, and the 1928 wreck of the timber ship *Pesuta*.

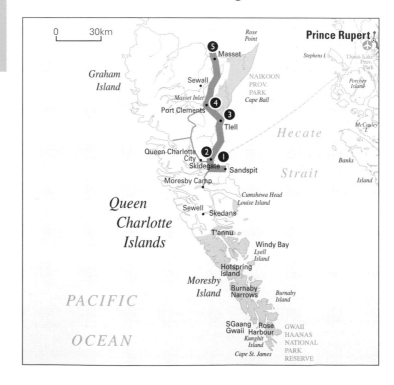

Cacilia's Bed &
Breakfast $$
*Tel: (250) 557-4664; www.
qcislands.net/ceebysea*

Tlell River House $$$
*Tel: (250) 789-9494;
www.tlellriverhouse.com,* is
Tlell's only hotel.

Sandspit

This scattered village has
the Charlottes' major
airport.

**Sandspit/North
Moresby Chamber of
Commerce** *PO Box
148, Sandspit, BC V0T
1T0; tel: (250) 637-2466;
www.sandspitqci.com*

**Accommodation in
Sandspit**

Sandspit Inn $$$
Tel: (250) 637-5334, is
next to the airport.

Suggested tour

Total distance: 300km.
Time: 2–4 days by road; 7–10 days by water.
Links: BC Ferries to Prince Rupert (*see page 206*) or air to Vancouver
(*see page 42*).

Route: From the airport at **Sandspit ❶**, drive east along **Shingle Bay**
to the ferry at **Alliford Bay**. If time allows, take an hour to walk the
Dover Trail, just west of **Haans Creek**. The ferry to **Skidegate
Landing** is free, the return ferry is $$.

From the landing, follow traffic uphill and around to Hwy 16, the
Yellowhead Hwy. Queen Charlotte City is 4km to the right (west);
Skidegate, Tlell, Port Clements and Masset to the left (east).

North of **SKIDEGATE ❷**, the highway passes **Balance Rock**. Continue
north along **Jungle Beach**, a tangle of driftwood. The road follows the
shoreline to **TLELL ❸**, near **Naikoon Provincial Park**.

From Tlell, Hwy 16 turns inland to **PORT CLEMENTS ❹**. The Golden
Spruce Trail and the Haida Canoe are just south of town. Return to Port
Clements and continue 38km to **MASSET ❺**.

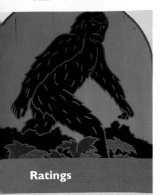

Lower Fraser Valley

Ratings

Children	●●●●●
Gardens	●●●●●
History	●●●●●
Scenery	●●●●●
Museums	●●●●○
Outdoor activities	●●●●○
Parks	●●●●○
Beaches	●●●○○

The lower section of the Fraser River Valley is the heart of BC, and not just for the flat, rich farmlands that keep Vancouver well supplied with milk and vegetables. BC began along the Fraser with the creation of the Hudson's Bay Company post at Fort Langley in 1827. The Fraser River gold rush in the 1850s opened the interior to the outside world and transformed BC into a Crown Colony in 1858 to thwart American expansion from the south.

The Lower Fraser is a microcosm of BC. It was the first section of the mainland to be explored by Whites, the first to be settled and the first to feel the impact of over-development. Half of BC's population lives, works and plays in the Lower Fraser River Valley, yet despite population and pollution, the Fraser remains the most productive salmon stream in the world.

FORT LANGLEY

ⓘ Vancouver, Coast & Mountains Tourism Region *Suite 600, 210 W Broadway, Vancouver, BC V5Y 3W2; tel: (800) 667-3306 or (604) 739-9011; http://vcmbc.com*

Tourism Langley *9234 Glover Rd, Fort Langley; tel: (604) 888-1477; www.tourism-langley.com. Open daily Jul–Aug, Sep–Jun Mon–Fri 0900–1700.*

This small rural town began as a Hudson's Bay Company trading fort in 1827. The original site was about 4km downstream, but the fort was moved a decade later to be closer to HBC's rich grain fields and pastures. When word of gold deposits on the Fraser finally leaked out in the 1850s (HBC had tried to downplay earlier reports in order to retain control), Fort Langley was promptly overrun by 30,000 goldseekers, most of them Americans. With only a handful of HBC men on the scene, the company worried that their mainland holdings would be annexed by the US. On a rainy November day in 1858, BC was declared a Crown Colony at the fort's 'Big House' and the British government took control.

The gold rushes eventually declined and HBC closed its fort, but the town thrived as an agricultural and residential centre. Today, a rebuilt Fort Langley National Historic Site is the centrepiece of a thriving tourism trade. The 4.6km **Fort to Fort Trail** connects the 1827 HBC

British Columbia Farm Machinery and Agricultural Museum $ *9131 King St; tel: (604) 888-2273; www.bcfma.com. Open daily Apr–early Oct 1000–1630.*

Domaine de Chaberton Estates $ *1064 216 St, Langley; tel: (604) 530-1736 or (888) 332-9463; www. domainedechaberton.com*

Fort Langley National Historic Site $ *23433 Mavis Ave; tel: (604) 513-4777; www.pc.gc.ca/lhn-nhs/bc/langley/index_e.asp. Open daily Sep–Jun 1000–1700, Jul–Aug 0900–2000.*

Langley Centennial Museum & National Exhibition Centre $ *Mavis St at 9135 King St; tel: (604) 888-3922; http://langleymuseum.org. Open Mon–Sat 1000–1645, Sun 1300–1645.*

site in present-day Derby Reach Regional Park with the Fort Langley National Historic Site.

The collection at the **British Columbia Farm Machinery and Agricultural Museum** emphasises 20th-century farm machinery, most of it used locally and much of it displayed outdoors. Inside displays concentrate on household items and logging equipment.

Domaine de Chaberton Estates, an estate winery in the Fraser Valley, features French and some German varietals.

Fort Langley National Historic Site was established by the Hudson's Bay Company as a fur-trading centre, but the local fur supply was quickly trapped out and the fort was moved to its present location in a lush agricultural region adjacent to a traditional First Nations trading site. With help from local Sto:lo bands, HBC created the salmon-packing industry, shipping 300kg barrels of salted salmon to markets across the Pacific and creating BC's first major export trade. HBC farmers fed customers from Hawaii and Alaska to California and the Company's own inland settlements.

News of gold deposits along the Fraser changed BC forever. American miners flooded north from California, some of them stopping in Victoria to obtain the required mining permits, others simply sailing up the Fraser River to the head of navigation at Fort Langley. The HBC found itself in a quandary: as the only source of food, supplies and transport, the Company was profiting hugely. But the influx of Americans threatened annexation by the US.

The HBC's solution was to turn its mainland holdings into a Crown Colony and let London deal with the American problem. British

Columbia was declared in November 1858, at a ceremony in the Chief Trader's house, the 'Big House', at Fort Langley.

Colonial status was the death of Fort Langley. Competitors moved into fishing, farming and commerce. Navigation was extended to Hope, then to Yale, destroying the fort's role in shipping. BC's capital moved to New Westminster, then Victoria, eclipsing the fort's political power. The fort finally went out of business in 1886 and fell into ruin.

The site became a National Historic Site in 1955 and was reconstructed for BC's centenary in 1958. Most of the storehouse is original (the building was used as a barn for decades), but the rest of today's Fort Langley, from the log palisade to the imposing white Big House and Blacksmith's shop, is modern reconstruction. Living-history volunteers conduct tours year-round, with regular demonstrations of barrel-making, blacksmithing, cooking, clerking and trading. A small Visitor Centre museum just outside the palisade covers the history of the fort.

Langley Centennial Museum offers more complete explanations of Sto:lo First Nations settlements in the lower Fraser Valley and later agricultural expansion than the Fort Langley visitor centre, as well as a look at local agricultural history. Don't skip the re-created general store, Victorian parlour and homesteader's kitchen.

Below
Trading beaver pelts at Fort Langley

Accommodation and food in Fort Langley

Planet Java $ *9178 Glover Rd; tel: (604) 882-5057; www.planetjava50s. com*, has Elvis Presley artefacts in 1950s diner décor.

Wendel's Bookstore & Café $ *103-9233 Glover Rd; tel: (604) 513-2238; www.wendelsonline.com*, has Fort Langley's best selection of local-interest books as well as a popular all-day café.

Bedford House Restaurant $$ *9272 Glover Rd; tel: (604) 888-2333* is a restored lumber baron's home set in expansive gardens, for evening dinner or Sunday brunch.

Sandman Hotel Langley $$ *8855 202nd St, Langley; tel: (604) 888-7263* or *(800) 726-3626; www.sandmanhotels.com/en/hotel/bc/langley*, is a reliable chain choice in the neighbouring town of Langley.

HARRISON HOT SPRINGS

ⓘ Tourism Harrison
499 Hot Springs Rd; tel: (604) 796-5581; http://tourismharrison.com

ⓝ Sasquatch Provincial Park $
Rockwell Dr; tel: (604) 466-8325; www.env.gov.bc.ca/ bcparks/explore/parkpgs/ sasquatc.html. Open daily except for periodic closure for heavy snowfall.

Harrison Public Hot Pool $ *Hot Springs Rd and Esplanade Ave; tel: (604) 796-2244. Open daily 0900–2100.*

There's been a hotel and mineral baths at Harrison Lake since the 1880s, but the hot springs themselves are out of sight along the western lakeside, a 10-minute walk from the Harrison Hot Springs Resort & Spa. The lake has a broad sandy beach, boating and fishing, with camping and hiking along the water and up nearby mountainsides. A small tourist town sits on the south shore. Surrounding forests are the haunt of Sasquatch, a legendary hairy forest giant that has been reported as far south as the Trinity Alps in Northern California. Hikers are more likely to spot deer, squirrels, Canada geese and the occasional beaver.

Although named after the shy, oversized creature of the northern forests, **Sasquatch Provincial Park** is actually one of the more popular spots for camping, hiking and boating on the lower mainland. Attractions include four lakes surrounded by rugged mountains. Look for mountain goats on the **Slollicum Bluffs** just north of **Deer Lake**.

Harrison Lake is 60km long and favoured by windsurfers and sailors for the heavy winds blowing southward most afternoons. Lake tour boats depart daily from the dock in front of the Harrison Hot Springs Resort & Spa in summer. There's a wide swimming beach directly in front of the town as well as marina facilities.

The actual hot springs supplying **Harrison Public Hot Pool** are about 2km away, but the sulphur- and potassium-rich water is too hot to touch. The indoor soaking and swimming pool is cooled to 38°C.

Accommodation and food in Harrison Hot Springs

Cookin' Kim's Country Cafe $ *105–196 Esplanade Ave; tel: (604) 796-8424*, lures locals for simple but filling meals.

Above
Harrison Hot Springs

Executive Hotel $$ *190 Lillooet Ave; tel: (888) 265-1155 or (604) 796-5555; www.harrisonhotsprings.com*, is the best value in town, across the street from the lake.

Kitami Restaurant $$ *318 Hot Springs Rd; tel: (604) 796-2728*, serves great Japanese food, including sushi, and gets plenty of visiting Vancouverites who want a taste of home.

Harrison Beach Hotel $$$ *160 Esplanade Ave; tel: (604) 796-1111 or (866) 338-8111; www.harrisonbeachhotel.com*, is comfortable and just across from the beach.

Harrison Hot Springs Resort & Spa $$$ *100 Esplanade Ave; tel: (866) 638-5075; www.harrisonresort.com*, is a full-service resort and spa on the shores of Harrison Lake.

HOPE

Hope & District Chamber of Commerce *895 3rd Ave; tel: (604) 869-3111; www.hopechamber.bc.ca*

Hope Museum $ *Info Centre 919 Water Ave; tel: (604) 869-7322. Open daily May–Sep 0800–2000, winter 0900–1700.*

Japanese Friendship Gardens *Memorial Park, Third and Park streets. Free.*

Minter Gardens $$ *52892 Bunker Rd, Rosedale (exit 135 off Hwy 1); tel: (604) 794-7191 or (888) 646-8377; www.mintergardens.com. Open daily Apr and Oct 1000–1700, May and Sep 0900–1730, Jun 0900–1800, Jul–Aug 0900–1900.*

Coquihalla Canyon Provincial Park and Othello Tunnels $ *10km east from Kawkawa Lake; tel: (604) 986-9371; www.env.gov.bc.ca/bcparks/explore/parkpgs/coquih_can.html. Closed in winter due to ice, Nov–Mar.*

Sitting at the head of the lower Fraser River Valley, Hope was long the head of navigation upriver and an important transfer point for goods and gold moving between the interior and coast. Navigation eventually moved upstream to Yale, but railway traffic revitalised the town, which has developed into a centre for hiking, rafting, cycling, fishing, soaring, mountain biking and other outdoor activities. Hollywood and Vancouver camera crews regularly use Hope for film shoots.

Highlight of **Hope Museum** is a restored ball mill from a nearby mine. Other displays cover Sto:lo life in the area, early White settlers and Canada's treatment of its Japanese citizens during World War II. The calm meditation garden in the **Japanese Friendship Gardens** is dedicated to the 2,300 Japanese-Canadians who were interned in barns at Tashme, 24km east, during World War II.

Minter Gardens doesn't have quite the advertising budget or the formality of Victoria's Butchart Gardens (*see page 66*), but Butchart can't begin to match Minter's setting against the Cascade Range. Eleven themed areas include rose gardens, the largest collection of Penjing rock bonsai outside China, a maze and Canada's largest floral flag.

Coquihalla Canyon Provincial Park & Othello Tunnels This is the canyon where Rambo blazed his name in *First Blood*. It's also one of the most famous sets of railway tunnels in Canada, carved through solid granite for the Kettle Valley Railway to the Kootenay region between 1910 and 1916. The almost flat 2.8km return stroll includes four tunnels and pleasant views of the rushing Coquihalla River.

The KVR ran between Hope and Nelson (*see page 246*), but was plagued by snow, washouts and rock slides. A 130m washout just north of the Othello Tunnels closed the railway permanently in 1959. Most of today's Coquihalla Highway (*see page 144*) follows the old KVR railbed, including one section which cost $300,000 per mile to build in 1914.

Accommodation and food in Hope

Blue Moose Coffee House $ *322 Wallace St; tel: (604) 869-0729; www.bluemoosecafe.com*, serves panini sandwiches and fair-trade coffee daily with live music on Friday night.

Quality Inn $ *350 Old Hope-Princeton Way; tel: (604) 869-9951 or (877) 424-6423; www.qualityinn.com*, is on the outskirts of Hope.

Skagit Motor Inn $$ *655 3rd Ave; tel: (604) 869-5220 or (888) 869-5228; www.skagit-motor-inn.com*, is quiet and central.

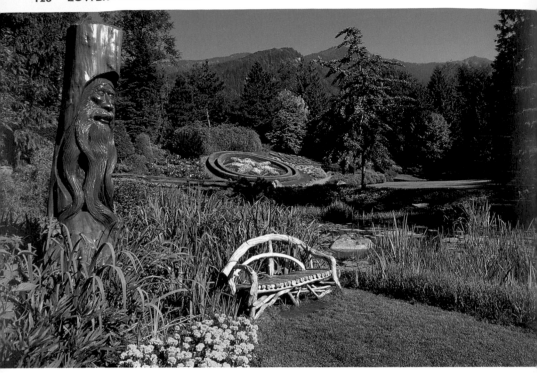

Above
Minter Gardens

Suggested tour

Total distance: 130km, or 260km as a long day trip from Vancouver.

Time: Allow 2 hours to drive to Hope, plus at least 2 hours each for Fort Langley and Minter Gardens and time to soak in Harrison Hot Springs.

Links: This route links with **Vancouver** (*see page 42*) to the west and the **Cascade Mountains** (*see page 130*) or the **Gold Rush Trail** (*see page 186*) to the east.

Route: From Central **Vancouver**, take either Broadway or Hwy 7A east to Hwy 1, the TransCanada Highway, eastbound towards Hope. Once across the **Fraser River**, the freeway runs through a mixture of rural farmland and small towns in the **Lower Fraser Valley**.

The flat plain stretching from the river to the base of the Cascades is one of BC's prime agricultural areas. Dairy herds alternate with fields of raspberries, blueberries, strawberries and grain, with the occasional horse farm and llama pasture. Try to resist the temptation to speed along the freeway – the RCMP set up frequent radar speed traps in both directions. Drivers who keep within 8–10kph of the posted speed limit may get a stern warning, but seldom a speeding ticket. Many Vancouver radio stations include speed trap locations in their traffic reports.

**Albion Ferry/
Fraser River
Marine Transportation**
*http://translink.bc.ca/
Transportation_Services/
Albion_Ferry/schedules.asp,
has ferry schedules.*

Circle Farm Tour
*http://circlefarmtour.com,
describe and provide maps
online for rural tourism,
including farmers' markets,
farms, fairs and local
production dining
experiences for
Abbotsford, Agassiz-
Harrison Mills, Chilliwack,
Langley, Maple Ridge-Pitt
Meadows and Mission.*

**Xa:ytem Longhouse
Interpretive Centre $$**
*35087 Lougheed Hwy,
Mission; tel: (604) 820-
9725; www.xaytem.ca. Open
Mon–Sat 0900–1630, on a
site where 9,000-year-old
buildings were excavated,
explains Sto:lo First
Nations culture in a
traditional cedar longhouse
with artists in residence
carving a house post.*

Much of the farming land east of **Langley** has gone into agricultural preserve that gives owners tax incentives to continue farming rather than selling out to the suburban sprawl of Greater Vancouver. *Farm Fresh Guide (http://bcfarmfresh.com)*, available at tourist infocentres, petrol stations and tourist stops throughout the valley and in Vancouver, maps farms in the Langley area selling produce to the public. *The Harvest Guide*, with similar free distribution, covers the valley from **Abbotsford** east towards Hope. Six communities have map-brochures for self-drive agricultural Circle Farm Tours.

The town of **Langley** is a busy farming and commercial centre. Follow freeway signs to **FORT LANGLEY ❶**, its older, smaller and more sedate cousin.

Detour: From Fort Langley, drive north to the **Fraser River** and the free ferry to **Albion**, on the north side of the river. Take Hwy 7 to the east (right), following signs to Harrison Hot Springs to rejoin the route.

From Fort Langley, return to Hwy 1 and continue eastwards, stopping at **Xa:ytem Longhouse Interpretive Centre** in **Mission** before arriving in **Abbotsford**. Near Hope, Minter Gardens draws raves and visitors from around the world – exit north on to Hwy 9 and follow signs to the left (west) just after crossing the Fraser River.

Return to Hwy 9 and turn left (north) through maize fields and dairy pastures toward **Agassiz**, which fancies itself the 'Corn Capital of BC'. Follow signs towards Hwy 7 and **HARRISON HOT SPRINGS ❷**, then return to Hwy 1 and continue east to **HOPE ❸**.

The Cascade Mountains

Ratings

History	●●●●●
Mountains	●●●●●
Scenery	●●●●●
Children	●●●●○
Nature	●●●●○
Outdoor activities	●●●●○
Walking	●●●○○
Wildlife	●●●○○

The Cascades aren't the tallest mountains in BC, nor the highest, but they're far and away the most scenic, the most rugged and the most inaccessible by road. Only one highway crosses the range east–west, the Crowsnest, which follows a gold-rush trail built for pack mules in the 1860s. The modern roadway is wider, smoother and not nearly as steep as the early track, but the snowcapped peaks, rushing rivers and dense forests that gradually give way to cacti and desert sand are as memorable today as they were to early surveyors.

The Cascades also form one of BC's most obvious political and economic barriers. Nearly the entire population of the province lives west of the mountains. With a few exceptions, such as the Okanagan Valley and isolated towns on major highways, the countryside from Hope eastwards becomes increasingly wild, rugged and invitingly empty.

APEX MOUNTAIN RESORT

Apex Mountain Resort $$$ *Green Mountain Rd, Apex Mountain Recreation Area; tel: (250) 292-8222 or (877) 777-2739; www.apexresort.com. Open all year.*

With a reputation as the sunniest of Canada's Cascade ski resorts, Apex also has some of the best alpine skiing – with dry powder – and snowboarding near the Okanagan Valley. The main lift is open in summer to carry walkers, mountain bikers and sightseers up to alpine meadows. Camping, horse riding and back-country trail trips are also available in summer.

HEDLEY

Mascot Mine Tours $$$ *Tel: (888) 799-8733 or (250) 292-8733; www.mascotmine.com; tours start from Snaza'ist Visitor Centre, Hwy 3. Call for summer season hours.*

This is one of the best preserved of BC's Cascades boom towns. Hedley has dwindled to less than a tenth of its pre-World-War-I population of 5,000, but many of its old buildings remain. So does the **Mascot Mine**, perched on a mountain slope 1,000m above the town. A 3km aerial tramway hauled a bonanza in gold, silver and copper down to mills in Hedley, but the good times were cut short by falling commodity prices

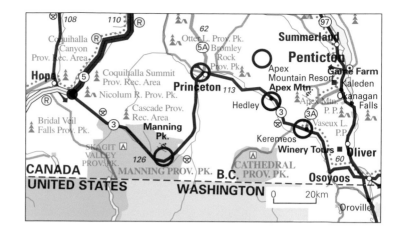

Hedley Heritage Museum 712 Daly Ave, Hedley, BC V0X 1K0; tel: (250) 292-8787; www.hedleybc.ca. Open summer. Call for hours.

Mascot Tea Room and Wild Goat Book Shop Hedley Heritage Museum, has snacks and small meals when the museum is open.

and World War I labour shortages. Surviving Mascot Mine buildings looming far above Hedley have been restored and are open for guided tours in summer. The **Hedley Heritage Museum** has a fine collection of local mining artefacts and period photographs explained by costumed interpreters. Gold panning is still allowed in the Similkameen River just south of town, but trout fishing is likely to be more productive.

KEREMEOS

Similkameen Country Keremeos; tel: (250) 499-5225; http:// similkameencountry.org. Information centre open in Memorial Park in summer.

Crowsnest Vineyards $ Surprise Dr, just east of Cawston; tel: (250) 499-5129; http://crowsnestvineyards.com. Open daily. A seven-room Country Inn is above the restaurant.

The Grist Mill at Keremeos $ 2691 Upper Bench Rd; tel: (250) 499-2888; www.tsa.gov.bc.ca/ heritage/historic_sites/grist_ mill.htm. Open daily.

Perched on a bench above the Similkameen River, Keremeos still looks and feels like the frontier town it once was. Orchards and pastures stretch nearly to the main street, which is lined with false-front wooden buildings and well-used pick-up trucks. The village began as a First Nations town big enough to convince the Hudson's Bay Company to build a trading post, and slowly grew as settlers started cattle ranches, fruit orchards and, more recently, vineyards. **Crowsnest Vineyards** offers broad mountain vistas from the tasting room, and German food.

The **Grist Mill at Keremeos**, an 1877 water-powered mill, is BC's only surviving 19th-century mill with the original machinery intact and working. Built next to Keremeos Creek, the grounds have been turned into a heritage garden surrounded by more modern orchards. The BC Heritage Trust site is open all year, but costumed interpreters operate the mill and demonstrate period farming and household tasks in summer. The tea room is an excellent summer lunch stop.

South Similkameen Museum fills the former Provincial Police building and gaol with its pioneer artefacts and antique police uniforms.

Cliffs of basalt columns (geologically like Wyoming's Devil's Tower or Northern Ireland's Giant Causeway) soar 30m in the blazing sun at **Keremeos Columns Provincial Park**. A survey error in the 1930s left

South Similkameen Museum $ *604 6th Ave; tel: (250) 499-5445; http://keremeos.net/museum. Call for hours.*

Keremeos Columns Provincial Park *North on Hwy 3A, east at the cemetery, a 16km return hike from the end of the pavement; www.env.gov.bc.ca/bcparks/explore/parkpgs/keremeos.html*

The Red Bridge *Just west of Keremeos and south of Hwy 3; http://keremeos.net/redbridge.html*

St Laszlo Estate Winery $ *Hwy 3 East, Upper Bench Rd; tel: (250) 499-2856. Open daily.*

the columns on private land outside park boundaries; ask permission to hike the 8km trail from the house at the end of the paved road.

The faded **Red Bridge** over the Similkameen River was built as a railway bridge around 1907. When the line was abandoned, the covered bridge was converted to highway use. Deep pools just below the bridge are popular local swimming holes during the blazing days of summer.

St Laszlo Estate Winery spreads across the upper bench above the Similkameen River providing expansive views of Cascade peaks in every direction. The wines are largely Hungarian- and German-inspired.

Right
Keremeos Mill

MANNING PROVINCIAL PARK

Manning Provincial Park Visitor Centre *Hwy 3, 1km east from Manning Park Resort. Open daily Jun–Labour Day 0900–1430.*

Manning Provincial Park $ *Hwy 3; tel: (604) 476-9069; www.env.gov.bc.ca/bcparks/explore/parkpgs/manning.html*

Originally created as a game preserve, Manning displays jagged, snow-capped peaks, alpine meadows, deep valleys, teal-blue lakes and dense forests. Vegetation and wildlife are as varied as the terrain, from wild rhododendrons and magnificent stands of red cedar to bears foraging along the highway, deer, beaver, chipmunks, and hoary marmots, the park symbol carved into a gigantic sign at the western entrance.

Hwy 3 bisects the park, with the primary facilities, the **Manning Park Resort** and the **Visitor Centre**, midway between Hope and Princeton, 68km in either direction. Resort facilities include the only indoor accommodation (chalets, cabins and hotel rooms), restaurants and supply/gift shop in the park. The Visitor Centre has a small natural history museum with free trail guides and other park information.

Manning Park Resort $$
7500, Hwy 3 Manning
Provincial Park;
tel: (250) 840-8822 or
(800) 330-3321; www.
manningpark.com

Beaver Pond South side
of the highway, 500m east
of the Visitor Centre. Open
all year.

Cascade Lookout Paved
road from Manning Park
Resort area. Open in
summer only.

Heather Trail Trail head
at Blackwall Peak Meadows.
Open in summer only.

Rein Orchid Trail Trail
head 100m west of
Amphitheatre car park off
Gibson Pass Rd.

Rhododendron Flats $
South side of the highway,
just beyond the Summallo
Grove.

Summallo Grove South
side of the highway, 9km
from the west park entrance.

Manning is a year-round outdoor recreation centre, with alpine and Nordic skiing, skating and snowboarding in winter and extensive trails for hiking, mountain biking and horse riding in summer. There are also several short, self-guiding nature trails, many accessible only in summer, as well as multi-day backpacking routes and several campgrounds accessible by car.

Two major rivers rise from the Cascades within Manning. The Skagit River curls westward through the park and the adjoining **Skagit Valley Provincial Park** (tel: (604) 986-9371; www.env.gov.bc.ca/bcparks/explore/parkpgs/skagit), then disappears into a series of hydroelectric reservoirs south of the US border to drain into Puget Sound near Seattle. The Similkameen River runs east through the Cascades and eventually drains into the Okanagan River and then into the Columbia River in Washington State.

In Manning Provincial Park, **Beaver Pond**, created by beavers damming a small stream, offers excellent birdwatching during May and June. The sometimes paved, sometimes gravel trail stretches 500m.

A summer-only paved road leads 9km from the highway at the Lodge to **Cascade Lookout**, with grand views back to the valley surrounding the Manning Park Lodge and Visitor Centre and nearby mountains. A good gravel road climbs another 6km to **Blackwall Peak Alpine Meadows** and sublime vistas invisible from lower lookouts. The meadows shimmer with wild flowers from late July to mid-August.

Heather Trail follows a carpet of wild flowers more than 21km long and up to 5km wide stretching from Blackwall Peak to Third Brother Mountain and beyond. Road access is from the Blackwall Peak Alpine Meadows car park.

Rein Orchid Trail explores bog and riverside terrain filled with native orchids, ferns and other wetland flora. The flat, 15-minute trail is only 500m long.

Rhododendron Flats, a flat 0.5km walking trail, goes through one of the few naturally occurring groves of rhododendrons in the Cascades. Red blossoms are at their height early–mid-June most years.

A 700m trail (wheelchair accessible in most seasons) in **Summallo Grove** circles through a towering riverside grove of red cedar and Douglas fir.

PRINCETON

Princeton Visitor Information
Centre 105 Hwy 3 East;
tel: (250) 295-3103;
www.princeton.ca

The town was originally called Vermillion Forks for the red pigment mined by First Nations bands. The name 'Princeton' dates from an 1860 visit to Eastern Canada by the Prince of Wales. Once a mining and cattle town, Princeton has become the commercial centre of the south Cascades region. Most of the major mines have closed in recent years, prompting residents to turn their colourful history into profitable tourism. Several downtown buildings sport western-themed

ⓘ Princeton and District Pioneer Museum and Archives
$ *167 Vermillion Ave; tel: (250) 295-7588; www.princetonmuseum.com. Call for hours.*

Gold panning $
Check with the Visitor Information Centre for location and pan hire.

Vermillion Bluffs $
Behind Home Hardware, Bridge St and Fenchurch Ave.

murals, while the town of Princeton promotes trails, cycling, hiking, fishing, local lakes, and proximity to Similkameen wine county and orchards.

Princeton and District Pioneer Museum and Archives has an outstanding collection of fossils in the Pollard Wing, including some of the earliest known examples of fossilised citrus trees, apple trees and salmon. There are also exhibitions of local mining equipment, fluorescent minerals and pioneer artefacts.

Gold prospectors followed the Similkameen River northward in the 1850s, panning and dredging as they went, but small flakes of gold continue to wash out of the Cascades with every spring melt. The Visitor Information Centre can recommend where to pan on the river.

The Okanagan First Nations bands who lived at **Vermillion Bluffs**, when Hudson's Bay Company explorers first appeared in the early 1800s, called the place *Yak Tulameen*, 'place where red earth is sold'. The band mined red ochre, vermillion sulphate, from cliffs along the Tulameen River, just west, and sold it at a well-established market-place where Princeton now stands.

Accommodation and food in Princeton

Santo's Steak & Pizza $$ *117 Bridge St; tel: (250) 295-6644*, has indoor or outdoor dining, daily.

The Villager Inn $$ *244 4th St; tel: (877) 295-6996* or *(250) 295-6996*, includes breakfast at this motel.

The Dewdney Trail

In the 1860s, it was easier to travel east–west through the United States than through BC, and easier still to travel north–south along the many river valleys that connected the two countries. When gold was discovered at Wild Horse Creek, near **Cranbrook** (*see page 250*), American miners and merchants flooded north, threatening to undermine already tenuous British authority. The solution: Surveyor Edgar Dewdney blasted a mule trail 1.2m wide through 400km of mountains, desert and forests from Hope to the East Kootenays in just seven months.

The Dewdney Trail opened the southern reaches of BC to the coast for the first time. As mining grew, so did the trail, expanding from mule trail to wagon road and automobile road, Hwy 3. With a boost from the Kettle Valley Railway, road access slowly focused the province's southern communities on Vancouver and Victoria and away from closer, more accessible commercial centres in the United States.

Opposite
Coquihalla Highway

Above
Keremeos Mill

Thompson Okanagan Tourism Association
2280-D Leckie Road, Kelowna, BC V1X 6G6; tel: (250) 860-5999 or (800) 567-2275; www.totabc.com, has information on the region and individual communities.

Suggested tour

Total distance: 240km.

Time: Allow half a day to drive from Hope through the Cascades to the Okanagan Valley and 2–4 days to explore Manning Provincial Park.

Links: Go west to the **Lower Fraser River Valley** (*see page 122*) and Vancouver (*see page 42*), north to **Kamloops** (*see page 138*), the **Gold Rush Trail** (*see page 186*) or the **Okanagan Valley** (*see page 148*).

Route: From **HOPE** ❶ *(see page 127)*, go east on Hwy 3, the Crowsnest Highway, named after the Crowsnest Pass near the BC–Alberta border. The freeway turns north toward **Kamloops** at Hwy 5, the **Coquihalla Highway** *(see page 144)*, while Hwy 3 reverts to two lanes. Hwy 3 largely follows the **Dewdney Trail**, the first rough mule track cut through the wilderness to supply Kootenay gold fields in the 1860s.

Look for the raw scar of the **Hope Slide** looming above the north side of the highway 10km beyond the junction. One side of the mountain, 1,983m high by 1km wide, slid into the valley in 1965. The slide raised the valley floor by 70m and blocked the highway for weeks.

Continue east past the wooden carving of a hoary marmot into **MANNING PROVINCIAL PARK** ❷, the most scenic (and the slowest) section of the Crowsnest. The road is winding and occasionally steep, the scenery distracting and the wildlife sometimes close enough to cause traffic jams.

The road turns north after leaving the park, heading for the former mining town of **PRINCETON** ❸. The highway follows the Similkameen River as it cuts through increasingly dry terrain eastward toward **HEDLEY** ❹. By **KEREMEOS** ❺, the mountains have taken on the look of desert, although streambeds and river courses are still lined with green – as are growing tracts of fruit orchards and vineyards. The highway takes a final plunge over **Richter Pass** (682m) before dropping into the true desert of the **Okanagan Valley** *(see page 148)* at Osoyoos ❻ *(see page 152)*.

Detour: From Keremeos, take Hwy 3A north and east to **Skaha Lake** *(see page 153)* in the central **Okanagan Valley**.

Ratings

Cowboys	●●●●●
First Nations	●●●●●
History	●●●●○
Outdoor activities	●●●●○
Scenery	●●●●○
Beaches	●●●○○
Parks	●●●○○
Sport	●●●○○

Kamloops

B C's largest city, at least in terms of area, takes its name from a Secwepemc First Nations word, *Tk'emlups*, the 'meeting place'. Straddling the junction of the North Thompson and South Thompson rivers, Kamloops spreads across 31sq km of river valley and hillside that have become the centre of BC's ranching industry.

In prior decades, scarlet-clad huntsmen rode to hounds across the rolling hills in noisy pursuit of wild foxes (or coyotes, depending on the luck of the hunt). Those same hills today are sprouting housing estates or provincial parks, depending on the luck of conservationists.

In the old city centre, on the low south bank of the Thompson River, dozens of stately brick buildings rise along shady streets that lead to sandy riverfront beaches. Outlying districts have more ice rinks, playing fields, gymnasiums and tennis courts than many countries can claim.

Kamloops, proud of being the Tournament Capital of Canada, holds at least one major sport competition every weekend of the year and boasts 13 golf courses.

Sights

ⓘ **Tourism Kamloops/ Kamloops Visitor Information Centre** *1290 W TransCanada Hwy (exit 368); tel: (250) 374-3377 or (800) 662-1994; http://tourismkamloops.com. Open Jan–May & Sep–Dec Mon–Fri 0900–1700; Jun daily 0900–1800; Jul–Aug daily 0900–1900.*

🅑 **BC Wildlife Park** *$$ 9077 Dallas Dr; tel: (250) 573-3242; www.bczoo.org. Open daily Mar–Sep, weekends the rest of the year. Call for hours.*

BC Wildlife Park
The province's premier spot for wildlife rehabilitation and captive breeding of endangered species is spread over 50ha in rainforest, grasslands, mountain, plateau and Northern zones. Spot indigenous wildlife, including grizzly bears, mountain lions, timber wolves, moose, mountain goats, falcons and snakes, with the option of viewing some denizens from the Wildlife Express miniature train.

City of Kamloops Fire Hall Museum
The museum is part of the city's active main fire hall with fire-fighters on hand

City of Kamloops Fire Hall Museum $
1205 Summit Dr; tel: (250) 372-5131. Open daily during business hours.

Farmers Market $
Tel: (250) 577-3461. Open Apr–Oct Sat 0800–1200, 2nd Ave and St Paul St; Wed 0800–1400 5th Ave and Victoria St. Tourism Kamloops has a brochure: Kamloops and Area Farm Fresh. Your Guide to Discover Agriculture, Fresh Food and Agri Tourism in the Kamloops Region.

to explain the intricacies of fire suppression equipment and technologies dating back to 1884.

Farmers Market

The regional farmers market started as a place for local farmers to sell their products, but has become a popular cultural and educational venue. Look for anything from a 4-H Club parade with chickens and rabbits to live music, square dancing and suggestions on how to control garden bugs without pesticides – plus a better selection of fresh fruits, vegetables, breads, cheese and picnic supplies than any store in town.

Harper Mountain

Kamloops' traditional family ski hill is a short drive from town with alpine and Nordic skiing in winter. There are day-use only facilities and a tube park. Lifts are less developed than competitor Sun Peaks, but prices are also considerably lower.

Harper Mountain
$$ *2580 Harper Mountain Rd; tel: (250) 372-2119; www.harpermountain. com. Open approx. early Dec–late Mar.*

Kamloops Art Gallery $ *465 Victoria St; tel: (250) 377-2400; www.kag.bc.ca. Call for hours.*

Kamloops Bike Ranch
Tel: (250) 828 3695; www.kamloops.ca/bikeranch/ index.shtml

Kamloops Heritage Railway $$ *510 Lorne St; tel: (250) 374-2141; www.kamrail.com. Various trains operate Jun–Sep.*

Kamloops Indian Band
200-355 Yellowhead Hwy; tel: (250) 828-9700; www.kib.ca

Kamloops Museum and Archives $ *207 Seymour St; tel: (250) 828-3576; www.kamloops.ca/museum/ index.shtml. Open Tue–Sat 0930–1630, Thu to 1930.*

Kamloops Symphony $$ *510 Lorne St; tel: (250) 372-5000; www.kamloopssymphony.com. Concerts Sep–May.*

Kenna Cartwright Park *TransCanada Hwy to Exit 366 north on Copperhead Dr, west on Hillside Dr; tel: (250) 828-3695; www.kamloops.ca/ parkgardens/kenna.shtml. Open daily.*

Kamloops Art Gallery

The gallery, probably the largest public art exhibition in interior BC, concentrates on local artists and publishes a free walking tour to private downtown galleries.

Kamloops Bike Ranch

Canada's largest municipal mountain bike park is sandwiched between two neighbourhoods with pineland, sagebrush and grasslands terrain.

Kamloops Heritage Railway

Summer weekends are the time to board for the 70-minute carriage or open-air car trips pulled by the restored steam engine No 2141, *The Spirit of Kamloops*. A restoration shop is located one block away in Pioneer Park. The *Armstrong Explorer* steam-powered train makes several summertime 185km round-trip excursions to Armstrong.

Kamloops Indian Band

The Kamloops Band is one of 17 modern Secwepemc (Shuswap) bands and the most economically successful. Much of the Band's land along the North Thompson and South Thompson rivers has been leased out to thriving industrial parks, farming and grazing operations. Profits support a successful Band community as well as the **Kamloopa PowWow**, held each August, one of the largest First Nations gatherings in North America.

Kamloops Museum and Archives

Three floors of displays explore local Secwepemc First Nations history, Hudson's Bay Company activities, gold rushes, ranching and cowboy history, local Chinese culture, Victoriana and natural history. The museum's collection of Secwepemc baskets is one of the best in the province. Exhibits include an 1842 log building from the HBC fort on what is now the Kamloops Indian Reserve on the north bank of the South Thompson River, two Victorian-era house interiors, a Victorian medical office and a late 19th-century general store.

Kamloops Symphony

The 50-member orchestra presents at least one concert monthly from autumn to spring.

Kenna Cartwright Park

BC's largest municipal park (800 hectares) is in the southwestern section of Kamloops, spread around Mount Dufferin. A number of nature trails offer hikers year-round views of the convergence of the North and South Thompson Rivers, Kamloops Lake and the Thompson Valley. It's mixed grassland–forest wilderness within the city, home to bears, coyotes, deer, and several provincially identified vulnerable species, including the Great Basin spadefoot toad.

McArthur Island
North Kamloops via McKenzie Ave or 12th St; tel: (250) 828-3695; www.kamloops.ca/ parkgardens/macisland.shtml. Open daily.

Riverside Park *South bank, Thompson River, east and west from the foot of 3rd Ave; tel: (250) 828-3695; www.kamloops.ca/ parkgardens/riversidepark. shtml. Summer music concerts nightly 1900–2030.*

Secwepemc Museum & Heritage Park $
355 Yellowhead Hwy; tel: (250) 828-9749; www. secwepemc.org/museum. Open Labour Day–mid-Jun 0800–1600, mid-Jun–Labour Day Mon–Fri 0800–1600.

St Joseph's Church
Off Chilcotin Avenue, Kamloops Indian Band Reserve; tel: (250) 374-7323. Open Jul–early Sep Wed–Sat; year-round for services.

McArthur Island

Recreation is big business in Kamloops, with baseball diamonds, soccer fields, tennis courts, ice arenas, gymnasia, golf courses ... and McArthur Island. The North Shore island is all recreation, with a nine-hole golf course, cycling trails, swimming, tennis, football, soccer, rugby, curling, lawn bowling, baseball, a skate park and more. McArthur is also a wildlife mecca, with a butterfly garden, viewing platform to spot beavers, muskrats, yellow-bellied marmots, squirrels, red foxes and river otters, hides for birdwatching and a Xeriscape Demonstration Garden.

Riverside Park

The city's first riverfront park features a rose garden, tennis, swimming, walking trails, children's water park and 5,000-seat Interior Savings Centre coliseum.

Secwepemc Museum & Heritage Park

The Secwepemc (pronounced 'shh-kwep-mm') or Shuswap First Nations controlled a vast territory from Kamloops west to the Fraser River, north to Soda Springs and east to the Rockies for millennia before the Hudson's Bay Company built its first fur-trading fort at Kamloops in 1812.

The Secwepemc traditionally lived a semi-nomadic life, following fish, game and food plants from spring to autumn and returning to permanent villages with the first winter snows. One of the largest and oldest of the villages occupied the northeastern shore of the confluence of the two Thompson Rivers, land that eventually became the Kamloops Indian Reserve.

A 4-hectare Heritage Park covers the ancient village site, which includes remains of dwellings at least 2,000 years old. Reconstructed houses and archaeological excavations show changes in house styles and sizes from 5,000 years ago to first contact with the HBC in the early 19th century. The Park also has exhibits of heritage and native food plants in a **Secwepemc Ethnobotanical Garden**, and a traditional salmon fishery. In summer, band performers offer traditional song, dancing, theatre and story-telling as well as salmon barbecues in a traditional summer lodge.

The museum building was once part of the Kamloops Indian Residential School. Exhibits include most of the artefacts found in the Heritage Park outside, as well as artefacts from digs throughout traditional Secwepemc lands and a fine collection of archival photographs. Museum displays put a distinctly Secwepemc spin on local history, detailing the legal and moral transgressions committed by White settlers that are largely ignored by the Kamloops Museum.

St Joseph's Church

The white steeple of St Joseph's was first raised in 1846, but the current building has been restored to its early 1900s look, complete with stained-glass windows and bright interior paintings. Don't miss the cemetery, directly across the car park, with grave markers ranging from simple wooden crosses to ornate totemic carvings.

⓪ Sun Peaks Resort
$$$ 50km and 45 minutes north of Kamloops off Hwy 5; tel: (800) 807-3257; http://sunpeaksresort.com. Open all year.

Tranquille Marsh
10km west of North Kamloops on Tranquille Rd; tel: (250) 371-6200. Open daily.

⬤ Western Canada Theatre Company
$$ Pavilion Theatre, 1025 Lorne St; tel: (250) 372-3216 or Sagebrush Theatre, 1300 9th Ave; tel: (866) 374-5483; www. westerncanadatheatre.bc.ca. Regular productions Sep–Apr.

Sun Peaks Resort
Sun Peaks has skiing in winter (881m vertical drop), groomed runs, open glades, Nordic skiing, dogsledding tours, sleigh rides, ice skating, tubing and snowboarding. Fishing, golf, hiking, horse riding, canoeing, kayaking, mountain biking, music festival, swimming and tennis are summer activities. Base facilities include hotels, condominiums, lodges, restaurants and shopping.

Tranquille Marsh
This BC Wildlife Watch viewing site overlooks an extremely active waterfowl habitat. Look for trumpeter swans, Canada and snow geese, herons, ducks and dozens of other species, especially during the spring and autumn migrations. Follow Red Lake Road a few kilometres to spot bighorn sheep.

Western Canada Theatre Company
Kamloops has one of the few professional theatre companies – in two venues – in the province outside Vancouver and Victoria. The programme emphasises well-known productions that have already garnered a following in London or New York.

Accommodation and food

Accommodation is usually easy to find, although advance booking is wise during the summer holiday period. Motels are concentrated along Hwy 5 and off Hwy 1 at exits 366–369. For more expensive digs, try along Columbia St (exit 369), which curves from the highway down to the old town centre near the river.

A growing population has enlivened Kamloops' restaurants. Don't expect the cutting-edge Northwestern cuisine found in Vancouver and Victoria, but there's more than steaks, burgers and meatballs.

Hello Toast $ *428 Victoria St; tel: (250) 372-9332*, is for people-watching while downing breakfast until 1500.

Mauryas Fine Indian Cuisine $ *165 Victoria St; tel: (250) 377-4969; http://mauryasfineindiancuisine.com*, has a varied menu.

Chapters Viewpoint Restaurant $$ *610 W Columbia St at the Howard Johnson Panorama Inn; tel: (250) 374-3244; www.chaptersviewpoint.com*, has panoramic views and the menu includes Mexican, New Mexican, and standard steakhouse dishes.

Taka $$ *270-1210 Summit Dr (Columbia Place Mall); tel: (250) 828-0806*, has Kamloops' best Japanese cuisine.

Bistro 3.2.6 $$$ *326 Victoria St; tel: (250) 374-2913*, is known for fine dining with innovative ingredient combinations.

Brownstone Restaurant $$$ *118 Victoria St; tel: (250) 851-9939; www.brownstone-restaurant.com*, in the 1904 Canadian Imperial Bank of

Commerce building, offers dinner choices from duck, quail or lamb to Arctic char, served inside or on an outdoor patio in good weather.

South Thompson Inn & Conference Centre $$$ *3438 Shuswap Rd, North of the South Thompson River, 15 minutes east off Hwy 1; tel: (250) 573-3777 or (800) 797-7713; www.stigr.com,* is an expansive horse-farm-cum-resort next to the **Rivershore Executive Golf Links** – guests get preferred tee times.

Below
Kamloops countryside

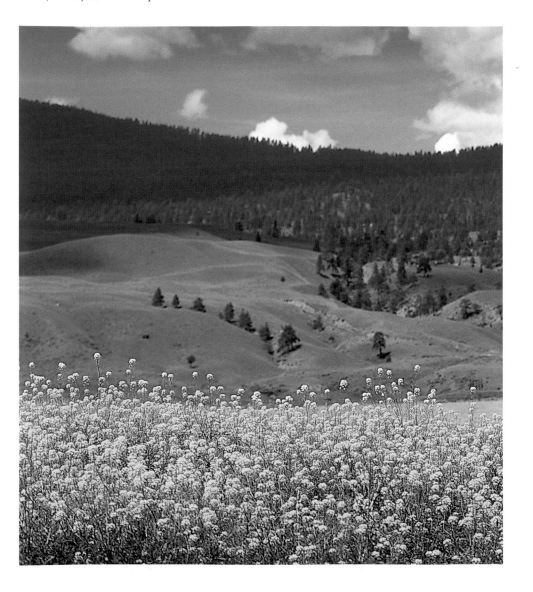

Weather The BC interior
is given to extremes that
may exceed 33°C (92°F)
and sun in summer; −20°C
(−4°F) and drifting snow in
winter. Both extremes are
arid.

Suggested tours

Total distance: 3km.

Time: 2 hours' walking, 4 hours' cycling. The Kamloops Museum has self-guiding maps and brochures for both tours.

Route: The North Kamloops cycle tour has seven stops between Riverside Park and the **Tranquille Sanitarium** by way of McARTHUR ISLAND ❶.

The museum's recommended walking tour includes 30 stops in the old city centre, Nicola Street–Riverside Park and Fourth Street–Lee Road. Start at the old **Calvary Temple** (*185 Seymour Street, across 2nd Avenue* from the **KAMLOOPS MUSEUM AND ARCHIVES** ❷), the oldest public building in town. It opened in 1887 as St Andrew's Presbyterian Church. Just uphill was Kamloops' posh residential district between the 1880s and 1914, with imposing residences along St Paul, Battle and Nicola streets between 1st Avenue and Lee Road.

Walk west along Seymour Street to the 1904 English-Gothic-style **OLD COURTHOUSE** ❸ (*7 W Seymour Street*). Diagonally across 1st Avenue is the **Cigar Factory** (*297 1st Avenue*), built in 1895 and converted to a bakery in 1913. Go back up 1st Avenue to the (Canadian Imperial) **Bank of Commerce** (*118 Victoria Street*), which looks almost as it did when built in 1904. Straight ahead is **RIVERSIDE PARK** ❹, originally the site of a sawmill, gristmill and brickyard.

Victoria Street is one of the most scenic sections of Kamloops, lined with well-preserved buildings. One of the most imposing is the **Fuoco**

Coquihalla Highway

Created for Expo '88, the World's Fair that put Vancouver on the international map, the Coquihalla shaves 90 minutes and uncounted grey hairs off the drive between Hope and Kamloops. Cruise smoothly from four-lane Hwy 1 on to four-lane Hwy 5 at Hope and you can make the run from Vancouver to BC's inland capital in a comfortable 4–5 hours – without bending a single speed limit!

BC's only toll road is actually a second attempt to conquer the Cascade Range between Hope and Kamloops. The first try, the Kettle Valley Railway (*see page 151*), was plagued by runaway trains, washouts, rockslides, avalanches and massive snowfalls until Canadian Pacific Railways finally gave up and closed the line in 1959. The Coquihalla follows much of the old KVR route through the Cascades, but a panoply of modern engineering marvels keeps the highway open through the same choke-points where the railway failed year after year: massive snow sheds, avalanche diversion channels, snow dams, arcing bridges and howitzer emplacements to blast hanging snowpacks are well worth the $10 toll.

The highway is a microcosm of BC scenery. From the lush forests and rough coastal mountains around Hope, the roadway climbs sharply into the older, more rounded peaks of the Cascades. As the climate becomes drier toward the interior, trees become smaller and moss is displaced by the sparse, semi-arid grasses of the Fraser Plateau.

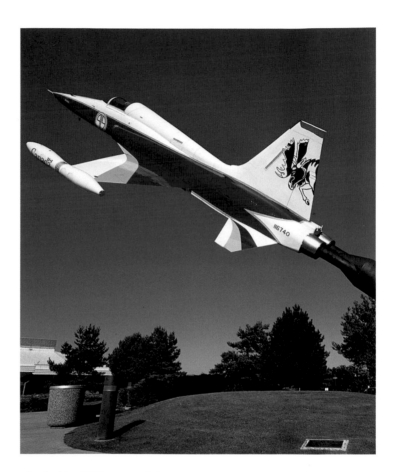

Right
Snowbird jet at Kamloops
Airport

Block (No 219), erected during the boom years between 1910 and 1914. The 1905 **Kamloops Inn** (No 345) was the site of the city's first fire hall. The **Ellis Goodman Block** (No 371) was home to a successful drugstore partnership, with an apothecary shop at street level and professional offices on the floors above. The **Plaza Hotel** (No 405), opened in 1927 in pseudo-Spanish style, was the first hotel in Kamloops built specifically for automobile traffic. Turn uphill along 4th Avenue to Seymour Street. The **Elks Lodge** (409 Seymour Street), also built in 1927, shows similar Spanish design details. Continue west along Seymour Street back to the Calvary Temple.

Also worth visiting

Lac du Bois Grasslands Protected Area *Northwest of Kamloops; www.env.gov.bc.ca/bcparks/explore/parkpgs/lacduboi.html.* Open daily, no developed facilities or water.

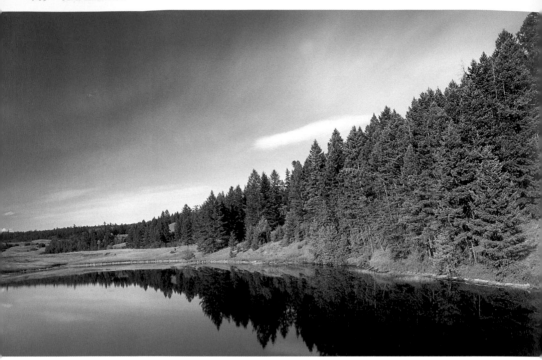

Above
Lac du Bois

Eastern unit Take exit 374 from Hwy 1 at Kamloops. Follow Hwy 5 north over the South Thompson River to Halston Avenue (second set of traffic lights). Take Halston west (left) over the North Thompson River. At the first traffic signal beyond the river, turn right (uphill) to Westsyde Road. Move to the left-hand lane and drive straight up the hill through the housing estates on Lac du Bois Road. Enter the park when the road turns to gravel at the cattle guard.

Western Unit Take Hwy 1 exit 369 or 374 towards the Kamloops Airport via Tranquille Road. From the airport, continue west towards Tranquille. At the Tranquille Sanatorium, turn right, over the railway tracks, and up a long hill.

Dewdrop Lake is straight ahead, along the flats; **Tranquille River Canyon** is uphill.

To explore the grasslands, head for the eastern unit, accessible from Hwy 5. For lakes and canyons, drive the western unit, off Tranquille Road beyond the Kamloops Airport. Either way, Lac du Bois is what Kamloops looked like before it was Kamloops, complete with sweeping vistas, red lava cliffs, canyons ringing with waterfalls, arid grasslands, dry forests, hidden lakes and rolling fields of wild flowers stretching to the horizon.

Lac du Bois is also BC's largest publicly owned grassland. Established in 1996, it accommodates multiple and not always compatible uses, from walking and mountain biking to grazing, logging, all-terrain vehicle driving, fishing, hunting and no-entry ecological preserves in three separate grassland communities.

Ecologists go dewy-eyed over the only-in-Kamloops opportunity to see all three types of bunchgrass native to North America west of the Rocky Mountains. Flower lovers rave about the variety: buttercups, biscuit root, mariposa daisies and yellow sagebrush are only the beginning, with flowering seasons that can range from May into July, depending on rainfall, exposure and elevation.

Birdwatchers think they're in heaven: sharp-tailed grouse, sapsuckers, hairy woodpeckers, flammulated owls and dozens of other species use the grasslands in every season. It's nearly impossible not to see cows, or at least evidence of their recent presence; visitors who know where to look can expect to spot California bighorn sheep, coyotes, foxes, moose, mule deer, rattlesnakes and waterfowl.

Okanagan Valley

Ratings

Food and drink	●●●●●
Wineries	●●●●●
History	●●●●○
Scenery	●●●●○
Beaches	●●●○○
Children	●●●○○
Outdoor activities	●●●○○
Wildlife	●●●○○

The Okanagan Valley is touted as one of Canada's two true deserts (the other is in the Yukon Territory), but leave the sand shoes at home – true desert is all but impossible to find anywhere in the valley. Decades of irrigation have pushed cacti and other desert creatures into a few isolated ecological reserves and Xeriscape gardens, as lush fruit orchards, vegetable fields and vineyards spread from the Okanagan River up every arable hillside, bench and plateau.

The valley itself follows a string of lakes linked together by the Okanagan River, the remnants of an immense glacial river that carved a broad north–south rift through the mountains. The Cascade Range blocks most rain-bearing clouds from the Pacific Ocean; the even higher Monashee Mountains to the east capture what moisture remains. The Okanagan sits in the rain shadow of both ranges, a desert that has blossomed into BC's fruit basket, wine cellar and most popular interior holiday destination.

BRITISH COLUMBIA WINE INFORMATION CENTRE

ⓘ Thompson Okanagan Tourism Association *2280-D Leckie Rd, Kelowna; tel: (250) 860-5999 or (800) 567-2275; www.totabc.com, has information on the region, individual communities and wineries.*

This is a complete source of information about wine in BC, with a tasting room and possibly the best commercial selection of BC wine in the province. **British Columbia Wine Information Centre** $ *553 Railway St, Penticton; tel: (250) 490-2006; www.bcwineinfo.net. Open Jul–Aug 0900–1900, Sep–Jun Mon–Sat 1000–1800, Sun 1000–1600.* Also try the **British Columbia Wine Institute** *107 1726 Dolphin Ave, Kelowna, tel: (250) 762-9744 or (800) 661-2294; www.winebc.com; call for hours*, which has information on wineries, detailed self-touring wine routes for the province and a list of events.

DOMINION RADIO ASTROPHYSICAL OBSERVATORY

Sitting at the bottom of a shallow valley, DRAO's towering white radio dish, surrounded by an array of smaller antennae, looks more like *Star*

Wars than the Okanagan. **Dominion Radio Astrophysical Observatory** $ *White Lake Rd, 9km from Kaleden Jct; tel: (250) 493-2277; www.drao-ofr.hia-iha.nrc-cnrc.gc.ca. Open Mon–Fri 1000–1700 and weekends Easter–Thanksgiving.*

KELOWNA

Tourism Kelowna Visitor Info Centre
544 Harvey Ave (Hwy 97), Kelowna, BC VIY 6C9; tel: (250) 861-1515 or (800) 663-4345; www.tourismkelowna.com. Open Mon–Fri 0900–1700, Sat–Sun 1000–1500.

Kelowna (pronounced 'Keh-low-nuh') began as an 1850s Roman Catholic mission, but soon moved into lumber and fruit. The 110sq km expanse of Okanagan Lake moderates winter weather while the dry, sunny climate produces dependable crops of apples, peaches and grapes.

Lake and sun have also made Kelowna a popular holiday destination. Vast areas of beaches, parks and mountain forests offer sailing, fishing, hiking, houseboating and skiing.

The 1917 Laurel Packinghouse contains the **British Columbia Orchard Industry Museum**, and displays the history of Okanagan

ℹ Kelowna's Cultural District *A self-guided walking tour brochure of this 6-block arts centre is available at the Visitor Info Centre by request: tel: (866) 903-3384 or online at www. kelownasculturaldistrict.com*

ℹ British Columbia Orchard Industry Museum $ *1304 Ellis St; tel: (250) 763-0433; www.kelownamuseums.ca/bc-orchard-museum/index.html. Open Mon–Fri 1000–1700, Sat 1000–1600.*

City Park $ *Lakeshore, from the floating bridge to the white sculpture 'The Sail'.*

Father Pandosy Mission *3685 Benvoulin Dr, southeast from the city centre; tel: (250) 860-8369; www.okanaganhistoricalsociety. org. Open daily Easter–Thanksgiving.*

Geert Maas Sculpture Gardens and Gallery $ *250 Reynolds Rd; tel: (250) 860-7012; www.geertmaas.org. Open daily 1000–1700.*

Kelowna Art Gallery $ *1315 Water St; tel: (250) 762-2226; www.kelownaartgallery. com. Open Tue–Sat 1000–1700, Thu to 2100, Sun 1300–1600.*

Okanagan Heritage Museum $ *470 Queensway; tel: (250) 763-2417; www. kelownamuseum.ca. Open Mon–Fri 1000–1700, Sat 1000–1600.*

Kelowna Land & Orchard $ *3002 Dunster Rd; tel: (250) 763-1091; www.k-l-o.com. Tours daily Easter–Oct.*

Right
Kettle Valley Railway bike trail

fruit growing and packing with period photographs and hands-on equipment displays. The **British Columbia Wine Museum & VQA Wine Shop** (*1304 Ellis St, also inside the Laurel Packinghouse; tel: (250) 868-0441; www.kelownamuseums.ca/bc-wine-museum/index.html. Open Mon–Fri 1000–1800, Sat 1000–1700, Sun 1100–1700*) follow exhibits with retail wine tasting.

Pleasant **City Park** stretches 1km from the foot of the floating bridge across Okanagan Lake to the white sculpture, *The Sail*, merging into the waterfront and marina.

Father Pandosy Mission, a rough-hewn Oblate Mission, founded in 1859 by Fr Charles Pandosy, was the first non-Native settlement in the Okanagan. The original log buildings have been heavily but accurately restored.

The **Geert Maas Sculpture Gardens and Gallery** complements the sculptor's more traditional indoor gallery, while the **Kelowna Art Gallery** has a growing collection of BC art and artists. Exhibits at **Okanagan Heritage Museum** include an 1861 trading post, a traditional First Nations pit house and Kelowna's first radio station.

One of the Okanagan's orchard giants, **Kelowna Land & Orchard**, offers regular tours, fruit and juice samples, Raven Ridge Cidery, a petting zoo, a small museum and Ridge Restaurant (lunch).

KVR Bike Trails, railbeds from the abandoned **Kettle Valley Railway**, with recently restored trestles and pathway, offer spectacular canyon and mountain views for walkers and mountain bikers with a maximum 2 per cent grade. **Myra Canyon** offers the best views; the first trestle is an easy 15-minute walk from the car park. The next 12km to **June Springs** crosses 17 trestles and two tunnels.

Elysium Garden–Nursery transformed an apple orchard with mountain views into display gardens and a Japanese garden, with a water-efficient xeriscape garden using plants from this desert region.

Most of the dozen or so **wineries** in the area offer free tours and tastings. **Gray Monk** is one of the oldest wineries in the Okanagan and still among the best. **Mission Hill Family Estate**, with Tuscan-inspired architecture, has spectacular views across Okanagan Lake from the winery tasting room and Terrace (*open May–Oct*). **Quails'**

KVR Bike Trails
A KVR Trail Map is online at www.penticton.ca

Elysium Garden–Nursery $$
2834 Belgo Rd; tel: (250) 491-1368; http://elysiumgardennursery.com. Open Apr–Sep Tue–Sun 0900–1700.

Gray Monk Estate Winery *1055 Camp Rd; tel: (250) 766-3168; www.graymonk.com. Open daily.*

Mission Hill Family Estate *1730 Mission Hill Rd; tel: (250) 768-7611; www.missionhillwinery.com. Open daily.*

Quails' Gate Okanagan Valley *3303 Boucherie Rd; tel: (250) 769-4451; http://quailsgate.com. Open daily.*

Summerhill Pyramid Winery *4870 Chute Lake Rd; tel: (250) 764-8000; http://summerhill.bc.ca. Open daily.*

Gate Okanagan Valley makes some of the wine region's grandest ice wines while offering tours, a wine shop and **Old Vines Restaurant ($$** *tel: (800) 420-9463 ex. 252 or (250) 769-2500)*. **Summerhill Pyramid Winery**, BC's largest producer of sparkling wines, also has stunning views across the valley from a deck just outside, and a four-storey pyramid-shaped aging cellar.

Accommodation and food in Kelowna

Kelowna, the largest population centre in this part of BC, has a wide selection of hotels, motels and bed and breakfasts to choose from. Book accommodation well in advance for this popular wine country destination; the same applies for winery restaurants with fine dining and views.

Bohemian Café & Catering Co. $ *524 Bernard Ave; tel: (250) 862-3517; www.bohemiancater.com*, is family-owned and known for speciality coffees.

Wood Fire Bakery $ *2041 Harvey Ave; tel: (250) 762-2626*, is a local favourite for breakfast and lunch, huge portions and casual self-service.

Ric's Grill $$ *210 Lawrence St; tel: (250) 869-1586; www.ricsgrill.com*, is a great place to have steak.

El Dorado $$$ *500 Cook Rd; tel: (866) 608-7500 or (250) 763-7500; www.hoteleldoradokelowna.com*, on Okanagan Lake, has boutique and heritage rooms.

KETTLE VALLEY STEAM RAILWAY

Kettle Valley Steam Railway $$
18404 Bathville Rd, Summerland; tel: (250) 494-8422 or (877) 494-8424; http://kettlevalleyrail.org. Operates varying schedule mid-May–mid-Oct. Reservations required.

This 16km section of track is all that remains of the Kettle Valley Railway that once linked Nelson with Hope. The train, pulled by a 1912 locomotive or a 1924 Shay steam locomotive engine, offers stupendous views across the Okanagan Valley, on two-hour tours.

O'KEEFE RANCH

O'Keefe Ranch $$
9380 Hwy 97 N; 12km north of Vernon; tel: (250) 542-2178; www.okeeferanch.ca. Open daily late Apr–Thanksgiving 0900–1800.

Started in 1867, the O'Keefe became one of the largest cattle ranches in the region. The ranch headquarters (*Hwy 97, 12km north of Vernon*) grew into a small town with church, general store and post office. Living history interpreters sound as if they just stepped off the range. There's a model train and rare farm animal breeds, while a blacksmith, potter, saddlery and other artisans show how craft skills were once put to use.

OLIVER

Oliver & District Chamber of Commerce and Visitor Info Centre *End of 36205 93rd St near Okanagan River; tel: (250) 498-6321 or (866) 498-6321; http://oliverchamber.bc.ca*

Oliver and District Museum $ *9728 356 Ave; tel: (250) 498-4027. Open Mon–Sat 0900–1600 in summer.*

Wine Country Welcome Centre *34881 97th St; tel: (250) 498-4867 or (888) 880-9463; www.winecountry-canada.com,* the **Toasted Oak Wine Bar & Grill** *$$* offers sampling of 370 local wines.

This orchard and vineyard town lived by ranching until a Provincial irrigation project turned jobless World War I veterans into farmers. **The Ditch**, the original irrigation canal, is still used. Most of the Okanagan River was canalised in the 1950s for more irrigation and flood control. Exhibits in **Oliver and District Museum**, the former Provincial Police building, cover natural history, early mining activities and irrigation.

Wineries: Oliver created the **Golden Mile** as a marketing ploy to lure visitors to a string of award-winning wineries located on the west side of Hwy 97 just south of town. **Gehringer Bros** leans toward traditional German-type wines. **Hester Creek Estate Winery** produces more modern styles influenced by California rather than Europe. **Inniskillin Okanagan Vineyards**, co-owned by the Inkameep Indian Band (Okanaqueen Tribe), produces intense, flavourful wines. **Tinhorn Creek** shines with reds and has Valley views from the winery deck.

Okanagan wine

Wine has been a familiar Okanagan product for decades, but high-quality wine is a new arrival. The change started in 1988, when Provincial authorities encouraged grape growers to pull out old vineyards that were filled with table grapes and high-yield, low-quality wine grapes. The replacements were Cabernet Sauvignon, Chardonnay, Riesling, Merlot, Sauvignon Blanc, Pinot Noir and similar varieties. The province also revised antiquated licensing laws that favoured high production over high quality and introduced the **VQA**, the Vintners Quality Alliance, BC's answer to appellation and quality control schemes in France, Germany, Italy and California. In summer, many major wineries host special events and concerts.

Wineries:
Gehringer Bros Estate Winery *Hwy 97 at Road 8; tel: (250) 498-3537 or (800) 784-6304.*
Hester Creek Estate Winery *13163 326th Ave; tel: (250) 498-4435; www.hestercreek.com*
Inniskillin Okanagan Vineyards $ *Road 11 West, Oliver; tel: (250) 498-6663 or (800) 498-6211; www.inniskillin.com/en/visit/okanagan.asp. Open summer daily 1000–1800; winter 1100–1600.*
Tinhorn Creek *Road 7, Oliver; tel: (250) 498-3743 or (888) 484-6467; www.tinhorn.com*

OSOYOOS

Osoyoos Chamber of Commerce *7610 Veterans Way; tel: (250) 495-7142; www.osoyooschamber.bc.ca. Open Mon–Fri 1000–1600.*

Beaches $ *Downtown and lakeside parks.*

Just north of the US border, Osoyoos sits in the same Sonoran desert made famous by Sonora, Mexico. Osoyoos Lake draws visitors eager to bake on sandy beaches and water-ski in almost-warm water, but irrigation has turned the desert into a literal fruit basket: apples, peaches, pears, grapes, plums and cherries from surrounding hillsides appear on roadside fruit stands in summer.

Sandy strands are a way of life. **Gyro Beach** and **Community Beach** are in the centre of town. **Desert Centre**, one of the Okanagan's few

Desert Centre $
West on 146 Ave; tel: (250) 495-2470 or (877) 899-0897; www.desert.org. Open May–Oct.

Nk'Mip Desert Cultural Centre $$ 1000 Rancher Creek Rd, Hwy 3 east of downtown;
tel: (250) 495-7901 or (888) 495-8555;
www.nkmipdesert.com. Call for hours.

Osoyoos Oxbows Fish and Wildlife Management Reserve Road 22 E, 7.5km north from Osoyoos; tel: (250) 490-8200. Open daily.

surviving pockets of desert, has 3km of boardwalks and interpretative kiosks. Look for greasewood, rabbit brush, sage, burrowing owls, spadefoot toads, yellow badgers and rattlesnakes. **The Nk'Mip Desert Cultural Centre** is the Okanagan First Nation's own desert interpretation, with self-guided trail walks, reptile encounters, a rattlesnake research centre, traditional village, and craft demonstrations.

There are marshlands and bird sanctuaries. **Osoyoos Oxbows Fish and Wildlife Management Reserve** is all that remains of the natural Okanagan River, with marshes, ponds and open channels providing vital wildlife habitat and birdwatching for rare species like the burrowing owl.

Accommodation and food in Osoyoos

Motels are concentrated along Hwy 3 E (Main St), the spit crossing Osoyoos Lake at the south end of town.

Best Western Sunrise Inn $$ 5506 Main St; tel: (250) 495-4000 or (877) 878-2200; http://bestwesternosoyoos.com, is close to Osoyoos Lake. Continental breakfast is included.

Campomarina Café and Restaurant $$ 5907 Main St; tel: (250) 495-7650; http://campomarina.com; open daily from 1700, has arguably the best Italian food in the South Okanagan.

Observatory B&B $$ #3 Observatory Rd on Anarchist Mountain; tel: (250) 495-6745; www.jacknewton.com/canada.htm. From mid-April to early October, Jack and Alice Newton operate a 3-suite bed and breakfast 500m above the valley, with Jack's expertise in viewing the sky through telescopes a bonus.

PENTICTON

Penticton & Wine Country Visitors Information Centre
553 Railway St; tel: (250) 493-4055 or (800) 663-5052; www.tourismpenticton.com. Open mid-May–early Sep 0800–2000, early Sep–mid-May Mon–Sat 0900–1800, Sun 1000–1700.

Penticton Museum and Archives $
785 Main St; tel: (250) 490-2451; www.penticton.ca/museum. Open Sep–Jun Tue–Sat 1000–1700, Jul–Aug Mon–Sat, same hours.

Sitting between Okanagan Lake and Skaha Lake, Penticton has sandy beaches at both ends of town and mountains behind. The traditional lure – peaches and beaches – is being pre-empted by vineyards, wineries and outdoor recreation.

Look for First Nations artefacts and pioneer memorabilia in the **Penticton Museum and Archives**. **Penticton Art Gallery** along Okanagan Lake has changing exhibits of local and nationally known artists and a Japanese garden behind the gallery.

The screams of summer delight are coming from tyre tubes and rafts floating 7km down the Penticton River Channel from Okanagan Lake to Skaha Lake. Operators set up temporary shop on the south shore of Okanagan Lake; prices include transport back to the starting point.

Skaha Lake is popular for sailing, boating, fishing, sightseeing and swimming off beaches at the north end, near Penticton. **Skaha Bluffs** are a renowned climbing venue.

Penticton Art Gallery $ *199 Marina Way; tel: (250) 493-2928; www.galleries.bc.ca/agso. Open Tue–Fri 1000–1700, Sat–Sun 1200–1700.*

Beaches *Lakeside parks at the north and south ends of Penticton.*

Rafting $ *Channel Float. Summer only.*

Skaha Lake $ *South of Penticton.*

SS *Sicamous* $ *On the beach off Lakeshore Dr; tel: (250) 492-0403 or (866) 492-0403; www.sssicamous.com. Open daily Apr–Oct, Nov–Mar Mon–Fri; call for hours.*

Opposite
O'Keefe Ranch, near Vernon

The 72m restored sternwheeler **SS *Sicamous***, at the Okanagan Inland Marine Heritage Park, sailed Okanagan Lake between 1914 and 1935.

Accommodation and food in Penticton

God's Mountain Estate $$ *4898 Lakeside/Eastside Rd; south of town above Skaha Lake; tel: (250) 490-4800; www.godsmountain.com*, is a whimsical, whitewashed villa perched between vineyards and a sheer drop into Skaha Lake. There is even a roofless room with a hot tub.

Penticton Lakeside Resort Convention Centre & Casino $$ *21 Lakeshore Dr W; tel: (250) 493-8221 or (800) 663-9400; http://rpbhotels. com*, spreads along Okanagan Lake.

Amante Bistro $$$ *483 Main St; tel: (250) 493-1961*, has 'upscale casual global cuisine' and is a popular local stop.

Black Pearl Lounge & Oyster Bar $$$ *1000 W Lakeshore Dr, upstairs at Salty's Beach House; tel: (250) 493-5001; www.saltysbeachhouse.com/ blackpearl*, is the place to have a Martini with fresh oysters.

Naramata Heritage Inn & Spa $$$ *3625 1st St, 19km north of Penticton, east side of Okanagan Lake; tel: (250) 496-6808 or (866) 617-1188; www.naramatainn.com*, is ultimate luxury in a restored heritage hotel.

Theo's Greek Restaurant $$$ *687 Main St; tel: (250) 492-4019 or (866) 861-4214; www.eatsquid.com*, is famed for its Cretan-influenced Greek food and sense of fun.

SUMMERLAND

Summerland Chamber of Economic Development Tourism *15600 Hwy 97, Summerland; tel: (250) 494-2686; www. summerlandchamber.bc.ca*

Pacific Agri-food Research Centre $ *4200 Hwy 97 S (across from Sunoka Beach); tel: (250) 494-7711; call for Gardens' opening hours.*

The small town, complete with town crier, is a major fruit-growing centre, sitting at the junction of three fertile valleys. The name was coined by an early developer who made a fortune subdividing the lakeside, adding irrigation and luring winter-weary farmers from Manitoba and Alberta. The Kettle Valley Steam Railway (*see page 151*) still steams over 11km of track.

Right
Summerland peaches

Summerland Museum $
9521 Wharton St;
tel: (250) 494-9395; www.summerlandmuseum.org.
Open mid-Jun–mid-Sep Tue–Sat 1000–1600, mid-Sep–mid-Jun Wed–Fri 1300–1600, Sat 1000–1600.

Cellar Door Bistro
$$ Sumac Ridge Estate Winery; tel: (250) 494-0451, offers Northwest dishes and picnic items. Open daily May–Dec, Mar–Apr Tue–Sat.

The **Pacific Agri-food Research Centre** opened as Dominion experimental farm in 1914 to develop fruit varieties better suited to the semi-arid Okanagan climate. English-style Ornamental Gardens soon followed, all open to the public.

The hilltop **Sumac Ridge Estate Winery** (*17403 Hwy 97 north of town; tel: (250) 494-0451; www.sumacridge.com, open daily*) is worth a visit just for the valley view – the outstanding wines are a bonus.

If it's sweet and based on fruit, you'll find it at **Summerland Sweets** (*6206 Canyon View Dr; tel: (250) 494-0377 or (800) 577-1277; www.summerlandsweets.com*): candies, syrups, jams, wines and more, all from local orchards. (*They are open most of the year for sampling and tours.*)

The artefacts at the **Summerland Museum** are local, but the KVR, irrigation and fruit-growing history are valley-wide.

VERNON

Tourism Greater Vernon 701 Hwy 97 S; tel: (250) 542-1415 or (800) 665-0795; www.vernontourism.com. Open daily.

Greater Vernon Museum & Archives $ 3009 32nd Ave; tel: (250) 542-3142; www.vernonmuseum.ca. Open Tue–Sat 1000–1700.

Outdoor recreation and original red-brick buildings at affordable rents have turned Vernon into a thriving and surprisingly trendy town at the north end of the Okanagan Valley. The city sits between three lakes, **Kalamalka**, **Okanagan** and **Swan**, all lined with sandy beaches. The acclaimed O'Keefe Ranch (*see page 151*) is northwest.

Greater Vernon Museum & Archives is the best place for agricultural history, including the region's first commercial orchards, planted in 1891 by Lord Aberdeen, later Governor-General of Canada. Downtown Vernon has a large outdoor art gallery with 27 murals depicting the history and culture of the town.

Above
Kalamalka Lake looking towards Vernon

Accommodation and food in Vernon

Best Western Vernon Lodge $$ *3914 32nd St; tel: (250) 545-3385 or (800) 663-9400; http://bestwesternvernonlodge.com,* has a real stream, BX Creek, running through the lobby.

Eclectic Med $$ *2915 30th St; tel: (250) 558-4646,* serves specialities like Moroccan roast lamb by candlelight.

Italian Kitchen Company $$ *2916 30th Ave; tel: (250) 558-7899,* offers unalloyed Italian, with a wine bar.

Suggested tour

Total distance: 160km.

Time: 4 hours to drive; 2–5 days for winery touring.

Links: The Okanagan Valley connects west through the **Cascade Mountains** *(see page 130)* to **Vancouver** *(see page 42),* via Hwy 97C to **Kamloops** *(see page 138)* or via Hwy 97/97A to the **Shuswap Lakes** *(see page 158).*

Route: From **OSOYOOS ❶** , take Hwy 97 north through a mixture of fruit orchards, vegetable fields and vineyards coaxed from the desert by intensive irrigation. Irrigation projects have been so successful that Canada's 'arid' desert has been reduced to a few endangered pockets of cacti and burrowing owls. Continue north to Oliver.

Detour: From the Osoyoos Oxbows Fish and Wildlife Management Reserve, continue east a few hundred metres to the main road and turn left. Follow the eastern shore of the river past some of the newest vineyards and wineries in the Okanagan to **OLIVER** ❷.

From Oliver, the Okanagan Valley narrows toward **Vaseux Lake**, a bird, mountain goat and California bighorn sheep sanctuary. Beyond the lake lies **Okanagan Falls**, now a minor rapid at the south end of Skaha Lake. The road climbs the hillside above the lake before dropping back down to water level at **PENTICTON** ❸, perched between **Skaha Lake** and **Okanagan Lake**.

Detour: From Penticton, follow secondary roads to the east of Okanagan Lake to **Naramata** for additional winery visits.

Continue north on Hwy 97 past **SUMMERLAND** ❹ and **Peachland** to **KELOWNA** ❺ and **VERNON** ❻.

Ratings

Lakes	●●●●●
Mountain scenery	●●●●●
Children	●●●●○
Outdoor activities	●●●●○
Parks	●●●●○
History	●●●○○
Nature	●●●○○
Towns	●●●○○

Shuswap Lakes

There's more than meets the eye – or the main highway – in the Shuswap Lakes region: lakes, long and narrow, more like flat, calm rivers than broad lakes, but also soaring mountains, breathtaking runs of salmon, sandy beaches and eye-popping scenery that is easy to reach and forever beyond the touch of even rough logging roads.

The Shuswap is arguably the most scenic section of the entire 8,047km stretch of Highway 1 between St Johns, Newfoundland and Victoria, BC. Wild, historic, filled with tiny towns, the Shuswap welcomes bald eagles and grizzly bears with the same equanimity it shows to fleets of luxury houseboats and some of the best ice cream on either side of the Rocky Mountains. Highways follow rail lines, which traced lakeshores and river canyons past rugged peaks and foaming waterfalls. If you can't find it in the Shuswap, it may not exist.

CHASE

ⓘ Chase and District Chamber of Commerce Visitor Information Centre
400 Shuswap Ave;
tel: (250) 679-8432;
www.chasechamber.com.
Open daily late May– Aug;
Sep–Jun Mon–Fri.

Ⓟ Niskonlith Lake Provincial Park $
8km northwest from Chase on Niskonlith Lake;
tel: (250) 955-0861;
www.env.gov.bc.ca/bcparks/
explore/parkpgs/niskonli.html

A carpenter from New York who was lucky enough *not* to strike gold in the Cariboo instead found fortune building a timber and cattle town. Chase is better known today for its outdoor recreation opportunities – canoeing down 58km of calm water to Kamloops, fishing, houseboating, hiking, swimming and golf. The town is surrounded by calm pine forests at the head of Little Shuswap Lake. The municipal beach is particularly scenic and popular.

The **Chase & District Museum & Archives**, the former Blessed Sacrament church, is filled to the rafters with the town's first physician's office, the gleaming mahogany bar from an early hotel, an antique barber's chair and everything in between. (**Chase & District Museum & Archives $** *1042 Shuswap Ave; tel: (250) 679-8847; www.chasemuseum.ca. Open mid-May–Sep 1000–1600.*)

Niskonlith Lake Provincial Park has camping, magnificent wildflower displays from May to June and good rainbow-trout fishing year-round.

Accommodation and food in Chase

Simply De Vine Coffee & Bistro $ *809 Shuswap Ave; tel: (250) 679-1186; www.simplydevinecoffee.com*, combines a coffeehouse with an art gallery of local artists' work, including limited-edition prints.

The Edge B&B $$ *340 Juniper St; tel: (250) 679-8791 or (250) 819-8242; www.theedge4fun.com/luxury_bb*, has quiet rooms near Chase Creek and also books ATV and boat rides.

CRAIGELLACHIE

A stone cairn and railway-station-type souvenir shop commemorates the driving of the last spike to complete the Canadian Pacific Railway in 1885 ($ *Hwy 1, east from Sicamous at a place named after a Morayshire, Scotland, peak*).

LITTLE SHUSWAP LAKE

Little Shuswap is the smallest of the Shuswap Lakes, but has the most accessible beaches from Hwy 1 ($ *North and east from Chase to the Adams River and Little River*).

MONTE CREEK

The small town and railway station are best known as the site of an abortive railway robbery by 'Gentleman Bandit' Bill Miner in 1906 that netted around $15. Miner was captured, sentenced to life in

Monte Creek $
Hwy 1, 31km east from Kamloops.

prison, escaped, and eventually landed in a US prison for later robberies. A romantic version of his story surfaced in a 1980s Hollywood film, *The Grey Fox*, filmed in the area.

RODERICK HAIG-BROWN PROVINCIAL PARK & ADAMS RIVER

Roderick Haig-Brown Provincial Park & Adams River
North from Hwy 1 at Squilax; tel: (250) 955-0861; www.env.gov.bc.ca/bcparks/ explore/parkpgs/roderick.html

The park surrounds and protects 11km of the Adams River between Adams Lake and Little Shuswap Lake. The river has one of the heaviest runs of sockeye salmon in the world, well over a million of the bright-red fish fighting their way up the Fraser and North Thompson rivers to spawn every fourth year. (The next major, or dominant, run occurs in 2010.) Off-years merely feature a few hundred thousand salmon, plus attendant bears, eagles, ravens, mink, gulls and other wildlife. Observation decks provide a clear view of spawning with naturalists on hand during the height of the late summer–autumn salmon runs. Hikers have 26km of trails used for wintertime cross-country skiing.

SALMON ARM

Salmon Arm & District Chamber of Commerce Visitor Info Centre *10120 Hudson Ave NE; tel: (250) 832-2230 or (877) 725-6667; www.sachamber.bc.ca*

RJ Haney Heritage Park & Museum $
751 Hwy 97B NE, 4km east from Salmon Arm; tel: (250) 832-5243; www.salmonarmmuseum.org. (with dinner theatre $$). Call for hours.

Rotary Peace Park and Public Wharf *Marine Park Dr at the lake.*

Larch Hills $
Larch Hills Nordic Society, Box 218, Salmon Arm; http://skilarchhills.ca

The commercial centre of the Shuswap Lakes region, Salmon Arm was born as a fruit and dairy town on the rich flood plain of the Salmon River, which enters Shuswap Lake here. The town and the south arm of Shuswap Lake were named 'salmon' for the massive runs of salmon that made their way from the Pacific Ocean each year. The salmon disappeared when faulty railway construction blocked the Fraser River at Hell's Gate (*see page 190*) in 1912, destroying the fish run. Even without the salmon, Salmon Arm is a popular port to hire houseboats to explore the far reaches of Shuswap Lake.

The **RJ Haney Heritage Park & Museum** includes a historic church, farm buildings, schoolhouse, and a rebuilt forest lookout tower with fine views of farmland to Bastion Mountain.

Rotary Peace Park and Public Wharf, a 250m pier and walkway, curves out from the park with excellent views of shorebirds and waterfowl. At least 150 different species of birds nest around the mouth of the Salmon River each spring. Best breeding displays are April to June.

Twenty kilometres east of Salmon Arm is **Larch Hills**, a cross-country ski area with 125km ski trails that include 43km of track.

Accommodation and food in Salmon Arm

Motels line Hwy 1 through town, there is some lakeside lodging, or, to explore Shuswap Lake by water, hire a houseboat:

Barley Station Brewpub $$ *20 Shuswap St S; tel: (250) 832-0999,* serves a variety of its brewed-in-house beers with good-size servings of halibut burgers and chicken wraps.

Ironwood Restaurant at Salmon Arm Golf Club $$ *3641 Hwy 97B S; tel: (250) 832-3773; www.salmonarmgolf.com/ironwoodrestaurant/menu. php,* has a reassuring comfort food menu, from starters to peppercorn steak.

Twin Anchors Houseboats $$ *Tel: (250) 836-2450 or (800) 663-4026; www.twinanchors.com,* is the largest of several local operators.

SEYMOUR ARM

A few old buildings still line the streets, but the restaurant, pub, general store and a small hotel are all at the wharf on Bughouse Bay. The town is accessible by road in summer and by ferry from Sicamous all year. (**Seymour Arm** *North end of Seymour Arm, the northernmost arm of Shuswap Lake, 47km north from Anglemont by logging road.*)

SHUSWAP LAKE

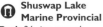

Shuswap Lake $
The lake stretches from Sorento, south to Salmon Arm, east to Sicamous and north to Seymour Arm.

The narrow, H-shaped lake is the most popular houseboating destination in BC, perhaps in Canada. The 1,000km of shoreline tends to be steep with no shoals or reefs, or soft and sandy. Warm summer weather means few storms and no heavy waves. Nineteen species of fish keep anglers busy all year.

SHUSWAP LAKE MARINE PROVINCIAL PARK

Shuswap Lake Marine Provincial Park *26 sites around Shuswap Lake; tel: (250) 955-0861; www.env.gov.bc.ca/ bcparks/explore/parkpgs/ shu_lk_m*

The park has less than 1,000 hectares, but is scattered around 26 sites on the shores of Shuswap Lake. Most of the units are accessible only by water and are extremely popular with summer houseboaters.

Right
Shuswap Lake

David Thompson

The Thompson River is named after David Thompson, Canada's most important and least acknowledged White explorer. In two decades of travel, this North West Company trader logged 90,000km by canoe, foot and horse, mapping four million square kilometres of Western Canada plus major sections of Washington, Idaho, Oregon and Montana in the US.

Along the way, Thompson found the source of the Columbia River at Columbia Lake (1807), pioneered Athabasca Pass through the Rockies (1811) and mapped the entire length of the Columbia River.

Thompson's greatest achievement, travelling the Columbia River to the Pacific Ocean, was also his greatest disappointment. He arrived just in time to find American fur traders, who had sailed from Boston, feverishly building Fort Astoria. Their 1811 post eclipsed British claims to what would become Oregon and Washington and led to the division of Western America along the 49th parallel. Thompson's precise maps were used well into the 20th century, but the explorer, having retired to Montreal, died in poverty.

SICAMOUS

ⓘ Sicamous and District Chamber of Commerce
*110 Finlayson St (near Government Dock);
tel: (250) 836-3313;
www.sicamouschamber.bc.ca.
Open Jul–Aug daily, Mon–Fri in winter 0900–1700.*

ⓘ 'D' Dutchmen Dairy $ *Hwy 1, 1km east from Sicamous;
tel: (250) 836-4304;
www.dutchmendairy.ca.
Open daily 0900–2100.*

ⓘ Shuswap Lake Ferry Service $$
Tel: (250) 836-2200. Service to Seymour Arm all year.

The name comes from a Secwepemc word that means 'narrow' or 'squeezed in the middle', a good name for the tiny narrows between Mara and Shuswap lakes. The one-time railway camp has become a resort town that is especially popular with houseboaters – local operators have more than 300 vessels for hire, no experience required. **'D' Dutchmen Dairy**, a local dairy, has 50 flavours of what aficionados call BC's best commercial ice cream. Even coach tours stop for a cone – highly recommended is the banana and black walnut.

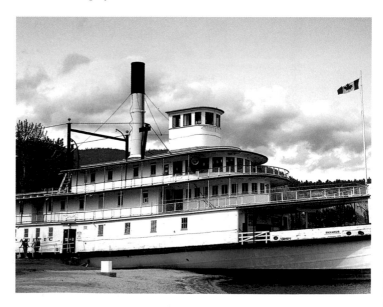

Right
The SS *Sicamous*

For those who don't want to drive their own boats, **Shuswap Lake Ferry Service** offers regular vehicle and passenger ferry (all year) services on the tug, *Stephanie*, between Sicamous and Seymour Arm.

Accommodation and food in Sicamous

Motels and restaurants line Hwy 1 and Hwy 97A from Vernon.

Best Western Sicamous Inn $$ *806 TransCanada Hwy E; tel: (250) 836-4117* or *(800) 485-7698; www.sicamousinn.ca*, is the largest in town, with the best facilities.

YARD CREEK PROVINCIAL PARK

Yard Creek Provincial Park $
*Hwy 1, 15km east from Sicamous;
www.env.gov.bc.ca/bcparks/explore/parkpgs/yard_creek*

This wet, upland forest has excellent birdwatching and pleasant hiking trails beneath hemlock and cedars along a sparkling creek, and is a popular camping and picnic spot.

Suggested tour

Total distance: 160km.

Time: 3 hours to drive; 2–5 days to explore.

Links: Kamloops (*see page 138*) is just west on Hwy 1; **Revelstoke** (*see page 236*) and the **Columbia River** (*see page 230*) just west.

Route: Hwy 1 follows the **South Thompson River** east past **MONTE CREEK ❶**. The high cliffs on the north side of the river have been eroded into an irregular series of columns and buttresses that can take on fantastic shapes in the late afternoon light. The earliest known human remains in BC, a man trapped in a mudflow about 8,000 years ago, were found along **Gore Creek**, near the north end of the bridge at **Pritchard**.

Road and river climb slowly to **CHASE ❷**, a ranching and lumber town on the south shore of Little Shuswap Lake, the west end of a vast lake system that extends north (Adams Lake) and east (Shuswap Lake).

Just east of Chase is a lay-by for **Chase Falls**, an easy and popular short hike. Just beyond is **Squilax Mountain**, home to a herd of Rocky Mountain bighorn sheep which often descend the bluffs on the south side of Hwy 1. The **Jade Mountain Lookout**, 2km east, offers broad views of Little Shuswap Lake. Just beyond is the **North Shuswap (Squilax) Bridge** over the **Little River**. The 4km river between the two Shuswap lakes was once a thriving trade centre for Secwepemc (Shuswap) First Nations. The river is better known today for trout fishing in February, March and October.

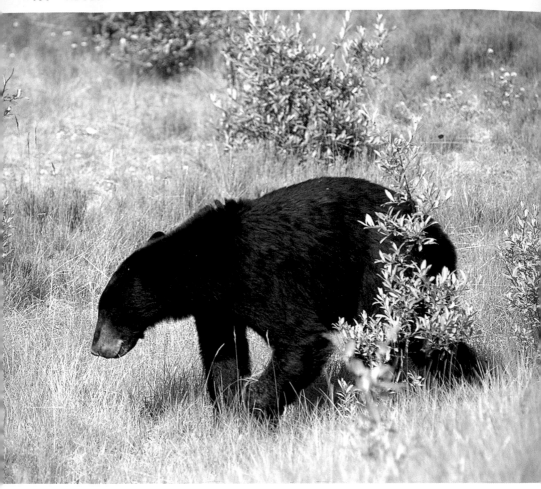

Above
Black bear, a denizen of this area

Quaaout Lodge & Conference Centre $$ *PO Box 1215 Chase, BC; tel: (800) 663-4303 or (250) 679-3090; http://quaaout.com.* Camp in a teepee in summer, an alternative to a hotel room.

Detour: Little Shuswap Lake Road runs east around the north side of Little Shuswap Lake to **Quaaout Lodge & Conference Centre**, a resort and outdoor recreation centre owned by the Squilax/Little Shuswap First Nation. The popular spot is jammed mid-July when the Nation hosts the annual **Squilax Pow-Wow**, drawing attendees from across North America.

Squilax-Anglemont Road runs northeast from the bridge to a turn for the **RODERICK HAIG-BROWN PROVINCIAL PARK ❸** and the Adams River, or continue along the north shore of **SHUSWAP LAKE ❹**.

A 40km paved road links the hamlets of **Lee Creek**, **Scotch Creek**, **Magna Bay** and **Anglemont**, all with campgrounds, bed and breakfasts and cabins for rent. **SEYMOUR ARM ❺** is another 45km north on a good gravel road. Return to Hwy 1 at the Squilax Bridge or take the Shuswap Lake Ferry to Hwy 1 at Sicamous.

Hwy 1 continues east from the bridge to **Squilax**, little more than a general store and hostel, and on to **Sorrento**. The tiny community swells to more than 4,000 in summer when motels, resorts, RV parks and campgrounds fill up. Hwy 1 climbs south from Sorrento.

Also worth visiting

Turn downhill at **Canoe Point Road** to Shuswap Lake at **Sunnybrae Provincial Park, Herald Provincial Park** and **Paradise Point**, one of the few sites in **SHUSWAP LAKE MARINE PROVINCIAL PARK** **6** that can be reached by land. Return to Hwy 1.

The main highway emerges on a hillside high above Shuswap Lake and sweeps down into the rich agricultural valley leading to **SALMON ARM 7**. Continue along the lakeshore past the junction with Hwy 97B, which leads south to **Vernon** and the **Okanagan Valley** (*see page 148*). If the valley seems hazy, blame the lumber mill at Canoe, which still burns sawdust and other waste. The best place to admire Shuswap Lake is the **Shuswap Rest Area**, a picnic area 15km east from Canoe on the north side of Hwy 1.

SICAMOUS 8 is just beyond, straddling the narrow junction of Shuswap Lake and **Mara Lake**, stretching southward. Hwy 97A leads south into the Okanagan Valley. Hwy 9 continues eastward past the 'D' Dutchmen Dairy, a must-taste ice-cream stop, following the **Eagle River** past **YARD CREEK PROVINCIAL PARK 9**. Stop at **CRAIGELLACHIE 10**, where the transcontinental Canadian Pacific Railway was completed in 1885.

Railway journeys

Ratings

Children	●●●●●
Heritage	●●●●●
Railways	●●●●●
Scenery	●●●●●
Mountains	●●●●○
Desert	●●●○○
Food and drink	●●●○○
Forests	●●●○○

No industry was more influential in the development of Southwestern Canada, especially British Columbia, than the railways. Settlers, miners, gold rush prospectors and immigrants raced west to claim land or resources; many took the trains. Returning to developed Eastern Canada were the raw materials from the land, forests, ocean and rivers, along with cultivated crops and cattle. The *quid pro quo* for BC's entry into the Canadian Confederation as a province in 1871 was the assurance from the Canadian Pacific Railway and the Federal government in Ottawa that a transcontinental railway would be built. Fifteen years later, Vancouver was quickly transformed from a backwater to a full-fledged city when the promise was fulfilled and it became the terminus railway hub controlling the overland flow of passengers and freight.

Present-day routes, demarcated by Mile Markers, wind through craggy mountain massifs, crawl through river canyons, traverse deserts and ranchlands, and skirt shimmering lakes.

THE CANADIAN

The Canadian $$
VIA Rail Canada, 1150 Station St, Vancouver; tel: (604) 640-3741 or (888) 842-7245; www.viarail.ca

Route: Jasper–Kamloops–Vancouver

The Canadian is Canada's original transcontinental rail line stretching from Toronto to Vancouver that convinced British Columbia to join the nascent Canadian Confederation in the first place. The complete journey takes three days and four nights, in either direction, but the scenic section between Jasper and Vancouver is scheduled for daylight viewing, with a stop in Kamloops.

The VIA Rail train rides the same rails as the Rocky Mountaineer, but without the frills of steady narration, a printed guide to the route and travel timed to provide the best views of the stunning mountain scenery both westbound and eastbound. But for travellers on a budget, VIA Rail is less expensive.

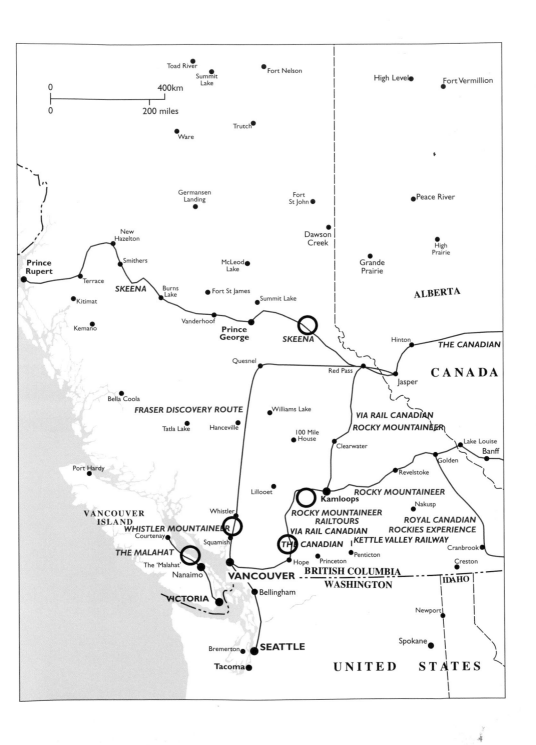

The Malahat

The Malahat $$
VIA Rail Canada, 450
Pandora Ave, Victoria;
tel: (888) 842-7245;
http://www.viarail.ca/trains/
en_trai_roch_vico.html.
Runs once daily in each
direction. There is no
baggage check.

Route: Victoria–Duncan–Nanaimo–Parksville–Courtenay

The Malahat has been running up and down Vancouver Island since the E & N, Esquimalt and Nanaimo Railway, began operations in 1886. It provided the first predictable land link between Victoria and Nanaimo. Service was later extended north to Courtenay. The train is named after The Malahat Ridge, a steep mountain range west of Saanich Inlet that frustrated road builders and limited travel north from Victoria for decades.

Just what the Saanich Indian word 'malahat' means is open to debate. One camp says, 'infested with caterpillars', referring to a year when an infestation of tent caterpillars stripped trees of their leaves. Another camp prefers 'place where one gets bait'.

Either way, *The Malahat* makes scheduled stops on its 4½-hour point-to-point journey, a fine way to venture beyond Duncan's totem poles, Nanaimo's Bastion near the marina and Parksville's swimming beach. The Chemainus murals are worth a stop, a wall-side composite history of First Nations, first settlers, Chinese merchants, lumberjacks, fishers, and the rails.

It's a train remarkable for its engineering and its scenic route. Instead of a locomotive engine, *The Malahat* uses lightweight, self-propelled passenger cars called Budd Cars. Unlimited stopovers are permitted with standard ticketing, but there is no provision to check baggage, so travel light. Bring your own provisions and non-alcoholic beverages, or get them at the Nanaimo stop.

ROCKY MOUNTAINEER

ℹ️ Rocky Mountaineer Vacations $$$ *1755 Cottrell St at Terminal Ave, Vancouver; tel: (604) 606-7245 or (800) 665-7245; www.rockymountaineer.com. Runs Apr–mid-Oct.*

Routes: Yellowhead: Vancouver–Kamloops–Jasper; **Kicking Horse:** Vancouver–Kamloops–Banff–Calgary; **Fraser Discovery:** Whistler–Quesnel–Jasper.

The *Rocky Mountaineer* trains, always photographed against stunning Banff National Park scenery in brochures, live up to their billing as the 'Most Spectacular Train Trip in the World'. Self-adulation aside, the *RM* took a route abandoned by VIA Rail in 1989 and in a decade built a heavily booked tourist train which offers good steward service, food and, above all, stunning scenery. Stewards called Onboard Attendants also provide a narrated history of points of interest en route, interpret natural history, provide books and talk about their personal research of the region.

Expect occasional stops or slow-downs for wildlife spotting. The *RM* waits for commercial traffic, so schedules are not precise, enhancing

Below
The *Rocky Mountaineer* train passes through Banff National Park

the feeling of travelling back in time when nature (rockslide, avalanche or flood) or business (a railway with more priority) could affect railway operations.

GoldLeaf Service, with roomy seats, has much-coveted dome car views, kept clean despite often misty or rainy weather. White linen and flower-vase dining is below the dome car level. RedLeaf Service passengers see the view from closer to ground level and can access landings between cars, a spot favoured by photographers. Meals served at the seat are box lunches of excellent quality. Snacks are non-stop.

The *Rocky Mountaineer* provides a tabloid newspaper upon boarding, a Mile Marker by Mile Marker key to the routes, scenery, historic men, engineering feats, commercial development and ethnology the train passes through. With the tabloid guide, it's impossible to be lost even though the *RM* traverses about 1,000km over track controlled by two railway companies, the Canadian National and Canadian Pacific.

The *RM* trains to Jasper or to Banff follow the same route from Vancouver as far as Kamloops. Leaving Vancouver, the train also leaves urban density behind for the green grass suburbs and lakes east. At Hope, the *RM* travels up the Fraser River Canyon, gathering a collective gasp at gondolas moving across the river almost into the train at Hell's Gate. As the train crisscrosses the Fraser and Thompson River Canyons, who can resist the sight of an occasional raft upriver near Suicide Rapids or the evocatively named Jaws of Death Gorge?

The route turns east to Kamloops where passengers disembark, have dinner, take in the local Two River Junction musical review, and spend the night.

Below
VIA Rail train crossing the North Thompson River at Kamloops

Kamloops–Jasper Along the Yellowhead Route on the second day, the *RM* follows the North Thompson River past Blue River and halts briefly at the lovely Pyramid Falls for photographers. Mountains begin to fill the view, with the Premier and Cariboo Ranges to the west and the Monashees to the east. Eastward, the *RM* approaches the Rockies and enters Mount Robson Provincial Park, with 3,954m Mount Robson ahead. Yellowhead Pass, used by the Grand Trunk Pacific and Canadian Northern Pacific Railways in prior days, is the crossing rejected by the CPR as not southerly enough to protect Canadian interests against American railways. Mount Edith Cavell is on the right as the train approaches Jasper.

Kamloops–Banff The Kicking Horse route to Banff from Kamloops skirts the edge of the Shuswap Lakes and Sicamous' houseboat population. Eighteen kilometres east at Craigellachie, a cairn commemorates the driving of the final spike to inaugurate the transcontinental railway by the CPR in 1885. A graceful bridge crosses the Columbia River to Revelstoke, gateway to Mount Revelstoke and Glacier National Parks. Lights dimmed, the *RM* heads through the arrow-straight 8km-long Connaught Tunnel through Mount MacDonald, built in 1913 to avoid the avalanche disasters constantly plaguing Rogers Pass. There is another pause to admire the 149m-long Stoney Creek Bridge arching 100m over the creek. Having crossed the Columbia Mountains, the route briefly follows the Columbia River south to Golden.

The *RM* moves east up into Yoho National Park to Field along the Kicking Horse River. There is a short train stop at Field, which is surrounded by dramatic golden mountains with hanging glaciers where fossils are rife (*see sidebar on page 266*). The CPR used the town as a stopping point for transcontinental trains and passengers. *RM* passengers stay aboard the train, this being merely a short wait for clearance on the track for the final haul over the Rockies.

Just east of Field are the Lower and Upper Spiral Tunnels, the double figure-8 solution to a too-steep grade up a mountain called the Big Hill. The Lower Spiral through Mount Ogden turns 230 degrees over its 900m, and the 1,001m-long Upper Spiral Tunnel through Cathedral Mountain swivels 250 degrees – before both emerge 15m higher than when the train entered either tunnel. The RM crosses into Alberta and Banff National Park at the Continental Divide, passing close to but not within viewing distance of Lake Louise before heading down the Bow River Valley to the town of Banff.

Passengers not returning by train to Vancouver can continue to Calgary on the *Rocky Mountaineer*.

An exhausting but rewarding nine-hour coach tour (*www. sightseeingtourscanada.ca*) taking in the Icefields Parkway and the TransCanada Hwy to between Banff and Jasper can be booked in either direction, with stops at Athabasca Falls, Sunwapta Falls, Peyto Lake and Lake Louise.

Fraser Discovery: Whistler–Quesnel–Jasper.
As a Whistler Mountaineer route extension or an independent add-on, this route moves north from Whistler into the Cariboo Gold Rush region along the Fraser River, with an overnight stop in Quesnel (*see page 192*). The next morning, the train crosses the Rocky Mountain Trench (*see page 237*) and sights Mount Robson (*see page 262*) as it approaches Jasper.

Below
Royal Hudson steam train

Royal Canadian Pacific $$$ *Tel: (877) 665-3044 or (403) 508-1400; www. cprtours.com. One trip per month, Jul–Sep.*

Royal Canadian Rockies Experience

Five nights of luxury – three on the train – start in Calgary. The train proceeds to stops in Banff, Lake Louise, crosses the Continental Divide, traverses the Spiral Tunnels to Field, and stops for the night by Golden. A coach ride to Kicking Horse Resort, and a gondola up to a vista-filled breakfast is followed by the train's southward journey along the Columbia River Valley to Cranbrook. Eastward is the Continental Divide at Crowsnest Pass and attractions on Alberta's prairies, including a ranch excursion, before returning to the Calgary railway station.

THE SKEENA

The Skeena $$$ *Tel: (888) 842-7245; www.viarail.ca. Runs three times weekly, year-round. Prince George accommodations must be booked independently.*

Route: Jasper–Prince Rupert.

A stop in Prince George is a welcome pause along the 1,160km route that follows the track of the early 20th-century Grand Trunk Pacific Railway. *The Skeena* leaves Jasper National Park heading west over the Yellowhead Pass. West is the land of First Nations and the Gitxsan, preserving the world's largest collection of standing totem poles in the Hazeltons. For the last 225km to Prince Rupert, *The Skeena* threads through its namesake river canyon, often giving credence to the Skeena's meaning as 'a river of mists'.

WHISTLER MOUNTAINEER

Whistler Mountaineer $$$ *Rocky Mountaineer Vacations; tel: (888) 687-7245 or (604) 606-8460; www.whistlermountaineer. com. Operates daily Apr–mid-Oct.*

A three-hour ride between Vancouver and Whistler winds along the spectacular mountain-lined fjords of Howe Sound and forests of the Sea-to-Sky route. The Glacier Dome Coach shows off the scenery, while breakfast is served out of Vancouver, or afternoon tea appears on the return route from Whistler. Both Glacier Dome and Coach Classic passengers can access the Henry Pickering Open Observation Car and are transferred between stations in Vancouver and Whistler.

Other railway rides in BC

British Columbia has a number of lovingly preserved or restored trains still in operation. One of the most beloved is the **Royal Hudson**, now at the West Coast Railway Heritage Park (*see page 180*) in Squamish. The CPR steam locomotive engine No 2860, built in 1940, carries the royal British coat of arms because King George VI and Queen Elizabeth had this class of engine to pull their train on a 1939 Canadian visit, and the king designated its type 'Royal Hudson'.

The **Alberni Pacific Railway** restored 1929 2-8-2 Baldwin Locomotive No 7 pulls a steam train to the McLean Mill National Historic Site on central Vancouver Island in summer (*see page 91*).

BC Railway Museums: Canadian Museum of Rail Travel *Cranbrook* (see **The Crowsnest** *page 250*); **Kwinitsa Railway Station Museum** *Prince Rupert* (see **Prince Rupert** *page 208*); **Prince George Railway and Forestry Museum** *Prince George* (see **Prince George** *page 225*); **Revelstoke Railway Museum** *Revelstoke* (see **Columbia River** *page 236*); **West Coast Railway Heritage Park** *Squamish* (see **Howe Sound & Whistler** *page 180*).

BC Ferries *Tel: (888) 223-3779 or (250) 386-3431; www.bcferries.com. Provides connections with* The Skeena *at Prince Rupert, and Vancouver Island's* The Malahat *to Vancouver.*

A 1924 Shay steam locomotive engine plies the last 16km of track remaining on the **Kettle Valley Steam Railway** (*see page 151*) route through the Okanagan Valley. Even older is the **Fort George Railway** (*see page 224*) 1912 six-tonne Davenport 0-4-0 locomotive engine operating on a narrow-gauge railway on summer weekends in Prince George. A **Fort Steele steam train** ride (*see page 253*) is one of the highlights at Fort Steele Heritage Town in eastern British Columbia. Not far away, alpine Kimberley uses **Kimberley's Underground Mining Railway** (*see page 254*) cars for a scenic 9km train ride to the Sullivan Mine. **Kamloops Heritage Railway** service includes a Bill Miner train robbery on some *Spirit of Kamloops* departures and occasional summer runs of the *Armstrong Explorer* steam train (*see page 140*).

Suggested tours

Time: 4–7 days depending on connections and season.

Links: For major stations, see **Vancouver** (*see page 42*), **Victoria** (*see page 62*), **Kamloops** (*see page 138*), **Jasper** and **Banff** (*see **Alberta Rockies** page 270*), **Prince George** (*see page 222*) and **Prince Rupert** (*see page 206*). **Central Vancouver Island** (*see page 86*) covers stops on *The Malahat*. At Prince Rupert, disembarking *Skeena* passengers can take an Inside Passage **Ferry Voyage** (*see page 113*) to Port Hardy, then a coach to Courtenay to board *The Malahat*.

Route: The railway companies offer combination packages with each other, as well as motorcoach and ferry connections where appropriate. Most tourist rail excursions run from approximately May to September. Regular trains such as VIA Rail's transcontinental *Canadian* run between Vancouver to Toronto with several stops en route.

A cross-province railway excursion provides an excellent introduction to geography before hiring a car and taking to the road. Rail buffs will want to take the train to see the two western provinces.

Coast to Rockies Triangle: Eastern Loop
Fly or drive from **Vancouver** to **Prince George**. The next morning, board **THE SKEENA ❶**, continuing its run to **Jasper**. The following day, board the **ROCKY MOUNTAINEER ❷** on its northern route from **Jasper** to **Kamloops**. Overnight and re-board the Rocky Mountaineer to **Vancouver**.

Interior to Coast: Western Loop
Fly or drive from **Vancouver** to **Prince George**. Board **THE SKEENA ❸** going northwest. At **New Hazelton**, the route begins to follow the curls and curves of the broad, high-walled super-scenic **Skeena River Valley** to **Prince Rupert**. Catch a **BC Ferry** to **Port Hardy** at the north end of **Vancouver Island**. Take a motor coach to **Courtenay** and board the **THE MALAHAT ❹** to **Victoria**. BC Ferries connect **Victoria** and **Vancouver**.

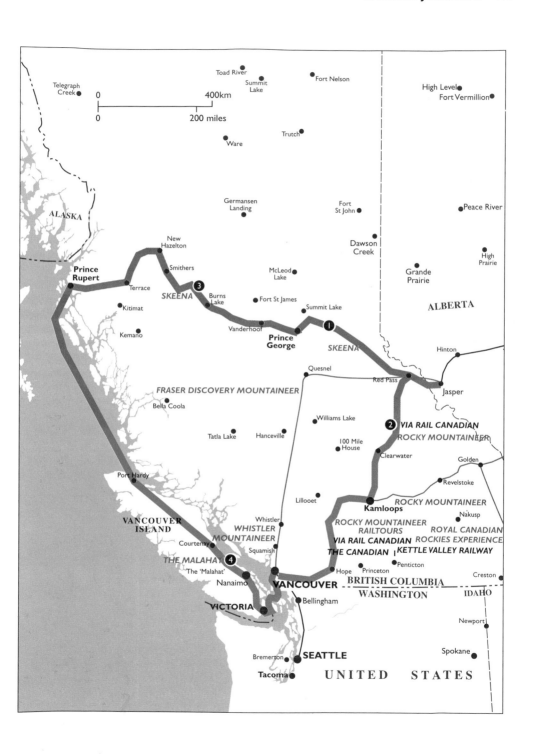

Telegraph Creek ●

Toad River ●

Summit Lake ●

Fort Nelson ●

High Level ●

Fort Vermillion ●

0   400km
0   200 miles

Ware ●

Trutch ●

ALASKA

Germansen Landing ●

Fort St John ●

Peace River ●

New Hazelton ●

High Prairie ●

Prince Rupert

Smithers ●

McLeod Lake ●

Dawson Creek ●

Terrace ●

③

SKEENA

Burns Lake ●

Fort St James ●

Grande Prairie ●

Kitimat ●

Vanderhoof ●

Summit Lake ●

①

ALBERTA

Kemano ●

Prince George

SKEENA

Hinton ●

Quesnel ●

Red Pass ●

FRASER DISCOVERY MOUNTAINEER

Jasper ●

Bella Coola ●

Williams Lake ●

② *VIA RAIL CANADIAN*

ROCKY MOUNTAINEER

Tatla Lake ●

Hanceville ●

100 Mile House ●

Clearwater ●

Golden ●

Port Hardy ●

Revelstoke ●

Lillooet ●

Kamloops ●

ROCKY MOUNTAINEER

Nakusp ●

VANCOUVER ISLAND

Whistler ●

ROCKY MOUNTAINEER RAILTOURS

ROYAL CANADIAN ROCKIES EXPERIENCE

Courtenay ●

WHISTLER MOUNTAINEER

Squamish ●

VIA RAIL CANADIAN

THE CANADIAN

KETTLE VALLEY RAILWAY

THE MALAHAT

'The 'Malahat'

④

Hope ● Princeton ●

Penticton ●

Creston ●

Nanaimo ●

VANCOUVER

BRITISH COLUMBIA

WASHINGTON

IDAHO

VICTORIA

Bellingham ●

Newport ●

Bremerton ●

SEATTLE

Spokane ●

Tacoma ●

UNITED STATES

Howe Sound and Whistler

They call it the Sea-to-Sky Highway, Hwy 99 on most maps. By either name, it curls and twists along the glacier-carved shores of Howe Sound, north from Vancouver, to the base of Whistler Mountain, one of North America's most acclaimed, most visited and most challenging mountain resorts. It is also one of the most scenic drives in southern BC, if not the easiest, that technically extends northeast on Hwy to Lillooet and Hat Creek.

Much of the roadway is carved into the sheer cliffs hugging Howe Sound. Signs warn of rockfalls and avalanche hazard, not lack of lay-bys. The few legal stopping spots provide picture-postcard views of BC Ferries plying the protected waters of the sound with trackless mountains rising barely beyond reach. More mountains rise just behind the highway, some pocked with the remains of enormous mining operations, some never touched and all cut by streams rushing from the sky back to the sea.

The Sea-to-Sky Highway is currently undergoing reconstruction (*tel: (877) 472-3399* or *(604) 775-1100; www.seatoskyhighwayimprovements.ca*) to widen it from two to four lanes and straighten the route, all in anticipation of traffic for the 2010 Olympic and Paralympic Winter Games. It is due to be completed by late 2009. Allow extra time to reach your destination.

Ratings

Coastal scenery	●●●●●
Outdoor activities	●●●●●
Skiing	●●●●●
Children	●●●●○
Nature	●●●●○
Entertainment	●●●○○
Food and drink	●●●○○
Villages	●●●○○

BRACKENDALE EAGLES PROVINCIAL PARK

Brackendale Eagles Provincial Park *Brackendale, Government Rd; www.env.gov.bc.ca/bcparks/explore/parkpgs/brackend.html.* Best eagle viewing Dec–Feb.

The 550ha Eagle Reserve lies along both banks of the Squamish River north of Squamish, providing winter habitat and food for between 2,000 and 3,000 bald eagles in mid-winter. Eagles flock to the river to feed on spawning salmon, a feeding frenzy that usually peaks around Christmas and tapers into mid-February, when the eagles disperse. Eagles can be observed from a riverside walk and observation point on the east bank or from the water with rafting and kayaking operators out of Squamish.

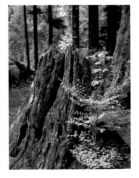

Brackendale Art Gallery *41950 Government Rd; tel: (604) 898-3333; www. brackendaleartgallery. com. Open daily Dec–Jan 1200–1700, weekends 1200–2200.* The gallery spearheaded the eagle reserve creation, hosts annual January eagle counts, and is the information centre.

BRANDYWINE FALLS PROVINCIAL PARK

Centrepiece of the park is Brandywine Falls, a 70m cataract erupting from atop an ancient lava bed. The falls viewpoint is an easy 10-minute walk through the forest. The name may date from an early brandy versus wine bet over the height of the falls by two early railway surveyors – neither had cash, so one bet brandy and the other wine. (**Brandywine Falls Provincial Park** *Hwy 99, 47km north of Squamish; tel: (604) 986-9371; www.env.gov.bc.ca/bcparks/explore/parkpgs/brandywi.html. Open daily.*)

BRITANNIA BEACH

This wide spot in the beach along Howe Sound was once a busy support and supply town for the Britannia Mine, the largest producer of copper in the British Empire between 1930 and 1935. Today, it's a centre for arts and crafts shops, small galleries, a general store and an ever-changing list of restaurants and bistros.

Britannia Beach
Hwy 99, 33km north of Horseshoe Bay.

BC Museum of Mining National Historic Site
$$ Tel: (604) 896-2233 or (800) 896-4044; http://bcmuseumofmining.org. Open daily Spring–mid-Oct 0900–1630; no underground railway in winter; check online for schedule.

During 70 years of operation, the massive Britannia Beach Mine produced more than 600 million kg of copper. The facility closed in 1974 but has re-emerged as the **BC Museum of Mining National Historic Site**, with nearly the entire plant battered but intact. Facilities include mining museum displays in the heritage support buildings just off the highway to the east. Outdoor displays include a 235-tonne 'Super Haul' truck and other massive equipment. Guided tours take visitors inside the 1910 mine underground and through tunnels to see slushers, muckers, drills and one of the last surviving gravity-fed ore concentrators in the world. If the site looks familiar, it probably is. The spooky, rust-stained shop that seems to spill down the mountainside has starred in nearly 100 cinema and TV productions in recent years. The **EPCOR Britannia Mine Water Treatment Plant Discovery Centre** (*www.epcor.ca*) shows visitors and schoolchildren a successful environmental clean-up.

Brohm Lake Interpretive Forest

Brohm Lake Interpretive Forest
Hwy 99, 13km north of Squamish; tel: (604) 898-2100; www.for.gov.bc.ca/dsq/interpForests/interpretive.htm #Brohm_Lake_Interpretive_Forest

There's fishing in the shallow lake and swimming in clear water that seldom warms to more than frigid. Eleven kilometres of trails lead through 400 hectares of forest with spreading views of the **Tantalus Mountain Range** and one of the largest ice fields in North America.

Garibaldi Provincial Park

Garibaldi Provincial Park *East of Hwy 99, Squamish–Whistler; tel: (604) 898-3678; www.env.gov.bc.ca/bcparks/explore/parkpgs/garibald.html. Highway signs indicate trail access. Open daily but weather may make access difficult.*

There is no road access into the wilderness park, but well-developed trail systems lead to five of the most popular camping and hiking areas – **Black Tusk/Garibaldi Lake**, **Cheakamus Lake**, **Diamond Head**, **Singing Pass** and **Wedgemount Lake**. In summer, look for azure-blue lakes, vast meadows of wild flowers, untouched stands of Douglas fir, yellow and red cedar, mountain hemlock and lodgepole pine.

Right
Timber bridge

The park gets heavy snow in winter, but Diamond Head is particularly popular with experienced Nordic skiers and snow campers.

HORSESHOE BAY

ⓘ North Vancouver Chamber of Commerce *102–124 W 1st St, Horseshoe Bay, North Vancouver; tel: (604) 987-4488; www.nvchamber.ca. Open Mon–Fri 1000–1700.*

Named after its shape, this protected bay opens on to the head of Howe Sound, a convenient terminal for service to **Nanaimo** (*see page 90*) on Vancouver Island, as well as more local services from **BC Ferries**. The small town just above the ferry docks offers restaurants, pubs, shopping and a pleasant park with views across the harbour from beneath spreading shade trees. (**BC Ferries** *End of Hwy 1; tel: (250) 386-3431 or (888) 223-3779; www.bcferries.com*)

MURRIN PROVINCIAL PARK

ⓘ Murrin Provincial Park *Hwy 99, 3km north of Britannia Beach; tel: (604) 986-9371; www.env.gov.bc.ca/bcparks/explore/parkpgs/murrin.html*

The park was named after a former general superintendent of the Britannia Beach Mine, who shared his summer cottage, tiny Brown Lake and surrounding trails with mine employees. It is popular for walking, picnicking, swimming, fishing, sunbathing and novice to intermediate rock climbing. More experienced climbers head for **Stawamus Chief** (*see page 181*).

PEMBERTON

ⓘ Pemberton and District Visitor Info Centre *Junction of Hwy 99 and Portage Rd; tel: (604) 894-6175; www.pembertonchamber.com. Open early May–Sep 0900–1700.*

North of Whistler, with Mount Currie as a backdrop, is a town known for potatoes and horse riding, set in a transition zone between sky-capped peaks and the Gold Rush Trail. Pemberton is a lodging alternative to Whistler, with golf, canoeing, kayaking, fishing, mountain-biking, jet boating, paragliding and gorgeous lakes rimmed by glaciers and ice fields. **Joffre Lakes Provincial Park** (*Duffey Lake Rd, off Hwy 99; www.env.gov.bc.ca/bcparks/explore/parkpgs/joffre.html*) has glacier-blue lakes and challenging trails for experienced winter-equipped hikers as well as summer wildflower viewing.

PORTEAU COVE PROVINCIAL PARK

ⓘ Porteau Cove Provincial Park *Hwy 99, 25km north of Horseshoe Bay; tel: (604) 986-9371; www.env.gov.bc.ca/bcparks/explore/parkpgs/porteau*

Once an important ferry landing on Howe Sound, today the cove is known for beachcombing, fishing and scuba diving. Several ships have been scuttled just off the beach north of the pier, marked by buoys, for divers to explore. Call to verify that the park is open.

SHANNON FALLS PROVINCIAL PARK

Shannon Falls Provincial Park
Hwy 99, 7km north of Britannia Beach; tel: (604) 986-9371; www.env.gov.bc.ca/bcparks/explore/parkpgs/shannon

You can hear Shannon Falls, the third highest in BC, from the car park. The 335m cataract is a five-minute walk along a pleasant but well-worn forest trail. Best time to visit is shortly after noon, when the sun highlights the falls dropping from the cliff high above.

SQUAMISH

Tourism Squamish Visitor Information Centre *102-38551 Loggers Lane (Squamish Adventure Centre); tel: (604) 815-4994 or (866) 333-2010; www.tourismsquamish.com*

West Coast Railway Heritage Park $$
3km north on Hwy 99 to Centennial Way, then 1km west at 39645 Government Rd; tel: (604) 898-9336; www.wcra.org/heritage. Open daily 1000–1700.

The word *squamish* means 'Mother of the Winds' in the language of the Coast Salish, the local First Nations group – it's an accurate description of local weather. Daytime sun heats the sheer rock faces surrounding Squamish, creating afternoon updraughts that build into world-championship windsurfing gusts.

Squamish is also a timber town of two minds. Forestry jobs and incomes are slowly declining while hiking, kayaking, cycling, fishing, rock climbing and other outdoor activities are growing in economic importance – and luring a growing number of outsiders who hate nothing so much as the sight of logging trucks, pulp mills and clearcuts. Outdoor recreation is winning, but timber interests are stringing out their measured withdrawal as long and as gracefully as possible.

The **West Coast Railway Heritage Park** is a must-see for rail buffs, with more than four dozen vintage railway carriages and locomotive engines. Highlights include a gleaming 1890 Executive Business Carriage

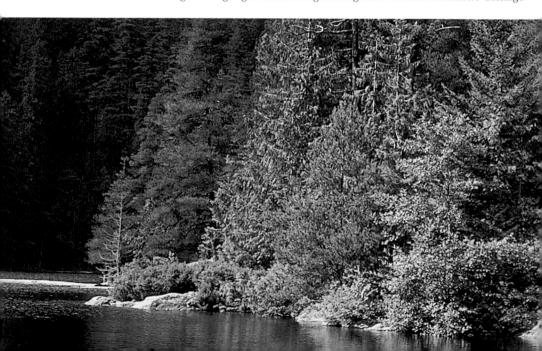

Squamish Estuary
West from Third Ave beyond Vancouver St, just southwest of town.

Squamish Estuary Conservation Society
www.naturesquamish.ca

panelled in hand-rubbed teak, a restored Colonist Car that once carried migrants across the prairies on hard benches, the Royal Hudson, the only surviving steam locomotive engine from the Pacific Great Eastern Railway that once served Howe Sound, and a gargantuan orange snowplough.

Squamish Estuary has excellent birdwatching, especially during the spring and autumn migrations.

Accommodation and food in Squamish

Howe Sound Inn & Brewing Company $$ *37801 Cleveland Ave; tel: (604) 892-2603 or (800) 919-2537; www.howesound.com*, the only brewpub on the Sound. Local fish, seasonal vegetables, rooms upstairs.

STAWAMUS CHIEF PROVINCIAL PARK

Stawamus Chief Provincial Park
Just north of Shannon Falls; tel: (604) 898-3678; www.env.gov.bc.ca/bcparks/ explore/parkpgs/stawamus

Below
Howe Sound

The 652m Chief lures thousands of climbers and hikers every year. There are at least 180 different ascent routes, including a rugged walking trail that gains 550m in just 2.5km. The rocky plug is the second-largest granite monolith in the world after Gibraltar. Best spot to watch rock climbers is from a lay-by on the eastern side of the highway, about 1km north of the park entrance. Some climbing routes are closed March to July for peregrine falcon nesting.

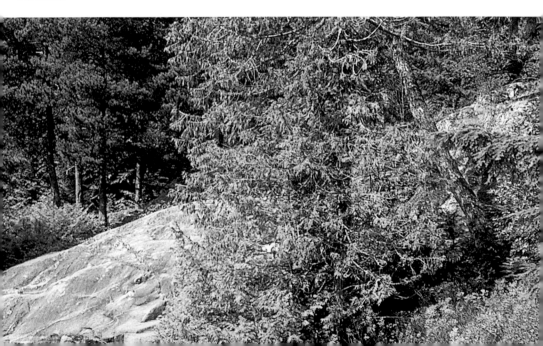

WHISTLER

Tourism Whistler
*4010 Whistler Way,
Whistler, BC V0N 1B4;
tel: (800) 944-7853;
international callers find
country-specific numbers at
www.whistler.com/contact;
general tourism information
at www.whistler.com. Visitor
centre open Mon–Fri
0800–2000, Sat–Sun to
1900.*

**Whistler 2010 Info
Centre** *Whistler Village on
walkway between Brewhouse
and Esquire's Coffee; tel:
(604) 932-2010; open daily
1100–1700. 2010 Olympic
and Paralympic Winter
Games website:
www.vancouver2010.com and
www.whistler.com/olympics*

**Whistler Blackcomb
Ski Resort** *Tel: (604) 904-
8134 or (866) 218-9690;
www.whistlerblackcomb.com
has detailed on-mountain
information for skiing and
summer activities.*

**Whistler Mountaineer
$$$** *Tel: (888) 687-7245 or
(604) 606-8460; www
whistlermountaineer.com,
offer 2-hour North
Vancouver to Whistler deluxe
rail service from late
Apr–mid-Oct.* **Rocky
Mountaineer Vacations**
*'Fraser Discovery Route' rail
tour (tel: (800) 665-7245,
(877) 460-3200 or (604)
606-7245; www.
rockymountaineer.com/our_
trains/rocky_mountaineer/
fraser_discovery_route.aspx)
travels north from Whistler
for an overnight stop in
Quesnel, then goes east to
Jasper National Park in
Alberta mid-May–early Oct.
Routes can be combined.*

Created in the hope of luring the Olympic Winter Games to Canada in the 1960s, Whistler developers scored as the alpine and sliding Nordic events venue for the 2010 Olympiad. North America's most successful mountain development has become just as successful – and just as busy – in summer.

Two mountains, Whistler and Blackcomb, have been trimmed and groomed for just about every mountain activity known to man or estate developer: skiing, golf, hiking, mountain biking, fishing, kayaking, rafting, canoeing, shopping, eating, drinking, mountain climbing, rock climbing, zip lining, dogsledding, rapelling face foward off a rock face and snowboarding are only the beginning. The winter season extends well into summer, thanks to lifts that access high-altitude glaciers. The year-round **Peak to Peak Gondola** travels 4.4km in 11 minutes from Whistler's Roundhouse Lodge to Blackcomb Mountain's Rendezvous Lodge. A few hundred metres below, families with hiking boots and backpacks can watch for deer, marmots, bears and other wildlife amid alpine meadows and open forest.

At the base is Whistler Village, an entirely artificial and hugely successful European-style pedestrian village packed with hotels, restaurants, shops, cafés, clubs, plazas, bridges, creeks, gazebos, musicians and magicians, none of them more than a 10-minute stroll away. Relaxing? No, but Whistler was designed for excitement, glamour and glitz and has very largely succeeded.

The original activity centre was Whistler Village, at the foot of Whistler Mountain. The Village still has more restaurants, more shops and more variety than the rest of the resort. A short walk across the valley is Upper Village, a more expensive, more exclusive and less frenetic enclave surrounding Fairmont Chateau Whistler. Smaller valleys to the south are filled with condominium developments that rely largely on the Village for services and entertainment.

Whistler Museum and Archives $
Tel: (604) 932-2019;
www.whistlermuseum.org

Golf Whistler $$$
boast four highly rated championship designer courses; tel: (800) 944-7853; www.golfwhistler.com

Whistler Blackcomb Mountain Bike Park $$
has 1,200m of vertical run, with more than 200km of lift-served track, two jump parks and three levels of skill centres; tel: (866) 218-9690 or (604) 904-8134; www.whistlerbike.com. Open late May–early Oct; verify online. Downhill bike rental and protective equipment are available at the bike park or in several Whistler Village shops.

Squamish Lil'wat Cultural Centre $
Fitzsimmons Creek, Whistler Village; tel: (604) 898-1822; www.slcc.ca

For activity information in any season, contact the **Tourism Whistler** and the **Whistler Activity and Information Centre** in front of the **TELUS Whistler Conference Centre** and next to the bus loop. Shops near the gondola base in Whistler Village hire out bikes and other equipment in summer and skis, snowboards and snowshoes in winter.

Summer is Whistler's value season, as well as its most active. At the base, five lakes are strung like turquoise and green beads on a necklace, woven together with 35km of paved trails for easy walking, cycling and rollerblading. Six lakeside parks offer broad lawns, sandy beaches and full picnicking facilities with sailing, swimming, windsurfing, boating and fishing.

Both Whistler and Blackcomb lifts remain open (except for short maintenance periods in autumn), with summer skiing on Blackcomb Glacier until July and hiking or mountain biking on Whistler Mountain until mid-October. Other possibilities include golf, climbing, backpacking, jet boating, flightseeing, rafting, horseback riding, heli-biking and ATVs.

Winter is Whistler's *raison d'être*, with 200-plus named runs and 38 lifts. Blackcomb has the longest lift-serviced vertical in North America, 1,609m, as well as the longest uninterrupted fall-line skiing on the continent. Whistler comes a close second, with 1,530m of vertical served by lifts. Then there's Nordic skiing at Whistler Olympic Park on valley golf courses and trails, ice-skating, snow shoeing, sleigh rides, dog-sledging, heli-skiing and guided 'sno-limo' sledge rides.

Even if you're only spending the day at Whistler, check out **Fairmont Chateau Whistler** at the base of Blackcomb Mountain. An enormous castle-like building beneath a copper-green roof manages to feel comfortable, thanks to touches such as Mennonite hooked rugs and quilts and First-Nations-inspired twig furniture. The Great Hall and the Mallard Lounge are best for gawking.

The **Whistler Museum and Archives** makes the best of skiing gear from the 1960s, fishing souvenirs from the 1920s and local logging paraphernalia. The **Squamish Lil'wat Cultural Centre**, configured as a Squamish (First Nation) longhouse and a Lil'wat (First Nation) earthen dwelling with a fire pit, presents the aboriginal history of these two nations: coastal Salish and interior BC Lil'wat. Cedar basket makers, blanket weavers and other artisans demonstrate traditional crafts. Guided or self-guided tours of a museum and the carved and decorated building complex show another side of Whistler.

Outdoor adventure fans of Nordic and cross-country skiing play in the **Callaghan Valley** west of Whistler at **Whistler Blackcomb Ski Resort**.

Accommodation and food in Whistler

Most Whistler hotels, inns and other accommodation have their own booking number, but it's easier to book through **Tourism Whistler** (*tel: (800) 944-7853; www.whistler.com*). Expect two- to three-night

Opposite
Whistler Mountain

minimum stays in high season (Dec–Mar), the lowest rates Sept–Nov and Apr–Jun, and mid-range rates the rest of the year. Find dining details for 90 restaurants, eateries, fast food and coffee spots online at *www.whistler.com/dining*

Roundhouse Lodge $–$$$ *Top of Whistler Mountain; tel: (604) 932-3434*, is dining with a view and a wide choice of types of food and prices, including the most formal, **Steeps**.

Caramba! $$ *12-4314 Main St, Town Plaza; tel: (604) 938-1879; www.caramba-restaurante.com*, is the liveliest Italian restaurant at Whistler.

Thai One On $$ *108-4557 Blackcomb Way, Upper Village; tel: (604) 932-4822*, is a calm refuge with Thai dishes as good as any in Vancouver.

The Wild Wood Café $$ *4-1085 Millar Creek Rd in Function Junction; tel: (604) 905-5066; www.wildwoodrestaurants.ca/htm/cafe.html*, is a place to have a tasty breakfast or lunch with locals.

Araxi Ristorante $$$ *Whistler Village; tel: (604) 932-4540; www.araxi.com*, gets justified raves for its menu, service and wine list.

Fairmont Chateau Whistler $$$ *4599 Chateau Blvd, Upper Village; tel: (604) 938-8000 or (800) 257-7544; http://fairmont.com/whistler*, is one of the Queens of the Mountain.

Pan Pacific Whistler Mountainside $$$ *4320 Sundial Cres, Whistler Village; tel: (604) 905-2999 or (888) 905-9995; www.panpacific.com*, has full-kitchen suites a few steps from both Whistler and Blackcomb gondolas.

Pan Pacific Whistler Village Centre $$$ *4299 Blackcomb Way; (604) 966-5500*, is a sister property.

Residence Inn by Marriott Whistler $$$ *4899 Painted Cliff Rd, Upper Village; tel: (604) 905-3400 or (888) 905-3400; http://whistler-marriott.com*, has a prime ski-in, ski-out location midway up the base of Blackcomb Mountain.

Rimrock Café $$$ *2117 Whistler Rd; tel: (877) 932-5589 or (604) 932 5565; www.rimrockwhistler.com*, is a locals' favourite, specialising in fish and game.

WHISTLER INTERPRETIVE FOREST

Whistler Interpretive Forest
Hwy 99, 9km north of Brandywine Falls Provincial Park across Hwy 99 from Function Junction; tel: (604) 898-2100 or (604) 932-5535; www.for.gov.bc.ca/dsq/ interpForests/interpretive.htm #Whistler_Interpretive_Forest

There's an extensive and well-marked network of hiking and mountain biking trails throughout a working forest between Hwy 99 and Garibaldi Provincial Park. Watch for logging trucks and be sure to park entirely off the roadway. Almost directly across Hwy 99 is **Function Junction**, a catchy name for a perfectly ordinary service area for Whistler Resort. There are bakeries, hardware stores, plumbers, electrical supplies and all the other mechanical and service functions that resorts like to keep out of sight and out of mind.

Suggested tour

Total distance: 120km.

Time: 2–4 hours, depending on traffic.

Links: The Sea-to-Sky Highway connects to **Vancouver** (*see page 42*) to the south, or continue north on Hwy 99 to the **Gold Rush Trail** (*see page 186*) near **Hat Creek Ranch** (*see page 190*).

Route: From Vancouver, take the **Lion's Gate Bridge** north over the First Narrows to **West Vancouver**. Take Hwy 1, the TransCanada Highway, westbound, following signs for the BC Ferries terminal at **HORSESHOE BAY** ❶, Squamish and **WHISTLER**.

Hwy 99, the **Sea-to-Sky Highway** (*see page 176*), continues north, hugging the cliffs above **Howe Sound**. There are a number of scenic lay-bys, none of them accessible northbound. If time permits, continue to **PORTEAU COVE**, north of Horseshoe Bay, and turn back for the views.

The roadway opens up just south of Porteau Cove, a one-time ferry landing for Howe Sound that has become a popular park for beachcombing, fishing, boating and scuba diving. Eight kilometres north is **BRITANNIA BEACH** and the Britannia Mine, once the largest copper producer in the British Empire. Just north is **SHANNON FALLS PROVINCIAL PARK**, with one of the highest waterfalls in BC, a five-minute walk from the car park, and **STAWAMUS CHIEF**, a massive peak that is a favourite with rock climbers.

Continue north to **SQUAMISH** ❷. The road turns inland past **BROHM LAKE**, **BRANDYWINE FALLS PROVINCIAL PARK** and Function Junction, a small service community for **WHISTLER** ❸.

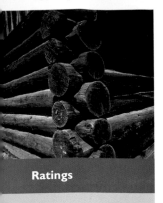

The Gold Rush Trail

Ratings

Historical sights	●●●●●
History	●●●●●
Outdoor activities	●●●●●
Scenery	●●●●●
Children	●●●●○
Museums	●●●●○
Parks	●●●●○
Nature	●●●○○

The Fraser River and Cariboo Gold Rush (1858–1863) transformed BC from a distant source of furs into a major presence on the world stage. Nearly every product, every place, every attitude that is a part of BC today has its roots in Gold Rush. Most of the province's major highways began as Gold Rush trails, many interior towns exist because they once filled Gold Rush needs. Even timber, largest of BC's traditional industries, owes much to the insatiable Gold Rush demand for wooden buildings, railway sleepers and fuel.

Who made the first gold discovery and where may never be known. First Nations traders brought small amounts of gold to the Hudson's Bay Company for years, but the fur-trading giant hid its shining secret, rightly fearing that an influx of gold miners would disrupt its profitable monopoly. The Gold Rush that created the province broke the company.

ALEXANDRA BRIDGE PROVINCIAL PARK

ⓘ Alexandra Bridge Provincial Park $
Hwy 1, 22km north from Yale; tel: (604) 466-8325; www. env.gov.bc.ca/bcparks/explore/ parkpgs/alexandra.html. Access on the park's west side only. Open May–early Oct.

The small park surrounds the 1926 **Alexandra Suspension Bridge** that still spans the Fraser Canyon. An easy walking path follows the original roadbed down to the old bridge and across the foaming river visible through an open grating. The suspension bridge replaces an 1863 bridge at the same spot, which itself replaced a ferry downstream at Spuzzum. The new Alexandra Bridge is 2km north of Spuzzum.

BARKERVILLE HISTORIC TOWN

For most of the 1860s, Barkerville was the biggest town north of San Francisco and west of Chicago. More than 100,000 hopeful miners and hangers-on travelled the Cariboo Wagon Road to Barkerville between 1862 and 1870. They turned what had been a shanty town into a city

Barkerville Historic Town $$ *Hwy 26, 8km east from Wells; tel: (250) 994-3332 or (888) 994-3332; www.barkerville.ca. Open daily mid-May–Sep 0800–2000; costumed interpreters and full services mid-Jun–Sep.*

Kelly & King House B&Bs $$ *Tel: (250) 994-3328; www.kellyhouse.ca, and* **St George Hotel $$** *Tel: (888) 246-7690 or (250) 994-0008; www.stgeorgehotel. bc.ca, offer the only overnight accommodations in a Canadian heritage site.*

so rich and so confident that it very nearly outdid Victoria in a bid to become the capital of BC.

The gold along Williams Creek ran out in little more than a decade, but the town survived to become a thriving heritage site. More than 125 buildings remain, most of them original, if heavily restored. The bordellos and dance halls never reopened, but restaurants, theatres, churches, stores, bakeries, photographers and a Chinese grocery are back in business during the summer months. In winter, the only residents are park wardens and ground squirrels.

For a better sense of just how far Barkerville lies from the rest of BC, walk (or ski in winter) the last 1.6km of the old wagon road west to Richfield with *A Walk to Richfield*, a self-guiding map keyed to 18 historic sites. The map is available at the Barkerville Visitor Centre. Most visitor facilities are in Wells (*tel: (877) 451-9355; www.wellsbc.com*).

BOSTON BAR

Boston Bar *Hwy 1, 11km north from Hell's Gate.*

Local First Nation residents named the settlement after the 'Boston men', or Americans, who swarmed over the gravel bar in search of gold. The town survived as a supply centre for later traffic and is now a lumber town.

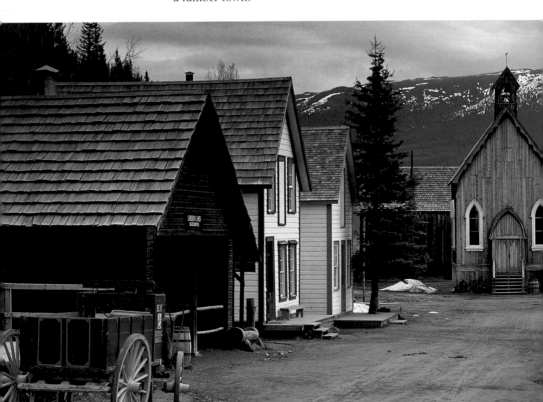

Food in Boston Bar

Elvis Rocks the Canyon Café $–$$ *Trans-Canada Hwy 1; tel: (604) 867-9260; www.travelthecanyon.com/elvisrocksthecanyon.html,* is a family diner serving 1950s-style breakfast and lunch. Comfort food includes a 4-egg omelette Jail House Special, served amidst Elvis Presley memorabilia lining the walls, with occasional Elvis-themed entertainment.

CHASM PROVINCIAL PARK

① Chasm Provincial Park *Hwy 97, 20km northeast from Clinton; tel: (250) 397-2523; www.env.gov.bc.ca/bcparks/explore/parkpgs/chasm.html*

The Painted Chasm is an enormous orange-pink river-carved gash through 120m and 15 million years of lava atop the Fraser Plateau. The 1.5km gorge shows multiple layers of reds and yellows that are especially brilliant in late afternoon sun.

CLINTON

① Village of Clinton *1423 Cariboo Hwy; tel: (250) 459-2261; www.village.clinton.bc.ca*

① Clinton Museum $ *1419 Cariboo Hwy; tel: (250) 459-2442; call for hours.*

Straddling the junction of two wagon roads, Clinton was originally called Junction, a name discarded when Queen Victoria decided her Colonial Secretary needed a town named in his honour. Little has changed in the years since.

Clinton remains a quintessential cowboy town where everyone knows everyone else and if you have to ask directions, you most definitely don't belong. Most of the horseback trail riding, hiking, rafting and other outdoor activities take place at guest ranches scattered in the hills and valleys to the west.

The **Clinton Museum**, set in an 1890s schoolhouse, chronicles the transition from Gold Rush to cowboy country. Most of the people featured in displays can be found at the **Pioneer Cemetery**, just north of the town.

Accommodation and food in Clinton

Many area ranches have discovered that guests are more profitable (and less laborious) than huge cattle herds. The self-proclaimed Guest Ranch Capital of BC has facilities ranging from rustic to ritzy.

Big Bar Guest Ranch $$$ *Tel: (250) 459-2333 or (877) 655-2333; http://bigbarranch.com,* was one of the first and is still among the best for families – horse riding, hiking, river rafting, backcountry camping trips, Nordic skiing and similar activities are geared for beginners.

Moondance Guest Ranch $$$ *Tel: (250) 459-7775 or (888) 459-7775; http://moondanceguestranch.com,* is a luxury ranch with a lodge, private cabins, gourmet meals and wood-fired saunas.

Opposite
Barkerville's main street

COTTONWOOD HOUSE HISTORIC SITE

Another of the roadhouses en route to Barkerville, Cottonwood was a family residence from 1874 to 1951. Period buildings include the main house, root cellar and a double barn, all explained by costumed interpreters (*$ Hwy 26, 28km east from Hwy 97; tel: (250) 992-2071 or (250) 983-6911; http://cottonwoodhouse.ca; open daily late May–early Sep*).

EMORY CREEK PROVINCIAL PARK

Once the site of Emory City, the park commemorates the thousands of Chinese workers who built the Canadian Pacific Railway. When White miners abandoned the town, Chinese workers moved in and reportedly recovered twice as much gold from tailings, the refuse left from mining operations, as the Whites had found in the first pass (*$ Hwy 1, 18km north from Hope; tel: Yale First Nation (604) 863-2443; www.env.gov.bc.ca/ bcparks/explore/parkpgs/emory.html; campgrounds open May–Oct*).

HAT CREEK RANCH

Hat Creek Ranch $$
Hwys 99 & 97 11 km north of Cache Creek; tel: (800) 782-0922; www. hatcreekranch.com and www.tsa.gov.bc.ca/heritage/ historic_sites/hat_creek.htm. Open May–Sep 0900–1700; Jul–Aug to 1800.

Still a working ranch, Hat Creek is the last intact roadhouse on the Cariboo Wagon Road. The 20 heritage buildings include one of the largest barns in BC. Stagecoaches and wagon trains used ranch facilities until automobiles began using the road in 1916. Facilities include trail rides, ranching demonstrations, museum displays and a summer Shuswap First Nation village.

HELL'S GATE

Hell's Gate Airtram $$ *Hwy 1, 10.5km north from Alexandra Bridge Provincial Park, Boston Bar; tel: (604) 867-9277; www.hellsgateairtram.com. Open early Apr–mid-Oct.*

An average of 850,000 cubic metres of water blasts through a space about the width of a city street every second. River rafters run the rapids daily in summer, but only one steamboat, the *Skuzzy*, ever made it upstream, winching through the raging narrows with bolts driven into the rock.

The rapids are more fearsome now. In 1913, a careless Canadian National Railway construction crew touched off a landslide that choked the river and blocked the salmon run for years. Fish ladders built between 1945 and 1946 helped, but modern salmon runs are less than one-third the pre-1913 volume, even in the best of years.

For the best view of the rapids, ride the **Airtram** 152m down and across the canyon to a museum, restaurant, gift shop and viewing

Opposite
Hell's Gate mural

platform. A suspension bridge crosses the river just downstream and railway trains pass every half-hour.

100 MILE HOUSE

ⓘ South Cariboo Visitor Info Centre
422 Cariboo Hwy 97; tel: (250) 395-5353 or (877) 511-5353; www. southcaribootourism.com. Look for the 12m Karhu racing skis that mark the VIC.

This small town is the service centre for the Central Cariboo and a major Nordic skiing area in winter. It began as a Cariboo Road stage stop in the 1860s. Seventy years later, Lord Martin Cecil, Marquis of Exeter, began and headquartered his Emissaries of Divine Light here. The Marsh Wildlife Sanctuary, adjacent to the Visitor Info Centre, has bird identification signage, helpful when spotting bald eagles and sandhill cranes.

108 MILE RANCH

ⓘ South Cariboo Visitor Info Centre
(see 100 Mile House) has information for 108 Mile Ranch and nearby resorts. Find more information online: www.108ranch.com

The one-time roadhouse has become a museum with a collection of heritage buildings moved to the site, including one of the largest log barns in Canada (**$** *Hwy 97, 13km north from 100 Mile House; www. historical.bc.ca/main.html; open late May–early Sep 1000–1700*). The **Hills Health Ranch** (*tel: (250) 791-5225 or (800) 668-2233; www.spabc.com*) has lodging, a spa using rose hips grown on the ranch, plus winter skiing and other activities. There are beaches at 108 and Sepa Lakes.

LILLOOET

ⓘ District of Lillooet Visitor Centre
790 Main St; tel: (250) 256-4289; http://lillooetbc.com. Open daily Jul–Aug 0900–1900; May–Jun and Sep–Oct Tue–Sat 1000–1600.

🏛 Lillooet Museum $
In the Visitor Centre (790 Main St); tel: (250) 256-4308.

🅒 Mile-0-Motel $$
616 Main St; tel: (250) 256-7511 or (888) 766-4530; www.mileomotel.com, is central and comfortable.

The main streets of Lillooet are extraordinarily wide to allow the 20-team ox wagons that worked the Cariboo Wagon Road to turn around. The **Mile Zero Cairn** opposite the Visitor Centre is Mile 0 for the roadhouses and supply points north.

Lillooet Museum shares a former Anglican church with the Visitor Centre and a trove of mining and pioneer artefacts. One self-guiding museum map lists 15 historical sites on Main Street alone; another follows the **Jade Trail** history of First Nations and Chinese railway workers, and sometime miners who excavated the area's jade.

LYTTON

ⓘ Lytton Visitor Centre *400 Fraser St;*
tel: (250) 455-2523;
www.lytton.ca

Lytton lives by logging and **river rafting**. Various companies based where the rivers meet run trips up and down the Fraser and North Thompson rivers that last between a few hours and a few days. Five kilometres of riverfront have also been set aside as a **Gold Panning Recreational Reserve** with hand-panning only. Ask for information and pans at the **Lytton Museum**, which is devoted to the Cariboo Wagon Road and mining history (*$ 425 Fraser St, next to the Visitor Centre; tel: (250) 455-2254; open daily in summer*).

QUESNEL

ⓘ Quesnel & District Chamber of Commerce and Visitor Info Centre *679-B Hwy 97 S; tel: (250) 747-0125; www.quesnelchamber.com or www.northcariboo.com*

ⓗ Heritage Corner *Carson and Front Sts; tel: (250) 992-3522 or (866) 783-7635.*

Quesnel & District Museum & Archives $ *Hwy 97; tel: (250) 992-9580; www.quesnelmuseum.ca. Open daily May–Aug and Sep–Apr Tue–Sat.*

Sitting at the confluence of the Quesnel and Fraser rivers, Quesnel was the last river town before the final overland trek to the gold fields at Barkerville. There's still enough gold in the rivers to keep prospectors busy. Much of the river has been staked, or claimed, but there's public panning at the river junction.

Heritage Corner is the centre of town, marked by massive steamboat and mining machinery in the riverfront park and a scenic 1929 bridge across the Fraser River.

Highlight of the **Quesnel & District Museum & Archives** is an extraordinary collection of area photographs from 1865 onwards; in August, join a narrated Quesnel Pioneer Cemetery Tour.

Accommodation and food in Quesnel

Billy Barker Casino Hotel $$ *308 McLean St; tel: (250) 992-5533 or (888) 992-4255; www.billybarkercasino.com*, looking like a river paddle steamer, offers lodging, gambling and a licensed restaurant.

Cariboo Hotel $$ *254 Front St; tel: (250) 992-2333*, is central.

Talisman Inn $$ *753 Front St; tel: (250) 992-7247 or (800) 663-8090; http://talismaninn.bc.ca*, has refrigerators, microwaves, ovens and high-speed internet connections.

Below
Hell's Gate

YALE

Historic Yale Museum $ *31179 Douglas St; tel: (604) 863-2324; www.tsa.gov.bc.ca/heritage/ historic_sites/yale.htm* and *www.historicyale.ca. Open daily May–mid-Oct 1000–1700.*

St John the Divine Church *Next to the museum.*

A handful of people still live in this Gold Rush boom town, though most of the town centre is a pleasant historic district. The interior of the 1863 Anglican **St John the Divine Church** remains almost unchanged since its consecration. It's the oldest church in BC still on its original foundations. **Yale Museum**, in an 1868 house, is filled with period photographs and exhibits concentrating on the two Sto:lo villages that were once here and Gold Rush memorabilia. Ask about gold panning at **Foreshore Park**, on the riverfront. Costumed interpreters give guided tours in summer, including lantern tours of the pioneer cemetery.

Suggested tour

Total distance: 600km.

Time: Allow 2 days to drive from Hope to Barkerville and a week to explore along the way.

Links: From Hope, Hwy 3 runs east through the **Lower Fraser River Valley** (*see page 122*) to **Vancouver** (*see page 42*) and west to the **Cascades** (*see page 130*) and the **Okanagan Valley** (*see page 148*). From Cache Creek, Hwy 1 leads east to **Kamloops** (*see page 138*) and the **Shuswap Lakes** (*see page 158*). At Quesnel, Hwy 97 continues north to **Prince George** (*see page 222*).

Route: From **Hope** ❶ (*see page 127*), Hwy 1 follows the **Fraser River** north into the **Fraser River Canyon** past EMORY CREEK PROVINCIAL PARK to YALE ❷, as far upriver as First Nations canoes and later steamboats ever travelled. Simon Fraser walked down the Fraser Canyon in 1806, complaining that 'We had to pass where no human being should venture. Yet in those places there is a regular footpath impressed, or rather indented, by frequent travelling upon the very rocks.' Gold discoveries along the Fraser River and further north brought calls for a road through the canyon.

By 1864, Royal Engineers had blasted the **Cariboo Wagon Road** through to Lytton, opening the interior to miners, loggers and settlers. Hwy 1 follows the same route, and usually the same roadbed.

Hwy 1 continues north past **ALEXANDRA BRIDGE PROVINCIAL PARK** ❸ to **HELL'S GATE** ❹, the narrowest spot along an already narrow canyon. The Sto:lo First Nation pegged logs to the canyon wall to create a trail along the sheer rock face. Today, a tram crosses the narrow rapids, a popular summer destination for kayakers and river rafters.

BOSTON BAR ❺ is one of the few Gold Rush towns along the Fraser River to survive into the modern era. Hwy 1 snakes high above the

ⓘ Skihist Provincial Park Tel: (250) 455-2708 or (250) 378-5334; www.env.gov.bc.ca/bcparks/explore/parkpgs/skihist

river towards **Siska**, one of 11 Nlaka'pamux Nation communities along the Fraser Canyon. Several tribal artists are building worldwide reputations carving soapstone from traditional quarries nearby. **Siska Art Gallery and Band Museum** (tel: (250) 455-0072) displays and sells local art as well as CDs by the Siska Halaw Singers and Drummers.

The highway continues along the canyon to **LYTTON** ⑥, at the confluence of the coffee-coloured Fraser and the icy-blue Thompson rivers. The Gold Rush wagon road crosses the river to Hwy 12, climbing through increasingly arid country along the Fraser to **LILLOOET** ⑦ and **HAT CREEK**.

Alternative route to Hat Creek: Continue north on Hwy 1 along the canyon of the **North Thompson River**. **Skihist Provincial Park**, 8km north, has fine views of the semi-desert canyon, rafters floating downstream and trains passing on the opposite bank. Lay-bys 5km north overlook **Little Hell's Gate**, a popular spot to watch salmon leaping upstream in autumn and rafters shooting the same rapids in summer. Most rafts launch just upstream from **Goldpan Provincial Park**.

BC gold rushes

Hollywood epics have cast trappers, farmers and Mounties as the romantic heroes of Western Canada, but gold miners deserve the credit for transforming a frontier into a Province.

The story begins with the Hudson's Bay Company, which occasionally accepted bits of gold from its First Nations trading partners but decided not to publicise its steady trickle of mineral wealth. HBC governors feared the kind of rush that had spelt disaster for established businesses in California, which had been wrecked by the tens of thousands of Argonauts who flooded west in 1849.

In early 1858, the HBC relented and shipped about 20kg of raw gold to the nearest mint, San Francisco. The shipment ignited a frenzy. Every craft that could float sailed north, jammed with miners headed for the Fraser River to Hope and beyond.

More than 30,000 miners flooded through Victoria between May and July 1858, nearly all of them Americans. Business prospered, but Government trembled. British authority was little more than a thin line of HBC trading posts. There was nothing to prevent the unruly American mobs from seizing BC as easily as they had taken California from Mexico a decade before.

Britain replaced HBC commercial control with direct rule in November 1858, throwing the company into a decline from which it never recovered. James Douglas, former chief agent for HBC, then governor of Vancouver Island, became governor of the newly created Crown Colony of British Columbia. He promptly requested British road builders, British troops and British magistrates to enforce British law.

The gambit succeeded. Bewigged justices backed by a handful of soldiers, and eventually the Royal Canadian Mounted Police, kept BC British through waves of miners rushing north to mineral strikes on the Boundary, Similkameen and Thompson rivers, the Okanagan Valley, Cariboo Mountains, the Yukon and the Kootenay Mountains. By the time the dust had settled around the turn of the 20th century, Gold Rush trails had grown into a network of roads, railways and ferry routes that are still recognisable today.

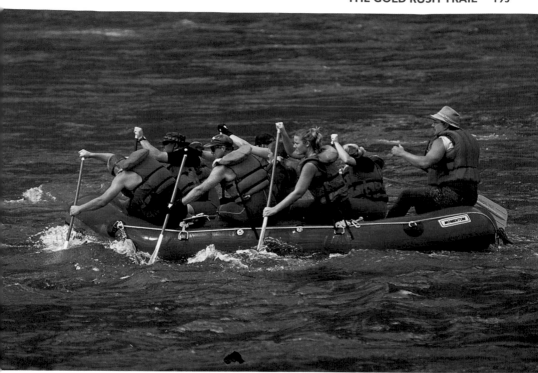

Above
Fraser Canyon

Goldpan Provincial Park *Tel: (250) 455-2708 or (250) 378-5334; www.env.gov.bc.ca/bcparks/ explore/parkpgs/goldpan*

Eleven kilometres north are **Spences Bridge** and **Murray Falls**, tumbling over red cliffs directly into the river. Watch for ospreys nesting in tall trees along the river (the nests look like untidy piles of sticks) and California bighorn sheep on nearby cliffs. In winter, sheep often descend to lick salt from the highway. There are several seasonal ice-cream and fruit stands north of town.

Continuing north, there is a welcome splash of shady green against the desert hills on the way to **Cache Creek** and the junction with Hwy 97. Hwy 1 turns east toward **Kamloops** (*see page 138*). Continue north on Hwy 97 to Hat Creek Ranch.

At **Lillooet,** turn on to Hwy 99, which corkscrews up rolling benchlands along the original wagon road track. Some of the natural terraces are irrigated, others are covered by low black sheets of plastic that shade crops of ginseng. Near the top of the grade is the hamlet of **Pavilion** and the **Pavilion General Store**, one of the oldest buildings in BC still on its original site. The mountain vistas are stunning and the store is the only ice-cream and cold-drink stop in the dusty summer heat.

The Cariboo Wagon Road continues north to **Kelly Lake** and Clinton as Pavilion Mountain Road, a steep gravel road that is passable in good weather. The highway loops east and south into **Marble Canyon**, named after 1,000m cliffs of red and yellow marble, before emerging at **HAT CREEK RANCH** ❽ and Hwy 97.

The hills turn green as the road climbs and conifers replace sagebrush on the way to **CLINTON** ❾, a centre for cattle and guest ranches. Just north is **CHASM PROVINCIAL PARK** ❿, a vast gorge cut through 15 million years of lava eruptions. Increasing rainfall brings denser forests on the way north to **100 MILE HOUSE** ⓫ and **108 MILE RANCH** ⓬, one-time roadhouses named after the distance from Lillooet on the Cariboo Wagon Road.

Further north through the forests is **150 Mile House**, the last stop before **Williams Lake** (*see page 202*) and Hwy 20 west across the Chilcotin to **Bella Coola** (*see page 200*).

Hwy 97 continues north to **Soda Creek**, the terminus of the Cariboo Wagon Road and the head of navigation along 650km of the Upper Fraser River to Quesnel and **Prince George** (*see page 222*). Rails replaced steamboats in the 1920s, but carbon dioxide still bubbles into the creek from calcium carbonate in the streambed.

There are few signs of settlement to the north until **Marguerite Ferry**, an unpowered ferry across the Fraser and the **Fort Alexandria Monument**. The monument marks the end of Alexander Mackenzie's 1793 journey down the Fraser and the site of an 1821 North West Company trading post. Mackenzie turned back on the advice of Dalkeh traders, and returned upstream to **QUESNEL** ⓭ and struck out overland to reach the Pacific Ocean at Bella Coola.

From Quesnel, turn east on Hwy 26 through the mountains to **COTTONWOOD HOUSE HISTORIC SITE** ⓮, another Gold Rush roadhouse. Eleven kilometres east is **Blessing's Grave Historic Park**, surrounding the isolated grave of one of the handful of miners murdered during the hectic years of the Cariboo Gold Rush. Just east is **Wells**, born in a second Cariboo Gold Rush during the 1930s, and **BARKERVILLE** ⓯, the gold mining centre so many thousands of miners laboured so long to reach.

Publican creates backwater

Williams Lake (*see page 202*) missed the Cariboo Gold Rush when a pub owner declined a short-term loan to Cariboo Wagon Road builders. Instead, the contractors built through 150 Mile House, where a more obliging publican made the loan and a quick fortune on the new road traffic. Williams Lake languished until the 1920s when the railway, now known as BC Rail, arrived from Lillooet, on the way north to Prince George.

Cariboo–Chilcotin

Ratings

Mountains	●●●●●
Nature	●●●●●
Outdoor activities	●●●●●
Parks	●●●●●
Scenery	●●●●●
Children	●●●● ○
History	●●●● ○
Wildlife	●●●● ○

This is Canada's answer to the Wild West, a semi-wilderness of forests, mountains, lakes and prairies, a land where towns are small, few and *very* far between. It's a land where ghosts of gold seekers haunt decaying ghost towns that once eclipsed Vancouver, a land where cattle outnumber people and dreams grow as big as the sky is wide.

The Cariboo lies east, dense forests that stretch from the Cariboo Mountains, in eastern BC, to the Fraser River. The Chilcotin is west, a great grassy plain rising from the Fraser and running to the feet of the Coast Range, home to some of the largest cattle ranches on earth and vast tracts that have yet to be properly mapped.

West again is the glacial crest of the Coast Range, dropping precipitously into the Pacific Ocean. It's hard to get here, and once arrived, even harder to forget.

ALEXIS CREEK

🛈 **Cariboo Chilcotin Coast Tourism Association** 204, 350 Barnard St, Williams Lake; tel: (800) 663-5885 or (250) 392-2226; www.landwithoutlimits.com

 Alexis Creek 112km west of Williams Lake.

With nearly 250 people, this Chilcotin metropolis has petrol, an RCMP station, post office, grocery store and a BC Forest Service office.

Accommodation in Alexis Creek

Chilcotin Hotel $ Tel: (250) 394-4400 or (866) 251-4404; http://chilcotinhotel.com, is the only hotel and restaurant in town.

ANAHIM LAKE

This largely First Nations village is the largest in the West Chilcotin and a centre for fishing the Dean and other

AC Christensen General Store
663a Christensen Rd;
tel: (250) 742-3266, is the
best source of area
information and supplies.

nearby rivers. **Anahim Lake Resort** (*$$ Hwy 20; tel: (800) 667-7212 or (250) 742-3242; www.anahimlakeresort.com*) offers fishing, air taxi service, hiking, riding and general relaxation. The renowned July Stampede is authentic, less commercial than July's Calgary Stampede.

BELLA COOLA

❶ **Bella Coola Valley Tourism** Tel: (866) 799-5202 or (250) 799-5202; www.bellacoola.ca.
Cariboo Chilcotin Coast Tourism Association Tel: (800) 663-5885 or (250) 392-2226; www. landwithoutlimits.com

🏛 **Acwsalcta Nuxalk Nation School**
4km east off Hwy 20; tel: (250) 799-5911; www. nuxalknation.org/content/ view/33/71

The Art House $
Hagensborg; contact the Bella Coola Valley Arts Council for hours and directions; tel: (250) 982-2229

Hagensborg Hwy 20, 18km east of Bella Coola.

Sir Alexander Mackenzie Provincial Park and Mackenzie Rock 65km northwest on Dean Channel; www.env.gov.bc.ca/bcparks/ explore/parkpgs/alex_mack. html

Thorsen Creek Petroglyphs Off Hwy 20, east of Bella Coola. Ask for directions at the museum.

Captain George Vancouver sailed up fjord-like North Bentinck Arm to Bella Coola in 1793, just weeks before Alexander Mackenzie walked down the narrow valley to the sea. Norwegian farmers arrived in 1894 to share the valley with Nuxalk (Bella Coola) First Nations. Town and fjord are ringed by sheer mountains, providing endless opportunities for fishing, hiking and outdoor adventure.

The **Acwsalcta Nuxalk Nation School** has some of the finest First Nations artwork on public display along the coast. **The Art House** combines gallery and teahouse in the former Principal's Residence. Works by local artists are for sale and the views are hard to beat.

Bella Coola Valley Museum (*$ 269 Hwy 20; tel: (250) 799-5767; www.bellacoolamuseum.ca, open Jun–mid-Sep Wed–Mon 1000–1700*), in a 19th-century schoolhouse and surveyor's cabin, has Hudson's Bay Company relics and Norwegian goods. Norwegian farmers at **Hagensborg** were Bella Coola's first non-Native residents in modern times. Many of the century-old homes and barns show adze marks produced by the original builders.

Mackenzie Rock in **Sir Alexander Mackenzie Provincial Park** was the final stop of Mackenzie's 1793 trek across Canada. He painted a message in vermillion and bear grease, *Alexander Mackenzie, from Canada, by land, the twenty-second of July, one thousand, seven hundred and ninety-three*, later chiselled into the rock. The **Thorsen Creek Petroglyphs** are dozens of carvings lining rocks along the creek. Engage a Nuxalk First Nation guide for safety.

Accommodation and food in Bella Coola

Bella Coola Valley Inn $$ *441 Mackenzie St; tel: (250) 799-5316 or (888) 799-5316; http://bellacoolavalleyinn.com*, is the best motel in town and the closest to the BC Ferries dock.

Tallheo Cannery Inn $$ *Across the harbour from Bella Coola; tel: (250) 982-2344; http://centralcoastbc.com/tallheocannery*, has 15 rooms.

BULL CANYON PROVINCIAL PARK

This pleasant picnic and camping stop (*$ Hwy 20, 6km west of Alexis Creek; tel: (250) 397-2523; www.env.gov.bc.ca/bcparks/explore/parkpgs/*

bullcan.html, open mid-May–Sep) was a cattle round-up point and the site of a decisive battle between Tsilhqot'in and Secwepemc bands.

CHILANKO FORKS

Chilanko Forks *62km west of Alexis Creek.*

Chilanko Forks is a traditional Chilcotin town with a general store and petrol station. A marsh by the airport access road is good for beaver and muskrat-spotting.

FARWELL CANYON

Farwell Canyon *19km south of Hwy 20 from Riske Creek.*

The Chilcotin River has cut a deep canyon through soft golden cliffs, creating flat-topped hoodoos (columns of rock formed by erosion) capped by sand dunes that shift with the wind.

THE HILL

The Hill *Hwy 20, east of Bella Coola.*

The final barrier to land travel between Bella Coola and the rest of BC was finally breached in 1953 – by local bulldozer operators who were tired of government highway engineers saying a road down the sheer western face of the Coast Range was impossible. Views from the single-track gravel road are stupendous, but there are no verges or lay-bys.

Right
Farwell Canyon

JUNCTION SHEEP RANGE PROVINCIAL PARK

This isolated park with grasslands at the junction of the Fraser and Chilcotin rivers protects one of the world's largest herds of California bighorn sheep, as well as some 40 or so butterfly species and countless birds (\$ *15km south of Hwy 20; www.env.gov.bc.ca/bcparks/explore/parkpgs/junction.html; a high-clearance vehicle is recommended*).

NIMPO LAKE

The Dean on Nimpo *\$\$ 1145 Hwy 20 West; tel: (888) 646-7655 or (250) 742-3332; http://thedeanonnimpo.com*

This 12km lake claims to be BC's floatplane capital for the many daily charter flights to remote rivers and lakes. **The Dean on Nimpo** is the most comfortable of several lake-front fishing resorts.

RISKE CREEK

 Riske Creek 46km
west of Williams Lake.

The tiny farming town of Riske Creek is named after a 19th-century Polish farmer, an early settler in the area.

Accommodation and food in Riske Creek

Chilcotin Lodge $$ *Riske Creek; tel: (250) 659-5646 or (888) 659-5688; www.chilcotinlodge.com,* is a former hunting lodge turned B&B, restaurant and campground, *open May–Dec.*

TATLA LAKE

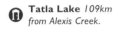 **Tatla Lake** 109km
from Alexis Creek.

Tatla Lake and the 400-resident town provide the halfway point between Williams Lake and Bella Coola. Nordic skiing is a popular winter activity, rivalling lake diving in the summer for appeal.

TS'IL?OS PROVINCIAL PARK

Lakes and streams in this undeveloped wilderness (pronounced 'sigh-loss') produce a quarter of the entire Fraser River salmon run. Apart from two gravel roads off Hwy 20, the only access is by air, boat, horse or foot (*100km south of Hwy 20 from Lees Corner; www.env.gov.bc.ca/bcparks/explore/parkpgs/tsilos*).

TWEEDSMUIR PROVINCIAL PARK

Tweedsmuir is 981,000 hectares of wilderness outside a narrow corridor along Hwy 20. The best easy walks are on the Bella Coola side along the **Atnarko River Spawning Channels**, where grizzly and black bears *always* have the right of way (*$ Headquarters on Hwy 20 east of Bella Coola; www.env.gov.bc.ca/bcparks/explore/parkpgs/tweeds_n* [Tweedsmuir North Provincial Park and Protected Area] and *www.env.gov.bc.ca/bcparks/explore/parkpgs/tweeds_s* [Tweedsmuir South Provincial Park]). Within the park, **Tweedsmuir Park Lodge** (*tel: (877) 982-2407 or (250) 982-2407; www.tweedsmuirparklodge.com*) offer heli-skiing, salmon fishing, grizzly bear viewing and a variety of other activities and a stay in a chalet or cabin.

WILLIAMS LAKE

This is the only real town between Hope and Quesnel, a cowboy city that has expanded into forestry, mining, agriculture and tourism.

**Williams Lake &
District Chamber
of Commerce** *1660 S
Broadway (Hwy 97, south end
of town); tel: (250)
392-5025; www.
williamslakechamber.com*

**Blackbird Bay Bed
& Breakfast $$** *1397
Borland Rd; tel: (250) 392-
7395; www.blackbirdbay.com,
is a bed and breakfast a
short walk from Scout
Island.*

**Fraser Inn Hotel
$$** *285 Donald Rd;
tel: (250) 398-7055, (800)
452-6789 or (888) 311-
8863; www.fraserinn.com, is
the largest hotel in town.*

**Station House
Gallery $**
*1 N Mackenzie Ave
(old BC Rail Station);
tel: (250) 392-6113;
www.stationhousegallery.com.
Open daily.*

**Museum of the Cariboo
Chilcotin $** *113 N 4th Ave;
tel: (250) 392-7404;
www.cowboy-museum.com.
Open Jun–Aug Mon–Sat
1000–1600; Sep–May
1100–1600.*

**Scout Island Nature
Centre** *West end of town,
off Hwy 97 east of city centre;
tel: (250) 398-8532.
Open daily.*

**Xats'ull Heritage
Village $$** *3405 Mountain
House Rd (Hwy 97 37km
north of Williams Lake);
tel: (250) 989-2323;
www.xatsull.com/Businesses/
XatsullHeritageVillage/tabid/
69/Default.aspx*

Williams Lake's public gallery, the **Station House Gallery**, concentrates on BC artists, while the **Museum of the Cariboo Chilcotin** focuses on the ranching, rodeo and cowboy history of the Cariboo–Chilcotin region.

Scout Island Nature Centre, a small marsh, has lakeside walking paths, wildlife watching and a summer nature centre. **Xats'ull Heritage Village**, a short drive from town, has daily cultural tours and programmes and extended educational stays in a pit house or tepee.

Suggested tour

Total distance: 465km.

Time: Allow 10–12 hours to drive; 2–5 days to explore.

Links: From Bella Coola, BC Ferries **Discovery Coast** route (*see page 106*) leads south to **Port Hardy** and **North Vancouver Island** (*see page 96*). From Williams Lake, the **Gold Rush Trail** (*see page 186*) leads north toward **Prince George** (*see page 222*) or south toward **Hope** (*see page 127*).

Route: From **WILLIAMS LAKE ❶**, take Hwy 20 west to the **Fraser River**. The river marks the edge of the **Chilcotin Plateau**, which stretches west towards the **Coast Range**. **Becher's Prairie** forms the eastern section of the plateau, rolling grasslands dotted with boulders deposited by retreating glaciers. Nest boxes on fence posts help attract birds which feast on the clouds of mosquitoes hovering above the thousands of tiny lakes and ponds scattered across the Chilcotin.

The enormous antennae rising from the prairie form part of the Loran-C navigation system. A good gravel road 9.5km west leads 16km south to the fairy-tale hoodoos of Farwell Canyon and **JUNCTION SHEEP RANGE PROVINCIAL PARK ❷**.

Detour: Follow the gravel road along the rolling curves of the almost treeless plain to **FARWELL CANYON ❸** and a wooden bridge over the **Chilcotin River**. There are early First Nations rock paintings on the overhang at the south end of the bridge. Local Tsilhqot'in fishers net salmon from the river in summer and autumn, drying their catch on racks nearby. The road loops 50km back to Hwy 20 at **Lees Corner**.

The bright yellow log buildings 1.5km west of the turn-off are the town of **Riske Creek ❹**. Continue west, following traditional wooden fences snaking along the road. One of the best views across the Chilcotin is from a hilltop rest area 35km west of Chilcotin Lodge and Riske Creek. Another gravel road leads south to **Hanceville**, named after Tom Hance, the first rancher in the area, and **TS'IL?OS PROVINCIAL PARK ❺**.

Hwy 20 continues westwards to **ALEXIS CREEK ❻**, the largest town in eastern Chilcotin, 10km west. **BULL CANYON PROVINCIAL PARK ❼** is another 9km west. Views westward are stunning as the road gradually rises towards **CHILANKO FORKS ❽** and a section of gravel highway.

Continue west towards Tatla Lake. There's a wonderful view across the lake and valley from a hilltop viewpoint 15km west of Chilanko Forks. **Pollywog Marsh**, 12km west of the lay-by, is a pleasant lakeside rest stop. **TATLA LAKE ❾**, another 10km west, is the edge of the Chilcotin Plateau and halfway to Bella Coola. It's a pleasant drive in summer, but don't be taken in by the weather. Winter temperatures regularly hit −50°C with 50kph winds driving blinding blizzards.

Kleena Kleene is well into the slowly rising foothills of the Coast Range. The road continues up towards **NIMPO LAKE ❿**, where the paved road begins again for the benefit of several lakeside fishing lodges.

Just west is the **Dean River**, famed for fine steelhead and trout fishing. A highway marker commemorates the 1864 **Chilcotin War**, when Tsilhqo'tin warriors killed 18 roadbuilders, packers and settlers who were attempting to cut a route from Bute Inlet (opposite Campbell River on Vancouver Island) across the Chilcotin to the Cariboo gold fields. Five of the warriors, including the war chief, were executed by Colonial troops, but the road was abandoned, sparing the Chilcotin from smallpox and land-hungry settlers for a few more years. A provincial enquiry in 1993 granted five posthumous pardons and a memorial was erected.

The paved road disappears again at **ANAHIM LAKE ⓫**, the closest the Chilcotin has to a modern town. Gravel roads lead north along the Dean River, but check locally for conditions before setting out. Beyond the last tyre tracks lies the Nuxalk-Carrier Grease Trail east to the Fraser and west to Bella Coola.

From Anahim Lake, the gravel road climbs into the Coast Range and **TWEEDSMUIR PROVINCIAL PARK ⓬**, which begins at 1,524m **Heckman Pass**. There are good views of the multicoloured **Rainbow Mountains** from the **Tsulko River**, east of the pass. Local First Nations bands mined obsidian from the Rainbows, a string of ancient volcanoes stained red, yellow and purple by mineral deposits.

Alexander Mackenzie and the Grease Trail

North West Company explorer Alexander Mackenzie has gone down in Canadian history as 'The First Man West' for his 1793 overland crossing to the Pacific Ocean at Bella Coola. Mackenzie was the first non-Native to cross North America beyond Mexico and return to tell the tale, but it was hardly a trail-breaking wilderness expedition. Mackenzie and company were shepherded every step of the way along an ancient network of trails and trade routes that spanned the continent. In the Chilcotin, he followed the Great Road, the Nuxalk-Carrier Grease Trail linking coastal Heiltsuk, Kwakwaka'wakw and Nuxalk First Nations with the interior. The trail was named after the Dakelh (or Carrier) peoples who traded oolichan oil for furs, obsidian and other goods from the Coast Range to the Rockies. Part of the rugged route has been reborn as the **Alexander Mackenzie Heritage Trail/Nuxalk-Carrier Grease Trail**, 420km from Quesnel (see *page 192*), on the Fraser River, to Bella Coola. The foot and horse track parallels Hwy 20 from Tweedsmuir Provincial Park at **Burnt Bridge**, 49km east of Bella Coola, to the sea.

Just west of Heckman Pass is a brake check stop at the top of **THE HILL** ⑬. There are no verges, no guardrails and no lay-bys in a 19km stack of single-track, hairpin turns that drops 1,300m to the head of the Bella Coola Valley. Use low gear to creep down (or up) the 18 per cent grade to prevent brakes from overheating and failing.

A hard road surface begins again at the bottom of The Hill, running through dense forest along the Atnarko and Bella Coola rivers. The valley opens and broadens toward the sea. **Hagensborg** still has many of the square-cut, hand-hewn buildings left by early Norwegian settlers a century ago. The town of **BELLA COOLA** ⑭ sits at the mouth of the Bella Coola River, at the head of **North Bentinck Arm**.

Ratings

Children	●●●●●
Nature	●●●●●
Scenery	●●●●●
Art	●●●●○
History	●●●●○
Museums	●●●●○
Outdoor activities	●●●○○
Parks	●●●○○

Prince Rupert

Prince Rupert is BC's most famous transit hub, the city that everyone goes through. Convoys of RVers and independent travellers drive through the city on the way to and from Vancouver Island or the Queen Charlotte Islands via BC Ferries. Schools of sport fishers fly through on the way to isolated lodges up and down the BC coast and along interior mountain rivers. Wildlife observation has begun to rival sport fishing, with whale watching for humpback, grey and orca whales matching bald eagle and black bear spotting in popularity. New cruise-ship facilities have increased summertime day trippers. Even the train passengers who roll through the centre of town are on the way to somewhere else, usually a circular tour that combines rail, motor coach and ferry from Vancouver to Vancouver by way of Vancouver Island and Prince Rupert.

What they're missing is a pleasant, albeit damp, city ensconced in Canada's Northern rainforest that is big enough to offer good food, good coffee and good internet connections but small enough to be walkable and friendly. It's a hub worth exploring.

Getting there

① Tourism Prince Rupert Visitor Info Centre *Atlin Terminal, 100–215 Cow Bay Rd, Prince Rupert, BC V8J 1A2; tel: (800) 667-1994 or (250) 624-5637; www.tourismprincerupert.com*

Weather Bring rain gear. Prince Rupert gets more than twice as much rain as Vancouver, an average of 2,552mm annually.

Air Prince Rupert Airport *(tel: (250) 624-6274; www.ypr.ca)* is on Digby Island, west of downtown, with ferry *(Digby Island Ferry; tel: (250) 624-1027; www.ypr.ca/html/ferry.html)* and bus connections to the city-centre locations. If leaving by air, be sure to check bus schedules as well as airline schedules – miss the bus and you miss the flight.

Floatplane flights use the **Seal Cove Seaplane Base** east from downtown.

BC Ferries *Ferry Terminal at the end of Hwy 16, 2km west of downtown; tel: (877) 223-8778, (250) 386-3431 or (888) 223-3779; http://bcferries.com.* BC Ferries connect with **Port Hardy** *(see page 101)* on Vancouver Island and **Skidegate** *(see page 120)* in the Queen Charlotte Islands.

Alaska Marine Highway Terminal *near the BC Ferries Terminal at the end of Hwy 16; tel: (800) 642-0066; www.dot.state.ak.us/amhs/index.html.* Prince Rupert is the southern terminus of the Alaska State Ferry system, on the Inside Passage/Southeast [Alaska] Route.

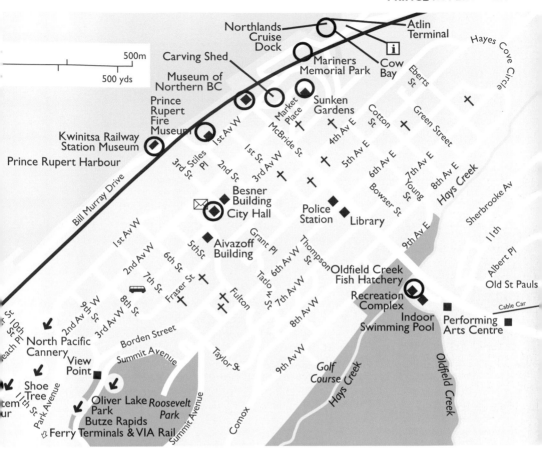

Road *Hwy 16*, the *Yellowhead Highway*, is the only road link with the rest of BC.

VIA Rail *2000 Park Ave; tel: (250) 627-7304 or (888) 842-7245; www.viarail.ca.* The *Skeena* runs between Prince Rupert and Jasper, with an overnight stop in Prince George.

Cruise Ship Ocean-going cruise ships plying between southern BC and Alaska during the summer arrive at **Northlands Cruise Dock**, *Cow Bay*.

Sights

Butze Rapids $
Off Hwy 16, 6km southeast of town.

Butze Rapids

The narrow rapids reverse flow with the tide, with the boiling, foaming water at its most scenic as the tide falls. The Tsimshian called the white foam floating from the rapids *kaien*, which became the name of the island Prince Rupert occupies. The 4.8km Butze Rapids Trail loop leads through old-growth forest to a view of the rapids.

Dreams delayed

Prince Rupert is a speculator's dream become reality, albeit several decades delayed. In the early years of the 20th century, railway baron Charles Hays envisioned a great port and gleaming city amid the rain forests of Northern BC. The commercial lure was location, days closer to Asian markets than Vancouver.

Hays sailed to England to raise capital for his grand project, then capped a successful trip by sailing home aboard the maiden voyage of the grandest ship afloat, the *Titanic*. When the *Titanic* sank, so did Hays' dreams. Planned hotels were never built. Trains rolled into Prince Rupert just in time to hit World War I. The Grand Trunk Pacific Railway came to Prince Rupert, but then disappeared in 1919, absorbed by the Canadian National Railway. Prince Rupert became a halibut fishing port and built freighters and minesweepers deployed in World War II. It took 50 years for transpacific shipping to catch up with Hays' vision. Cargo ships can dock at the railway terminal in Prince Rupert and have their cargoes halfway across the continent by the time competitors dock in Vancouver.

Carving Shed $
One block east from the Museum of Northern BC; tel: (250) 624-3207. Open irregular hours Jun–Aug.

City Hall *3rd Ave W and 3rd St.*

Cow Bay *East from downtown.*

Kwinitsa Railway Station Museum $
Pacific Place, 1st Ave and Bill Murray Drive; tel: (250) 627-1915. Open Jun–Aug daily; 0900–1200, 1300–1700.

Laxspa'aws Pike Island Archaeological & Cultural Tour $$
Tour begins at Atlin Terminal near the Visitor Information Centre; tel: (800) 667-4393 or (250) 624-5645; www.seashorecharters.com. Call to verify tour dates.

Carving Shed
Part of the Museum of Northern BC, the carving shed houses totem poles and other works in wood in the making. Carvers are usually happy to explain the significance of the traditional designs and images.

City Hall
Inside are ordinary municipal offices, but the outside is art deco. To the side is a small plaza with a fine totem pole and statue of city founder Charles Hays.

Cow Bay
Named after cattle that were made to swim ashore to a dairy in 1906, Cow Bay is a combination fishing harbour, trendy haven and repository of historic buildings. Look for coffee shops, bistros, restaurants and boats. Mailboxes, rubbish bins and other surfaces are decorated with Jersey spots and similar bovine motifs.

Kwinitsa Railway Station Museum
The 1911 building was one of 400 identical stations built on the Grand Trunk Pacific Railway line between Prince Rupert and Winnipeg, Manitoba. Only four stations survive; this one was barged 75km down the Skeena River in 1985 and restored as a railway museum.

Laxspa'aws Pike Island Tour
In the late 1700s, ten Tsimshian First Nation bands, around 7,000 people, lived in some 60 villages around present-day Prince Rupert harbour, one of the largest population centres on the entire continent. The village sites are still there, complete with petroglyphs, middens and spectacular island scenery. The 4.5-hour excursion to Pike Island at Venn Passage begins with an orientation and a 40-minute enclosed ferry ride. After an on-island briefing, there is a 1.3km guided walk on

Mariners Memorial Park *North and east from the Museum of Northern BC, overlooking the harbour.*

Museum of Northern BC $ *100 1st Ave W and McBride St; tel: (250) 624-3207; www.museumofnorthernbc. com. Open Mon–Sat 0900–2000, Sun 0900–1700 in summer; Sep–May Mon–Sat 0900–1700.*

North Pacific Cannery $$ *1889 Skeena Dr, Port Edward (11km off Hwy 16 at south end of Kaien Island); tel: (250) 628-3538; http://web. mac.com/andrewcthamilton/ iWeb/NPC/welcome.html*

Oldfield Creek Fish Hatchery *Off Wantage Rd from Hwy 16; tel: (250) 624-6733. Open daily.*

groomed cedar-chip covered forest trails. Three of five 2,000-year-old archaeological village sites, middens, and beaches with canoe run marks and rock carvings are featured, though the flora of the lush rainforest alone is a great introduction to the area.

Mariners Memorial Park

This harbour-front park commemorates a local fishing boat that disappeared in a storm with all hands. Displays include a statue depicting a fisherman at his wheel surrounded by a wall listing local sailors lost at sea and the restored Kazu Maru, a small Japanese fishing boat that drifted from Japan to BC in the 1980s.

Museum of Northern BC

The airy, longhouse-style building is one of the finest museums in BC; the focus is 10,000 years of local Tsimshian history (the name means 'people going into the river of mists'), stretching from islands off Prince Rupert and up the Skeena River as far as Kitselas Canyon above Terrace (*see page 219*), and the museum covers Northwest Coast aboriginal culture in detail. Tribal Councils are heavily involved in museum research and displays, documenting village sites, artefacts and oral histories, creating databases and publishing a variety of scientific and popular books.

North Pacific Cannery

BC's oldest and largest surviving salmon cannery (North Pacific Cannery National Historic Site) is the last of 19 salmon canneries that once dotted the shores of the lower Skeena River. More than 1,200 canneries from Alaska south to Sacramento, California, were part of the trade at its height in the early 20th century before refrigeration and fish farms made fresh salmon fillets an everyday commodity. The 1889 cannery has been restored to show the fishing and canning process as well as daily life a century ago. The setting, a long waterfront boardwalk, docks and employee housing overlooking Inverness Pass, is one of the most scenic in the area. Don't miss the large model railroad collection in the transit shed.

Oldfield Creek Fish Hatchery

Started as a classroom project in the late 1970s when local coho salmon runs had dwindled to just nine spawning fish, the hatchery has played a visible role in increasing the salmon population and heightening local concern over the impact that logging and other human activities can have on fish habitat and survival. Local high-school students convinced city authorities and local service organisations to contribute time, labour and money to build a small salmon hatchery and restore spawning beds in Oldfield Creek. Salmon spawned at Oldfield have been used to re-create runs on other local streams that had lost their entire native fish population.

From mainland Alaska to Yellowstone National Park, the land of the Great Bear is sacred to native peoples and wildlife lovers. Forty-five kilometres northeast of Prince Rupert, 50 north-coast grizzly bears live in an undisturbed ecosystem necessary for their survival, the **Khutzeymateen Grizzly Bear Sanctuary** (*www.env.gov.bc.ca/bcparks/ explore/parkpgs/khutz.html*). Human visitation is severely limited for the animals' protection, with two authorised tour operators permitted several days of boat access to the area from May to September. **Ocean Light II Adventures** (*tel: (604) 328-5339; www.oceanlight2.bc.ca*) sails a 22m ketch; **Sun Chaser Charters** (*tel: (250) 624-5472; www.citytel.net/sunchaser*) has a 12.5m sailing boat.

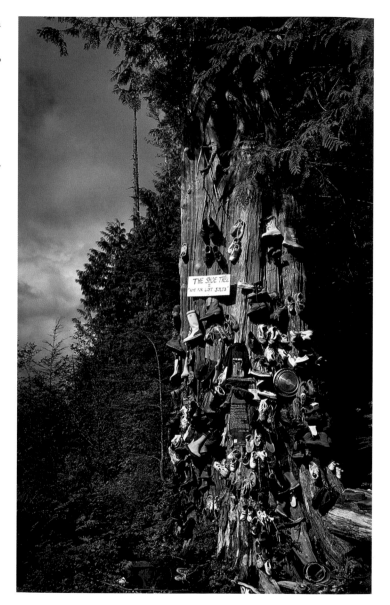

Right
Prince Rupert's shoe tree

Oliver Lake Dwarf Forest $ *Off Hwy 16, 6km south of Prince Rupert.*

Oliver Lake Dwarf Forest

This small park protects a section of muskeg and wet forest that includes carnivorous plants and naturally stunted lodgepole pine trees (visible from boardwalks) that look like carefully tended bonsai specimens.

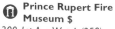

Prince Rupert Fire Museum $
200 1st Ave W; tel: (250) 624-2211; www. princerupertlibrary.ca/fire. Open daily in summer; by appointment in winter.

Shoe Tree *Hwy 16 south of Prince Rupert. Ask for directions at the Info Centre.*

Sunken Gardens *East from the Carving Shed.*

Totem Tour *Self-guided walking tour.*

Prince Rupert Fire Museum
Fire buffs make a pilgrimage just to see Prince Rupert's beautifully restored 1925 REO Speedwagon fire truck. The museum, next to the Prince Rupert Fire Hall, displays dozens of badges, patches and pins donated by visiting firemen from around the world and firefighting equipment dating back to the town's beginnings in 1906.

Shoe Tree
No one is quite sure how or when the *Tree of Lost Soles* got its start, but decades of mis-matched shoes have ended up nailed to the trunk, draped in the branches and piled around the base of this huge tree, although locals say it is unimportant.

Sunken Gardens
The gardens were originally dug as the foundation for a 1920s provincial courthouse that was later moved a few hundred metres closer to town. The site was used for storage during World War II and later turned into a public garden.

Totem Tour
Tsimshian carvers have created dozens of totem poles and other wooden carvings that have been erected around Prince Rupert. The Info Centre and Museum have self-guided tour brochures to totems throughout Kaien Island.

Accommodation and food

Hotels, motels and bed and breakfasts are scattered throughout Prince Rupert.

Cowpuccino's $ *25 Cow Bay Rd, Cow Bay; tel: (250) 627-1395*, specialises in desserts and coffees.

Breaker's Pub $$ *117 George Hills Way, Cow Bay; tel: (250) 624-5990*, is the liveliest waterfront restaurant in town.

Cow Bay Café $$ *205 Cow Bay Rd, Cow Bay; tel: (250) 627-1212*, uses local fish in Trinidadian-inspired dishes.

Eagle Bluff Bed & Breakfast $$ *201 Cow Bay Rd, Cow Bay; tel: (800) 833-1550* or *(250) 627-4955; www.citytel.net/eaglebluff*, has superb harbour views.

Smile's Seafood Café $$ *113 Cow Bay Rd, Cow Bay; tel: (250) 624-3072*, is the oldest and best-known fish restaurant in Prince Rupert.

The Crest Hotel $$$ *222 First Ave W; tel: (250) 624-6771* or *(800) 663-8150; www.cresthotel.bc.ca*, has the best water views and the most expensive hotel rooms in town.

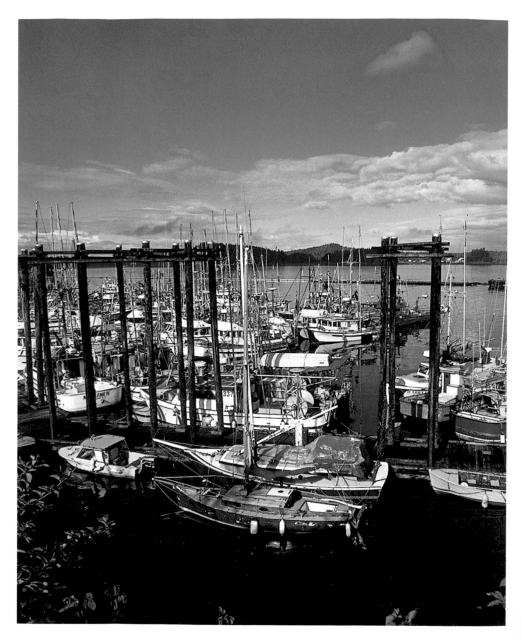

Above
Prince Rupert harbour

Waterfront Restaurant $$$ *222 First Ave W (Crest Hotel); tel: (800) 663-8150 or (250) 624-6771*, is the most elegant eatery on the North Coast. If dinner is too dear, soak up the sunset views for the price of a drink.

Suggested tour

Total distance: 3km.

Time: 2–3 hours on foot.

Route: Prince Rupert's origins as a planned town are still obvious, at least in the downtown area, where streets are wide and boulevards grand. From the **KWINITSA RAILWAY STATION MUSEUM** ❶ on the waterfront, walk up Bill Murray Drive to 1st Avenue W. Turn right, or west (1st Avenue W becomes Stiles Place) and walk one block to 3rd Street and left (south) two blocks to 3rd Avenue W. **CITY HALL** ❷ is on the right with its totems and statue of Prince Rupert founder Charles Hays.

Prince Rupert Archives

100 1st Ave E;
tel: (250) 624-3326;
http://princerupertarchives.ca.
City and regional archives relating to the history and culture of Prince Rupert and the surrounding area.

Follow 3rd Avenue W to the left (east) to McBride Street (Hwy 16). Turn left (north) to another totem. To the right are the **SUNKEN GARDENS** ❸, **CARVING SHED** and **PRINCE RUPERT ARCHIVES**. The **MUSEUM OF NORTHERN BC** ❹ is ahead, next to **MARINERS MEMORIAL PARK**, with the **FIRE MUSEUM** to the left on 1st Avenue W. The Visitor Information Centre and Museum of Northern BC have an excellent self-guided walking-tour brochure with more details and route suggestions. In summer, the museum operates guided walking tours with local tales at historic sites.

FOR
20
km

Ratings

First Nations art	●●●●●
History	●●●●●
Mountains	●●●●●
River scenery	●●●●●
Children	●●●●○
Geology	●●●●○
Outdoor activities	●●●●○
Parks	●●●●○

The Yellowhead Highway: Prince Rupert to Prince George

The northern interior is a vast plateau, in parts heavily forested, elsewhere rolling grasslands, all of it ringed by jumbled mountains that remain impassable outside the occasional river valley twisting towards the Pacific Ocean. To the west lies the Skeena, the 'River of Mists', the mystical, half-seen heartland of a vibrant First Nations enclave and a traditional route through the Coast Range. Further east lie rolling farm and forest lands dotted with lakes and marshes that eventually drain into the mighty Fraser River.

A century of logging, mining and agriculture has wrought visible changes, but the human population is as scattered today as it was when Simon Fraser paddled through on his way south in 1806. Wilderness is seldom more than a few minutes away from even the largest towns, a region where moose, deer, bears, cougars and wolves still roam a largely empty land at will.

EXCHAMSIKS RIVER PROVINCIAL PARK

An old-growth Sitka spruce forest dominates this small park at the confluence of the Exchamsiks and Sitka rivers. It's crowded during salmon season (thanks to excellent fishing), nearly deserted the rest of the year. (**Exchamsiks River Provincial Park** $ *Hwy 16, 56km west of Terrace; tel: (250) 638-8490; www.env. gov.bc.ca/bcparks/explore/ parkpgs/exchamsi.html.*)

Right
Totem in Exchamsiks River Provincial Park

The Yellow Head

Hwy 16, the Yellowhead Highway, is named after an enigmatic French Canadian trapper, Pierre Hatsinaton. Called Tête Jaune, or Yellow Head, for his brilliant blond hair, Hatsinaton popularised a Fur Brigade route along the **Yellowhead Pass** (see page 263) through the Rocky Mountains that still serves as BC's main land link to the east. Local legend says Yellow Head hid a rich cache of furs near **Tête Jaune Cache** (see page 263), just east of today's **Mount Robson Provincial Park** (see page 262), in the early 19th century, but disappeared before he could carry them east. Both man and legend were popularised in the 1939 film classic *Tay John*, directed by Howard O'Haggan.

FORT ST JAMES

ⓘ Fort St James Chamber of Commerce Visitor Information Centre 115 Douglas Ave; tel: (250) 996-7023 or (800) 608-7698; http://fortstjameschamber.com. Open daily.

ⓝ Fort St James National Historic Site $ Hwy 27, 68km north from Hwy 16; tel: (250) 996-7191; www.pc.gc.ca/lhn-nhs/bc/stjames/index_e.asp. Open mid-May–Sep 0900–1700.

Originally called Nak'azdli, the town has been a major Dakelh (Carrier) settlement for millennia. Today, it lives on timber and tourism.

Simon Fraser paddled down Stuart Lake to Nak'azdli in 1806. He liked the 300km string of rivers and lakes so much he dubbed it 'New Caledonia' and established the first White trading post in the territory of the Dakelh, the widest-ranging traders in interior BC. When the Hudson's Bay Company absorbed Fraser's North West Company in 1821, Fort St James became the chief post for the entire mainland area. Despite its importance, the harsh winters, gruelling isolation and monotonous diet of fresh salmon, smoked salmon and dried salmon made Fort St James the Siberia of the North American fur trade.

The HBC post, now **Fort St James National Historic Site**, survived until the 1930s and was later restored to its 1896 appearance. The major buildings are original, including the fur warehouse, fish cache, men's house, officers' quarters and dairy, all staffed by living-history interpreters in period costume. The Visitor Centre museum has excellent displays on the Dakelh people.

GITWANGAK

⊘ Hwys 16 and 37 junction, 50km southwest of New Hazelton.

The town and Gitwangak First Nation name means 'place of rabbits', but you're more likely to see **totem poles** dating back to the 1870s across the street from **St Paul's Anglican Church**, with 400-year-old stained-glass windows and a Norse-style bell tower.

GITWANGAK BATTLE HILL NATIONAL HISTORIC SITE

Gitwangak Battle Hill National Historic Site Hwy 37, 5km north of Hwy 16; tel: (250) 559-8818; www.pc.gc.ca/lhn-nhs/ bc/kitwanga/index_e.asp

This sculpted hill held one of the largest Tsimshian fortifications in the Skeena River region. The cedar plank redoubts and wood palisade protected a Grease Trail leading 100km north to the Nass River. A flaming battle in the early 1800s destroyed the complex. Spiked logs were rolled down from wooden palisades to fight off invaders. A self-guiding walking trail interprets the Gitwangak Battle Hill site.

THE HAZELTONS

ⓘ New Hazelton Visitor Information Centre Hwys 16 and 62, 4070 9th Ave, New Hazelton; tel: (250) 842-6071. Open mid-May–Sep.

There's a trio of towns: **South Hazelton**, a modern highway settlement; **New Hazelton**, an early railway town; and **Hazelton**, the original riverside settlement on the banks of the upper Skeena River. All three are dominated by **Mt Rocher Déboulé**, the mountain of rolling stones, named by early miners who dodged frequent rockfalls.

Bulkley Valley Motel $$ *4444 Hwy 16, New Hazelton; tel: (250) 842-6817, is in the town centre.*

28 Inn $$ *New Hazelton; tel: (250) 842-6006 or (877) 842-2828; www.28inn.com, is the largest motel in the area.*

Below
Fort St James

The Gitxsan call it **Stii Kyo Kin**, 'Stands Alone', the centrepiece of an ancient city-state and still the Gitxsan cultural capital, heart and soul. There are more standing totem poles in the Hazeltons than anywhere else in BC, as well as a 'Hands of History' 113km driving loop to **Kitwanga** – follow the information signs showing a stylised hand with an all-seeing eye in the palm.

Hazelton, a busy river port from the 1860s until the Grand Trunk Pacific Railway arrived in 1912, could be a film set today. The slow-paced town is filled with false-front wooden buildings from the more prosperous Victorian era. The Chamber of Commerce has maps of self-guiding driving and walking tours that begin at the main Visitor Information Centre on Hwy 16.

KISPIOX

Kispiox *Hwy 62, 13km north of Hazelton. Contact* **Kispiox Band** *tel: (877) 842-5911 or (250) 842-7057; www.kispioxadventures.com, for Gitxsan-guided cultural and ecotours and river rafting.*

This ancient (and now tiny) Gitxsan village, at the confluence of the Kispiox and Skeena Rivers, has a magnificent stand of 15 totem poles, including a rare carving of a crying woman, inside a grassy enclosure. Wander into galleries, both open most days in summer, which feature fine local carving and other artworks. Anglers may recognise the name from the world-class salmon and steelhead fishing along the Kispiox River.

'KSAN HISTORICAL VILLAGE

'Ksan Historical Village $ *Hwy 62, 7km north of New Hazelton; tel: (250) 842-5544 or (877) 842-5518; www.ksan.org. Open daily Apr–Sep 0900–1800, shorter hours, Mon–Fri in winter.*

'Ksan is the visible heart of Gitxsan culture. The model village and museum occupy the site of Gitanmaax, a cluster of villages at the junction of the Skeena and Bulkley rivers that has been settled for at least 7,000 years. A short, shady forest walk from the car park leads to seven brightly decorated cedar plank longhouses and a growing collection of totem poles. The buildings house a museum, gift and art shop, carving shed and band meeting rooms.

SMITHERS

ℹ Tourism Smithers
*1411 Court St;
tel: (250) 847-5072 or
(800) 542-6673; www.
tourismsmithers.com*

**🏛 Bulkley Valley
Museum** $ *Hwy 16
and Main St, Central Park
Building; tel: (250) 847-
5322. Call for hours.*

Smithers Art Gallery
*Hwy 16 and Main St;
tel: (250) 847-3898;
http://smithersart.org. Open
Tue–Sat 1200–1600.*

**Babine Mountains
Provincial Park** *Old
Babine Lake Rd;
www.env.gov.bc.ca/bcparks/
explore/parkpgs/babmtn.html*

**Driftwood Canyon
Provincial Park** *Old
Babine Lake Road, 11km
northeast of Smithers;
tel: (250) 638-8490;
www.env.gov.bc.ca/bcparks/
explore/parkpgs/driftwood.html*

**Tyhee Lake Provincial
Park** *On Tyhee Lake, 16km
southeast of Smithers;
tel: (250) 638-8490;
www.env.gov.bc.ca/bcparks/
explore/parkpgs/tyhee.html*

☾ Chez Josette B&B
$$ *4259 McCabe
Road; tel: (250) 847-8743;
www.bcnorth.ca/chezjosette,
is a quiet bed and breakfast
that opens on to hiking
and skiing trails.*

Hudson Bay Lodge $$
*3251 Hwy 16 E; tel: (250)
847-4581 or (800) 663-
5040; www.hudsonbaylodge.
com, is the largest hotel in
the region.*

The economic centre of the Bulkley River Valley, Smithers is dominated by the classic alpine form of **Hudson Bay Mountain**, 2,621m. The faux-Alpine décor along the main street, complete with red-brick pavements and a statue of a man playing an alpenhorn, adds a kitschy touch. Like most interior towns, Smithers grew up on timber, but has diversified into agriculture, sport fishing and outdoor recreation in recent years, including winter alpine and Nordic skiing.

Bulkley Valley Museum highlights development in the Bulkley Valley. Look for local artists and local themes at the **Smithers Art Gallery**.

The 32,000-hectare **Babine Mountains Provincial Park** offers some of central BC's finest hiking through sub-alpine meadows, glacial-fed lakes and rugged peaks, with snowshoeing and cross-country skiing in winter.

Created to protect slate cliffs filled with plant, animal and insect fossils 50 million years old, **Driftwood Canyon Provincial Park** also offers picnicking and pleasant forest walks. The good gravel road continues 35km west to Hwy 16 at Moricetown. Watch for moose and deer, especially early and late in the day.

Tyhee Lake Provincial Park, a small bit of Bulkley River Valley along Tyhee Lake, provides a habitat for a variety of birds, squirrels, beaver, black bears and moose. The beach and campground are popular local getaways.

TERRACE

ⓘ Terrace & District Chamber of Commerce Visitor Centre *4511 Keith Ave; tel: (250) 635-2063 or (800) 499-1637; www. terracechamber.com. Open Mon–Fri 0830–1600, daily 0800–1700 in summer.*

ⓜ Heritage Park Museum $ *4702 Kerby Ave; tel: (250) 635-4546; http:// heritageparkmuseum.com. Open Jun–Aug 1000–1800; winter Mon–Thu 1000–1600.*

House of Sim-Oi-Ghets *Hwy 16 at W Kalum Rd; tel: (250) 638-1629; www. kitsumkalum.bc.ca/hos.html. Open daily in summer. Call for hours.*

George Little House *3100 Kalum St; tel: (250) 638-8887; www.city.terrace. bc.ca/departments/pr-georgelittlehouse.html*

Once a major steamboat stop, Terrace is better known now for salmon and bears. World-record salmon have been caught in the Skeena River within walking distance of the town centre. The municipal emblem, the white Kermode bear, tends to keep to the woods, but is occasionally spotted along quiet side roads.

Eight original log buildings have been collected into an excellent regional museum, **Heritage Park**, filled with period photographs and artefacts. Costumed guides lead tours in summer.

Watch First Nations Nisga'a carvers work in a communal space in the restored 1914 home of Terrace's founder, **George Little House**.

House of Sim-Oi-Ghets, a gallery run by the Kitsumkalum Band, offers the best selection of First Nations arts and crafts in the area.

Accommodation and food in Terrace

Kasiks Wilderness Resort $$ *5720 Hwy 16 W; tel: (250) 615-3521; http://kasiks.ca*, has camping to luxury lodging 60km west of Terrace.

Sandman Inn Terrace $$ *4828 W Hwy 16; tel: (250) 635-9151 or (800) 726-3626; www.sandmanhotels.com/en/hotel/bc/terrace*, is full service close to the city centre.

Sonbadas Steak House $$ *4402 Lakelse Ave; tel: (250) 638-1503*, provides a good selection of Greek dishes plus steaks and seafood.

Suggested tour

Total distance: 740km.

Time: One very long day driving, 3–4 days to explore.

Links: The Yellowhead Highway links with **Prince Rupert** (*see page 206*) and the **Queen Charlotte Islands** (*see page 116*) to the east and the **Gold Rush Trail** (*see page 186*) to the south via Hwy 97.

Route: From **Prince Rupert**, take Hwy 16 south. The highway passes several scenic parks with fishing, hiking and grand vistas before reaching the **Skeena River**. The name means 'river of mists' in the language of the Tsimshian and Gitxsan First Nations. Swirling mists and low-hanging clouds often hide surrounding mountain peaks and the opposite shore.

The Skeena Canyon has been a highway for thousands of years, first for First Nations canoes, then paddlewheel steamboats, the Grand Trunk Pacific Railway and now Hwy 16. Bald eagles, bears, ravens and other predators/scavengers are common sights. The best river viewpoints are **Basalt Creek**, about 20km east from the first sight of the river, and **Telegraph Point**, 33km beyond.

Opposite Bulkley River

Above
Terrace Heritage Park

The highway passes **TERRACE ❶**, named after the natural terraces along the Skeena River, a major steamboat stop until the GTP arrived in 1912. The small timber and sport fishing town is a good place to see **Kermode** (ker-mode-ee) bears, a subspecies of black bear that is honey-blond-white in colour. The Kermode is a spirit bear in local First Nations lore, given to punishing evil-doers and rescuing the deserving in distress. These days, it's the Kermode that needs help as logging and other human activities cut into its wild habitat.

From Terrace, the road swings north past **Usk**, a steamboat town that has all but disappeared, to **GITWAN̲GAK ❷**, with a turn to **GITWAN̲GAK BATTLE HILL NATIONAL HISTORIC SITE ❸**, and continues on to the three **HAZELTONS ❹**.

Detour to Kispiox: From the Visitor InfoCentre at New Hazelton, take Hwy 62 left (north) to cross over the single-track **Hagwilget Bridge**, hanging 76m above the boiling Bulkley River. The Git̲xsan and Wet'suwet'en First Nations built a bridge of wooden poles lashed together with cedar bark rope over the gorge at the same site.

The highway crosses gently rolling pastures to '**KSAN HISTORICAL VILLAGE ❺** and on to Hazelton, the head of navigation on the Skeena River. The road narrows and follows the Kispiox River north to the Git̲xsan village of **KISPIOX ❻**. Return to Hwy 16.

The highway leaves the Skeena just west of the Hazeltons to follow the **Bulkley River** southeastwards. The river is squeezed to just 15m at **Moricetown**, which has been a traditional Wet'suwet'en fishing spot for at least the last 4,000 years. The small town is named after an early missionary priest.

SMITHERS ❼ is the largest town in the Bulkley Valley, laced by several small rivers and streams. The Yellowhead climbs out of the valley to **Houston**, a sport fishing town that proudly proclaims its number-one money spinner with an 18m fly-fishing rod cocked above the **Houston Chamber of Commerce** (*3289 Hwy 16; tel: (250) 845-7640; www.houstonchamber.ca*). The highest point on the entire Yellowhead Hwy is 40km east at **Six Mile Summit**, 1,423m. Downhill lies the **Lake Country**, filled with lakes, meadows and second-growth forests.

Detour: From a turn-off just west of **Vanderhoof**, take Hwy 27 north for 68km to **Stuart Lake** and **FORT ST JAMES**, the former HBC post. Return to Hwy 16.

The highway rolls east through **Vanderhoof**, a logging town that has turned to ranching. The geographic centre of BC is 10km east, marked by a roadside cairn. The highway continues east through rolling forests to **Prince George** (*see page 222*).

Prince George

Ratings

Children	●●●●
Geology	●●●●
History	●●●●
Parks	●●●●
Mountains	●●●
Outdoor activities	●●●
Scenery	●●●
Wildlife	●●

Alexander Mackenzie paddled past the junction of the Fraser and Nechako rivers in 1793 without even noticing the massive confluence in a heavy morning mist. Simon Fraser had better visibility in 1807; he stopped long enough to build a small trading post on the flat bowl below looming cliffs cut by the two rivers. And that was the last most of the outside world heard of the place until the Grand Trunk Pacific Railway arrived on the way west to Prince Rupert.

Almost a century later, Prince George remains an isolated, if vital, crossroads. Roads, railways and air routes have replaced river conduits for people, goods and information, but road and rail seldom stray far from river routes in BC's rugged interior. A smoothly undulating carpet of forest cloaks a rolling plateau dotted with lakes and laced by sparkling rivers tumbling towards the Pacific.

Getting there

ⓘ Tourism Prince George Visitor Information Centre *1300 1st Ave; tel: (250) 562-3700 or (800) 668-7646; www.tourismpg.com. Open Mon–Fri 0830–1700, can book BC Ferries and VIA Rail.*

Northern BC Tourism *1274 5th Ave, Prince George; tel: (250) 561-0432 or (800) 663-8843; http://nbctourism.com*

Prince George is the primary transportation hub for northern BC. Air, rail and road routes headed north–south and east–west all cross at the junction of the Fraser and Nechako rivers.

Air

Prince George Airport (YXS) *4141 Airport Rd, 10km south of downtown off Hwy 97 S; tel: (250) 963-2400; http://pgairport.ca/yxs.* Prince George is one of the busiest inland airports in BC, with frequent service from Vancouver and other major cities around the western side of North America. A shuttle bus and taxis serve downtown, or hire a car at the airport.

Rail

VIA Rail *1300 1st Ave; tel: (888) 842-7245; www.viarail.ca,* runs west to Prince Rupert and east to Jasper, Alberta, aboard the **Skeena**, which runs through the Skeena River Valley and through the Yellowhead Pass. The entire 1,160km trip takes two days.

Road

Prince George sits at the junction of Hwys 97/16, two of Western Canada's most important highway corridors. Hwy 97 runs south to Hwy 1 and Vancouver and north to Dawson Creek, Fort Nelson and into Alaska. Hwy 16, the Yellowhead Highway, runs west to Prince Rupert (and, via a ferry, to the Queen Charlotte Islands) and east through the Yellowhead Pass to Jasper, Alberta, and on to Eastern Canada.

Sights

Connaught Hill Park *Centre of town, off Queensway St, vehicles prohibited in winter. Open mid-May–mid-Oct.*

Connaught Hill Park

This volcanic plug overlooking downtown has become one of the most popular parks in Prince George for its easy walking trails and 360-degree views. The park is most crowded at noontime in good weather when workers from city offices flock to the summit for an outdoor lunch and to admire floral displays.

Cottonwood Island Nature Park *Off River Road, 2km northeast from downtown.*

Fort George Park $ *17th Ave and Taylor Dr.*

Fort George Railway $ *Fort George Park. Operates weekends and holidays May–Sep.*

The Exploration Place Science Centre and Museum $$ *Fort George Park, 333 Becott Pl; tel: (250) 562-1612 or (866) 562-1612; www.theexplorationplace.com. Open daily late May–Oct 1000–1700; Nov–Apr Wed–Sun.*

Cottonwood Island Nature Park

Look for a variety of migratory birds in this 32-hectare wildlife reserve skirting the Nechako River just west of its confluence with the Fraser.

Fort George Park

Fort George was the name Simon Fraser gave to the small post he built over the winter of 1807–8, located on today's riverside park site. The park also holds the traditional burial grounds for the Lheidle T'enneh First Nations. Nearby South Fort George was the head of navigation on the upper Fraser River where paddlewheel steamboats unloaded cargo and passengers well into the 20th century.

The park has become a well-loved family playground, in large part thanks to the **Fort George Railway**. The narrow-gauge railway opened in 1978, but the 1912 six-tonne Davenport 0-4-0 Locomotive engine, a dinky in railway terminology, was used to build the Grand Trunk Pacific Railway Line. The station is modelled on one of GTP's standard designs that was used for more than 200 stations across BC and Alberta. Most of the original stations were built on the north side of the tracks in order to maximise sun and warmth on the south-facing platforms and block frigid winds from the north and west.

Also in the park is **The Exploration Place Science Centre and Museum**, a hands-on experience for children who can be members of a paddleboat crew, have their photo taken with a *Tyrannosaurus Rex* skull model, play sports in a sports hall of fame, sit inside a jail cell, and watch insects and other creatures dine on custom-prepared goodies from a sophisticated menu that would do justice to any fine restaurant.

Below
Fort George Railway

Heritage River Trail System

An 11km loop of broad gravel trails follows the Nechako River from the Cameron Street Bridge east around Cottonwood Island Nature Park, past the confluence of the Fraser River and south to Fort George Park. The trail turns inland along Hudson Bay Slough, then cuts through town to Carrie Jane Gray Park. Follow Camey Street N back to the Cameron Street overpass.

Huble Homestead – Giscome Portage Regional Park

A vital roadhouse in the early years of the 20th century, the Homestead stood at the south end of the Giscome Portage, which connects the Arctic and Pacific watersheds over the Continental Divide. The homestead declined in importance after a 1919 road cut the portage out of commercial transportation routes. Costumed interpreters provide guided tours of the homestead, general store and blacksmithy.

Moose Viewing Area

A forest fire in 1961 turned Grover Forest into rolling meadows filled with the kind of tender new growth that moose love to browse. The best views are from a raised platform an easy five-minute walk from the car park.

Native Art Gallery

This is the best (but not the only) selection of both Interior and Coastal First Nations art products in the area.

Prince George Railway and Forestry Museum

Heaven for steam buffs, the museum celebrates the history of the GTP (now part of the Canadian National Railway) and the Pacific Great Eastern (now part of BC Rail). The site shows a restored section house, GTP's 1914 Penny Station, a railway worker's bunkhouse, an early BC Telephone building and a heritage fire hall. Rolling stock includes a 1903 Russell snowplough and a 1913 CPR steam crane, both in working order.

Sugarbowl-Grizzly Den Provincial Park & Protected Area

Hikers can park by trailheads along Hwy 16, to enter a wilderness area where caribou and grizzly bears are protected amid forests of old-growth interior cedar-hemlock. Cross-country skiers use the same ungroomed trails in winter. In 1862, one group of Overlanders suffered hypothermia, overturned canoes, loss of provisions and death when they encountered the Grand Canyon of the Fraser here on their attempt to use the river to reach Quesnel.

Tabor Mountain Ski Resort

Tabor Mountain is Prince George's own ski hill, a 244m vertical drop with lifts, a busy day lodge, and organised mountain biking in summer.

ⓘ Two Rivers Gallery
$ 725 Civic Plaza; tel:
(250) 614-7800 or (888)
221-1155; www.
tworiversartgallery.com.
Open Mon–Wed, Fri–Sat
1000–1700, Thu
1000–2100 (free
1500–2100), Sun
1200–1700.

**University of Northern
British Columbia**
3333 University Way;
tel: (250) 960-5555;
www.unbc.ca

**Willow River
Interpretative Trail**
Hwy 16, 34km east from
Prince George.

Right
Ice climbing

Two Rivers Gallery

Prince George's biggest gallery space shows touring exhibitions as well as local and regional artists. The striking civic centre building is worth a visit just for the exterior and crest (totem) pole.

University of Northern British Columbia

Canada's newest autonomous university has planted its futuristic campus atop Cranbrook Hill, overlooking Prince George from the south. Choose from a self-guided indoor tour that weaves through the main buildings all year or an outdoor walk better taken in summer than in winter.

Willow River Interpretative Trail

The Canadian Institute of Forestry has created an excellent series of forest and streamside walking trails that explore several different hardwood, softwood and stream habitats. Allow between 45 minutes and 2 hours for the signed trails.

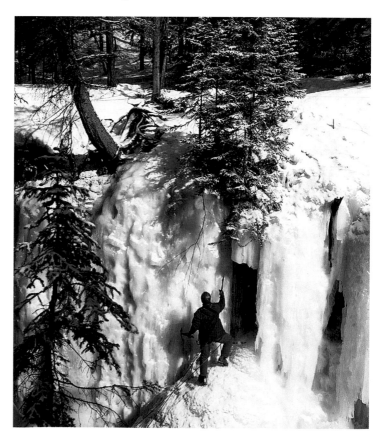

Accommodation and food

The University and a booming economy have given Prince George a better selection of accommodation and restaurants than might be expected in the middle of the northern forests.

Downtown Motel $ *650 Dominion St; tel: (250) 563-9241 or (800) 663-5729; www.downtownmotel.ca*, is just a block from the civic centre.

Pastry Chef Bakery $ *380 George St; tel: (250) 564-7034*, Prince George's oldest bakery, uses no preservatives and bakes everything from scratch.

Alekos Greek Taverna $$ *1232 4th Ave; tel: (250) 562-8661*, brings an authentic taste of Greece with superb service to Northern BC.

Credo Manor $$ *6872 O'Grady Road; tel: (250) 964-8142*, is a quiet, comfortable bed and breakfast near the University campus.

Ramada Hotel Downtown Prince George $$ *444 George St; tel: (250) 563-0055 or (800) 272-6232; http://ramadaprincegeorge.com*, is a large city-centre hotel.

Coast Inn of the North $$$ *770 Brunswick St; tel: (250) 563-0121 or (800) 716-6199; www.coasthotels.com*, is the best hotel in town.

Ric's Grill $$$ *547 George St; tel: (250) 614-9096; www.ricsgrill.com*, specialises in premium quality steak, but offers a wide menu selection.

Shogun $$$ *770 Brunswick St (Coast Inn of the North); tel: (250) 563-0121*, serves Japanese sushi and teppan dishes.

Suggested tour

Total distance: 260km.

Time: Allow 1 long day or 2 days for easier sightseeing.

Links: From Prince George, the **Yellowhead Hwy** (*see page 214*) links with **Prince Rupert** (*see page 206*) to the west and the **BC Rockies** (*see page 258*) to the east. To the south, Hwy 16 links to the **Gold Rush Trail** (*see page 186*) at Quesnel.

Route: This circular tour runs north to one of the only waterfalls in north-central BC, through forest and muskeg (bog) to Fort St James and back to Prince Rupert along the Yellowhead Highway.

Take Hwy 97 north through pastoral farmlands to the **Salmon River**. About 36km north of Prince George is a marked sideroad to the **HUBLE HOMESTEAD ❶** and **Giscome Portage Trail**. The homestead was established in 1904 as a waystation for travellers crossing the Arctic–Pacific Continental Divide. Waterways north of the divide, which runs between **Teapot Mountain** and **SUMMIT LAKE ❷**, 15km

**Crooked River
Provincial Park**
*Tel: (250) 964-3489;
www.env.gov.bc.ca/bcparks/
explore/parkpgs/crooked.html*

north, flow into the Arctic Ocean; waterways south of the divide flow into the Pacific.

At **Bear Lake**, head west on the Davie Bear Forest Service Road, an excellent gravel road that leads to the **CROOKED RIVER PROVINCIAL PARK ❸** and beyond. The meandering river was a major transport route for the Sekanni and other First Nations, as well as Alexander Mackenzie, Simon Fraser and other explorer/traders. The many lakes, rivers and streams support a wide variety of wildlife, from Canada geese, loons, blue-winged teal, ospreys, bald eagles and hawks to bears, beavers, muskrats, moose and deer. **Fisher Lake** and **Merton Lake** have particularly scenic picnic and camping sites.

Logging roads offer clear views of logging practices, including clearcuts, in which broad swathes of forest are stripped of all trees. The logged areas may be replanted or left to regenerate naturally, but either way end up looking like a disaster zone for decades. The one useful effect is to reveal the landforms hidden by dense forest. Just past the Weedon Forest Service Road (Road 300) is an area of long narrow ridges formed during the last Ice Age, around 10,000 years ago, when glaciers 1km thick covered this northern plateau.

The road forks just west of the **Muskeg River**. Take the south fork (1500 Road) to continue the tour. The north fork, Davie Muskeg Forest Service Road, leads 7km to **Muskeg Falls**. A short, easy trail leads from the car park to the 20m falls, one of the few waterfalls that has developed in the area since the glaciers retreated.

The tour continues to the south end of **GREAT BEAVER LAKE ❹**, one of the most scenic lakes in the area accessible by road. Continue west, past the **MURRAY RIDGE SKI HILL ❺** to a logging truck weighing station. Take the sharp turn south to **FORT ST JAMES ❻** (*see page 216*) and Hwy 27. Follow Hwy 27 south to Hwy 16, the Yellowhead Hwy, just west of **VANDERHOOF ❼**, and turn left (east) back to Prince George.

Gravel road precautions

Some public highways are part-paved, part-gravel, while other major roads, including Forest Service roads and logging roads, are entirely gravel. Gravel roads important enough to be shown on highway and tourist maps are well maintained, but require special driving precautions, particularly in areas with active logging.

Logging trucks and other industrial vehicles *always* have the right of way. Most are equipped with radios.

In an active logging area, try to follow a log truck so the driver can notify oncoming traffic. Don't follow so close as to choke on dust, but don't fall back so far the driver loses sight of you.

Don't pass a logging truck unless the driver signals you to go around.

If a logging truck pulls over beside the road and stops, you should, too – there's almost certainly another truck headed your way along a section of road too narrow for two vehicles to pass safely.

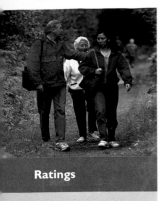

Ratings

Mountains	●●●●●
National parks	●●●●●
Nature	●●●●●
Scenery	●●●●●
Outdoor activities	●●●●○
Children	●●●○○
Geology	●●●○○
History	●●●○○

Columbia River

Subtly, the long and mighty Columbia River begins its much-dammed and thwarted route 2,044km to the Pacific Ocean from Columbia Lake, a long but unprepossessing body of water visible from a lay-by along Hwy 93/95. Bird migration along the Columbia Valley is awesome in spring and autumn; migration of humans over one of the world's snowiest mountain areas at Rogers Pass is almost as awe-inspiring because of the sheer technical skill it takes to keep the pass open against avalanche.

While Parks Canada wages 'snow wars', this is railway country, from the hub at Golden at the north end of the Columbia Valley to Revelstoke west of the Selkirk Mountains along the fast-flowing Columbia River, west of Golden over Rogers Pass. Glaciers, old-growth cedars and wild-flower meadows lie in between the two towns, each claiming the distinction of Gateway to the Columbia.

CANAL FLATS

ⓘ **Kootenay Rockies**
*1905 Warren Ave,
Kimberley;
tel: (250) 427-4838;
www.kootenayrockies.com*

**Canal Flats Provincial
Park** *South end of Columbia
Lake; www.env.gov.bc.ca/
bcparks/explore/parkpgs/
canal.html*

There is a small lumbering community here, but the area's claim to fame is twofold: the Kootenay River and the source of the Columbia River in Columbia Lake, separated only by 2km of land (they actually join at Castlegar, *see page 241*), and an 1889 canal built to divert Kootenay River water away from valley farms. Too narrow locks were the canal's downfall. The *North Star*, only the second vessel to pass through, wrecked the locks and system in 1902. (**Canal Flats** *historic point, Hwy 93/95 at south end of Columbia Lake*.) The tiny, 6ha **Canal Flats Provincial Park** is a mecca for windsurfers.

COLUMBIA LAKE

Columbia Lake
South of Fairmont Hot Springs on the east side of Hwy 93/95.

Look for a lay-by on the east side of Hwy 93/95 and a sign announcing '*Columbia Lake–Source of Columbia River Which Empties into Pacific Ocean at Astoria-Oregon*', that is, 2,044km southwest of the headwaters! Spiky golden hoodoos (eroded columns of rock) rise sheer above Dutch Creek at the lake's north end.

FAIRMONT HOT SPRINGS

Here you can soak in the 43°–48°C odourless hot springs, Canada's largest natural hot pools, long used by Ktunaxa (Kootenay) peoples. From several vantage points, including the Mountainside Golf Course, the forest-bound resort looks westward to the craggy line of the Purcell

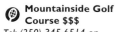

Fairmont Hot Springs $$ *5225 Fairmont Resort Rd; off Hwy 93/95; tel: (250) 345-6000 or (800) 663-4979; www.fairmonthotsprings.com. Open year-round* with a **Ski Hill** $$.

Hot Pools $ *Open daily 0800–2000.*

Mountainside Golf Course $$$ *Tel: (250) 345-6514 or (800) 663-4979, one of two 18-hole courses, offering magnificent views over the Columbia River Valley. Open mid-Mar–late Oct.*

Mountain Range. Hiking, biking, horse riding and winter downhill skiing and snowboarding supplement the pools' attraction for the RVers, lodge guests and another 750,000 visitors who make an annual pilgrimage to the resort.

Where there's a will

Ornery Major A B Rogers, described by Parks Canada as 'short, sharp and rough-tongued', was driven to find a pass over the Rockies suitable for a railway. In 1881, he tried the pass's west side, and 'Many a time I wished myself dead.' In 1882, he approached from the east and 'felt like a piece of liver'. He had found a viable pass through the mountains. The impetus? The CPR had promised to name the pass after him and paid a $5,000 bonus. In ornery style he never cashed the cheque.

GLACIER NATIONAL PARK

Glacier National Park $ *Mount Revelstoke and Glacier National Parks Headquarters, 301B 3rd St W (Post Office Bldg) Revelstoke; tel: (250) 837-7500; www.pc.gc.ca/pn-np/bc/glacier/index_e.asp. Open Mon–Fri 0830–1200, 1300–1630.*

Rogers Pass National Historic Site *69km east of Revelstoke, 72km west of Golden, on Hwy 1 in Glacier National Park.*

Rogers Pass Discovery Centre *Rogers Pass; tel: (250) 837-7500; www.pc.gc.ca. Open summer daily 0730–2000; spring & autumn daily 0830–1630 (closed Tue & Wed Nov); winter daily 0700–1700.*

The northern Selkirk Mountain Range, the birthplace of North American technical climbing – mountaineering – in 1888, is a land of snow and around 400 active glaciers, including **Illecillewaet Glacier**, visible from Hwy 1 on a clear day. Waterfalls and wild flowers are abundant in season. If travelling east, you will see 14.6km Mount Macdonald Tunnel, North America's longest railway tunnel, built after hundreds died between 1885 and 1911 trying to keep the Rogers Pass open on the surface. A series of snowsheds protects traffic from avalanches as 'Snow Wars' keep Rogers Pass open in winter. The twin keys: constant monitoring and 105mm howitzers deployed to blast snow along avalanche paths.

Rogers Pass National Historic Site's many peaks poke the sky at 3,700m, catching shrouds of snow which avalanche dangerously below. Major A B Rogers, who discovered the 1,382m pass, noted, 'Our eyesight caromed from one bold peak to another for miles in all directions. The wind blew fiercely across the ridge and scuddy clouds were whirled in eddies behind the great towering peaks of bare rock. Everything was covered with a shroud of white, giving the whole landscape the appearance of snow-clad desolation.' **Rogers Pass Discovery Centre** offers excellent explanations of the Snow Wars waged by the CPR and more currently by Parks Canada and the Royal Canadian Horse Artillery to keep the TransCanada Highway open. **Abandoned Rails Trail** follows Hwy 1 past side-paths and snowsheds 1.3km to the **Rogers Pass Discovery Monument**, which commemorates completion of the TransCanada Highway in 1962, the first alternative to rail transit over the pass.

Accommodation and food in Glacier National Park

Glacier Park Lodge $$$ *Rogers Pass; tel: (250) 837-2126; www.glacierparklodge.ca.* The only non-camping accommodation provides 50 rooms next to the Rogers Pass Discovery Centre, with a restaurant, 24-hour cafeteria and petrol station.

GOLDEN

🛈 Kicking Horse Country Chamber of Commerce Visitor InfoCentre *500 10th Ave N; tel: (250) 344-7125 or (800) 622-4653; http://goldenchamber.bc.ca. Open Mon–Fri 1000–1600.*

Trains, lorries, rivers, an active sawmill, tourists and outdoor enthusiasts (hang-gliders, rock climbers, whitewater kayakers and rafters, mountain bikers, hikers and anglers) all use Golden as a convenient valley-floor base. Here is the confluence of the Columbia and Kicking Horse rivers and access to Yoho National Park (*see page 264*) or Glacier National Park (*see page 232*). Mountains rise along both sides of the valley, causing spectacular sunsets over the Purcells, a drama much needed in this rather pedestrian service centre.

Accommodation and food in Golden

Legendz $ *1405 W TransCanada Hwy; tel: (250) 344-5059,* serves delicious steak and creamy eggs, with other Marilyn Monroe and James Dean era specialities.

Below
Glacier National Park

Sportsman Lodge $ *1200 12th St N; tel: (250) 344-2915 or (888) 989-5566; http://sportsmanlodge.ca,* is quiet and away from the highway.

Golden Rim Motor Inn $$ *1416 Golden View Rd; tel: (250) 344-2216* or *(877) 311-2216; www.goldenrim.ca,* has views of the Columbia River Valley.

Kicking Horse Mountain Resort $$$ *13km west of Golden, 1500 Kicking Horse Trail; tel: (250) 439-5424 or (866) 754-5425; http:// kickinghorseresort.com* off Hwy 1, is an all-year mountain resort with winter skiing down a 1,280m slope, the second longest in Canada, or hiking and mountain biking in summer. More than half of the ski runs are either expert or advanced. At any time, it's worth a ride up the mountain just for the panorama from **The Eagle's Eye $$$**, the highest restaurant in Canada at 2,335m.

INVERMERE

ⓘ Invermere/ Columbia Valley Chamber of Commerce Visitor InfoCentre *651 Hwy 93/95 Crossroads, Invermere; tel: (250) 342-2844; www. cvchamber.ca. Open Mon–Fri 0830–1630.*

ⓘ James Chabot Provincial Park *North end of Windermere Lake; tel: (250) 422-3003; www.env.gov.bc.ca/bcparks/ explore/parkpgs/james.html*

At the northwest corner of Windermere Lake, the area's commercial centre south of Golden boasts September to October kokanee salmon spawning in its end of the 15km-long lake. Lakeside **James Chabot Provincial Park** has a swimming beach, watersports and a 350m boardwalk over the wetlands.

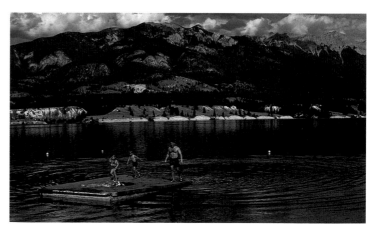

Right
Lake Windermere

Opposite
Revelstoke

MOBERLY MARSH/BURGES AND JAMES GADSDEN PROVINCIAL PARK

ⓘ Moberly Marsh/ Burges and James Gadsden Provincial Park *West of Hwy 1 north of Golden; www.env.gov.bc.ca/bcparks/ explore/parkpgs/burges.html*

Most drivers don't stop in the rush to and from Golden, but migratory waterfowl do along this stretch of Moberly Marsh between the TransCanada Hwy 1 and the Columbia River. Spot muskrats and ospreys from a 3.5km riverbank **Dyke Trail** in Burges and James Gadsden Provincial Park, which protects much of the marsh.

MOUNT REVELSTOKE NATIONAL PARK

Mount Revelstoke National Park $
Mount Revelstoke and Glacier National Parks Headquarters, 300 3rd St W (Post Office Bldg) Revelstoke; tel: (250) 837-7500; www.pc.gc.ca/pn-np/bc/revelstoke/index_e.asp. Open Mon–Fri 0830–1200, 1300–1630. Wardens at Meadows-in-the-Sky Parkway in summer have park information.

Giant Cedars Nature Trail *1km west of east boundary of Mount Revelstoke National Park.*

Meadows-in-the-Sky Parkway *3km east of Revelstoke in Mount Revelstoke National Park. Trailers are prohibited beyond the parkway trailer parking area 0.5km from Hwy 1.*

Unlike the Rockies National Parks, which were spurred on by the CPR and the need for an all-weather automobile route (Kootenay), this park was a result of the City of Revelstoke citizens' building a trail to the mountain's summit and lobbying for a road. That road, Meadows-in-the-Sky Parkway, draws thousands of mid-summer visitors to the rich displays of wild flowers.

Giant Cedars Nature Trail Rainforest in the interior of BC? Five- to eight-hundred-year-old Western red cedar trees along a 0.5km boardwalk tell the tale. The damp, mossy streambed is dim, but vibrant with many hues of green. Virgin old-growth forest boasts standing cedars so thick with branches that little water falls through when it rains.

Meadows in the Sky Stop at the elaborate archway Welcome Station entrance to the 26km Meadows-in-the-Sky Parkway for information. Depending on the severity of the past winter, the parkway may be closed part of the way up, even though the route is normally open early July to late September. Enjoy the winding, 16km switchback drive past fine views of Revelstoke and the Columbia River. Waterfalls plummet off rock walls covered with ferns and greenery as the parkway rises through forests of cedar, hemlock, fir and spruce. Park at Balsam Lake and take the Summit Shuttle to the wild-flower meadows or hike the colourful carpet by way of the 1km Summit Trail to an historic fire tower at the top.

Revelstoke Viewpoint

REVELSTOKE

ℹ Revelstoke Chamber of Commerce Visitor Info Centre *204 Campbell Ave; tel: (250) 837-5345 or (800) 487-1493; http://seerevelstoke.com*

Snow sports
www.seerevelstoke.com/snow

🎵 Revelstoke Nickelodeon Museum $$ *111 First St West; tel: (250) 837-5250; www.revelstokenickelodeon. com. Call for 1-hour tour by owner.*

Revelstoke Dam $
5km north of Revelstoke (in season); tel: (250) 814-6697; mid-Oct–late May (250) 814-6600; www. bchydro.com/recreation/ southern/southern1205.html

Revelstoke Railway Museum $ *719 Track St West; tel: (250) 837-6060 or (877) 837-6060; www.railwaymuseum.com. Open daily May–Oct; some days Nov–Apr. Call for hours.*

No one seems to know why there are bear statues and signs everywhere in this railway hub and recreation centre in the middle of the Selkirk and Monashee Mountains. Ask and the answer is there are lots of bears around here. Trains constantly roll, click and grind through town. **Grizzly Plaza** *(Mackenzie Ave, Victoria Rd and First St)* is the venue for nightly concerts in July and August. Rail and Columbia River transportation propelled Revelstoke into existence in the 1880s. The Chamber of Commerce has *Heritage Walking & Driving* and *Railway Heritage Driving Tour* brochures.

A 1911 one-time pool hall and bowling alley now houses the large personal mechanical music machine collection of three members of the Evans family from the UK. The **Revelstoke Nickelodeon Museum** has barrel organs, juke boxes, gramophones, magic lantern equipment and more, with a sampling demonstrated on a personal hour-long tour.

BC Hydro operates **Revelstoke Dam** and generating station, a must for those fascinated by waterway engineering and the intricacies of changes to the Columbia River. Get an individual talking wand at the entrance for a self-guiding tour through the two-storey visitor centre atop the powerhouse. Take a lift 165m up to the top crest of the dam and look both up and downstream.

It's not large, but the **Revelstoke Railway Museum** is a good introduction to the challenges faced by CPR engineers and officials who encountered avalanches, difficult soil, steep grades, harsh winters and labour strife while constructing and maintaining the railway. Prized are Business Car No 4 and Mikado P-2k class locomotive No 5468, on display in a replica of Victoria's E&N Roundhouse.

Right
Revelstoke Railway Museum

Accommodation and food in Revelstoke

Many Revelstoke motels are near the noisy railway track at the west end of town.

Chalet Bakery $ *415B Victoria St; tel: (250) 837-4556*, makes European-style breads and pastries.

Woolsey Creek Café $ *600 2nd St; tel: (250) 837-5500*, has delicious breakfast blueberry cornmeal and apple rhubarb muffins, and wraps and sandwiches for lunch.

Canyon Motor Inn $$ *1911 Fraser Dr, off Hwy 1 at Columbia River Bridge; tel: (250) 837-5221 or (877) 837-5221; www.canyonmotorinn.ca*, has small, very clean rooms in a quiet spot near the river.

Frisby Ridge Teriyaki Restaurant $$ *201A 1st St W; tel: (250) 837-5449*, serves Japanese and Korean food, in the BC mountains.

Griffin Lake Mountain Lodge Bed and Breakfast $$ *27km from Revelstoke, 7776 TransCanada Hwy; tel: (250) 837-7475 or (877) 603-2827; www.griffinlakelodge.com, open in summer* on a beautiful lake.

Regent Inn $$ *112 E 1st St; tel: (250) 837-2107 or (888) 245-5523; www.regentinn.com*, is in a downtown heritage building next to Grizzly Plaza.

ROCKY MOUNTAIN TRENCH

Rocky Mountain Trench dividing the Rocky and Cascade Mountain Ranges from Alaska to the central USA has the Columbia River at its bottom in this area.

Astronauts say this depression between mountain ranges which extends from Alaska along the western side of the Rocky Mountains into the central US is one of the most prominent features on Earth. The rift valley separates ancient Columbia Mountains from the craggier, younger Rocky Mountains on the eastern side, with lush wetlands and cultivated farmland in between.

WINDERMERE

St Peter's Anglican Church Kootenay St; tel: (250) 342-6644.

The town and its namesake lake are a resort getaway for locals, windsurfers and people from colder climes. **St Peter's Anglican Church** was stolen in 1897, removed via a railway flatcar from Donald, 160km north, by residents who wanted a ready-made church when most Donald inhabitants moved to Revelstoke along with the CPR operations.

ⓘ Columbia Valley Chamber of Commerce Visitor InfoCentre *651 Hwy 93/95 Crossroads, Invermere; tel: (250) 342-2844; www.cvchamber.ca. Open Mon–Fri 0830–1630.*

Suggested tour

Total distance: 310km.

Time: 2 days.

Links: South of Canal Flats on Hwy 93/95 to **The Crowsnest** (*see page 250*). At Radium Junction, go east to Kootenay National Park or at Golden go east to Yoho National Park in **BC Rockies Parks** (*see page 258*). At Revelstoke, continue west on Hwy 1 to the **Shuswap Lakes** (*see page 158*).

Route: From **CANAL FLATS ❶**, travel north through the **ROCKY MOUNTAIN TRENCH ❷** on Hwy 93/95 along the west side of **COLUMBIA LAKE ❸**, headwaters of the **Columbia River**. The wetlands that begin here are amongst the most extensive and richest on Earth, 26,000 hectares of protected space. From Canal Flats to **Donald**, north of Golden, is the least-developed section along the Columbia River. Beyond Columbia Lake's north end are the **Dutch Creek Hoodoos** looming mysteriously on the left, and **FAIRMONT HOT SPRINGS ❹**, for soaking, swimming, golfing, hiking and winter skiing with views of the Purcell Mountains to the west above the valley floor. North is **Windermere Lake**, which has **WINDERMERE ❺** along the highway side and **INVERMERE ❻** on the west side.

At Radium Junction, Hwy 93 splits off east from Hwy 95 to Radium Hot Springs in Kootenay National Park. Hwy 95 continues north along the Columbia River Valley to **GOLDEN ❼**, at the junction of Hwy 95 and TransCanada Hwy 1 from Yoho National Park.

Continue north on Hwy 1 past **BURGES AND JAMES GADSDEN PROVINCIAL PARK ❽** at **MOBERLY MARSH ❾** and **Donald**, where the CPR line first crossed the Columbia River.

Enter **GLACIER NATIONAL PARK ❿**. **Beaver Valley** has a lovely picnic spot and wild flowers in summer. Tunnels covering the TransCanada Hwy are snowsheds, built to deflect the hideous impact of avalanches. **Rogers Pass Discovery Centre** has a roaring fire, excellent exhibit and film depictions of avalanche control and snow management, and a well-stocked bookshop. One kilometre south is the **Rogers Pass Monument** arch to the 1962 TransCanada Highway completion. The **Illecillewaet Glacier** campground and trailhead to a series of trails near the glacier are accessible from Hwy 1, not far south of the monument.

There's a 16km gap between park boundaries. Almost immediately upon entering **MOUNT REVELSTOKE NATIONAL PARK ⑪**, stop and take the short 0.5km **Giant Cedars Nature Trail** for a view of BC rainforest. In May, walk the 1.2km **Skunk Cabbage Trail** for views of the odiferous plants flowering yellow along the **Illecillewaet River**. The park's jewel is the **Meadows in the Sky Parkway**, a 42km drive to **Balsam Lake** parking and a 2km shuttle ride or walk to Mount Revelstoke's summit, carpeted with wild flowers in mid-summer.

Opposite
Mount Revelstoke Mountain
Meadows in the Sky

Descending quickly from the park, enter **REVELSTOKE ⑫** to visit the Revelstoke Railway Museum and Revelstoke Dam.

The Kootenays

Ratings

Geology	●●●●●
History	●●●●●
Mountains	●●●●●
Children	●●●●○
Outdoor activities	●●●●○
Parks	●●●●○
Architecture	●●●○○
First Nations	●●○○○

This region takes in the West Kootenays through the Purcell, Selkirk and Monashee Ranges, heaven for lovers of rugged mountains and lakes. Linked by just one highway, which follows the first track hacked from Hope to Fort Steele during the 1860s, Southern BC is more vertical than horizontal. What little flat space exists between mountain ranges is filled with water more often than not.

Ghost towns abound, no surprise in a region best known for mineral rushes in search of gold, copper, silver and lead, as do smelter ruins, decaying mine shafts and long-abandoned graveyards slowly disappearing beneath encroaching forests.

The future is as bright as the past. Urban professionals from across Canada have transformed one-time backwaters into modern enclaves surrounded by splendid opportunities for boating, hiking, fishing, skiing and other outdoor recreation.

AINSWORTH HOT SPRINGS

Ainsworth Hot Springs Resort $$
Hwy 31, 36km north from Balfour; tel: (250) 229-4212 or (800) 668-1171; http://hotnaturally.com

The hot springs flow from a stalactite-filled 46m cave. Spa aficionados swear by the water, which has the highest mineral content of any natural hot springs in Canada. Everyone else swears by the stunning views across Kootenay Lake to the Purcell Mountains from the 45°C outdoor baths.

BOUNDARY CREEK PROVINCIAL PARK

Boundary Creek Provincial Park
Hwy 3, 4km west of Greenwood; tel: (250) 548-0076; http://www.env.gov.bc.ca/bcparks/explore/parkpgs/boundary.html. Open late May–Oct.

A slag heap and crumbling chimney are all that remain of the largest single producer of copper in the world between 1901 and 1918. The park also has pleasant camping and picnicking spots along Boundary Creek.

CASTLEGAR

ℹ️ **Castlegar and District Chamber of Commerce** 1995 6th Ave; tel: (250) 365-6313; http://castelgar.com. Open Mon–Fri 0900–1700; daily late May–Labour Day, Jul–Aug Thu–Fri to 1800.

🏢 **BC Hydro Hugh Keenleyside Dam** 8km north of Castlegar; tel: (250) 365-3115; www. bchydro.com/recreation/ southern/southern1202.html

Doukhobor Suspension Bridge National Heritage Site Base of Airport Hill. Park at the south end of the new Kootenay River Bridge and walk 500m down the old highway.

Castlegar Canadian Pacific Railway Museum $ 400 13th Ave; tel: (250) 365-6440; www.stationmuseum.ca/ museum. Open Mon–Sat 0900–1700.

Castlegar grew as a railway and mining town at the confluence of the Kootenay and Columbia rivers. Odorous fumes still waft from a pulp mill just below **BC Hydro Hugh Keenleyside Dam**, which backs the Columbia into Arrow Lakes, stretching 230km north to Revelstoke (see page 236). Doukhobor farms added an important agricultural element to the economy.

When local authorities ignored requests for a bridge across the Kootenay River, the Doukhobors (see page 242) designed and built their own span in 1913, which carried Hwy 3 traffic for decades. It forms part of the **Doukhobor Suspension Bridge National Heritage Site**.

Castlegar Canadian Pacific Railway Museum, an old CPR station, concentrates on area history from the early days of the 20th century.

Doukhobor Discovery Centre is a reproduction of a typical village and includes the communal main house, cottages and workrooms. The furnishings, photographs and artworks are authentic, as are the costumed guides who explain traditional Doukhobor life and beliefs.

The small river island which forms **Zuckerberg Island Heritage Park** was named after a local Russian teacher who built an onion-dome home in the forest. Zuckerberg's home has been restored, and there are trails and picnic tables.

Accommodation and food in Castlegar

Common Grounds Café $ 692 18th St (Castleaird Pl); tel: (250) 365-3883, is good for light meals and an internet check.

**Doukhobor
Discovery Centre $**
112 Heritage Way, across
from the Castlegar Airport;
tel: (250) 365-5327;
http://doukhobor-museum.org.
Open daily May–Sep
1000–1700.

**Zuckerberg Island
Heritage Park $**
9th St and 7th Ave;
tel: (250) 365-6440;
www.stationmuseum.ca/
zuckerberg. Open summer
Wed–Sat 1000–1700.

Flamingo Motel $ *1660 Columbia Ave; tel: (250) 365-7978; www.flamingomotel.ca,* has a park-like setting.

The Village Bistro $–$$ *At the Doukhobor Discovery Centre; tel: (250) 365-6643; http://doukhobor-museum.org, open daily May–Sep,* serves Doukhobor vegetarian specialities including borscht soup and vareniki as well as standard breakfasts and burgers.

Fireside Inn $$ *1810 8th Ave; tel: (250) 365-2128; www.firesideinn.ca,* is convenient and central.

The Doukhobors

The name means 'spirit wrestlers' in Russian. It's an apt name for a group of rabid pacifists who lived by the motto 'Toil and a Peaceful Life'. They successfully resisted the Russian Tsars only to be rent by internal divisions and bomb blasts.

Spiritual leader Peter Verigin led the Doukhobors to Canada, eventually settling on flat land across the Columbia River from Castlegar in 1908. Initially ignored by colonial authorities, the Doukhobors built many of the earliest bridges in Boundary Country, including the graceful Doukhobor Suspension Bridge over the Kootenay River. About two dozen villages eventually filled *Ootischenia*, the 'Valley of Consolation', most of which is now occupied by Castlegar's airport and golf course.

The new immigrants planted orchards, grain and vegetables while building sawmills, jam factories, pipe works and similar enterprises, but their communal living arrangements, outspoken pacifism and vocal opposition to meat, tobacco and alcohol won few friends locally.

Verigin was killed by a bomb blast in 1924, almost certainly planted by a faction who feared that he was leading the community into mainstream Canadian society. The Doukhobors, along with Hutterites and other communal religious groups, eventually ran foul of laws designed to break up their tightly knit communities. Communal villages have disappeared, but thousands of Doukhobors still live in Boundary Country from Castlegar to Grand Forks. Many of their distinctive farm buildings are still visible along country roads, and Russian restaurants – invariably Doukhobor – are local institutions.

CODY CAVES PROVINCIAL PARK

Except for a few ladders, the rugged cave looks much as Henry Cody, an early prospector, first saw it a century ago. Open for one-hour guided tours only. Paths snake through forests of stalactites, stalagmites and soda straws. (**Cody Caves Provincial Park $$** *North of Ainsworth Hot Springs; tel: (250) 353-7364; www.env.gov.bc.ca/bcparks/explore/parkpgs/codycaves.html. Open Jun–Sep.*)

CRESTON

Creston and District Chamber of Commerce
1607 Canyon St (Hwy 3);
tel: (250) 428-4342; or
(866) 528-4342;
www.crestonbc.com/chamber

Creston Museum $
219 Devon St;
tel: (250) 428-9262;
http://creston.museum.bc.ca.
Open daily mid-May–mid-Sep. Call for hours.

Creston Valley Wildlife Centre $ Hwy 3,
10km west from Creston;
tel: (250) 402-6908;
http://crestonwildlife.ca.
Open daily; call for hours.

A small farming town overlooks a plain where the Kootenay River once sprawled between the Purcell and Selkirk Mountains. The river has been dyked and channelled, creating fertile grain fields. Creston's rural past appears on murals in the town centre.

Highlight of the **Creston Museum** is a replica of a traditional Kootenay canoe, a 'sturgeon-nosed' craft with ends pointing down into the water.

Creston Valley Wildlife Centre, the interpretation centre for the 7,000-hectare Creston Valley Wildlife Management Area, offers guided canoe tours ($) of one of BC's richest wetland areas, and there are walking trails and educational displays. The area has the largest concentration of nesting ospreys in North America as well as massive bird migrations spring and autumn.

Accommodation and food in Creston

A Break in Time Caffé $ 1417 Canyon St; tel: (250) 428-5619, serves Mexican, vegetarian and international fare.

Valley View Motel $ 216 Valleyview Dr; tel: (250) 428-2336 or (800) 758-9334; www.valleyviewmotel.info, has cosy cabins near the Creston Valley Museum.

Downtowner Motor Inn $$ 1218 Canyon St; tel: (250) 428-2238 or (800) 665-9904; www.downtownercreston.com, is central.

Granny's Place Family Restaurant $$ 1230 Canyon St; tel: (250) 428-3990, serves breakfast through the day.

GRAND FORKS

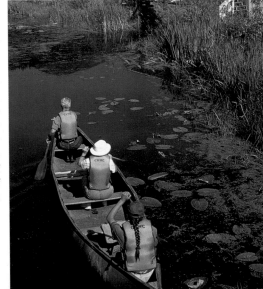

An agricultural enclave at the junction of the Kettle Valley and Granby rivers, Grand Forks boomed with the 1900 opening of the Granby Smelter. The smelter closed in 1919, but the glistening mountain of ebony-coloured slag off Granby Road, just north of town, remains.

Right
Creston Valley Wildlife Centre

Grand Forks Chamber of Commerce Visitor Information Centre *524 Central Ave at 5th St; tel: (250) 442-5835 or (866) 442-2833; http:// grandforkschamber.com. Open all year.*

Boundary Museum *$ (call for new location and details); tel: (250) 442-3737.*

Hardy Mountain Doukhobor Village Historic Site *$ 3655 Hardy Mountain Rd; tel: (250) 492-0173; www.conservancy.bc.ca/ content.asp?sectionid=181. Call for open dates.*

Phoenix Forest and History Tour *Phoenix Rd, 19.5km west from Grand Forks; self-guiding map online at www.phoenixforest. freehomepage.com/phdriving. htm. Drivable all year.*

Below
SS Moyie on Kootenay Lake

If rebuilt in a new location as anticipated, the **Boundary Museum** should house artefacts from First Nations to Doukhobors, miners and railways. See the overview, then take a **self-guided tour** of some of the 300-plus heritage buildings from the mining and railway era with a free museum map.

Hardy Mountain Doukhobor Village Historic Site, in a 1912 Doukhobor communal home, overflows with period artefacts and records. Many other Doukhobor buildings are visible along Hardy Mountain Road as it twists back to Hwy 3.

The **Phoenix Forest and History Tour**, a back-road route between Grand Forks and Greenwood, passes many of the former mines, towns and railways that made the Boundary rich in the early 20th century.

Accommodation and food in Grand Forks

Borscht Bowl $ *214 Market Ave; tel: (250) 442-5977, open Mon–Sat,* serves an interesting combination of Doukhobor and Mexican.

Grand Forks Hotel Restaurant $$ *7382 2nd St; tel: (250) 442-5944,* has Russian as well as non-vegetarian choices.

Ponderosa Pines Mountain Spa $$ *6700 Danshin Village Rd; tel: (250) 442-2547 or (800) 665-3211; www.ponderosaspa.bc.ca,* offers lodging, home-cooked meals, and spa and massage services.

Ramada Limited Grand Forks $$ *2729 Central Avenue, Hwy 3; tel: (250) 442-2127 or (888) 298-2054,* has free breakfast and wireless internet connections in the room.

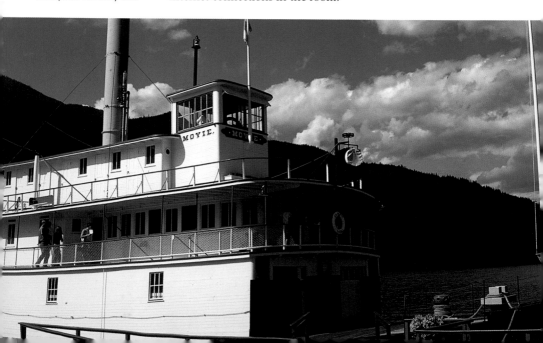

GREENWOOD

ⓝ Greenwood
Museum and
Visitor Centre $
214 S Copper St (Hwy 3);
tel: (250) 445-6355; www.
greenwoodmuseum.com.
Open May–Jun and Sep
1000–1600; Jul–Aug
0900–1700.

Lotzkar Park $ Hwy 3,
just south of town.

This booming mining town nearly died after the local mines closed, but was revived as a Japanese-Canadian internment camp during World War II. Some 20 historic buildings have been restored. **Greenwood Museum** packs a major punch in its telling of the mining boom and Japanese internment days. The museum can point out locations where some *Snow Falling on Cedars* (1999) scenes were filmed using area extras.

At **Lotzkar Park**, the best-preserved smelter ruins in North America rise above a barren ridge of black smelter slag that once glowed red-hot even at noon. Locals call it a 'corner of hell gone cold'.

KASLO

ⓘ Kaslo Visitor
Centre 324 Front St
by the SS Moyie; tel: (250)
353-2525; www.klhs.bc.ca.
Open mid-May–mid-Oct.

Kaslo was a lumber town before silver and lead strikes brought miners flooding into the Kootenays. Tourism is number one today, thanks to 60 historic buildings and spectacular hiking, mountain biking, fishing, camping and boating.

The beached and meticulously restored *Moyie*, at the **SS *Moyie* National Historic Site**, sailed Kootenay Lake until 1957, and was the last sternwheeler in regular passenger service in Canada ($ *Front St; tel: (250) 353-2525; www.klhs.bc.ca; open daily mid-May–mid-Oct 0900–1700 for self-guiding tours*).

KOKANEE CREEK PROVINCIAL PARK

Built on the site of a former lakeside estate, the park offers hiking, boating, camping, fishing and **Redfish Creek Spawning Channel**, an artificial spawning channel for Kokanee salmon. Best time to see the bright-red fish is mid-August to mid-September. The park also shelters a major osprey population (*Hwy 3A, 20km northeast from Nelson; tel: (250) 825-4212; www.env.gov.bc.ca/bcparks/explore/parkpgs/kokanee.html*).

KOOTENAY LAKE

ⓘ Kootenay Lake
Chamber of
Commerce Visitor Info
Centre Next to the
Crawford Bay Airstrip;
tel: (250) 227-9267;
www.kootenaylake.bc.ca.
Open in summer.

This long, narrow lake between the Purcell and Selkirk Mountains was a major navigation route long before it became a prime recreation area. Facilities lie along Hwy 3A, north from Creston to Kootenay Bay. There you can link to Balfour by the free Kootenay Lake Ferry, with more facilities along Hwy 3A west into Nelson.

Crawford Bay on the east shore of Kootenay Lake is a collection of artisans producing metalwork, brooms and similar crafts, and home to

Kootenay Lake Ferry *Tel: (250) 229-4215; www.kootenaylake. bc.ca/Ferry.shtml. Year-round, 40–50 minutes between Kootenay Bay and Balfour. Free.*

Kootenay Lake $ *North from Creston, east of Nelson.*

Crawford Bay *Hwy 3A, 78km north from Creston.*

Glass House $ *Hwy 3A, in Boswell, 25km north from Creston; tel: (250) 223-8372. Open May–Oct.*

Lockhart Beach Provincial Park $ *Hwy 3A, 40km north from Creston; tel: (250) 422-3003; www.env.gov.bc.ca/ bcparks/explore/parkpgs/ lock_beach.html. Lockhart Creek Provincial Park www.env.gov.bc.ca/bcparks/ explore/parkpgs/lockhart.html*

Right
Nelson wall mural depicting Steve Martin in *Roxanne*

Kokanee Springs Golf Course ($$ *tel: (250) 227-9226 or (800) 979-7999; http://kokaneesprings.com*).

Mortician David Brown built the **Glass House**, a scenic lakeside house, from 500,000 embalming fluid bottles in the 1950s, as he explained, 'to indulge a whim of a peculiar nature'.

There's excellent camping and hiking in **Lockhart Beach Provincial Park** and the adjacent Lockhart Creek Provincial Park.

NELSON

This sparkling Victorian-era mining town was the set for Steve Martin's 1987 film *Roxanne*, a modern version of *Cyrano de Bergerac*. Local painters have enshrined Martin on a mural at the end of Vernon Street. Film publicity helped Nelson reinforce its current incarnation as a rural refuge for urban professionals who expect wi-fi internet connections and the perfect *latte* after a tough day at the computer.

The imposing **courthouse** and **city hall** were designed by Francis Rattenbury, who built the Empress Hotel and Parliament Buildings in Victoria. Costumed guides from the Chamber of Commerce lead walking and driving tours of the town's 350 **heritage buildings** in summer, or visitors can follow self-guiding maps in any season.

Nelson & District Chamber of Commerce *225 Hall St; tel: (250) 352-3433 or (877) 663-5706; www. discovernelson.com. Open daily.* **Artwalk** *560 Baker St, Ste 5; tel: (250) 352-2402; http://ndac.ca/annual-events/artwalk. Monthly Jul–Sep.*

Nelson Mining Museum Chamber of Mines of Eastern BC *$ 215 Hall St; tel: (250) 352-5242. Open Mon–Fri 1000–1600.*

Touchstones Nelson: Museum of Art and History *$$ 502 Vernon St; tel: (250) 352-9813; www.nelsonmuseum.ca. Open mid-May–Sep Mon, Wed–Sat 1000–1800, Sun to 1600; winter closed Mon–Tue.*

Lakeside Park *Foot of the Nelson Bridge.*

Streetcar No 23 *$ downtown to Lakeside Park; tel: (250) 367-9564. Operates daily in summer, weekends Apr and autumn; http://streetcar.kics.bc.ca*

Kootenay Rockies Tourism *Tel: (250) 427-4838; www. kootenayrockies.com and* **Explore the Kootenays** *http://explorethekootenays. com offer web links to the entire Kootenay region.*

More than a dozen galleries stage monthly shows July to September by 70 local artists. Maps of **Artwalk** are available at the Info Centre.

The **Nelson Mining Museum Chamber of Mines of Eastern BC** has BC's biggest mineral collection. **Touchstones Nelson: Museum of Art and History**, a strictly local collection, emphasises steamboats, mines and local artists.

Lakeside Park is the most popular recreation area, with sandy beaches, canoe and boat rentals, lawns, playgrounds and greenhouse.

Streetcar No 23 is BC's only operating historic streetcar, making regular runs the length of the city along the lakeshore.

Accommodation and food in Nelson

All Seasons Café $$ *620 Herridge Lane; tel: (250) 352-0101; http://allseasonscafe.com*, offers outstanding Northwest cuisine and the best wine list in Nelson.

Cloudside Inn $$ *408 Victoria St; tel: (250) 352-3226 or (800) 596-2337; www.cloudside.ca*, is a cheerful bed and breakfast in an historic home.

Hume Hotel $$ *422 Vernon St; tel: (250) 352-5331 or (877) 568-0888; www.humehotel.com*, has been Nelson's landmark hotel since the 1890s.

Max & Irma's Kitchen $$ *515A Kootenay St; tel: (250) 352-2332*, serves Nelson's best pizza and Italian dishes.

Louie's Steakhouse $$$ *616 Vernon St in The New Grand Hotel; tel: (250) 352-7211; www.newgrandhotel.ca/louies.htm*, specialises in its carvery beef, Caesar salad and 28 versions of Martini.

Suggested tour

Total distance: 300km.

Time: It's possible to drive from Creston to Greenwood in one long day, but 2–3 days allows time to enjoy and explore.

Links: The **Okanagan Valley** (*see page 148*) and the **Cascade Mountains** (*see page 130*) lie west from Greenwood on Hwy 3. To the east, Hwy 3 leads to **The Crowsnest** (*see page 250*) and the **BC Rockies** (*see page 258*).

Route: The direct route follows Hwy 3 125km west from Creston past the **Creston Valley Wildlife Centre** and into the **Selkirk Mountains** to 1,774m **Kootenay Pass**, the highest paved highway pass in Canada.

The west side of Kootenay Pass twists and turns across five canyons and multiple avalanche chutes. Just west is **Burnt Flat Junction** and

Right
Ferry SS *Nasookin* converted to
a house on the shores of
Kootenay Lake

Hwy 6, which runs 10km south to the US border at **Nelway** (*open daily 0800–2400*).

Hwy 3 turns north to **Salmo**, then west to **Bombi Summit**, 1,214m, with a long descent to the **Columbia River** at Castlegar. The best view of the confluence of the Columbia and Kootenay rivers is from the **Ootischenia Lookout Rest Area**, 8km from the summit on the west side of the highway.

Scenic alternative: The more interesting 150km route to Castlegar follows Hwy 3A north from Creston along the shores of **KOOTENAY LAKE ❶**, passing **Glass House**, **Lockhart Creek Provincial Park** and **Crawford Bay** on the way to the Kootenay Lake Ferry at Kootenay Bay. The 35-minute crossing to **Balfour** is free, but the line-up can take most of the day, especially in summer.

Detour: From Balfour, turn north on Hwy 31 to **AINSWORTH HOT SPRINGS ❷** and **CODY CAVES PROVINCIAL PARK ❸** on the way to **KASLO ❹**. The tiny village has more than 60 heritage buildings, including the SS *Moyie*, a sternwheeler that once carried passengers on the lake. Return to Balfour.

Hwy 3A hugs the north shore of the West Arm of Kootenay Lake. The south shore is all but inaccessible except by boat. The waters between hold record-sized trout and kokanee (land-locked) salmon. What looks like a steamboat cabin perched on the north side of the highway was the upper saloon and wheelhouse of the SS *Nasookin*, once the largest steamboat on Kootenay Lake. The road crosses the bright orange **Nelson Bridge** into **NELSON ❺**, a mining town that has moved into the computer age.

Kootenay Lake empties into the **Kootenay River** just west of Nelson. The highway passes four hydroelectric dams along the river, built to take advantage of the 200m fall from Kootenay Lake at Nelson to the Columbia River at Castlegar. A lay-by 13km west of the junction with Hwy 6 offers a good view of **Lower Bonnington Dam**. A second lay-by 1,500m beyond overlooks **Brilliant Dam** and, just downstream toward the Columbia River, the disused (Doukhobor) Suspension Bridge. A modern bridge arcs over the river to **CASTLEGAR ❻**.

Hwy 3 climbs south from Castlegar, then turns west over dramatic canyons towards **Christina Lake**, an important winter range for deer and elk.

Hwy 395 leads south into Washington just beyond the lake, while Hwy 3 continues westbound into **Boundary Country**, a transition zone between the high Kootenay peaks and the drier, more fertile Okanagan Valley to the west.

GRAND FORKS ❼ is the commercial hub of the Boundary Country, an agricultural town that boomed with mineral strikes in nearby hills. Continue along Hwy 3 over **Eholt Summit**, named after an abandoned mining town, to **GREENWOOD ❽**, a one-time mine boom town, which claims modern fame as the smallest city in BC.

The Crowsnest

Ratings

Heritage	●●●●●
Historical sights	●●●●○
Scenery	●●●●○
Children	●●●○○
Museums	●●●○○
Architecture	●●○○○
Food	●●○○○
Railways	●○○○○

Perched on the east side of the Kootenay Rockies and south of the Columbia River Valley is a microcosm of BC, with a history of coal and gold mining, lumbering, important freight railway lines and scenic ski alps, complete with a purpose-built Bavarian town. The cheerful-looking crow on Crowsnest Highway signposts belies the massacre of horse-stealing Crow warriors by Blackfoot braves who resented thieves camping in their territory, their nest. Highway 3, called the Crowsnest, spans the Alberta–BC border at Crowsnest Pass and zigzags south and west for several hundred kilometres. A circuit from Cranbrook, the regional hub, links First Nations and Gold Rush town history with scenic recreation lakes, a magnificent falls and an alpine village, famed for accordions and alpenhorns. In winter, this southeast corner of BC is transformed into a winter wonderland of mountains and icy lakes, with major ski resorts at Kimberley and Fernie.

CRANBROOK

ⓘ Cranbrook and District Chamber of Commerce InfoCentre
2279 Cranbrook St N; tel: (250) 426-5914 or (800) 222-6174; www.cranbrookchamber.com

ⓜ Canadian Museum of Rail Travel $$
57 Van Horne St S at Baker St. (Hwy 3/95); tel: (250) 489-3918; www.trainsdeluxe.com. Open daily mid-Apr–mid-Oct 0945–1800; mid-Oct–mid-Apr call for hours.

Aboriginal Ktunaxa lost their camping ground to White settlers in 1870 and to a member of the BC Legislature. Cranbrook became a CPR divisional point and the railway its lifeblood.

Canadian Museum of Rail Travel Train buffs enjoy touring through the self-styled 'Canada's Orient Express', built in 1929 as a seven-car unit for CPR's Trans-Canada Limited for Montréal to Vancouver service. The museum is on Van Horne Street (named after the former CPR president, overseer of Canada's transcontinental railway) and accommodates five sets of trains from different eras of Canada's railway history.

Elizabeth Lake Sanctuary Wildlife Area 1101 1st Ave S.

Jimsmith Lake Provincial Park 5km west of Cranbrook on Jim Smith Lake Rd; tel: (250) 422-3003; www.env.gov.bc.ca/bcparks/explore/parkpgs/jimsmith.html

Canadian Rockies International Airport (YXC) Off Hwy 95A between Cranbrook and Kimberley; tel: (250) 426-7913; www.flycanadianrockies.com

Elizabeth Lake Sanctuary Wildlife Area A slice of the Rocky Mountain Trench protects 113 hectares of nature, with a lakeside trail, waterfowl viewing hides and a dip-netting pond to peruse fish closely. Coots, killdeer, Canada geese, ruddy ducks, wood ducks, buffleheads and black terns share the lake with muskrats, elk, moose and turtles.

Jimsmith Lake Provincial Park Join the locals swimming, canoeing, picnicking or camping. You can cross-country ski to the lake in winter and lace up some skates to enjoy the ice.

Accommodation and food in Cranbrook

Super 8 $ 2370 Cranbrook St N; tel: (250) 489-8028 or (800) 800-8000; www.super8.com. Across from the InfoCentre, this chain hotel is clean and comfortable at the quiet north end of town.

Heritage Inn $$ 803 Cranbrook St N; tel: (250) 489-4301 or (800) 888-4374; www.heritageinn.net/cranbrook.php. This motor inn has 100 rooms and a very central location.

Munro's At The Prestige $$ 209 Van Horne St S in the Prestige Rocky Mountain Resort; tel: (250) 417-0444, has home-made pies and pizza on the menu.

Singing Pines Bed and Breakfast $$ 5180 Kennedy Rd; tel: (800) 863-4969; www.singingpines.ca; open May–Sep, has two rooms, a Western décor, and views of the Purcells and Rocky Mountains.

Prestige Rocky Mountain Resort & Convention Centre $$$ 209 Van Horne St S; tel: (250) 417-0444 or (877) 737-8443; http://prestigeinn.com/cranbrook-prestige-hotel.php. A modern, posh railway-theme hotel has 108 rooms near the railway museum.

FERNIE

ⓘ Fernie Chamber of Commerce Visitor Information Centre
Hwy 3 at 102 Commerce Rd; tel: (250) 423-6868 or (877) 433-7643; http://ferniechamber.com. Open daily in summer, Mon–Fri autumn–spring.

⊕ Fernie Alpine Resort $$ *5339 Fernie Ski Hill Rd; tel: (250) 423-4655, (866) 633-7643 or (887) 333-2339; www.skifernie.com. Open year-round, with limited spring and autumn activities. Ski season: open daily approximately Dec–mid-Apr.*

Mountains and tourism services are the *raison d'être* for this all-season recreational area, once known for coal mining and rum-running.

At **Fernie Alpine Resort**, an annual 9m snowfall creates a paradise for alpine and Nordic skiers, snowshoers and snowmobilers. Sleigh-rides and dog sledging are other winter options. Mountain bike, ride a horse, kayak, raft, hike, fly fish or take a chairlift ride to scenic views in summer.

Accommodation and food in Fernie

Wolf's Den Lodge $$–$$$ *5339 Ski Hill Rd, Fernie Alpine Ski Resort; tel: (877) 333-2339; www.skifernie.com. Open all year,* the 42-room lodge offers ski-in, ski-out slope access.

Best Western Fernie Mountain Lodge $$$ *1622 7th Ave; tel: (250) 423-5500* or *(866) 423-5566; www.bestwesternfernie.com,* is next to the Fernie Golf and Country Club with views of the Three Sisters peaks.

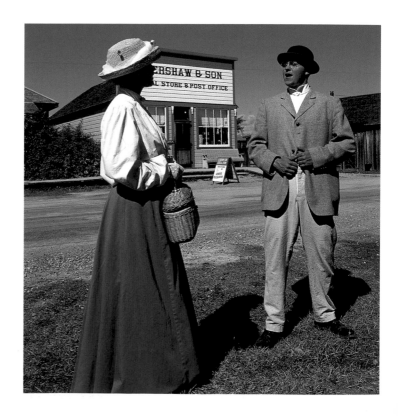

Right
Living history at Fort Steele

Above
Fort Steele steam train

Fernie Stanford Resort $$$ *100 Riverside Way; tel: (250) 423-5000 or (877) 423-5600; www.ferniestanfordresort.com*, has a 51m indoor waterslide and serves standard and Indian cuisine in the **Grizzly's Den $$** restaurant.

The Old Elevator Restaurant $$$ *291 1st Ave; tel: (250) 423-7115; http://oldelevator.com, open Tue–Sun*, is in a restored 1908 feed store, complete with the original elevator and loft, which has won awards for its décor and fine dining menu.

Fort Steele Heritage Town

Fort Steele Heritage Town $$
9851 Hwy 93/95 16km north of Cranbrook; tel: (250) 417-6000 or (250) 426-7352; www.fortsteele.ca. Open May–mid-Oct 0930–1800 (1700 May–Jun), with character actors in summer. Admission covers 2 consecutive days.

The 1864 Kootenay Gold Rush brought settlers to Galbraith's Ferry, later renamed after NWMP Superintendent Sam Steele who brought law and peace to the region. The *de facto* capital of the East Kootenays' rich mining economy lost out and declined when BC Legislator Colonel James Baker got the CPR to build the proposed divisional point in his Cranbrook holdings. The restoration is perfect, with summertime set pieces between neighbours on the street discussing the day's events and politics, all in costume. A bakery, tin-smithy, confectionery, heritage buildings, horse-drawn wagon rides and a steam train provide a well-rounded introduction to Fort Steele's golden years.

KIMBERLEY

ⓘ Kimberley Visitor InfoCentre
*270 Kimberley Ave;
tel: (250) 427-3666 or
(866) 913-3666;
http://kimberleychamber.ca.
Open daily Jul–early Sep
0900–1800, rest of year
Tue–Fri 1200–1700, Sat
1000–1700.*

ⓑ Kimberley's Underground Mining Railway $$$
*Sullivan Mine and Railroad
Historical Society; downtown
station at Gerry Sorensen
Way is next to the Kimberley
Visitor Centre; tel: (250)
427-0022;
www.kimberleysunderground
miningrailway.ca.
Loop from downtown with a
stop at Kimberley Alpine
Resort. Call for hours.*

ⓐ Kimberley Alpine Resort $$ *301 North
Star Blvd; tel: (250) 427-
4881, (877) 754-5462 or
(800) 258-7669;
http://skikimberley.com, is
open summer and winter.*

At 1,113m, Canada's highest city was dedicated to silver, zinc and lead mining production at Sullivan Mine (Cominco), which closed in 2001. Happy Hans, the world's largest cuckoo clock, Bavarian kitsch and **Kimberley Alpine Resort** have replaced the local mining industry.

Kimberley's Underground Mining Railway cars roll through scenic countryside to the former Sullivan Mine and the Underground Interpretive Centre where riders can work with real mining equipment in a show that demonstrates how mining was done. The rail tour also stops at Kimberley Alpine Resort. The mining company wanted to promote fertiliser in 1927. The resultant **Cominco Gardens $** (*306 3rd Ave; tel: (250) 427-2293. Open May–Sep dawn to dusk*) boast 45,000 blooms annually, with dedicated rose, prairie and Victorian gazebo areas.

In the **Platzl** (*T-shaped pedestrian street encircled by Wallinger Ave, Howard St, Kimberley Ave and Ross St*), Bavarian architecture, restaurants, shops, and depictions of the Happy Hans town mascot reflect the transition the town economy has made from mining lead to mining tourists.

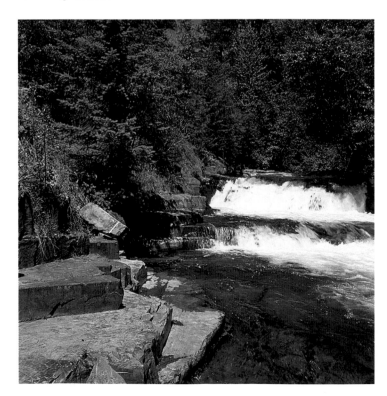

Right
Marysville Falls

Accommodation and food in Kimberley

Kimberley City Bakery $ *287 Spokane St; tel: (250) 427-2131 or (800) 335-3387; www.kimberleycitybakery.ca,* serves breads, pastries and chocolates in the tearoom or to take away.

Chef Bernard's $$ *170 Spokane St, on the Platzl; tel: (250) 427-4820.* The chef is well known and locally beloved in this Bavarian *schnitzelhaus* which serves excellent pasta dishes.

Old Bauernhaus $$$ *280 Norton Ave, up the ski hill; tel: (250) 427-5133.* Bavaria was never so authentic as in this 350-plus-year-old building dismantled and reassembled here.

Trickle Creek Residence Inn $$$ *500 Sternwinder Dr; tel: (877) 282-1200 or (250) 427-5175; www.marriott.com/hotels/travel/yqeri-residence-inn-kimberley-trickle-creek,* has a ski-in-ski-out location at the mountain base, full kitchens, breakfast and gas fireplaces.

MARYSVILLE FALLS

Marysville Falls $
7km south of Kimberley.

An easy 10-minute afternoon walk along rocky Mark Creek to a spectacular crashing 30m cascade is worth a brief stop.

MOYIE AND MOYIE LAKE PROVINCIAL PARK

Moyie and Moyie Lake Provincial Park $ *20km south of Cranbrook, Hwy 3; tel: (250) 422-3003; www.env.gov.bc.ca/bcparks/explore/parkpgs/moyie.html*

Bears roam around the popular windsurfing and swimming lake, which nestles within the Purcell Mountains. Explorer David Thompson's party was almost swept away by Moyie River floods in 1808, but today's 200 residents point with pride to lovely buildings and a well-preserved fire hall which served when the St Eugene Mine silver/lead mine owners became rich before 1898.

ST EUGENE MISSION

St Eugene Mission *515 Mission Rd, Cranbrook; tel: (250) 489-2372.*

St Eugene Golf Resort & Casino $$ *7777 Mission Rd; tel: (250) 420-2000 or (866) 292-2020; www.steugene.ca.* **Casino of the Rockies** *Tel: (250) 417-2772,* is adjacent.

The 1897 white Victorian gingerbread church in the middle of farms on Ktunaxa/Kinbasket St Mary's Reserve is as immaculate inside as out with stained-glass windows and interior supports resembling a barn. Stop by nearby Ktunaxa Tribal office for information and to go inside the church. The former Kootenay Indian Residential School complex 16km north of Cranbrook is now the **St Eugene Golf Resort & Casino**, with an 18-hole championship golf course (*tel: (877) 417-3133 for tee times*), and a base to enjoy the area's many outdoor activities. A Ktunaxa/Kinbasket Interpretive Centre is in the former school building.

Suggested tour

Total distance: 90km for a circuit from Cranbrook. Detours: 97km from Cranbrook to Fernie; 31km south to Moyie.

Time: 2 days.

Links: The **Columbia River** (*see page 230*) lies north of Wasa. Continue south and west of Moyie Lake Provincial Park on Hwy 3, the Crowsnest, to Creston and **The Kootenays** (*see page 240*). North of Fernie at Sparwood, Hwy 3 turns east to the Crowsnest Pass and enters Alberta.

Route: CRANBROOK ❶ makes a convenient base with services and facilities, but with this circuit, it's almost as convenient to stay in Kimberley.

Cranbrook's main attraction is the **Canadian Museum of Rail Travel** and the red wooden railway **Water Tower** nearby, situated along the Canadian Pacific Railway line where rolling stock provides a realistic background for the historic railway carriages. A graceful reconstructed red-brick **Rotary Clock Tower** (*Baker & Cranbrook Sts*) is the focal point for a Chamber of Commerce *Heritage Tour* brochure of Cranbrook's downtown and Baker Hill Residential Area buildings. **Elizabeth Lake Sanctuary Wildlife Area** is an utterly peaceful spot for picnicking and walking the lakeside trail accompanied by birdsong. Follow signs when crossing Hwy 3 to **Jimsmith Lake Provincial Park**, with non-powered watersports on offer.

Take Hwy 3 to the northeast end of Cranbrook and go left on to Hwy 95A. Be prepared to turn right almost immediately on to Old Airport Road to **ST EUGENE MISSION ❷** in the midst of the tribal headquarters for the Ktunaxa/Kinbasket First Nation **St Mary's Reserve**. The restored historic church is lovely. Continue along Old Airport Road to rejoin Hwy 95A.

Stop at the bridge in **Marysville** at the south edge of **KIMBERLEY ❸** and hike down Mark Creek for a view of magnificent **MARYSVILLE FALLS ❹**. Kimberley's heart is the Platzl, the Bavarian chalet-style pedestrian plaza, with a cuckoo clock that claims to be the world's largest. It chimes on the hour, revealing the ubiquitous Happy Hans yodelling. Catch Kimberley's Underground Mining Railway excursion train at the Platzl. A short drive up the ski hill offers vistas over the Kootenay River Valley. Before leaving town, take in the thousands of blooms at **Cominco Gardens**.

⓫ Wasa Lake Provincial Park
Tel: (250) 422-3003;
www.env.gov.bc.ca/bcparks/
explore/parkpgs/wasa_lk

Continue north on Hwy 95A past **Ta Ta Creek** and turn south at the Hwy 93/95 junction to **Wasa Lake Provincial Park** for swimming in the Kootenay's warmest lake (May–October). Follow Hwy 93/95 to **FORT STEELE ❺** for time travel in one of BC's best and most authentic historic site restorations. Return to Cranbrook.

Detour to Fernie: South of Fort Steele, go east on Hwy 3/93. North of Elko on Hwy 3 is the **Elk Valley** traversing the Elk River, named after the numerous wapiti spotted by settlers. Coal mining boomed around 1900 from the valley into Alberta, and Fernie and the surrounding area became rich, though plagued by a legendary curse on the mines. **FERNIE ALPINE RESORT 6** buzzes with summer and winter activity in a stunning range of mountains.

Detour to Moyie: Take Hwy 3/95 south of Cranbrook to **MOYIE 7**, a tiny town set on a scenic hillside. **MOYIE LAKE PROVINCIAL PARK 8** has watersports and sailing.

Demon King Coal

Fernie became rich on coal deposits, a seam which stretches across the Crowsnest Pass into Alberta at Frank Slide, site of a 1903 disaster when poor coal-mining techniques and water seepage caused 30 million cu m of limestone to slide down Turtle Mountain onto Frank Townsite.

Fernie, too, seemed cursed. Coal Creek Mine developer William Fernie, so the story goes, extracted information about coal deposits from a local Ktunaxa maiden, while pretending to woo her. When the lady was rejected by Fernie, the girl's mother placed a curse on Fernie. Curse or no, the Coal Creek Mine explosion in 1901 killed 128, followed by a 1904 fire which burned the town, and a flood in 1916. A 1964 ritual by local First Nations chiefs was enacted to counteract the curse. Since 1901, though, local people have seen the Ghostrider, said to be the spurned betrothed seated on a horse, and her mother chasing Fernie across the face of Mount Hosmer at the end of each day.

BC Rockies Parks

Ratings

Geology	●●●●●
Mountains	●●●●●
National parks	●●●●●
Nature	●●●●●
Outdoor activities	●●●●●
Scenery	●●●●●
Walking	●●●●●
Wildlife	●●●●●

The Rocky Mountains west of the Continental Divide shelter great rivers, exploding cataracts, emerald-green lakes, red-rock defiles, thick green forests and slashes of colour gushing forth from the earth. Disc-shaped trilobites, whose fossils were discovered in Yoho National Park, inhabited this raw, breathtaking landscape half a billion years ago. Kootenay National Park's Radium Hot Springs pools soothed First Nations bathers for centuries. An enduring symbol of the Rockies, Mount Robson, dominates eastward afternoon vistas, a snow-striated massif embraced by forest at its base.

Early explorers looking for fur trade routes west followed streams and whitewater rivers to their headwaters. The mountains required feats of railway engineering when the imperative to ship goods, settlers and tourists westward became financially irresistible. Despite a million visitors flowing through each year, there's enough high-country wilderness in the BC Rockies to leave memories of untrammelled vastness.

KOOTENAY NATIONAL PARK

Kootenay National Park $
Tel: (250) 347-9505;
www.pc.gc.ca/pn-np/bc/kootenay/index_e.asp

Kootenay National Park Visitor Centre 7556 Main Street East (at Redstreak Campground Rd), Radium Hot Springs; tel: (250) 347-9505. Open mid-May–mid-Jun and early Sep 0900–1700, mid-Jun–Labour Day 0900–1900.

Visitors who merely drive through without stopping inadvertently pay homage to the park's *raison d'être*. The Banff–Windermere Highway, Hwy 93, the route through Kootenay National Park, was built between 1912 and 1923 as an all-weather commercial transit road over the Rockies. Motorised touring and holidaymakers never looked back!

The 95km stretch of Hwy 93 in the park follows the meanderings of Sinclair and Swede creeks to the Kootenay and Vermillion rivers. The parkway rises east from the Columbia River Valley through a red-rock canyon and passes vistas of a ridge of peaks framing the Kootenay River before winding up to the Continental Divide at the 1,651m Vermillion Pass on the BC–Alberta boundary.

The Kootenay (pronounced 'coo-teh-knee' in Canada), 'people from beyond the hills', lived and gave character and names to a region from the peaks of the Rockies to southern interior BC. Descendants of a

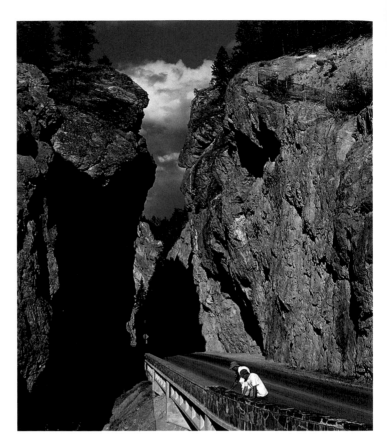

Right
Sinclair Canyon, Kootenay
National Park

🛈 **Kootenay Park
Lodge Visitor
Centre** *Vermillion Crossing,
68km northeast of Radium
Hot Springs; tel: (250) 762-
9196. Open daily mid-
May–early Oct.*

linguistically unique and part Plains, part (BC) Plateau group, the
Ktunaxa, Kootenae, Kootenai or Kootenay live in BC and in the USA
in Montana. Foods, hunting traditions, homes, clothing and
ceremonies resemble bits and pieces of neighbouring bands', but were
distinct. Whatever their origins, the Kootenay gathered the brightly
coloured mud running from the mountain streams and soaked weary
bones in the medicinal hot springs.

Kootenay peoples called the coloured earth 'The Place Where the
Red Spirit of the Earth is Taken'. Scientifically, iron oxide stains
water pushing up from three springs beneath the earth red and
yellow, sometimes mixing to brown or orange. The 'vermillion' after
which the park's river and pass (at the Continental Divide) are named
reflect the ochre paint pots' reddish colour.

Kootenays gathered the bright mud, formed and baked it into cakes,
then rubbed off powder as needed and mixed it with rendered animal
grease for face paint, clothing and tepee decoration and for medicine.
When White entrepreneurs started a short-lived ochre mining

Radium Hot Springs Chamber of Commerce and Visitor Centre *7556 Main St E, Radium Hot Springs; tel: (250) 347-9331 or (888) 347-9331; http://radiumhotsprings.com. Open daily 0900–1700, to 1900 in summer,* at the southwestern edge of Kootenay National Park, serves the area's population and services centre. There are also motels in the park above the Radium Hot Springs Pools.

Paint Pots *85km northeast of Radium.*

Radium Hot Springs Pools *$ 3km east of Radium; tel: (250) 347-9485 or (800) 767-1611; www.hotsprings.ca and www.pc.gc.ca/regional/ sourcesthermales-hotsprings/ itm2-/radium_E.asp. Open mid-May–mid-Oct 0900–2300; mid-Oct–mid-May Sun–Thu 1200–2100, Fri–Sat to 2200. Call to check hours before arrival.* Enquire about family rates and hire of swimsuits and towels. Massage and reflexology treatments available; *tel: (250) 347-2100.* There is a summertime poolside restaurant for drinks, sandwiches, burgers, ice cream and snacks.

operation for paint pigments in the early 1900s, they followed Kootenay trading practices by transporting the mud elsewhere, albeit by hand, to Castle Junction (Banff National Park) and on to Calgary by railway.

A 1.6km return trail traverses varied countryside before reaching the **Paint Pots**, actually three main pools – one red, one yellow and one bright green. Descend from the parking area into a sub-alpine forest with ferns and wild flowers growing beneath the trees. A swinging suspension bridge bounces and sways across the crashing pale blue waters of the Kootenay River. The land suddenly runs with rivulets of colour as the path ascends by the ruins of mining equipment to the three pots, an oasis of coloured, water-filled pockmarks surrounded by forest. A tiny wetland offers fine birdwatching.

The sheer golden-red walls of Sinclair Canyon shelter the site where groundwater sinking 2km down a fault in the earth returns to the surface heated to 44°C. Most of the park's 1.2 million annual visitors make a pilgrimage to the outdoor **Radium Hot Springs Pools**, to soak, swim or absorb the atmosphere of an unpretentious, not-quite-spa experience. The hot, semi-secluded soaking pool is a toasty 39°C; a lap in the swimming pool afterwards will seem almost bracing at 27°C. Mountain sheep are sometimes spotted clinging to nearby cliffs.

Radium? No, a misnomer, but there is radon, with a minuscule amount of radioactivity. Early 20th-century researchers presumed it was radium, and therapeutic, though a wristwatch emits more radium than the pools! Equally pleasant is the faint-to-odourless atmosphere distinctly lacking in the sulphur experienced in Banff's Cave and Basin National Historic Site (*see page 270*).

Accommodation and food in Kootenay National Park

Alpen Motel **$$** *5022 Hwy 93, Radium Hot Springs; tel: (250) 347-9823 or (888) 788-3891; www.alpenmotel.com,* is cheerful with flower-boxes, 14 spotless, no-pet, non-smoking rooms a block from the park portal, and free mineral hot pool passes.

Kootenay Park Lodge **$$** *Hwy 93 at Vermillion Crossing; tel: (403) 762-9196 or (403) 283-7482; www.kootenayparklodge.com; open mid-May–Sep.* To stay in the centre of the park in a log cabin is almost a wilderness experience. Canadian Pacific Railway built the lodge in 1923. There is a licensed restaurant; the gift-shop sandwiches are home-made and scrumptious.

Old Salzburg Restaurant **$$** *4943 Hwy 93; tel: (250) 347-6553; http://oldsalzburgrestaurant.com,* matches the style of many nearby alpine-chalet-style motels with Austrian specialities such as schnitzel and goulash soup.

MOUNT ROBSON PROVINCIAL PARK

ⓘ **Tourism Valemount/ Valemount Visitor Centre** *785 Cranberry Lake Rd; tel: (250) 566-4846; www.valemount.org/ Tourism/index.htm. Open mid-May–mid-Sep.*

Mount Robson Provincial Park Visitor Centre *At the west end of the park on Hwy 16; (Apr–Sep); www.env.gov.bc. ca/bcparks/explore/parkpgs/ mtrobson.html. Open daily May–Oct.*

The Texqakallt/Shuswap aboriginal name, *yuh-hai-has-kun,* says it all: the Mountain of the Spiral Road to Heaven. *If* Mount Robson is out from behind the often obscuring cloud cover, the sheer rise of its 3,954m height is stunningly beautiful. The highest peak in the Canadian Rockies was not scaled until 1913, an ascent which continues to lure only the most experienced climbers today. Whether driving by on the Yellowhead Hwy, Hwy 16, or stopping for a look, plan on going west in the morning or east in the afternoon for the best-lit views of Mount Robson's face.

The most famous view of Mount Robson and its only slightly less high neighbour, 3,426m Mount Resplendent, is from the Visitor Centre along Hwy 16 at the park's west end. **Berg Lake Trail** car park is 2km north of the Visitor Centre. From there, it's a several-day, advance-registration, 23km hike to Robson Pass, with limited pitches for self-contained camping along the trail. Short of that is Kinney Lake at 7km, famed for still morning reflections of Mount Robson. Beyond is the Valley of the Thousand Falls and no fewer than 15 glaciers, including the advancing Berg Glacier which 'calves' blue ice into Berg Lake.

East of the Visitor Centre is a short, easy hike through forest to the sheer drop of **Overlander Falls**, named after 1862 prospectors headed for the Cariboo gold fields with more determination than preparation.

Midway through the park, you will spot waterfalls across Moose Lake. Canoe through the rightly named **Moose Marsh**, a likely place to find the 450kg beasts browsing. The Fraser River, which has its headwaters at Fraser Pass in the provincial park, is popular with

Berg Lake Trail *Car park 2km north of Visitor Centre with trailhead.* Advance registration by phone, *tel: (800) 689-9025,* at Visitor Centre required for multiple-day hiking. 23km one-way to end; pre-book for a camp pitch en route. Carry all-weather gear and provisions. Part of trail may close to encourage caribou calving. For detailed trail information, *see: www.env.gov.bc.ca/bcparks/explore/parkpgs/mt_robs/berg.html#berg*

Moose Marsh *Southeast of Moose Lake.*

Overlander Falls *1.5km east of the Visitor Centre.*

Yellowhead Pass *Hwy 16 at the BC–Alberta boundary.*

Below
The Fraser River

whitewater rafters where it parallels the Yellowhead Hwy between Red Pass at the west end of Moose Lake and near the Visitor Centre, and below that spot on placid water.

The park's eastern boundary at the 1,146m **Yellowhead Pass** is also the Continental Divide and the provincial border with Alberta at Jasper National Park. The Yellowhead, the lowest pass in this section of the Rockies, was used for centuries by aboriginal peoples, trappers and hunters. Ironically, although it was surveyed in 1872 and known to be the best logistical engineering choice for building a railway line through the Rockies, in 1881 the CPR chose to build the railway over Kicking Horse Pass further to the south, to forestall American railroaders from stealing business from southern Canada.

Tête Jaune (*tay john*) **Cache**, Yellowhead's purported spot for hiding goods and furs, is at the junction of the eponymous Yellowhead Hwy (16) and Hwy 5. A few buildings and services suffice for the meeting of the roads named after trapper Pierre Hatsinaton's golden hair.

Accommodation and food in Mount Robson Provincial Park

There is a store for provisioning across from the Visitor Centre and two reservation-recommended campgrounds with 144 pitches in the park.

Mount Robson Lodge $$ *log cabins* and **Robson Shadows Campground $** *tel: (888) 566-4821* or *(250) 566-4821; www.mountrobsonlodge.com (open mid-May–mid-Oct)*, are 5km west of the park.

Valemount (*44km southwest of the park*) offers a range of motels.

Above
Emerald Lake, Yoho National Park

YOHO NATIONAL PARK

Yoho National Park Visitor Centre *South side, TransCanada Hwy 1, Field; tel: (250) 343-6783. Open May–late Jun, Sep, 0900–1700; late Jun–Labour Day 0900–1900; late Sep–Apr 0900–1600. There is an excellent selection of books and a Burgess Shale Fossil exhibit.*

Few places on earth have both yielded such a rich treasure trove of fossils and been the site of almost unimaginable modern engineering feats. First Nations Cree used the word *yoho* to express awe and wonder at a landscape that included rock escarpments, hanging glaciers, waterfalls, emerald lakes, crashing rivers and sheer ranges of mountains.

John Palliser's 1857 expedition took three years to scientifically survey Southern Alberta and what would become British Columbia. Geologist-naturalist James Hector was assigned to evaluate the river valley and its steep mountain pass. His skittish horse fell near Wapta Falls, knocking him out and frightening Hector's troupe. When he recovered, the relieved men named the river Kicking Horse.

Though Hector recommended against transportation across Kicking Horse Pass and in favour of the less precipitous Yellowhead Pass

**Yoho National
Park $** Tel: (250)
343-6783; www.pc.gc.ca/pn-
np/bc/yoho/index_e.asp

Emerald Lake 11km
north of Field.

Natural Bridge
3km southwest of Field along
the route to Emerald Lake.

Takakkaw Falls 17km
northeast of Field via Yoho
Valley Rd. Because of a
switchback section beyond
the Meeting of the Waters,
trailers are prohibited.
Yoho Valley Rd closed to
vehicles early Oct–late Jun.

further north, nationalist imperative dictated that Kicking Horse be chosen as the Canadian transcontinental railway route, to show encroaching American interests that Canadians could transport their own commodities.

Brilliant, cantankerous Major Albert Bowman Rogers surveyed the passes and recommended that, despite its slope, the Kicking Horse must connect to another pass in the unexplored Selkirk Range to the West (see Rogers Pass, page 232) and would be viable. Canadian Pacific Railway general manager, William Cornelius Van Horne, pleasing stockholders and covering up mismanagement scandals, pushed for the Kicking Horse route. The years from 1885 to 1905 saw runaway train crashes on the 4.5 per cent grade, until the spiral tunnels were built.

A CPR engineer taking a break near the railway hub in Field probably thought he was dreaming to see some discs of stone resembling horseshoe crabs in the dirt of Mount Stephen. He had found trilobites.

Smithsonian Institution palaeontologist Charles Walcott, conducting Rockies digs on Burgess Pass within view of Emerald Lake in 1909, recognised the trilobites for what they were: fossils from the Palaeozoic Cambrian period, 500–590 million years old. The Burgess Shale has since yielded 120 fossilised species, more than 65,000 specimens of hard-shelled animals which swam and ate in the sea and underwater reef which extended inland half a billion years ago.

Emerald Lake Greener than green, green enough to make blue sky pale in comparison, the glassy glacier-formed 28m-deep lake is perfect for canoeing. You can hike, or in winter (usually mid-November to mid-May) snowshoe or Nordic ski the 5km loop around the lake. Walk clockwise from the wooden car bridge near the parking area for the best views of the President Range northward. The trail's approach to the east and south sides is more lushly forested. Veterans allow a full day to hike a 21km triangular loop, north from the lake's north end up the Yoho Pass Trail, then south along the flanks of Wapta Mountain on the Burgess Highline Trail to Burgess Pass, then west back to the Lake Loop Trail.

Natural Bridge Two kilometres up the road to Emerald Lake is one of the most accessible and beautiful attractions in the Rockies parks. A rocky outcropping forms a grey rock tunnel for the green waters of the Kicking Horse River. An afternoon stop is best for drama and photos: walk across the man-made bridge spanning the water to take in alternative viewpoints.

Takakkaw Falls The winding 15km road through the Yoho River Valley is filled with waterfalls, a Spiral Tunnel viewpoint, a lay-by for the Meeting of the Waters at the confluence of the Yoho and Kicking Horse rivers, and a challenging switchback.

Takakkaw (the word means 'wonderful' or 'magnificent' in Cree) Falls consist of sheer, golden cliffs, tufted on the top ridge by a line of

Upper and Lower Spiral Tunnels
Lower Spiral Tunnel Viewpoint is 8km northeast of Field along TransCanada Hwy 1. Open mid-May–mid-Oct. Access another viewpoint along Yoho Valley Road, mid-Jun–mid-Sep, by the Kicking Horse River interpretive sign.

The Burgess Shale Geoscience Foundation *$$$ Tel: (800) 343-3006; www.burgess-shale.bc.ca, offers excellent interpretative hikes, including a long, rigorous Burgess Shale/Walcott Quarry Hike and a shorter Mount Stephen Fossil Beds Hike walk up Field's Mount Stephen, with numerous trilobite fossils. Access for groups limited to 15 persons is by guided tour only.*

dark green conifers, and water from Daly Glacier above exploding out into space before plunging 254m to the ground. The trail to the falls' base from the parking area crosses a bridge before winding up to a very chilly and thick misty zone, perfect for rainbows in the afternoon.

Upper and Lower Spiral Tunnels If there's a train traversing the tunnels, you're in luck! Most of the time, the vistas of the raw landscape surrounding the 992m Upper Spiral Tunnel and 891m Lower Spiral Tunnel have to suffice to evoke the interpretive sign descriptions.

Imagine the Big Hill west of Kicking Horse Pass, where, because the CPR got a government-granted variance to build track on a grade over 2.2 per cent, runaway trains were common, a potential deathtrap for those on the trains and those maintaining the lines.

For 20 years, death loomed any time a train went west down the Rockies' rise. In 1905, using engineering principles adapted from Switzerland's St Gotthard Railway Baischina Gorge Tunnels, the CPR completed a set of $1.5 million tunnels, so perfectly aligned when dug that the joining point varied by only 5cm.

And the innovation? Adding 7km of track in one straight and in a rough figure-8 pattern, two spirals within the mountain, reducing speed and eliminating the plunge down the 6.6km Big Hill.

Accommodation and food in Yoho National Park

The small town of **Field** has about a dozen bed and breakfasts. Enquire at the Field Visitor InfoCentre.

Yoho Brothers' Trading Post $$ Hwy 1, across from the InfoCentre, sells sandwiches, First-Nations-style souvenirs and books, and is the meeting place for the Yoho-Burgess Shale Foundation tours.

Cathedral Mountain Lodge $$$ *Yoho Valley Rd; tel: (250) 343-6442 or (866) 619-6442; http://cathedralmountain.com. Open mid-May–early Oct.* Log cabins with fireplaces along the pale blue Kicking Horse River and stunning views of the mountains near Field make this an alluring mid-park lodging. A grocery store is good for provisioning before Takakkaw Falls; the licensed Dining Room Restaurant serves crisp salads, tangy fresh tomato soup and delicately prepared fish.

Emerald Lake Lodge $$$ *At Emerald Lake; tel: (403) 410-7417, (800) 663-6336 or (250) 343-6321; www.crmr.com/emerald-lake-lodge.php.* Chalets surround the lodge-cum-resort, often booked out by executive conferences. The view of canoeists on the jewel-coloured lake is without equal. **Cilantro's $$** restaurant serves meals and drinks on an umbrella-decked terrace in summer.

Kicking Horse Lodge $$$ *100 Centre St, Field; tel: (250) 343-6303 or (800) 659-4944,* has 14 rooms year-round in a chalet-style building, a dining room and lounge.

Opposite
Kicking Horse Pass

Canada's Rocky Mountain National Parks

Parks Canada provides *The Mountain Guide*, a free tabloid-sized newspaper with a page of highlights from each of the six parks: Banff, Glacier, Jasper, Kootenay, Mount Revelstoke and Yoho. The same summaries can be found online: *www.pc.gc.ca/docs/v-g/ pm-mp/guidem-mguide/ index_e.asp*

Suggested tour

Total distance: 550km.

Time: 4 days to drive; can be divided into south (Kootenay and Yoho National Parks) and north (Mount Robson Provincial Park).

Links: The Rocky Mountain Trench along the **Columbia River** (*see page 230*) at Radium is a jumping-off point for Kootenay National Park, and is the gateway to Yoho National Park at Golden. Cross over to the **Alberta Rockies** (*see page 270*) for the transit between parks via the Castle Junction and Icefields Parkway links. From Tête Jaune Cache, continue on the Yellowhead Hwy to **Prince George** (*see page 222*).

Route: From **Radium**, take Hwy 93 east through Sinclair Canyon to the **Radium Hot Springs Pools**, and follow the Banff–Windermere Hwy through **KOOTENAY NATIONAL PARK ❶**. East of the pools, traverse a red-rock defile. Shallow **Olive Lake** shimmers blue-green with fish-beloved grasses. The highway rises immediately to a superb **Kootenay Valley Viewpoint**, then descends beneath an area favoured by mountain goats to **Vermillion Crossing**. The **Paint Pots** are 22km northwest. Hike a crisscross 0.8km trail up **Marble Canyon**. At the top of Vermillion Pass is the **Continental Divide** and the **Fireweed Trail** through a 1968 forest-fire area.

Cross into Alberta and **Banff National Park** (*see page 270*) at Castle Junction. Go north on TransCanada Hwy 1 to 3km beyond the Lake Louise exit, and continue on Hwy 1 veering left to the **Great [Continental] Divide** at the BC boundary and west into **YOHO NATIONAL PARK ❷** at **Kicking Horse Pass**. The **Lower Spiral**

Geological Rockies

Rockies' peaks and sideways-smashed mountains hint at the sliding and crashing which formed them. Inland seas lapped at the area which became the Western Rockies, silt trapping tiny lifeforms as fossils 500,000 years ago. In the Age of Dinosaurs, 160–60 million years ago, volcanoes erupted and faults thrust older rock on top of younger rock. At the bottom was granite; above was sedimentary rock, forming into the striated layers which streak faces of the Rocky Mountains.

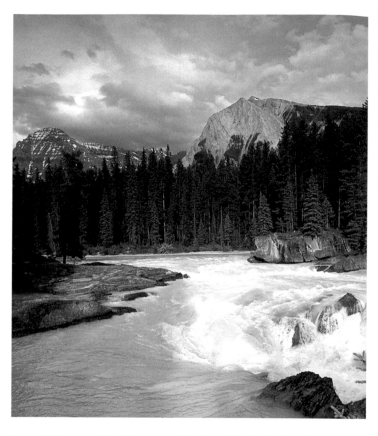

Right
Yoho National Park

Tunnel Viewpoint is 8km west. Take the Yoho Valley Road turn-off to **Takakkaw Falls**, with the **Upper Spiral Tunnel Viewpoint** and **Meeting of the Waters Exhibit** en route. Return to Hwy 1 and descend the Big Hill to **Field Park and Visitor InfoCentre** for the Burgess Shale Exhibit. Immediately south is the road to **Natural Bridge** and **Emerald Lake**. Rejoin Hwy 1 to **Faeder Lake**, with pristine mountain reflections, hike a steep 3km trail up the **Leanchoil Hoodoos** and to **Wapta Falls**, near where Hector's horse kicked.

To continue through the Rockies, retrace the route up Hwy 1 into Banff National Park, and take Hwy 93, the Icefields Parkway, north to Jasper via Jasper National Park. From Jasper, take Hwy 16, the Yellowhead Hwy, west over **Yellowhead Pass** through MOUNT ROBSON PROVINCIAL PARK ❸, passing **Yellowhead Lake** and Moose Marsh. Canoeists paddle **Moose Lake**; rafters take to the **Fraser River**. The best views of **Mount Robson** are from the **Visitor Centre**, near the trail to **Overlander Falls**. **Berg Trail** parking is just north. Continue west to **Tête Jaune Cache**.

ROCKY

WILLMORE
WILDERNESS
PARK

De Veber
7

sthaven Mtn.
98 m

Mt. Chown
3,331 m

The Ranee
2,939 m

ALTA.
BR. COL.

Mt. Robson
3,954 m

Resplendent Mtn.
3,426 m

Mt. Terry Fox
Prov. Park

Valemount

Yellowhead Pass
1,131 m

Jasper

MOUNT ROBSON
PROV. PARK

Marmot
Basin

Simon Pk.
3,322 m

Mt. Edith
Cavell
3,363 m

Athabasca
Falls

Jasper Tramway

Kerkeslin
Mtn.
2,956 m

Samson Pk.
3,081 m

NATIONAL

JASPER

William A.
Switzer
Provincial
Park

Hinton

Brûlé
Lake

Roche Miette
2,316 m

Luscar Mtn.
2,601 m

Sirdar Mtn. 2,804 m

Mt. Balinhard
3,130 m

PARK

Mt. Brazeau
3,470 m

Hornbeck Cr.
P.R.A.

Edson

125

WHITEHORSE
WILDLAND P. P.

Pembina

Nojack
P.R.A.

Nojack
59

BIGHORN

WILDLAND

Mt. Dalhousie
2,947 m

ROCKY
MOUNTAINS
FOREST
RESERVE

Brazeau
Reservoir

HAMBER
PROV. PARK

Hallam Pk.
3,219 m

Kinbasket L.

Cummins
Lakes Prov. Pk.

Mt. Alberta
3,619 m

Mt. Columbia
Highest Pt. in Alta.
3,747 m

Icefield Ctr.

Icefields

Sunwapta Pass
2,035 m

Mt. Cline
3,361 m

MOUNTAINS

RECREATION

AREA

Abraham
Lake

Clearwater

Mica Dam

Gordon Horne Pk.
2,885 m

338

Adamant Mtn.
3,355 m

Mt. Sir Sandford
3,522 m

Mt. Amery 3,329 m

Mt. Lyell 3,520 m

Mt. Forbes
3,612 m

Mt. Freshfield
3,336 m

Mt. Mummery
3,328 m

Mt. Willingdon
3,373 m

Condor Pk.
2,948 m

Wapiti Mtn
3,028 m

Barrier Mtn.
2,962 m

BANFF

Lake
Louise

NATIONAL

PARK

Sunshine
Vil.

The President
3,138 m

Emerald
Lake

Rogers Pass
1,327 m

GLACIER

148

Revelstoke Dam
Vis. Ctr.

Last Spike
Mon.

Lake
Revelstoke

Silver Beach
Provincial Park

Humamilt
L.

Shuswap
L.

Herald
Prov. Pk.

NATL. PK.

Vis. Ctr.

Mt. Dawson 3,390 m

White-
tooth

Leanchoil

Grand Mtn.
3,305 m

Golden

YOHO
NATIONAL
PARK

Banff
Mt. Norquay

102

Cave & Basin N.H.S.

Banff

(1A)

MT.
ASSINIBOINE
PROV. PK.

104

KOOTENAY

NATL. PARK

MOUNT
REVELSTOKE
N.P.

Martha Creek
Provincial Park

Revelstoke

Railway Mus.

Mt. Mackenzie

Yard Ck.
Prov. Pk.

Sicamous

Blanket Cr.
Prov. Pk.

Shelter Bay
Prov. Pk.

Duncan

mon
Arm

Coldstream

Armstrong

Spallumcheen

Silver Star Mtn.

Lumby

Salmon
Arm

SILVERSTAR P.P.

Mabel L.
Prov. Pk.

Upper
Arrow
Lake

MONASHEE
PROV. PK.

Sugar
L.

Monashee
Pass
1,189 m

Nakusp

McDonald Creek
Prov. Pk.

Summit
Lake

BUGABOO
PROV.
PARK

Mt. Templeman
3,070 m

Duncan
Dam

Dry Gulch Prov. Park

GOAT
RANGE
PROV.
PARK

Duncan
Lake

Mt. Hamill
3,243 m

Panorama

0   20km

Radium Hot
Springs

Windermere
Valley Mus.

Columbia Lake
Prov. Pk.

Canal Flat
Prov. Pk.

66

Alberta Rockies Parks

Ratings

Children	●●●●●
Mountains	●●●●●
National parks	●●●●●
Nature	●●●●●
Outdoor activities	●●●●●
Scenery	●●●●●
Walking	●●●●●
Wildlife	●●●●●

Canada's best-known natural icons don't disappoint. If anything, the peaks are higher and more pristine, the lakes a deeper aquamarine, the rivers an icier blue, the glaciers vaster and the animals more evident than seems possible.

The Alberta Rockies, primarily found in Banff and Jasper National Parks, are heaven for hikers and cyclists, canoeists, rafters, skiers and snowshoers, best when explored beyond the confines of a vehicle, motor coach or train window.

The icons also pack the parks with more than three million annual visitors, most driving through in July and August. They stop barely long enough to shop in Banff, stroll around the Banff Springs Hotel, walk around Lake Louise, dash to the Peyto Lake Viewpoint and haul along the Icefields Parkway. Traverse any trail to add a unique individual experience, and watch for bear, wapiti (elk), deer and Rocky Mountain sheep just beyond the next turn.

BANFF NATIONAL PARK

ℹ **Parks Canada Banff Information Centre** 224 Banff Ave; tel: (403) 762-1550; www.pc.gc.ca/pn-np/ab/banff/index_e.asp. Open winter 0900–1700; spring and autumn 0900–1900; summer 0800–2000.

Banff/Lake Louise Tourism Tel: (403) 762-8421; www.banfflakelouise.com

Town of Banff 110 Bear St (Town Hall); tel: (403) 762-1200; www.banff.ca. Open Mon–Fri 0830–1630.

Canada's first national park, established in 1885, splashes scenery around and between its two centres, the town of Banff and Lake Louise.

Banff Park Museum National Historic Site The 1903 'railroad pagoda' exterior and Douglas-fir interior, complete with balconies around an atrium, set off this fine Victorian-style collection of stuffed park birds, insects and animals.

Fairmont Banff Springs The 1888 tourist hotel (see page 274) was built by the CPR to lure railway passengers to its Scottish-looking baronial manor, and some details remain. Stroll the grounds, but find the best views from Tunnel Mountain Road across the Bow River.

Cave & Basin National Historic Site Found by CPR workers in 1883, the sulphuric hot springs were a gold mine for the Canadian government and the CPR, who both wanted to develop the area as a tourist stop. 'These springs will recuperate the patient and recoup the treasury,' commented Prime Minister Sir John A Macdonald obligingly.

Tourism Canmore
907 7th Ave; tel: (866)
226-6673 or (403) 678-
1295;
www.tourismcanmore.com

Banff's birthplace can be toured, but not bathed in. The free 0.6km **Marsh Trail Loop** is fine for bird-, elk- and orchid-spotting.

Lake Louise Emerald water, white Victoria Glacier, red canoes, a rainbow of Icelandic poppies, a carved winter ice palace, tea-time elegance. The modernised, buff-coloured, château-style hotel stands at the east end of the lake like a sentinel. In summer, hikers take the **Lake Agnes Trail** to one tea-house or follow the 10.5km return **Lakeshore Trail/Plain of the Six Glaciers Trail** to another.

Lake Louise Visitor Centre By Samson Mall; tel: (403) 522-3833. Open mid-Jun–Labour Day 0900–2000; early May–mid-Jun, late Sep 0900–1700; late Sep–Apr 0900–1600.

Banff Book & Art Den 94 Banff Ave; tel: (403) 762-3919 or (866) 418-6613; www.banffbooks.com, has a good selection of books on the Canadian Rockies and works by Canadian authors.

Banff Park Museum National Historic Site $ Banff Ave by Bow River Bridge; tel: (403) 762-1558; www.pc.gc.ca/lhn-nhs/ ab/banff/index_e.asp. Open daily mid-May–Sep 1000–1800; Oct–mid-May 1300–1700.

Cave & Basin National Historic Site $ 311 Cave Ave; tel: (403) 762-1566; www.pc.gc.ca/lhn-nhs/ ab/caveandbasin/index_e.asp. Open daily mid-May–Sep 0900–1800, and variable hours depending on day of the week Oct–mid-May.

Buffalo Nations Luxton Museum $ 1 Birch Ave; tel: (403) 762-2388; www.buffalonationsmuseum. ca. Open daily May–early Oct 1000–1730; 1300–1700 in winter.

Moraine Lake $ From Lake Louise Drive, turn south on Moraine Lake Road for 11km.

Left
Banff National Park's Johnston Canyon

Buffalo Nations Luxton Museum Plains First Nations people who followed and hunted buffalo accurately portray traditional culture in a wooden stockade museum building. Walk by the dioramas of tepee-dwellers and displays of peace pipes and elegant bead and porcupine quill clothing.

Moraine Lake Ten craggy peaks surround this icy blue lake, with surreal beauty, beloved by summer canoeists. At the north end, the **Rockpile Trail** boulders lead to a view of the peaks and moraine flow to the water.

Peyto Lake Hike up Bow Summit through a flower carpet of Indian paintbrush and heather during July and August. Cloud patterns constantly change the colour of the lake, as it spreads long and blue before the wooden balcony viewpoint. Look left for a classic glacier flow into Peyto Lake.

Banff Gondola The 8-minute ride up 2,281m Sulphur Mountain is lovely on a clear day, with unobstructed views of Banff townsite. The short **Vista Trail Walkway** to Sanson's Peak Meteorological Station at Cosmic Ray Station National Historic Site provides a chance to stretch your legs with fabulous views.

Accommodation and food in Banff National Park

Banff and Lake Louise accommodation does not begin to serve the millions of visitors who arrive and want to stay the night. East of the park, fast-growing **Canmore**, set amid stunning snowcapped peaks, provides an ever-increasing number of motels, posh lodges and bed and breakfasts catering to park visitors and local recreation enthusiasts. If you are arriving from Calgary en route to Banff National Park, stop at **Travel Alberta Visitor InfoCentre** 2801 Bow Valley Trail, Canmore; tel: (800) 252-3782 or (outside N America) (780) 427-4321; www1.travelalberta.com. Open daily.

Canadian Rockies Chalets $$ 1206 Bow Valley Trail, Canmore; tel: (800) 386-7248 or (403) 678-3799; www.canadianrockieschalets.com, has large, clean accommodation, cheerful owners and helpful touring advice.

The Crossing Resort $$ Saskatchewan River Crossing, Hwy 93 at Hwy 11; tel: (403) 761-7000; www.thecrossingresort.com. If you are driving between Banff and Jasper early March–late October, this is a convenient spot to stop and refresh with lodging, a cafeteria and gift shop.

Moraine Lake Lodge $$ End of Moraine Lake Rd at lakeside, 15km from Lake Louise; tel: (403) 522-3733 or (877) 522-2777; www.morainelake.com. Open Jun–Sep. While there can be snow even in summer, the 18 cabins and rooms in the lodge have spectacular mountain and lake views with complimentary tea-time pastries. Café snacks, lunches or fine dining are available in the glass-roof **Atrium** $$$ during summer season.

Peyto Lake $
*West of Hwy 93,
Icefields Parkway, 98km
northwest of Banff; 40km
northwest of Lake Louise.*

**Banff Gondola (up
Sulphur Mountain) $$$**
*End of Mountain Ave;
tel: (403) 762-2523; http://
banffgondola.com. Open
daily except a fortnight in
Jan. Call or check website
for hours.*

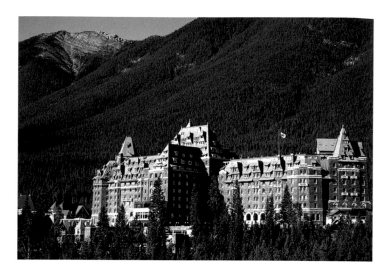

Right
Fairmont Banff Springs

SkiBig 3 *(Ski Banff
Lake Louise Sunshine)*
*225 Banff Ave, Banff;
tel: (403) 762-4754, (403)
762-4561 or (877) 754-
7080; http://skibig3.com.
Open Mon–Fri 0830–1700,
has skiing and
snowboarding information
and can make bookings for
Banff National Park's three
ski resorts: Ski Norquay
(Banff), Lake Louise
Mountain Resort and
Sunshine Village (Banff).*

Regal View Garden Restaurant $$ *Banff Gondola at Sulphur Mountain;
tel: (403) 762-2523; http://banffgondola.com/services.asp; open Jun–Sep,* is
a high dining experience at 2,281m, serving buffet breakfast, lunch
and dinner. The **Summit Restaurant $** serves light cafeteria fare.

Deer Lodge $$$ *109 Lake Louise Dr, Lake Louise; tel: (403) 522-3991 or
(800) 661-1595; www.crmr.com/deer-lodge.php,* has hand-hewn log
décor for its 73 rooms, Victoria Glacier views from the rooftop hot-
tub, and a fine restaurant serving Canadian wines with wild game,
berries and local ingredients.

Fairmont Banff Springs $$$ *405 Spray Ave, Banff; tel: (403) 762-2211
or (800) 257-7544; www.fairmont.com/banffsprings,* is the castle-like,
770-room icon set against the forested mountains, jammed with
guests and sightseers in summer. **Willow Stream Spa** and the 9- and
18-hole **Banff Springs Golf Courses** are enhanced by Bow Valley
vistas. Intimate **Grapes Wine Bar** *(mezzanine, open daily)* serves
delicious fondue. **Waldhaus Restaurant and Pub** *(tel: (403) 762-
6860),* in a Bavarian-style building near the golf course, serves hearty
dishes with lager and schnitzel. For Bow Valley views, have a
sundowner in the piano bar **Rundle Lounge**.

Fairmont Chateau Lake Louise $$$ *111 Lake Louise Dr; tel: (403) 522-
3511; or (800) 257-7544; www.fairmont.com/lakelouise,* is a 489-room
lakeside hotel with views across the lake to Victoria Glacier. In
summertime, tea ($$$, *tel: (403) 522-1818,* reservations recommended)
is served in the aptly named **Lakeview Lounge**. The 24-hour **Chateau
Deli $** prepares made-to-order sandwiches. The casual **Poppy
Brasserie $$** combines Lake Louise garden views with meals and a
breakfast buffet.

JASPER NATIONAL PARK

ⓘ Jasper National Park Information Centre *500 Connaught Dr;
tel: (780) 852-6176;
www.pc.gc.ca/pn-np/ab/
jasper/index_e.asp.
Open daily Apr–mid-Jun, Oct
0900–1700; mid-Jun–Labour
Day 0830–1900; Sep
0900–1800; Nov–Mar
0900–1600.*

Icefield InfoCentre *Icefields Parkway 123km
south of Jasper; tel: (780)
852-6288 or Ice Explorer
coach onto the glacier, tel:
(877) 423-7433;
www.columbiaicefield.com.
Open May–mid-Oct, daily.*

**Jasper Tourism &
Commerce** *409 Patricia
St; tel: (780) 852-3858;
www.
jaspercanadianrockies.com.
Open daily.*

ⓗ Athabasca Falls $ *Icefields Parkway,
30km south of Jasper.*

Columbia Icefield $$ *Icefield Centre, Icefields
Parkway; tel: (877) 423-7433.*

Icefields Parkway $ *3km west of the Lake Louise
exit, 230km north to Jasper
Townsite.*

Maligne Lake $ *48km from Jasper via
Maligne Lake Rd.*

Pyramid Lake $ *End of Pyramid Lake Rd.*

Jasper began in 1811 as a North West Company trading post outpost and was visited by Overlander gold prospectors in 1862. The park was designated in 1907 and Grand Trunk Pacific Railway passengers arrived *en masse* in 1911. Scenic attractions outweigh shopping and dining opportunities, but who cares when wildlife roams the streets and the edge of town is a 5-minute walk away?

Athabasca Falls Misty and mysterious, the falls descend 23m through pure quartzite. Hold on to railings to walk the 2-minute path to various viewpoints. Nordic skiers find a frozen shaft of ice and rock in winter.

Columbia Icefield A huge-tyred Ice Explorer coach hauls passengers over moraine gravel to the Continental-Divide-spanning icefield, for a 20-minute walk on a glacier and a sampling of glacial water. The Icefield InfoCentre has information on Athabasca Glacier Ice Walks (*tel: (800) 565-7547; www.icewalks.com*).

Icefields Parkway The 230km drive along Hwy 93 between Lake Louise and Jasper offers glaciers, waterfalls, wildlife and awesome vistas for several hours' drive by car or narrated Brewster coach tours.

Maligne Lake Though Jesuit missionary Fr Pierre de Smet lost horses and goods in the river he proclaimed 'wicked', the lake at the river's end is quite lovely. Take a 90-minute narrated boat tour to Spirit Island in the middle of the lake, fish for trout or canoe and kayak at this day-use lakeside retreat. En route to the lake, hike (snowshoe or ice climb) Maligne Canyon, take a look at Roche Bonhomme, a horizontal mountain profile that plausibly resembles a Native chief lying in profile, search the shores of green Medicine Lake for sunning wapiti, or join rafters bouncing downstream over Maligne River rapids.

Pyramid Lake A close 7km from Jasper townsite, this large, crystalline lake reflects a pyramid-shaped mountain. Kayaks, canoes, sailing boats and motorboats are for hire at Pyramid Lake Resort, while picnicking, horse riding, fishing, and skating and Nordic skiing in winter are other options.

Accommodation and food in Jasper National Park

Atha B Pub $ *Athabasca Hotel, 510 Patricia St; tel: (780) 852-3386 or (877) 542-8422,* is the drinking spot for locals, with live entertainment.

The Glass House $$ *715 Miette Ave; tel: (780) 852-3861; www.visit-jasper.com/glasshouse.html,* complete with a solarium, is a comfortable bed and breakfast serving home-made pastries, close to the town centre.

Fairmont Jasper Park Lodge $$$ *Tel: (800) 257-7544 or (780) 852-3301; http://fairmont.com/jasper,* has 446 rooms in chalets and log cabins, and adds a fine 18-hole golf course favoured by wandering wapiti. Splendid floor-to-ceiling views of Lac Beauvert are elegantly combined with rich meats, fish and wines in the adults-only **Edith Cavell Dining Room $$$** *tel: (780) 852-6052* (reservations required). For a panoply of Canadian décor and dishes such as buffalo skillet, there's the **Moose's Nook Northern Grill $$$**.

Icefield Chalet $$$ *Icefield InfoCentre; tel: (877) 423-7433; www.columbiaicefield.com/hotel.asp; open May–early Oct*, has 32 rooms on the third floor of the Icefield InfoCentre – ask for a glacier view room.

Below
Moraine Lake, Banff National Park

Rocky Mountain wildlife

Apart from iconic scenery, nothing draws people to the Rocky Mountains more seductively than the appearance of animals, most of them big and surprisingly active. The effect of several million visitors to Banff Jasper National Parks each year causes stress to the wildlife and frustrates drivers who park and line up in what park wardens refer to as 'animal jams' to get close to creatures while blocking the highways.

Yet the animals, such as bears and wapiti, which are close to the towns of Banff and Jasper, have adapted, looking for human food and, in the case of wapiti, getting protection from traditional predator wolves and cougars. They are wild animals, and when threatened retaliate with sharp teeth, horns, antlers, claws or hooves. Don't feed the animals, threaten their homes, food or young and force them to protect themselves. Such approaches usually end with the animal's death.

Though small, the Canadian and Parks Canada symbolic animal, the beaver, keeps streams, rivers and lakes healthy by damming. They were almost exterminated for their reddish pelts in the early 19th century.

There are probably no more than 300 straight-muzzle black bears and hump-shouldered grizzlies to be seen, grazing on berries and grass along roadsides. Fur colour can range from blond to red, brown or black for either species.

Bighorn sheep are easy to identify, front or back. Large, curling brown horns can crook 360 degrees on males. Brownish coats are accented by a large white patch on the rump, and all of them, young and old, love salt licks, especially in winter.

Listen at night around Banff and Jasper townsites for the plaintive, haunting howls of coyotes, those smart hunters who have avoided total decimation by those protecting cattle and sheep.

White-tail and mule deer are considerably smaller than elk, though both groups enjoy easy grazing near the towns. Mule deer have huge ears and white rumps; white-tail deer raise tails when they run, flashing the tail's white under-colouring.

Elk, or wapiti, are the size of horses, the males sporting many-pronged racks (antlers), and bellowing in combat with other males during the late autumn rut. They range in colour from light grey to light brown to ruddy, depending on the season, and sport a cream-colour rump patch.

There are few moose in the two parks, but the elongated big nose and solid thick brown antlers on these 450kg animals are hard to mistake, even if half-hidden in a marsh.

ⓘ Canada's Rocky Mountain National Parks Parks Canada provides *The Mountain Guide*, a free tabloid-sized newspaper with a page of highlights from each of the six parks: Banff, Glacier, Jasper, Kootenay, Mount Revelstoke and Yoho. The same summaries can be found online: *www.pc.gc.ca/docs/v-g/pm-mp/guidem-mguide/index_e.asp*

Suggested tour

Total distance: 305km.

Time: Minimum 2 days, stopping at Lake Louise or Saskatchewan River Crossing.

Links: The **BC Rockies** (*see page 258*) at Castle Junction for Kootenay National Park, at the Hwy 1 fork to Yoho National Park, and Hwy 16 west from Jasper to Mount Robson Provincial Park.

Route: TransCanada Hwy 1 runs from **BANFF NATIONAL PARK** ⓘ east gate by **Banff** to just north of the Lake Louise exit. Veer right to take the Icefields Parkway, Hwy 93, 230km to Jasper.

Above
Lake Louise

Lake Minnewanka
10km from town of Banff; 1.5-hour boat tours $$; tel: (403) 762-3473; www. minnewankaboattours.com, operate mid-May–early Oct.

Barriers along the roadside beyond Banff National Park's east gate protect wildlife from vehicles, but also restrict the natural range of elk and other migrating animals through this section of the **Bow Valley**. For boating and bighorn sheep spotting, turn right to drive the loop around **Lake Minnewanka**, 'Lake of the Water Spirits', or, in late spring to autumn, turn left on to Tunnel Mountain Road for views of the **Hoodoos** and the **Bow River Valley**.

Upper Hot Springs Pool $ *Mountain Ave, Banff; tel: (403) 762-1515 or (800) 767 1611; www. hotsprings.ca. Open late May–mid-Sep 0900–2300, mid-Sep–late May Sun–Thu 1000–2200, Fri–Sat to 2300.*

Whyte Museum of the Canadian Rockies $ *111 Bear St, Banff; tel: (403) 762-2291; www.whyte.org. Open daily 1000–1700.*

The main town of **Banff** turn-off is 1km further west on Hwy 1, across the highway from the winter-only **Ski Norquay Mount Norquay Ski Area**. Take the Vermillion Lakes Drive immediately right for reflections in grassy-shore lakes of surrounding mountains filled with birds and wandering elk. In Banff, tour the Fairmont Banff Springs Hotel, take pictures by **Bow Falls** below the hotel, canoe or play a round of golf. **Upper Hot Springs Pool**, near the parking area for the Banff Gondola to Sulphur Mountain, is the spot in Banff to soak up mountain views along with the mineral waters.

Banff's museums and historic site cover history, natural history and First Nations. Banff's origins are exposed at **Cave & Basin National Historic Site**; the **Whyte Museum of the Canadian Rockies** covers mountain-climbing feats; and the **Buffalo Nations Luxton Museum** shows the lives of local First Nations peoples. At the head of Banff Avenue, the main street, stroll around the Park Administration Building's flower-filled **Cascade Gardens**, with views across the **Bow River Bridge** and Banff Avenue to majestic **Cascade Mountain.**

Detour along Bow Valley Parkway: For 55km, Hwy 1A parallels the TransCanada Hwy, but is considered the more scenic, if slower (60kph), route. Traffic flow may be restricted because of animal movement in some seasons, but driving one or both segments – Banff to Castle Junction or Castle Junction to Lake Louise – in either direction is the best way to spot wildlife, enjoy wild flowers and experience river canyons by getting off the generally straight TransCanada.

Pick up the Bow Valley Parkway 5.5km west of Banff town. **Johnston Canyon**, at 23km, has a narrow 1km path, some of it boardwalk, along limestone wall and over a bright green river to the Lower Falls, above a blue pool. North, 2,766m **Castle Mountain** acts as a landmark for those getting off at **Castle Junction** to go west to Kootenay National Park (*see page 258*). Drive towards Lake Louise through a forest of lodgepole pine, with occasional glimpses of trains, backed by mountains, travelling along the railway line at the base of the Bow Valley.

Side-leaning **Mount Rundle** dominates the view south (left) for many kilometres along the Bow River Valley. For winter skiing and snowboarding, turn left from Hwy 1 on to Sunshine Road to **Sunshine Village.**

Castle Mountain is the golden rock massif on the right side of Hwy 1. Turn left, 58km from Banff to **Lake Louise**. Lake Louise Village, with its Visitor InfoCentre, petrol station, stores, restaurants and services, is just off the highway; the lake and **Fairmont Chateau Lake Louise** are 4km up a winding road, congested in summer. Turn left at Moraine Lake Road for left-hand side views of the **Valley of the 10 Peaks** before reaching **Moraine Lake.**

Follow signs right to the Icefields Parkway, Hwy 93. Mountains will appear higher and higher, less eroded. To the left is the **Crowfoot**

Simpson's Num-Ti-Jah Lodge $$$
Hwy 93, 40km north of Lake Louise; tel: (403) 522-2167; www.num-ti-jah.com. Closed Nov.

Ski Marmot Basin
Tel: (780) 852-3816 or (866) 952-3816; www.skimarmot.com

Jasper Tramway $$$
Tel: (780) 852-3093 or (866) 850-8726; www.jaspertramway.com. Open mid-Apr–mid-Oct, depending on weather. VIA Rail operates a winter Snow Train from Edmonton to Jasper; www.viarail.ca/classes/en_serv_clas_snow_train.html

Miette Hot Springs
$ 61km east of town of Jasper; tel: (780) 866-3939; www.pc.gc.ca/regional/sourcesthermales-hotsprings/itm2-/miette_e.asp. Open early May–mid-Oct.

Glacier, where two pale-blue 'toes' hang on the cliff's edge. Crystal-blue **Bow Lake** is below, with **Bow Glacier** distant across the lake, and red-roofed **Simpson's Num-Ti-Jah Lodge** at the north end.

Trees thin out at 2,088m **Bow Summit**, with a wild flower-filled forest trail up to the **Peyto Lake** viewpoint. **Mistaya Canyon**, 32km north, twists around its river a short hike away from Hwy 1. One of the Rockies' most beautiful waterways, the **North Saskatchewan River**, rushes pale green at The Crossing, where David Thompson explored the area from his base at Rocky Mountain House in 1807 (*see* **Shuswap Lakes** *page 158*).

The **Weeping Wall** on the right, rivulets of water with spring runoff, is enjoyed by Rocky Mountain sheep and ice climbers when the rock face freezes in winter. The **Big Bend** switchbacks wind up to Parker Ridge.

Sunwapta Pass at 2,035m marks **JASPER NATIONAL PARK ②** and the **Columbia Icefield**. Take the 2km trail to **Sunwapta Falls**, best for photography in the afternoon. Hwy 93 moves north along the Athabasca River, which creates a misty blanket over **Athabasca Falls**, frozen eerily in winter.

Mount Edith Cavell, standing regally to the west, is named after a brave British nurse executed in World War I for aiding prisoners. To ski **Marmot Basin** from December to April, take the marked winding road left from Hwy 93. Whistlers Road, named after the noisy hoary marmots in the area, leads to the **Jasper Tramway** for Jasper Townsite views and vistas of the Miette and Athabasca rivers.

Wapiti (elk) wander everywhere around **Jasper**, a relaxed, unpretentious tourist-catering community strung near the railway line along Connaught Drive. Drive out to Fairmont Jasper Park Lodge for a lovely series of watersports recreation lakes, epitomised by the lodge's own **Lac Beauvert**. **Pyramid Lake** is north of town. The chilly **Athabasca** and **Maligne rivers** offer challenging rafting and magnificent scenery.

Drive northeast of Jasper on Hwy 16, and turn right onto Maligne Lake Road. The wildlife-rich road traverses **Maligne Canyon**, favoured by ice climbers and snowshoers in winter, and passes the conical-shaped mountains around **Medicine Lake** before arriving at **Maligne Lake**.

Also worth exploring

Miette Hot Springs at the edge of Jasper National Park is one of three public soaks (along with Radium Hot Springs, *see page 261*, and Banff Upper Hot Springs) in the Rockies Parks. Look for wapiti and bighorn sheep along Hwy 16, the Yellowhead Hwy, for 43km northeast of Jasper. Turn right on to Fiddle Valley Road for 17km, past the ruined

Jasper Park Collieries and coal tailings and 360-million-year-old **Ashlar Ridge.** There are ruined buildings at the old hot springs bathhouse. The modern resort has 53.9°C sulphuric waters, a motel and bungalows, café, restaurant and picnicking.

How to talk Canadian

Back bacon: known as Canadian bacon in the USA and as peameal bacon elsewhere.

Bannock: a deep-fried bread usually eaten with such trail 'delicacies' as moose stew.

Beaver fever: *giardiasis*, severe diarrhoea and fever from drinking untreated ground water infected with *Giardia lamblia*.

Block heater: an electric engine heater attached to the other end of the plug dangling from the front bumper of most Canadian cars. The heater is plugged in on cold nights (–10°C or colder) to prevent the engine coolant and oil from freezing and cracking the engine block.

Brew: a beer, either in a bottle or on draught.

Canuck: a Canadian or a member of the Vancouver Canucks ice hockey team.

Chinook: a warm wind from west of the Rockies that melts winter snows as it passes over the mountains, warming Calgary and southwest Alberta.

Cow pie: cattle droppings, a hazard to walkers on open grazing lands.

Cowtown: Calgary.

Donair, donner kebab, gyro, schwarma: a sandwich made of shaved meat (usually lamb) wrapped in pitta bread.

Downtown: city or town centre.

Flapjacks: pancakes.

Flat (of beer): a case of 24 bottles or cans of beer.

Fries: chips, usually, but not always, made of potatoes.

Galapagos of Canada: the Queen Charlotte Islands, also called Haida Gwaii.

Gas: petrol.

Goeduck: pronounced 'gooey duck'; a large clam with a long, thick neck, usually used for soup.

Gorbie: someone not from the area; a tourist, usually someone asking questions such as 'How much does that mountain weigh?'

Holiday: a public holiday, not a private holiday, which is more often a vacation.

Hoser: a teasing term used by men, implying the person being needled is none too bright.

Ice fog: fog composed of ice crystals instead of water vapour.

Loonie: $1 coin, named after the Canadian bird, the common loon, one of Canada's symbols.

Métis: a person of mixed aboriginal and white ancestry, constitutionally recognised as one of three First Nations entities.

Ogopogo: mythical beast similar to the Loch Ness monster, believed to lurk beneath the waters of Okanagan Lake.

Parkade: a parking garage.

Parking lot: a car park or parking garage.

Road apple: cattle or buffalo droppings on the road.

Road kill: literally animals killed by passing automobiles, but also used to describe bad restaurant food.

Sasquatch: Bigfoot, the legendary man-like hairy giant of the woods.

Shooter: a raw oyster, usually swallowed whole.

Shredding: snowboarding.

Sundog: ring around the sun formed by ice crystals in the upper atmosphere.

Talking stick: originally a carved staff used in First Nations gatherings to signify that the holder was entitled to speak to the group; now used in non-Native meetings to focus attention on the speaker.

Texas gate or cattle gate: a grate of widely separated metal pipes set in the roadway to keep cattle and horses at bay.

Toonie or Twonie: the $2 bi-metal coin.

Toque: a winter hat, pronounced like 'spoke'.

Vamping: van camping.

Wapiti: elk.

Index

Acknowledgements

Project management: Cambridge Publishing Management Limited
Project editor: Karen Beaulah
Series design: Fox Design
Cover design: Liz Lyons Design
Layout and map work: Concept 5D and Cambridge Publishing Management Limited
Repro and image setting: PDQ Digital Media Solutions Ltd, and Cambridge Publishing Management Limited
Printed and bound in India by: Replika Press Pvt Ltd

We would like to thank the following for the photographs used in this book, to whom the copyright in the photographs belongs:

Maxine Cass (pages 21, 22, 36, 42A, 47, 50, 67, 70, 86, 90, 93, 164, 191, 192, 206, 226, 230B, 233, 235, 236, 250A, 250B, 252, 256, 264, 268, 272, 274, 276 and 278); **Dreamstime.com** (pages 35 – Fallsview, 53 – Stephen Rosset, 99 – Lksstock, 168 – Natalia Bratslavsky); **Fred Gebhart** (pages 3, 5, 14, 18, 24, 30, 32, 39, 41, 42B, 44, 48, 60, 62, 64, 68, 73, 74, 76, 77, 79, 80, 82, 84, 88, 96, 100, 102, 104, 106A, 106B, 110, 113, 116A, 116B, 119, 122, 124, 126, 128, 130, 132, 135, 136, 138A, 138B, 140, 142, 145, 146, 148, 150, 154, 155, 156, 158, 161, 162, 166, 170, 172, 176A, 176B, 178, 180, 182, 186, 188, 195, 198A, 198B, 201, 210, 212, 214A, 214B, 217, 218, 220, 222, 225, 230A, 234, 238, 240A, 240B, 243, 244, 246, 248, 253, 258, 260, 262 and 270); **Eddy Posthuma de Boer** (pages 6, 12 and 267); **Anne Vipond** (pages 56, 57, 58, 59 and 114).

Feedback form

We're committed to providing the very best up-to-date information in our travel guides and constantly strive to make them as useful as they can be. You can help us to improve future editions by letting us have your feedback. Just take a few minutes to complete and return this form to us.

When did you buy this book? ....
....

Where did you buy it? (Please give town/city and, if possible, name of retailer)
....
....

When did you/do you intend to travel in Vancouver and BC?......................................
....

For how long (approx)? ....

How many people in your party? ....

Which cities, national parks and other locations did you/do you intend mainly to visit?
....
....
....
....

Did you/will you:
❑ Make all your travel arrangements independently?
❑ Travel on a fly-drive package?
Please give brief details: ....
....

Did you/do you intend to use this book:
❑ For planning your trip?   ❑ Both?
❑ During the trip itself?

Did you/do you intend also to purchase any of the following travel publications for your trip?
Thomas Cook Travellers: Vancouver and BC..
A road map/atlas (please specify) ....
Other guidebooks (please specify) ....

Limerick
County Library

Have you used any other Thomas Cook guidebooks in the past? If so, which?

....

....

Please rate the following features of *Drive Around Vancouver & British Columbia* for their value to you (circle VU for 'very useful', U for 'useful', NU for 'little or no use'):

The *Travel Facts* section on pages 14–23	VU U NU
The *Driver's Guide* section on pages 24–29	VU U NU
The *Highlights and Touring Itineraries* on pages 40–41	VU U NU
The recommended driving routes throughout the book	VU U NU
Information on towns and cities, National Parks, etc	VU U NU
The maps of towns and cities, parks, etc	VU U NU

Please use this space to tell us about any features that in your opinion could be changed, improved, or added in future editions of the book, or any other comments you would like to make concerning the book:

....

....

....

....

....

....

....

....

Your age category: ❑ 21–30 ❑ 31–40 ❑ 41–50 ❑ over 50

Your name: Mr/Mrs/Miss/Ms ....

(First name or initials) ....

(Last name) ....

Your full address (please include postal or zip code):

....

....

....

....

....

Your daytime telephone number: ....

Please detach this page and send it to: Drive Around Series Editor, Thomas Cook Publishing, PO Box 227, The Thomas Cook Business Park, 9 Coningsby Road, Peterborough PE3 8SB.

Alternatively, you can e-mail us at: *books@thomascook.com*